# The Writer's Way

*Sixth Edition*
*Expanded Version*

JACK RAWLINS
California State University at Chico

with *Understanding Plagiarism: A Student Guide to Writing your Own Work*
by

ROSEMARIE MENAGER-BEELEY, ED.D
Foothill College

LYN PAULOS
Santa Barbara City College

HOUGHTON MIFFLIN COMPANY
BOSTON NEW YORK

THE WRITER'S WAY, SIXTH EDITION
by Jack Rawlins


Publisher: Pat Coryell
Senior Sponsoring Editor: Suzanne Phelps Weir
Development Editor: Kellie Cardone
Editorial Assistant: Peter Mooney
Associate Project Editor: Reba Libby
Editorial Assistant: Rachel Zanders
Senior Manufacturing Coordinator: Marie Barnes
Marketing Manager: Cindy Graff Cohen
Marketing Assistant: Wendy Thayer
Cover illustration: The Letter, 1993 by Patricia O'Brien. Private collection/Bridgeman Art Library.

TEXTCREDITS

"No Room for Children" by Rasa Gustaitus is reprinted by permission of the Pacific News Service and the author.
Excerpt from The Right Stuffby Tom Wolfe. Copyright © 1979 by Tom Wolfe. Reprinted by permission of Farrar, Straus & Giroux, LLC.
"The People Versus," by Steve Rubenstein, © San Francisco Chronicle, 1982. Reprinted by permission.
Excerpt originally appeared in, "Real Women Do Eat Food," by Warren Leight, Mademoiselle,August 1989. Reprinted by permission of the author.
"How Do It Know?" by Robert Schadewald, The TWA Ambassador,February 1979. Reprinted by permission of Paulsen Publishing Company.
Hochschild, Adam, "Protect Your Inalienable Right to Steer Tanks." Copyright © 1989 by Adam Hochschild. Reprinted by permission.

UNDERSTANDING PLAGIARISM: A STUDENT GUIDE TO WRITING YOUR OWN WORK
by Rosemarie Menager-Beele and Lyn Paulos


Vice President and Publisher: Patricia A. Coryell
Editor-in-Chief: Suzanne Phelps Weir
Senior Sponsoring Editor: Lisa Kimball
Development Manager: Sarah Helyar Chester
Editorial Associate: Peter Mooney
Editorial Assistant: Brett Pasinella
Manufacturing Coordinator: Priscilla Manchester
Senior marketing manager: Cindy Graff Cohen

Custom Publishing Editor: Dan Luciano
Custom Publishing Production Manager: Christina Battista
Project Coordinator: Katherine Roz

Cover Designer: Eric Hague
Cover Photograph: Brian Lary/Stock.Xchng

This book contains select works from existing Houghton Mifflin Company resources and was produced by Houghton Mifflin Custom Publishing for collegiate use. As such, those adopting and/or contributing to this work are responsible for editorial content, accuracy, continuity and completeness.



Printed in the United States of America.

ISBN-13: 978-0-547-00370-2
ISBN-10: 0-547-00370-6
1029089

1 2 3 4 5 6 7 8 9 – WP – 09 08 07

Houghton Mifflin
Custom Publishing

222 Berkeley Street • Boston, MA 02116

Address all correspondence and order information to the above address.

# Contents

# Part Three

## REVISING AND EDITING 65

# PREFACE

## The Approach

I've been teaching composition for thirty years. In the beginning, I would have students write, look at their product, and tell them what went wrong. That didn't go very well. I was too late.

So I tried to intervene earlier. I entered into their writing process, and offered advice and feedback as they drafted, outlined, and revised. Things went better, but not very well. I was still too late.

Finally I realized that the real work of writing takes place before the writer starts putting words on paper, when the writer makes a series of decisions about fundamental issues: Why am I writing at all? Who am I writing to? What am I trying to accomplish? In other words, the real work takes place when the writer defines the writing task and her role in it. And if I didn't intervene then, at the very beginning, I would always be too late.

So this book is an attempt to get in on the writing process at the very beginning and examine all the long-established assumptions from which you, the college student, and almost everyone else writes. My premise is simple: You can't write well if you're writing for the wrong reasons. If you think that writing is an exercise in "expressing yourself," hiding your ignorance, impressing a teacher, getting a good grade, avoiding grammar mistakes, following the rules, or demonstrating your extensive vocabulary or outlining skills, then every time you write you'll simply be reinforcing that misunderstanding. Until you write for the reasons successful writers write, teaching and practice and drill will only make the bad habits more entrenched.

*The Writer's Way* is based on two core principles, to which it returns again and again: 1) good writing begins when you write for the right reasons; and 2) good reasons to write will teach you everything you need to know about technique. A writer constantly makes choices: Should I do *this*, or *that*? Should I do it *this* way, or *that* way? Real writers don't answer such questions by asking themselves, "What's the rule?" or "What do good essays do?" Instead, they ask, "What am I trying to accomplish here?"; "Will this help me accomplish that?"; and, "Is there another way of doing it that will accomplish it better?" In short, the real writer asks, "Will this *work*?" The goal of *The Writer's Way* is to train you in this new way of thinking.

## How the Book Is Laid Out

This book is divided into seven parts. The Prologue is a two-part introduction to the art of going to college. The first part is a list of things good students do in order to get an A. The second part is an instruction manual on how to study. You'll want to have the Prologue down cold before you walk through the classroom door, or as soon thereafter as possible.

Part One is an introduction to the attitude toward learning to write that lies behind the rest of the book. I encourage you to read it before doing anything else.

Parts Two and Three are a step-by-step walk-through of the writing process: from first thoughts through brainstorming, drafting, rethinking, organizing, peer editing, stylistic polishing, cosmetic editing, and publishing. Part Two covers all the messy, creative steps from first thoughts through the first draft. Part Three is about ways to take that draft and revise it into something better. It would be lovely if you could know everything in Parts Two and Three before you wrote an essay, but you won't be able to wait, so you will probably find yourself writing essays while reading one chapter after another, and in fact you can read them in almost any order.

Part Four introduces you to the three main essay "modes": personal writing, writing to inform, and argument. You'll want to read these three chapters if your writing course gives assignments by mode ("Write an informative essay") or you're just looking for ways to break out of your old essay-writing rut. For each mode, there is a collection of sample essays in Part Six, the Treasury of Essays. You'll want to read those samples along with the chapter.

Part Five discusses writing for college courses. Here you'll learn how to approach traditional academic writing assignments (the research paper, the lab report, the essay test . . .) and how to perform basic scholastic writing skills: research, documentation, quotation, and the like. If your writing course gives assignments that use these forms and techniques, obviously you'll want to read these chapters, but even if it doesn't, these chapters will help you in every other course you take in college that involves writing. There are sample academic essays in the Treasury of Essays, and a complete term paper (on the physical afflictions associated with using computers) at the end of Chapter 25.

Part Six is the fun part. It's a collection of essays written by my students over recent years—twenty-eight essays to delight and inspire. You'll want to read them, because they're wonderful, and because the easiest way to help your writing is to read some great writing and fall in love with it. Then the most natural thing in the world is to go out and try to do something like the writing you love. The essays are grouped under five headings: personal essays, informative essays, argumentative essays, academic essays, and the Diet Set, a collection of four essays on dieting.

## Unusual Features

*The Writer's Way* has a number of features that set it apart from other composition textbooks:

The Prologue addresses questions you need answers to before you can begin any school work: What do good students do that poor students don't do? What does it mean to "study" a chapter in a book? How can I tell if I'm "learning" anything? What do good readers do beyond looking at the words and trying to remember them?

*The Writer's Way* contains *sixty-one complete essays*—about half sprinkled throughout the chapters to illustrate principles, and half collected at the end of the book in the Treasury of Essays (Part Six). Fifty-six of these essays are by my students, so you can see that your peers can and do write wonderful essays, and you can as well.

Most of the chapters end with *Writer's Workshop* sections. These workshops are similar to the lab sections of a science course: First you watch a hands-on demonstration of one of the concepts presented in the chapter; then you dig in and get your own hands dirty.

Almost all the chapters end with *exercises*. These obey the spirit of the book and the Writer's Workshop sections by avoiding drills and mechanical activities whenever possible and focusing on whole-language activities, in which you are asked to work with entire blocks of text. As often as possible, the text being worked with is your own, since anything one learns about someone else's writing is far less powerful than what one learns about his own.

A number of topics that often are not covered in composition textbooks are covered in this book. In addition to the Prologue, on how to go to school, and Part One, on how writing gets learned and what makes writing work, there are chapters on critical thinking, peer editing (including explicit instruction on how to do it well), publishing, essay test taking, collaborative assignments, titling, and how to make a too-short essay longer. The chapter on first-drafting examines writer's block, explores where it comes from, and offers two dozen strategies for overcoming it.

## What's New in the Sixth Edition

The most obvious new feature is the Prologue, an introduction to the art of going to school. I added it because in recent years I've watched my students prevent themselves from learning by believing in a toxic set of myths about how learning happens. The Prologue attempts to replace those myths with an attitude toward learning that makes learning likely.

The Sixth Edition has a new approach to revision, one based on tool-making. The central idea is that a writer revises not by staring at the draft and somehow trying to make it better, but by building revision tools, like thesis statements and outlines, and using them on the draft the way a carpenter uses a saw on a two-by-four. I'll show you how to make the tool, critique the tool so you know it works, and use the tool on the draft to get solid revision guidance.

The critical thinking chapter has a new beginning, one that discusses why humans as a rule don't do critical thinking very well. I added it because, for my students, the central issue around critical thinking isn't how to do it, but why should anyone want to do it?

There are ten new essays. Partly this is because instructors who work with the book year after year want to have some new fun. Four of the ten are in the Dict Set, in a new essay section in the Treasury of Essays. These essays offer four dramatically different approaches to dieting, a topic close to America's heart.

The methodologies of software-based research and documentation have continued to evolve, so all the material in the book on those subjects has been updated to keep pace.

The end-of-chapter exercises have been reworked. The new exercises are stronger, more numerous, and more holistic.

## Acknowledgments

Several new student writers have added their names to the list of generous classroom friends who let me use their essays for free. Their names are in the Treasury of Essays at the back of the book. I am grateful to the following reviewers for critiquing the sixth edition manuscript: Beth Gulley, Johnson County Community College; Elizabeth Kleinfeld, Red Rocks Community College; Emily Kretschmer, Minnesota State University, Mankato; Ron Mitchell, University of Southern Indiana; Shannon Mondor, Humboldt State University; Michael Soderlund, Central Lakes College; and Marianne Zarzana, Minnesota State University, Mankato.

*J. R.*

# THE WRITER'S WAY

# Prologue: How to Go to School

## How to Get a Good Grade

Here's a time-tested list of things good-grade getters do. There's some overlap with the Guide to Studying (p. P-2), since learning and grade-getting are related. I suggest you note which things you already do, mark the ones you don't, then pick two or three of those "don'ts" as personal goals for this semester.

"We hold these truths to be self-evident":

1. Go to class every day.
2. Be on time for class.
3. Do all the assigned reading, by the time it's due.
4. Hand in all assignments, on time.
5. Study the course syllabus.
6. Take part in class discussion.
7. Take notes during class.
8. Rewrite all papers.
9. Use a word processor for all essay-style assignments.
10. Follow directions slavishly.

Less self-evident truths.

11. Sit near the front of the room.
12. Become an expert on the course grading system.
13. Come to each class session with a question about the material.
14. Visit the instructor during office hours.
15. Study for tests over as long a period as possible.
16. Take notes recording your thoughts and reactions as you're doing the course reading—not after.
17. Write in your textbooks—highlight, underline, jot marginal notes.
18. After all assigned readings and all class sessions, write answers to these questions:

What happened? or What did it say?
What was the point? What am I supposed to learn from it?
Why does it matter?

19. Before each class session, remind yourself where the class left off last time.
20. Muse on assignments off and on, all the time, from the moment they're assigned until they're due.
21. Study by *talking* with classmates, not by reading or note-taking.
22. Act like a good employee; treat your teacher like a boss.
23. Strive to make the teacher's life easier and more rewarding.

## How to (Re)Learn in School: A Guide to Studying

The basic school experience is this: You hear a lecture, read a chapter of a book, or do an exercise in class, and the teacher says, "Go learn that." If you're like most students, despite having been in school for umpteen thousand years, you don't have a very clear notion of how to go about it. To help, here's an introduction to the art of studying. The first twelve principles are about the attitude you bring to the task, and the next nine are about what you actually do.

**1. Learning in school is relearning.** Learning when you're little is easy because you're writing on a blank slate. But by the time a person gets to age 16 or so, her worldview is complete and any teaching is reprogramming. You "know" what writing an essay is like, and you have to unlearn what you know and replace it with a new model. When I started to learn scuba diving, part of my worldview was "You can't breathe underwater—you'll drown." I had to unlearn that.

Relearning is harder than learning. Breaking an entrenched habit is much harder than picking up a new one. After I had been riding a bike for twenty years, a coach told me to ride with my heels down. That would have been easy if I hadn't already learned a different way. I'm still telling myself, "Keep your heels down, keep your heels down" as I ride, after a year of dogged reprogramming.

**2. Doing something teaches you nothing.** You don't learn by activity or exposure. You don't learn by reading the book, listening to the lecture, watching the video, doing the assignments, completing the exercises, or writing the essays. And repetition doesn't help—being married ten times doesn't make you better marriage material.

There are two reasons why we keep thinking that doing is learning. First, because it works with muscle learning: If you ride a bike for enough hours, you'll learn to ride a bike, without thinking about it.

Second, because school has been telling us doing is learning: "If you do the following drills, you'll learn." It doesn't work, as years of school drills prove to us.

**3. You learn by reflecting.** You begin by having an experience—you read, see, hear, or do something—and then you think about it. No reflecting means no learning. No one can reflect for you, which means no teacher can hand you the understanding or the insight or force you to have it. Learning goes on inside you, and it takes place in the quiet moment after the activity (or, less often, during the activity). You ride your mountain bike over a rocky spot; you fall; you stop and ask, "What went wrong?" You read a book; you stop and ask, "What did that mean? What are the consequences of accepting it as true?"

School rarely gives us time to reflect. It's always rushing on to the next activity. So the most difficult and most necessary part of learning is to *make time for reflection.*

Don't fall for the trap of performing actions that substitute for reflecting and calling them learning. For instance, taking notes in class, making up flash cards, or outlining assigned readings all *look* like learning, but if you aren't reflecting while you do those things, they're just more pointless motion.

**4. Learning can't be scheduled.** You can't know when insight will come or how to make it come. So don't schedule a time to study—"I'm going to have insights about my composition assignment between 6:00 P.M. and 7:00 P.M. tonight." Instead, *reflect all the time*—muse on the assignment or the course material constantly, with a part of your brain, while you go through your day.

Reflecting all the time sounds like work, but it isn't. Your mind works all the time whether you want it to or not, as we discover when something is worrying us. Any yogi will tell you that it takes years of practice to learn to turn the mind *off,* even for a minute or two. And it's physiologically impossible for your brain to get tired, which is why you can study or write all day, go to bed, and find your mind still racing while your body cries out for rest. With practice, keeping a part of your mind on a task becomes effortless—you just tell your brain to call you when something pops into it (like the chime that says, "You've got mail"), and it does.

**5. Learning equals changing.** Experiencing and reflecting are merely the first two in a series of five steps to learning: 1) you experience something; 2) you reflect on the experience; 3) you arrive at an insight ("Now I see what I did wrong!"); 4) you resolve to be different ("Next time I'll take water before I go into the desert"); and 5) you implement the change—you do it differently next time. Going through just some of the steps and stopping short of number 5 equals learning nothing. If you want to assess how much you've learned at the end of a lecture, book, or class, ask yourself, "How different am I from when I started?"

**6. All learning is self-teaching.** The five-step program goes on in your head, where no one but you can get at it. A teacher or textbook can encourage, guide, inspire, or bribe, but that's all in *support* of the teaching, it isn't the teaching itself. And self-teaching can't fail, if you stick with it. Let's assume you act, reflect, and come to an erroneous conclusion. You act on that conclusion and reflect on the outcome. You conclude that your first resolution was misguided. So you conclude that you should try something else. Then all you have to do is continue running the five-step program until by trial and error you've figured things out.

**7. Relearning is uncomfortable.** Change is momentarily destabilizing. You feel like your feet aren't firmly on the ground. And they aren't: Change is like stepping off a ledge into the dark. You can't be sure where the new path will take you, and it only makes sense to feel uneasy. Teachers or classrooms or textbooks lessen the discomfort but can't make it disappear, because they can't make the unknown safe. The only way to be totally comfortable is to remove the possibility of learning. When I was in the midst of unlearning the idea that I couldn't breathe underwater, I was terrified. Every scuba diver I've ever known had to go through the same terrifying reorientation, and no instructor has found a way to get around the moment of terror.

The discomfort is in proportion to the potential for change. If a teacher asks me to memorize the kings and queens of England in chronological order, I'm not afraid, because the knowledge doesn't involve any risk. But every time I've tried to learn something that altered me a lot—writing a book, playing in an orchestra, scuba diving—the fear and discomfort were mammoth. If you feel comfy in a classroom, leave—you aren't about to learn anything that matters.

You must learn this lesson well, because if you don't, every time you get close to important learning, you'll feel discomfort, assume something is wrong, and run away.

**8. Relearning feels wrong.** The old way feels "right" because it's familiar. We are so committed to the familiar that people will let their lives be ruined by alcohol or spousal abuse simply because that's what they're used to. You have to accept that period when the new feels wrong, wait it out, and give the new time to become the familiar.

**9. Relearning makes things go worse.** If you've been riding a bike or writing an essay in a familiar way, when you try a different way of doing it you don't do it better; your performance deteriorates—for a while. You're skilled at the old way but not at the new, so you handle the old way better. And you have to *think about* the new way as you try it—it isn't automatic—so self-consciousness gets in the way of your performance. But all that is temporary—soon you'll be riding or writing better than you were in the beginning. So don't judge a relearning lesson by the immediate results. When your teacher asks you to approach essay writing in a new way and the essay turns out worse, don't reject the lesson.

The adjustment can take some time. When Tiger Woods replaced his old golf grip with a new one, he had to use it for over a year before he was sure it was an improvement.

**10. You have to want to be different.** Relearning means becoming a different person, and you have to be willing to let the old person die so the new can be born.

The ego defines change in one of two ways. In the first, change is defined as a condemnation of the self: "I need to change because there's something wrong with the old me." The ego's only healthy response to that is to fight off the learning to avoid adopting the toxic message that comes with it. That's why dieting because you're fat and feel disgusting doesn't work. In the second way, change is defined as growth: "I want to change because I see a way to become a more enriched, more complete person." Now the ego can embrace the learning. Dieting because you love cycling and want to climb that big hill works.

**11. Learn by joining the club.** For every skill or body of knowledge, there is a club of people who practice or study it. Sometimes the club is a physical group of people with a clubhouse and dues—the Garden Club, the Chess Club. Just as often, the club is virtual—the club of writers or the club of fans of Tori Amos. In either case, you must join up. You can join literally, by paying dues and attending meetings, or you can sign up mentally, by calling yourself a writer and acting like one.

This act of joining is very powerful. Notice the difference between "I'm taking piano lessons" and "I'm a pianist"—wow! Joining means you stop defining yourself as a "student" and start defining yourself as a doer. All doers are learners—Tiger Woods is still learning how to play golf.

You're a member the moment you choose to be. How good you are or how much you know is irrelevant. No one ever said, "You have to shoot a round of 85 before you can be a member of the golf club." And I've known people who have published several books and are still saying in their hearts, "I'm not really a writer."

A member of a club flaunts membership—by wearing the uniform, talking the talk, reading the magazines devoted to the discipline, hanging with other members, talking shop, sharing work with colleagues, going to meetings. Think of ways you can flaunt your membership in the club of writers.

**12. Learn by imitating your teacher.** Your teacher may not be the person your hip young self most wants to be like, but learning is done by imitating the mentors, the older and wiser members of the club—every young golfer imagines she is Tiger Woods—and the nearest mentor is standing at the front of the classroom. You need a hero to model the new self you're trying to become.

*The less like you your teacher is, the more you stand to learn.* If your teacher is exactly like you, you won't get to travel any distance to become like her; you're already there.

So much for the learning attitude. Now let's talk nuts and bolts. Let's say you just read a chapter or heard a lecture and are setting out to "learn it." What does that actually mean?

**13. Learning means understanding.** If I know that $E=mc^2$, I know nothing unless I understand what that means. Let's divide understanding into three rounds. Round One consists of five basic questions about the experience you just had:

a. *What just happened?* (What did I/we do?) Answers sound like "We practiced outlining essays." Don't pooh pooh this question as somehow beneath you; whenever I ask my students, "What did we do in our last class session?", most of them can't say.
b. *What was the purpose?* (Why did I/we do it?) Answers sound like "We did it to understand how essay titles work." In school, "Why?" can be a threatening question because it's so powerful, which is why you need to ask it.
c. *What did it say?* (What was the content?) This question only works with texts (books, lectures, movies). What you're seeking is a *paraphrase,* a brief rewording of the content in your own words. *Don't react yet.* Reacting is a way of skipping over this step.
d. *What was the point?* What did it mean? What was the message? What lesson was I supposed to learn from it? Never do anything that's pointless, and never do anything until you're clear on what the point is. In school, the teacher typically has a point in mind. Know what his intended lesson is, but feel free to draw as many lessons of your own as possible.

   Because "point" is scary, people often want to substitute purpose. When I ask my students to explain the point of a previous exercise to me, they typically give me verbs: "The point was *to learn* how to outline." A verb is a purpose; a point must be *a sentence*: "The *point* was, outline *sentences.*"
e. *How can I use this?* Learning something is meaningless unless you can do something with it. How can you use the

things you learn in school? However tricky a question that may be, you must answer it.

Round One is the groundwork for understanding. Round Two is about bringing order to the material. If you're learning material that has no structural logic, such as the alphabet, you have to pound it into your brain via jingles, mnemonic gimmicks, or massive repetition. But that won't work with college lessons (chapters in a book or class lectures) because just one of them consists of literally thousands of parts: sentences, points, examples, explanations, statistics, formulas. No one is smart enough to make up a jingle for all that. But the thousands of bits have logical structure. Here are four ways to use that fact to your advantage:

**14. Reduce the material to something you can see at a glance.** In other words, make a *summary*. If you wrote a paraphrase for basic question c (p. P-6), you may already have done this. *The Writer's Way* offers you two concrete ways to do it on paper, the outline and the abstract (Chapters 6 and 7).

How small is small enough? Psychologists have an answer: seven items. Seven is the number of items a normal human mind can hold at one time. So shoot for a summary that's seven normal-size sentences or less. The Magic Number Seven never changes, so don't make the summary bigger if the original text is bigger. A summary of an essay is as long as the summary of a book.

**15. See the pattern.** The pattern, also known as the design, structure, organization, governing principle, logic, paradigm, system, map, model, template, outline, or algorithm, is the idea that arranges the pieces, explains why they're all there and arranged just so, and lets us see the whole thing at a glance.

Since we can only hold seven things in our brain at once, the only way we can master material larger than seven sentences is to see the structure—the organizing principle that makes a book, for instance, be *one* thing, made out of a certain number of chapters, thousands of paragraphs, and tens of thousands of sentences.

Everything that makes sense has a pattern. If I ask you to remember the following:

123456789

it's easy, because you see the pattern and therefore only have to remember one thing. If I ask you to remember this sequence of numbers:

112358132134

it's brutal slogging beyond seven numbers or so, until you see the pattern: Each number is the sum of the previous two numbers (what mathematicians call a Fibonacci series). Now there's only one thing to remember, and it's easy. And notice how size doesn't affect learning difficulty—if I add numbers to either series, the series doesn't get harder to learn as long as its generating principle remains the same.

Often the pattern is spelled out for you. Books have tables of contents, novels have Cliff Notes plot summaries, meetings have agendas, theme parks have maps, car manuals have wiring diagrams, houses have blueprints. When the pattern isn't handed to you, you have to figure it out.

**16. Make a branching tree diagram (BTD).** Of all the patterns in the world, it's the most common and most useful. Here are examples, the first for European languages and the second for popular music.

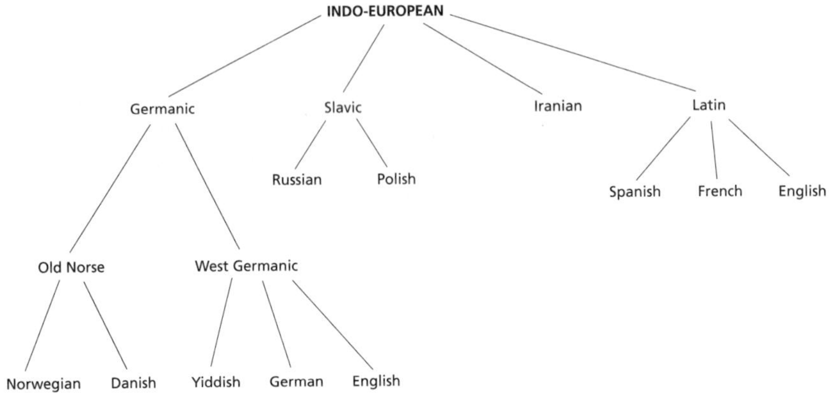


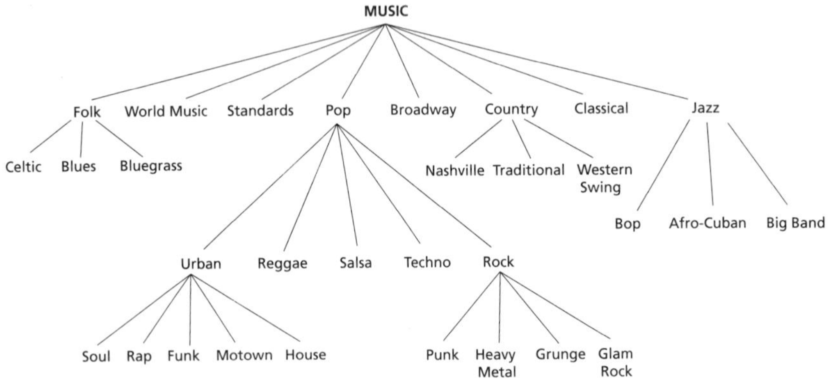


A table of contents is a BTD, printed left to right instead of top to bottom. The BTD shapes material into a pyramid, which allows you to choose how many parts you want to master. If you want to learn just one thing, study the peak of the pyramid; if you want to begin by learning seven things, move down a level or two.

**17. Learn from the top down.** Always begin your learning at the top of the BTD pyramid and work your way down. The reasons are obvious: There are fewer items at the top, which makes learning easier, and the pyramid only makes sense going down—each level explains the level beneath it. You have to understand what a boat is before you can define "dinghy."

In school, we often do the opposite. When we read a chapter in a book, we begin by reading the *words*—the very bottom of the bottom of the pyramid. Then we try to understand each of the sentences. From a sense of each sentence's meaning, we try to understand the paragraphs. And we build toward a sense of the chapter's whole meaning. If we start losing comprehension, we go back down the pyramid and start staring at sentences more intently. It gives you what reading theorists call "tunnel vision." Do the opposite: Skim the words, looking only for the largest meaning. When you're done, go directly to the top of the pyramid and ask the five basic questions of Round One (pp. P-6–P-7). Once you've mastered the top of the pyramid, you can start working down, rereading and seeking understanding of the chapter sections, then the paragraphs, and finally the sentences, always using your understanding of the larger parts to explain the smaller ones.

Once you've organized the material, Round Three takes you further:

**18. Connect the new to the old.** When you learn something new, it needs a place to attach itself on the network of knowledge in your head, like a mollusk that settles on the hull of an ocean liner. The more links you can find between new knowledge and old, the more you'll understand and the better you'll remember. If I ask you to remember a random number, that would take some mental work; but if I ask you to remember your age, which is also a number, you can remember it effortlessly.

The links are for you to invent, and you can construct a personal connection to anything. When I talk about learning by imitating your teacher, connect it to your mental map by imagining yourself imitating horrid Mr. Roarer in fifth grade.

**19. Consider the implications.** To understand something is to be aware of its logical consequences: "If X is true, then Y must be true." All ideas have implications. A lesson will lay down a principle, such as "Learn from the top down"; you make it real by deducing the logical consequences: "If you're having trouble reading a text, read faster, not slower." Understanding isn't about whether you like an idea or think it's true; it's about whether you can live with its consequences. In the 1950s America committed itself to the idea that blacks should have social and legal rights equal to those of whites. We've spent the last fifty-plus years working out the implications of that decision, and we haven't finished yet. Einstein said "$E=mc^2$," and most of the scientific and technological advances of the last century have resulted from exploring the practical applications of that simple equation. We'll talk about ideas and their consequences in detail in Chapter 16.

**20. Nouns are useless.** As you work toward understanding, don't work with nouns by themselves. They're *too easy,* and that includes noun phrases, however large. Nouns create the illusion of substance, but really they're just labels—and like the labels on boxes, they don't guarantee there's anything inside. If you say, "Composition, essay, revision, editing, brainstorming," you've done no work and learned nothing. Ask yourself what you want to say *about* the noun. What do you want to say *about* revision? In other words, *change the noun into a sentence* by adding a verb.

**21. Test your learning by talking.** When the learning process is over, how do you know it worked? That's easy; *say* what you've learned to someone. Tell the material to a classmate, partner, or friend. With knowledge, the proof of ownership isn't being able to write it or think it. Writing is too passive—it's too easy to transcribe without comprehension. And thinking is so insubstantial that we can always tell ourselves we think well. The proof of learning is being able to teach it. This is why generations of teachers have said, "The person who's really learning a lot in the classroom is the teacher."

# Part One

## INTRODUCTION TO WRITING

# Chapter 1

## LEARNING TO WRITE

In the rest of this book, we'll talk about what to do at the moment you're writing. But here in the beginning I want to talk about what you do *in your life* to learn to write well. Here's a lifelong approach to writing, one that makes good writers.

## Learn Like a Baby

As far as we know, the way a baby teaches itself to talk is an excellent way to learn language skills. Generally, people learn to speak effortlessly, happily, and voluminously in seven years or so, starting from nothing. And everyone gets it right; have you ever met a grownup who didn't know where the adjectives go or hadn't mastered his interrogatives?

What do we know about the baby's approach to language acquisition?

1. It takes a long time—years. *Learning to write also takes a while. There is no trick or device or weekend workshop that will hand good writing to you.*
2. The baby practices constantly—not fifteen minutes a day, not an hour a day, but all the time, as an ongoing part of living. *In the same way, writing must be a part of your daily life—you can't just write once a week or when an assignment is due.*
3. The baby works hard, but the work doesn't hurt, and it doesn't leave the baby exhausted, resentful, or hostile to talking. *Writing also takes work to learn, but the work shouldn't hurt.*
4. The baby needs constant exposure to models. He must be surrounded by adult speech, and the more he hears the easier it is to learn. There's no alternative to listening: If the baby doesn't hear English, he can't learn to speak English. *Thus you need constant exposure to examples of good writing. The*

*more you've read, the easier it is to learn to write. There's no alternative to reading: If you haven't read essays, you can't write an essay.*

5. The child wants speech desperately. You don't have to make him talk, and bribing him doesn't help much. He wants to learn for two reasons. First, language is powerful: If you can talk, you can get things you want. Second, language is a primal joy, like music. Babies babble long before they know sounds can "mean" things, just because it's fun. *So you have to want to write, and the only reasons to write that work are to get something you want and to have fun.*
6. The whole world expects the child to learn. Not talking is a sign of a disability or severe psychological trauma. The child is treated as a *talker* from before he utters his first word, not as a *person learning to someday talk. So the world must expect you to write and treat writing as an expected, normal human activity. You must call yourself a writer, not a person trying to learn how to write.* (See joining the club, p. P-8.)
7. It's easy to try too hard or care in the wrong way. If we tell the baby to try hard and to watch his speech carefully, he won't speak better; he'll become tongue-tied. *If you try too hard, you probably won't write better and you may give yourself writer's block. The more you write in fear or write to avoid error, the worse you'll write.*
8. Nobody tells the child how to do it; the child teaches himself. *You'll teach yourself to write. Teachers can encourage, but they can't explain how to do it.*
9. The child practices all aspects of talking at once, holistically. He never breaks language into pieces or steps. No child ever said, "First I'll master nouns, then move on to verbs; first I'll learn declarative sentences, then work on interrogatives." Instead, the child starts out trying to say the whole messages that matter to him the most. *Don't break writing into pieces or "work up to" writing with drills or mechanical exercises. If you want to learn to write essays, write whole essays.*

## The Four Basics

The Baby's Way can be reduced to four keys. To learn any language—Vietnamese or formal essay English—you need four things: exposure to models, motivation, practice, and feedback. But in each case you need the right sort—not just any kind of exposure, motivation, practice, or feedback will do.

## Exposure

Exposure, all by itself, will teach you most of what you need to write. Babies learn to talk by listening, not by talking. If I sent you to live in England for a year, you'd come back speaking with a British accent and using British vocabulary without consciously practicing, doing drills, or being corrected. Saturate yourself with eighteenth-century prose for a couple of months and you'll come out thinking in eighteenth-century prose.

We make language the way we see it made. We have no other choice. That's why we should expose ourselves to models that are written the way we want to write. And being exposed to one thing doesn't teach us to do another, so we must expose ourselves to exactly what we want to write. A lifetime of reading cartoons won't teach us how to write formal essays. If you want to write essays, read essays.

Exposure works faster than you'd imagine. It only takes a Western movie or two to catch on to how Western movies "go." If you read Dave Barry essays for twenty minutes every evening for three weeks, afterwards you could probably write a pretty good Barryian essay.

Ordinary reading will work, but a special kind of reading works better: *reading for the craft.* If someone loved to watch dance and went to a ballet, how much would she learn about dance by watching? A little. But if a practicing dancer went to the ballet, how much would she learn? A lot. The difference is in the way the two people watch. The first watches like an audience. The second watches like an apprentice. Experiencing art doesn't teach you to make art well by itself. Watching movies doesn't make you a director. But once you decide to study directing, every movie you watch is an education.

To write, you must read the way the dancer watches dance and the director watches movies: for the craft, not merely to experience the *effect* of the art, but to see how the effect is wrought. The masses see a movie like *Dumb and Dumber* and laugh; the artist sees *Dumb and Dumber* and, while laughing, studies how the director makes us laugh. How do essays end? Most people have seen it done hundreds of times but haven't noticed how. To learn, as you go on with your reading life, notice with a small part of your mind how each writer you read solves the problem of ending. After a while, you still won't be able to say how endings go, but you'll know, and when you write you'll do it like that.

You need a second kind of exposure as well: Besides exposure to the finished product, you need exposure to the writing process. If you wanted to learn to make automobile engines, you'd need to see more than just finished engines; you'd need to see people making engines, from initial brainstorming and design to final machining and testing. You need to see writers at work, reacting to prompts, doing research, organizing drafts, cutting, line editing. Writing is the only complex skill we're asked to master without spending a lot of time seeing someone do it.

This second kind of exposure is hard to get. When was the last time you watched a skilled writer rewrite a draft? For most of us, the answer is "Never." Where can you go to get such exposure? To a writer's colony. There's probably one meeting in your composition classroom.

## Motivation

To write well, you have to want to. How obvious. If someone hates tennis and plays only when he's forced to, we expect he won't play well. Yet in our world we usually accept hating to write and try to work around it: Of course you hate to write—doesn't everyone?—but we'll force you to write with grades or convince you to care by telling you no one will hire you if you can't write. That doesn't work. If you can't find real, personal reasons to write, you won't write well. Period.

Luckily, those reasons aren't hard to find. All humans love writing, the way we love music, dancing, or talking. All children are dying to write, and scribble long before they can make letters. We even love the supposedly unrewarding parts of writing, like spelling—as you know if you've ever done crossword puzzles or jumbles, or played Hangman, Scrabble, Word Search, Boggle, Perquacky, Spill and Spell, Four Letter Words, or any of the other spelling games that fascinate schoolkids and make game manufacturers rich. We love language as stuff and love to play with it like clay; we love puns, word games, tongue twisters, the latest slang phrase, rhymes, and secret codes like Pig Latin. Even the people who "hate English" in school write secret notes to each other in class the minute the teacher's back is turned and rush off to read the latest X-Men comic book or see a movie or listen to a rap album, all of which are forms of literature and are made out of "English."

Nor do we have to work hard to develop high standards. Children, when they begin writing, have to be taught to *lower* their standards, or they'll fuss over and polish every letter and every punctuation mark and never get beyond the first word or two.

But something gets in the way of all that natural love of language, because most people, by the time they're grown up, say they don't like to write. And when they try to motivate themselves, things get worse. They try harder and hate writing more. People usually write poorly not because they don't care enough, but because they care too much. Most people who "hate to write" care so much that they dare not do it—the chance of failure and pain is too high. I can prove it: You're at a party and find out the person you're talking to is an English teacher. Suddenly you realize that the way you use English "matters." Does that make you speak better, or worse?

We let fear of criticism and failure kill a lot of things we once loved. We all love to dance and sing as children, but when we grow up we learn to raise our standards, critique our dancing and singing sternly, and think about how we sound or look to others. As a result, we decide we "don't like" dancing and singing, and never do it where anyone can watch. But it's not the dancing and singing we don't like; it's the value system we've learned to impose on it.

So what can you do? First, *turn off the language cop in your head,* the voice that's policing you for errors and failure. Write the way you used to play with clay or paints—to see what comes of it, without fear of reprisal. Remember how badly you drive when a police car is on your tail? No one creates well in fear or when motivated by self-contempt. (Of course, you'll have to polish the writing before you send it to an editor.)

Second, *use writing to accomplish something you passionately want to do.* Some years ago my daughter and I began music lessons. She was nearly tone deaf, so the program started with very simple tunes like "Three Blind Mice." Molly was doing pretty well, pushed along by a bubbly teacher and a rabidly supportive parent. Then one day she came home from a friend's house. She had heard the soundtrack album from the Broadway musical *Annie.* She sang me "Tomorrow," a song of breathtaking difficulty. And she sang it beautifully. Suddenly her musical training took off, helped by the *Annie* album, which I immediately bought. Her standards for her own singing went through the ceiling. The moral: You learn by finding tasks worth the work. For most writers that means say something you care passionately about to an audience of real people, and get as a reward their thoughtful response to *what* you said—not how you said it.

Exposure and motivation will teach you to write pretty well by themselves. From his college days to his sixties, my father never wrote a word except to fill out insurance forms and write an occasional business letter. But he read voraciously all that time, mostly in anthropology and the sciences. In his sixties he went to Africa, encountered the Bushmen, and suddenly wanted to write a book about them, his own life spent hunting, and humankind's relationship to the wilderness. And he wrote a very nice book. Whether it won a Pulitzer Prize isn't the point; the point is he could write without much more than a lifetime of reading and a passionate need to say something.

## Practice

Of course, you have to write to learn how to write, and the more you write the better. But practice is vastly overrated as a teaching device—remember, doing something teaches you nothing (p. P-2). Babies will never learn to speak French, however much they "practice," if they never hear it spoken, and doing something over and over again won't make you remember it if you don't care, as every generation of sentence diagrammers has proved.

## Feedback

When you're learning, you try something and see what happens. You hit the tennis ball and watch where it lands. Where it lands tells you if the shot worked or not. That's feedback. Writing has no built-in feedback system. You write the essay and hand it in, and it's like playing tennis in the dark: You hit the ball, it flies off into the blackness, and you learn nothing. You need to know where the ball went. You need readers who will tell you: Were they convinced? Was the explanation clear? Did the opening paragraph capture their interest? Did they like the writer's voice? Were the jokes funny?

Feedback can go horribly wrong and maim the user. If you ask someone who "hates to write" where she learned to hate it, she'll probably say, "My Xth-grade teacher ripped every paper I wrote to shreds, covered every page in red ink, and I've been afraid to write ever since." We know the damage it does, yet against all evidence people remain convinced that mechanical error marking is the single most necessary element in a successful writing program. Many students demand that I mark their writing up, like patients who demand that the dentist's drill hurt so they know they're getting their money's worth.

Let me give you five reasons why you won't learn to write from error marking. First, error marking hurts most people so much that they can't stand to learn from it. Second, it overloads the writer: The essay comes back a blur of red, and the writer doesn't know where to begin. Third, it speaks to the what and not the how: It labels what's wrong but doesn't tell you why or how to prevent it. It's as if a tennis coach watched you serve for fifteen minutes and said, "You're serving into the net," and walked on. (I know that! Tell me how to fix it!) Fourth, because error marking works best on minor mechanical features (spelling, noun–pronoun agreement) and worst on big issues (thesis, structure, tone, intention), it implies that minor mechanical features are the most important aspect of writing. Fifth, it equates good writing with error-free writing, yet we all know that we get no pleasure at all as readers from writing that merely avoids errors. Both implications strip writing of its true purposes and rewards.

So what kind of feedback helps? Chapter 10 is all about that, and writers will tell you later in this chapter (beginning on p. 12), so I'll be brief now. Feedback helps when it is offered as suggestions (instead of orders) given to help accomplish what the writer wants to do (instead of to correct errors or follow rules or do what the teacher wants). Ideally, the writer says to the reader, "I'm trying to do *this;* how could

I accomplish that better?" And the reader says, "Maybe if you did a little of *that* it would work better."

## What Good Is a Composition Class?

In your pursuit of the Four Basics, a composition class can help:

### Exposure

A class can't give you the thousands of hours of reading you need, but it can help by exposing you to a world of great writing you might never encounter otherwise. And it can help you practice the art of reading for the craft, so the reading you do for the rest of your life will be writer's training. More important, it can expose you to models of the writing process. A writing class will surround you with other writers writing, so you can see how they do it.

### Motivation

A writing class can help you find real reasons to write, by introducing you to the great writers who inspire you and make you say, "Hey, I wish I could do that!" And it can help by giving you a real audience of classmates who will react enthusiastically and thoughtfully to your work—and by surrounding you with writing artisans who are excited by language and reading and writing and who will quicken your excitement for these things. The club of writers often holds its meetings in classrooms.

### Practice

A writing course may be the one time in your life when you can treat writing the way it should be treated, as an ever-present, integral part of your thinking, reading, and conversing. You'll never have it so good again, believe me.

### Feedback

Feedback is a writing course's best gift. A writer's most precious possession is a thoughtful colleague willing to read her writing carefully and offer considered advice. In life, you're lucky to find two; in a writing class, you should be surrounded by them. Think of it: The university goes to all the trouble of rounding up twenty-five people whose job it is for four months to help you write.

## How Can I Write Well Right Now?

The Four Basics are a lifelong journey; what if you have an essay due this Friday? We can use the principles of exposure, motivation, and feedback to find a way to write well today.

Since you need exposure, write in a language you already know—your speaking language. Or write in a form you've read a lot of: a comic strip, a sports column, a TV sitcom script, a personal narrative, an ad, a movie review.

Since you need motivation, write something you want to write; say something that matters to you; write to people you want to talk to; write something you'd love to read.

Since you need feedback, find a classmate—a fellow member of the club of writers—and two days before the essay is due spend an hour kicking a rough draft around. Ask your classmate what he thinks in response to what you said. Ask him how the essay could be made to work better. Pay him back by doing the same for his rough draft.

Sometimes you only have to do the first of these three. Here's a writer who learned to write well overnight by using the language she spoke. Her first draft began like this:

> The use of phonics as we discussed after reading Weller's book is like starting at the end of learning to read in which no meaning or insight is given to the context of the concept of reading.

In conference, I asked her to *say* to me what she meant. She did, in strong, plain English. I said to her, "Look—you talk easily and well. So trust your talk, and talk your papers." Her next essay (on how to teach spelling) began

> Spelling should be taught as a subject separate from reading. Good reading skills do not mean good spelling skills. Spelling is learned by writing.

Beautiful!

Now here's a writer who learned to write well overnight by writing in a form she knew well. Her first essay began like this:

> As a teacher of young children the act of censoring literature is an important task. This prevents bad material from entering the classroom. On the other hand, who has the right to judge what is considered "bad material"? However, our society has a set of basic human values and it is necessary to protect these morals through the act of censorship in regards to textbooks and other various forms of reading material.

That's in trouble. Her second essay was a narrative, and she wrote like this:

Finally, the moment had arrived. Summer was over and the first day of school was just three days away. Jennifer was so eager and anxious to go to school. She got up bright and early, put on her favorite jeans, her new tee-shirt, and her new blue tennis shoes. Her mom and dad were still asleep, so she made her own lunch and left a note telling them she went to school early because she did not want to be late for her first day. With her lunch pail in one hand, and her Pee-Chee folder in the other, she set out for her little journey to the bus stop alone.

# WRITER'S WORKSHOP

## What Helps, What Doesn't

Many of the chapters in this book end with "Writer's Workshop" sections like this one. If you would like a word on how they work and how you might read them, see the Preface, p. xv.

My first attempt at a "big" piece of writing was an adventure story I wrote in the sixth grade. I slaved on it for weeks and was hugely proud of how long it was. I gave it to my teacher and waited antsily for his reaction. After several weeks, I asked how it was going, and he took it from the filing cabinet where it had been lying since I gave it to him, wrote "AA" on it, and handed it back to me. He had never looked at it. The grade was just to shut me up. That was in 1957, and I've never written another story. It still hurts to think about it.

Chapter 1 is about the model for "good writing" and the image of ourselves as writers we carry around with us. We construct that model and that image from lessons learned in experiences like mine. Some of the lessons are good, and we should keep them. Sometimes they're poisonous and keep us from writing well, and we have to unlearn them. Every term I ask my students to examine their past for the events that shaped their attitudes toward writing, then turn the responses into conclusions: What works, what doesn't? What experiences make for strong, happy writers and what make for frightened, weak ones? Here are some typical responses:

> *In the eighth grade our teacher assigned an autobiography. We bought a blank photo album, filled it with old family photos, and wrote about each one. It was fantastic. There was no grade, no marks, just a comment: "It sounds like you led a very exciting life!" I still have that album and will always cherish it. The teacher could have ruined it with a grade and red pen marks.*

> *I can honestly say that I loved to write, until I had Mr. Del Rio in my junior year. The whole year was grammar. It wasn't terribly awful until he made us write papers to include certain types of phrases and clauses. They had to be underlined in red, so he could identify them quickly. The papers had no meaning at all.*

> *I never did believe that what I learned in school was writing. Real writing was the stuff that gave you goose bumps when you read it. I wrote at home and kept the products in a box in the closet. I certainly couldn't take it to school to be scrutinized for grammar mistakes.*

> *I remember my high school English teacher telling us that if he finds one grammar error, he will not finish reading your paper. It didn't matter if you had a terrific paper or not. Ever since, I have been dwelling on my sentence structure and where I should put a semicolon, instead of just writing. I wish I could have had a teacher who would have allowed me to write just for the heck of it.*

> *I wrote a poem that delighted me. I thought it would make the teacher laugh. I got an A on it. I didn't continue writing poems. An A is a lousy response to a poem.*

> *I enjoy writing because as far back as I can remember my dad read to me often, at least once each night. When I learned to write (not spelling correctly or with any punctuation to speak of) I would write stories that were take-offs from books my dad had read to me.*

> *In school I would hear the words "write a paper" and I would fill with dread. But I loved to write letters to my friends. Writing itself isn't what I fear, it's knowing it's going to be evaluated and scrutinized.*

*In college I tried to do exactly what my teachers asked. I stopped trying to please myself, in order to please them. My teachers chose the subjects, most of which I couldn't understand or had no meaning to me, and I knew I must say what they wanted me to say. After I spent hours on a paper, I'd look at it and hate it.*

*My earliest recollection of writing is the scribbles Mom and Dad would proudly send to Grandma and Aunt Mary. Mom and Dad were great models. They were prolific writers. Mom was always jotting things down: grocery lists, letters, notes to babysitters. Dad wrote forestry articles, lists of things to do around the home, 4-H lesson plans, checks. Armed with crayons and then pencils, my siblings and I were encouraged to draw or write, as long as we left the walls alone. A favorite writing assignment was writing our birthday menus. I also loved writing checks when playing house.*

*When I was exposed to Ken Macrorie's concept of "Engfish," I realized I had spent at least fifteen years of schooling perfecting a language I would never use again once I left school behind.*

*I've been writing a weekly newsletter for my church. When I began I was preoccupied with mechanical errors. After a while, I realized the audience wasn't interested in being grammar critics but was interested in what the newsletter said.*

*My teachers have always wanted the standard five-paragraph essays. I end up saying everything in the first two paragraphs, and everything else is a bunch of stuff even I don't understand.*

*Three friends and I decided to put together an underground newspaper. We were the talk of the school. No one knew who we were. I would love it when someone sitting in class would start laughing at some article. One of us overheard some students saying, "Okay, so we know they're in fourth-period PE and drive mini-trucks. Now all we got to do is find out who they are so we can kill them."*

*I never really liked writing until the fifth grade. Before that, all I wrote were book reports. Then one day the teacher told us to write an excuse for not doing our homework. I rambled on about how my pet dragon ate my assignment and how I got a Ferrari for my birthday and got arrested for going 140 miles an hour (pretty good lie for a ten-year-old). My teacher liked it so much she printed it in the school newspaper. I was really excited and wrote other stories just for fun. Next year, I had a teacher who made us diagram any grammar errors we made. I was turned off to writing until high school.*

*I remember when I first learned to hate writing. In the fourth grade I decided to write a fantasy story about a magic ring that would make me invisible. I was scribbling away when my teacher came by. She marked all the misspelled words and the punctuation mistakes in bright red ink. She lectured me on using good handwriting, not "chicken scratch." I never did finish that story.*

*For years after that I had trouble writing. I know it sounds ridiculous for such a small incident to have affected me so much, but it did. I would erase my first draft so many times I would wear holes in the paper. I wrote with my arm circled around my paper so no one could see what I was writing, and if someone tried to comment or correct it I would tear it up and throw it away.*

Obviously, many people are feeling a lot of pain about their writing. And the people in these histories are the system's *successes,* those who thrived and went to college, most of them intending to become teachers! But there's comfort to be taken here, too. All of us writers are having the same experiences, reacting the same way, thriving on the same things, and being curdled by the same things. We're all in this together, and we agree on what helps and what doesn't. For instance, being read to a lot by your parents helps; being forced to push your personal message into cookie-cutter patterns like five-paragraph essay paradigms doesn't. Critical feedback in the form of conversation with a mentor making suggestions about alternatives helps; critical feedback in the form of red-pen corrections doesn't. All we have to do is do the things that help and avoid the things that don't.

So what should you do to become a healthy writer? First, tell your own story. Get clear on what assumptions about writing you now own and where you got them. Second, using the histories in this section and your own experience, make a list of things that work and things that hurt. Third, reject the poisonous messages you've been fed. Finally, create for yourself a writing environment that nourishes you as a writer.

**Now it's your turn.** In this chapter you've been listening to a conversation about how people learn to write. It's time to join the conversation.

Step 1: Make your own contribution to the collection of tales in Writer's Workshop. Write a two-page narrative detailing everything you've done or had done to you that has helped form your writing or your view of yourself as a writer. Remember to go back to the beginning—most people's attitudes toward reading and writing are formed long before they get to school. And think about what isn't in your life as well as what is—sometimes lacks are profoundly educational, like never seeing your parents reading for pleasure.

Step 2: Make a list of experiences that promote writing and a list of experiences that curdle it. For instance, you might have "Mom puts sample of my writing on the fridge" in the plus list.

Step 3: As a class, pool your anecdotes and your lists, until you have answered this question: What would a person do if she were setting out to create for herself the perfect writer's upbringing and environment?

## EXERCISES

1. Write a two-page essay exploring how well your writing career up to now has provided you with each of the Four Basics (pp. 4–9). List changes you could make to improve the amount and type of each you're getting now.

2. For each of the nine principles in the Baby's Way (pp. 3–4), write a paragraph discussing how well your writing program up to this point in your life has followed that principle. List changes you could make to follow it better.

3. Write an essay discussing the kinds of feedback your writing has received throughout your life. Begin with your earliest memories of writing, and continue through recent school experiences. Rate each kind of feedback for effectiveness: Did it help, or did it hurt? How much healthy feedback have you received in school?

# Chapter 2

## WHAT MAKES WRITING GOOD?

In Chapter 1 we talked about how the bulk of your writing skills are acquired. Now let's talk about what the goal of writing is. When you set out to "write well," what exactly are you trying to accomplish? You can't write well until you know the answer, just as you can't play baseball well until you know that the objective is to run around the bases and reach home plate. The bad news is, many students are trying to "write well" by trying to accomplish the wrong things. The good news is, what makes writing good is something simple, something you already have.

Let's look at a piece of the real stuff and see what it's got. Here's a professional essay. What does it have that bad essays don't have?

## MAKING A BRAVE NEW WORLD WITH NO ROOM FOR CHILDREN

RASA GUSTAITUS

The man came running toward us as we were doing a few last stretches after a morning turn around the Golden Gate Park track. A small figure trailed behind him.

He came alongside and passed—a youngish man in excellent condition, with carefully groomed mustache, blue and red jogging shorts, appropriate shoes and socks. His companion, not nearly as sure-footed and falling farther behind every minute, turned out to be a little girl of maybe three, at most four, in a hooded green winter coat that flopped loosely around her. She too passed us. But a few dozen feet away, as she realized the man was receding hopelessly into the distance, she stopped, stretched her arms toward his back, and wailed: "Daddy!"

He was way out of hearing range now. Sobbing, she stood alone in the sand on the track that surrounds an enormous grassy playing field. More runners passed her, turned to glance, and ran on.

I went over and took her hand. "He'll be back," I said. "See, he's just turning the bend. Soon he'll come around again."

She stopped crying and I led her to the bleachers. Her nose was running, but I had nothing to wipe it with. After a while, the man passed again. "Thanks," he said to me; and, to the child, "I told you it's all right as long as you can see me." Again we watched his back recede.

"I have three daddies," the child said.

"Oh? And how many mommies?"

"Well, there's my mom, and you, and . . ."

"I'm not your mommy," I hastened to correct her, so as to avert yet another abandonment. "I'm just a friend."

We talked a bit more, but it was time for me to leave. So I advised her to sit there and watch, hoping the man was a two-mile and not an eight-mile daddy—whether or not his position in her family was daddy one, two, or three.

The scene stayed in my mind: the vigorous running man and the tiny sniffling girl, with the too-heavy coat slipping off her shoulders, left behind. It struck me that the image summed up what has happened in many American communities, in places where new gourmet bakeries and physical fitness studios open daily and families are increasingly scarce.

Most of the adults seem over-scheduled with personal self-improvement efforts. They're out there running, getting body work, practicing martial arts, writing novels, learning to paint after forty, dabbling in psychic studies. They are full of vigor and enthusiasm.

Meanwhile, the children are sent to McDonald's for dinner and parked endlessly in front of TV sets. They run their favorite movies through the videocassette player, and then turn on their radio stations. While the adults seek out wholesomeness to keep their aging systems at optimum levels, the children wind up with junk food for body, mind, and soul. They have multiple parents with whom they cannot keep up.

I tried, recently, to find a children's jazz dance class for my twelve-year-old daughter, only to discover that the two big studios nearby cater to adults.

"The parents are working; they don't have time to take the children around," explained one teacher. "You'll find some children's classes in Marin County or the East Bay."

One after another, the family neighborhoods of U.S. cities have taken this turn, toward a refinement that begs larger questions. The single people who move into houses vacated by dying Irish widows here have good taste. And childhood fantasies are not entirely absent: Among the new shops in my neighborhood is one specializing in handmade stuffed animals. But most customers are adults buying for other adults.

In a local flat, a single mother laid off from her job as a school-bus driver speaks of the isolation she feels as she struggles to get by with her two-year-old son. Nearby a feminist-established Women's Building boasts a lot of activities, and most of them have "child care provided"—an obligatory service for feminist events. "But how about something you do *with* children?" asks this mother. . . .

Congress has approved the expenditure of $177.1 billion for the MX missile, just for starters. Economies will be made on school lunches and educational support services. But armed defense may be irrelevant to a society that ignores its children. It is already on a fast-track, self-destructive course. ❖

*(Pacific News Service, 1985)*

## What Good Writing Isn't

Let's list the things that a good essay *doesn't* need:

*A large vocabulary.* We know all or almost all of Gustaitus's words.

*Complex sentences.*

*A brand new idea.* Gustaitus isn't saying anything that hasn't been said before.

*An argument that's absolutely and exclusively true.* The essay has a nice thesis, but the opposite—that our society is built around catering to children—is just as true.

*The last word on its topic.* The essay doesn't end discussion of how our society deals with its children; it just adds a little something to it.

*Profound thinking.* The ideas in the essay aren't subtle or brainy.

*Extensive research or expertise.* Gustaitus's only "research" she got off the front page of the newspaper—the MX missile budget.

*Extraordinary experience.* I've had experiences like Gustaitus's encounter on the jogging track several times. I bet you have too.

Since Gustaitus's essay doesn't have these things, they can't be what makes good writing good, and you don't need to have them either.

There are things Gustaitus's essay does have that make it *better* but that won't make the essay good by themselves: transition between ideas, overall organization, thesis, examples, conclusion, unambiguous language. They're not the heart of writing, the way reaching home is the heart of baseball—they won't make your writing good unless you have the "other thing" too.

There are also things the essay *must* have but for which it gets no credit at all: spelling, punctuation, sound usage, and the other mechanical aspects of writing. You'd never say to a friend, "Oh, I read the most wonderful article in the paper yesterday. Such comma placement! And every word spelled just right!" These things don't make your writing "good"—only legal.

## What Good Writing Is: The Sense of Audience

The key that separates good writing from bad is a sense of *audience.* Writers who write for the wrong reasons think of writing as a mechanical act with certain "good" surface features, and when they write, they try to make an essay that includes them: correct spelling, an outlineable structure, a thesis statement, a large vocabulary, complete documentation of sources, and so on. That approach produces essays like Dr. Frankenstein's early experiments: However meticulously you sew the bits and pieces together, it's never going to get up off the operating table and walk. The alternative, the only approach to writing that works, is to set out to *do something to the reader.*

You can do anything to your reader you want—move him to tears, bug him, convince him to vote for your candidate, convince him you're right, teach him how to make jambalaya, make him feel what growing up with your big brother was like. And you know you've succeeded when you get what you set out to get: He cries, he feels bugged, he votes your way, he thinks you're right, he learns how to make jambalaya, or he knows what growing up with your big brother was like.

You already know all this. And (here is the really wonderful thing) you already know how to do it, too. All children begin their writing careers by writing the messages they think will pack the biggest wallop for their readers: "I love you." "I am Ericka." "Come to my party." But somewhere along the line we forget we know it. A friend of mine once asked his students to write dialogues. He suggested to one student that if she had the speakers say less than the whole truth the scene might get more dramatically interesting, because the reader would then have to look behind the words. The writer replied, "But you didn't say we had to make the dialogues interesting." All we have to do is remind ourselves of the secret that writer forgot.

Once you get the secret of good writing firmly in your mind, you think in a different way about writers' decisions. Instead of saying, "What's the rule?" when a question arises, you say, "What works? What does my reader want? What am I trying to do to her?" For instance, let's say you're writing your way through an essay and you approach the conclusion. You have a decision to make: Should you summarize the essay in the final paragraph? With the old attitude, you recall someone telling you that in an essay you should "tell them what you're going to tell them, tell them, then tell them what you told them." So you summarize. With the new attitude, you ask yourself, "Does my reader want or need a summary? Will a summary conclusion read well?" For most essays the answer to both questions is no. Readers can remember what they've read and don't appreciate it if you tell them again. In other words, summary conclusions usually *don't work.*

### Having a Reader in Your Head

All writers have colleagues read their work and tell them how it reads. We'll practice doing that in Chapter 10. But no reader has the time to tell you how every line you write works, and you need to know, so you need an imaginary reader in your head. As you write every line, you imagine a first-time reader reading it and guess how she responds. The more you hear the reader's responses, the better you can decide how to react to and control them, and the better you'll write.

When I talk of hearing the writer's responses in your head, I mean it in the most literal way. If you're writing a recipe for novice cooks and you write, "Then add a tablespoon of oregano," you should hear your reader responding, "What's oregano? Where can I get some? What's a tablespoon?" If you write, "All U.S. presidents in this century have been owned by the oil companies," you should hear the reader responding, "How do you know? Can you prove it? That sounds awfully wild to me. Are you putting me on?" and so on. If you write, "Cleaning up our environment is a humongous task," you had better realize that some readers will respond, "This person talks like a kid," or "This guy doesn't speak my language."

You can never be sure how your reader is responding, because people are unpredictable and different readers have different values and knowledge. If you write, "Gun control violates the right to bear arms guaranteed by the Constitution," you'll evoke a firestorm of reactions:

> Right on!
> Just another gun nut.
> Not that old cliché!
> What does the Constitution say?
> Is that what the Constitution really means?
> So we can't control guns at all?
> Can't we change the Constitution?
> What's "the Constitution"? That old sailing ship?

You can't speak to all these voices, but you don't have to—as long as you're imagining your reader responding *in any way at all,* you're being a writer.

Nor does this mean you have to do what the reader wants. You may want to frustrate him, make him mad, trick him—but you have to know he's feeling frustrated, angered, or tricked, and you must be doing it to him for a reason. And the reader doesn't need to be *pleased* all the time; he just needs to be able to look back, when the reading is over, at what was done to him and see the reason for it—he says, "I see now why the writer refused to tell me what was going on until the end—he had his reasons."

So the good writer doesn't write and then ask herself what she wants to say next; she writes, asks herself what her reader says in response, then asks herself what she wants to say in response to that. The text becomes a dialogue. We'll see that dialogue written out on pp. 27–29, and again on pp. 112–113.

We depend on the dialogue more than we know, and writing is harder than speaking largely because the other participant has to be made up. When we talk, we know the listener is involved even when she's silent, because the body language tells us so. But to get in touch with how crucial the listener's response is to us, try talking to someone who seems to be asleep, or try talking to someone who is utterly quiet on the telephone. We become tongue-tied and have to prod the listener for assurance: "Are you still there? You listening to me?" When we write, we need the same assurance, but we have to construct a listener who gives it to us.

This does *not* mean that writing is good if it causes a reaction in the reader. Any and all writing causes readers to react—lousy writing often causes readers to react with confusion, frustration, boredom, and anger, for instance. The true principle is, Writing is good if it causes the reaction *the author set out to cause* in the reader, and then *works with* that reaction—hears it, reacts to it, addresses it, honors it.

## Giving the Readers What They Need

Good writers give readers everything they need to read them well. Good readers are busy doing lots of jobs; it's your job to assist them. For example,

*They're summarizing,* so you must give them an essay that's summarizable.

*They're trying to put what they're reading to personal use*—"What good is this to me?"—so you must give them something they can use.

*They're trying to understand how you got to your conclusion,* so you must include the evidence and reasoning that took you there.

*They're trying to understand,* so you have to explain.

*They're trying to connect with you,* so you have to be human on the page.

The clearer you are on what a reader's jobs are, the more you can help him do them and the better you'll write.

### Seeing Writing as Performance

Good writing knows it's a performance. Good writers are hams on the page. They feel the presence of the audience the way a stage actor does. The only difference is that the writer's audience must be imagined. People who read aloud well are usually good writers, and a simple way to write well is to *write something you'd love to read out loud.*

## It Really Works: Two Proofs

If good writing is all about having a reader firmly in mind, we should be able to take writers who are trying to "make essays" and tell them to write to real people instead, and their writing should get better instantly. And it works. Here's a passage from an essay on hypnotism, written by someone with no sense of humans reading him:

> For some types of material, learning while in an actual state of hypnosis is best, while for other types of material, it is better to study in a waking state with post-hypnotic suggestions providing the improvement. Rote memorization is best done in a hypnotic state, but material of a technical nature which requires integration into one's present knowledge of the subject area should be done in the waking state. The reason that technical material can't be effectively learned while under hypnosis is because the subconscious mind lacks the ability for critical and inductive reasoning. Only the conscious mind has this ability. However, post-hypnotic suggestions can help to improve the learning of technical material.

I asked the writer to rewrite it as if he were talking to real people, and he produced this lovely stuff:

> If you're trying to learn a foreign language, memorize a definition or a speech, or anything that requires rote memorization, then it is best to do it in an actual hypnotic state. However, technical material is another matter. You can memorize the material easily enough, but all you can do with it is repeat it, just like a parrot. With post-hypnotic suggestions, you can improve your ability to concentrate, retain, and recall the technical material.

We should also be able to find good writing that "breaks the rules" when breaking the rules does what the writer wants to do to the reader. Here are two examples. The first is a paragraph from *The Right Stuff* by Tom Wolfe, describing how navy pilots feel the first time they have to land on an aircraft carrier:

> This was a *skillet!*—a frying pan!—a short-order grill!—not gray but black, smeared with skid marks from one end to the other and glistening with pools of hydraulic fluid and the occasional jet-fuel slick, all of it still hot, sticky, greasy, runny, virulent from God knows what traumas—still ablaze!—consumed in detonations, explosions, flames, combustion, roars, shrieks, whines, blasts, horrible shudders, fracturing impacts, as little men in screaming red and yellow and purple and green shirts with black Mickey Mouse helmets over their ears skittered about on the surface as if for their very lives (You've said it now!), hooking fighter planes onto the catapault shuttles so that they can explode their afterburners and be slung off the deck in a red-mad fury with a *kaboom!* that pounds through the entire deck—a procedure that seems absolutely controlled, orderly, sublime, however, compared to what he is about to watch as aircraft return to the ship for what is known in the engineering stoicisms of the military as "recovery and arrest." . . . As the aircraft came closer and the carrier heaved on into the waves and the plane's speed did not diminish and the deck did not grow steady—indeed, it pitched up and down five or ten feet per greasy heave—one experienced a neural alarm that no lecture could have prepared him for: this is not an *airplane* coming toward me, it is a brick with some poor sonofabitch riding it (*someone much like myself!*), and it is not *gliding,* it is *falling,* a thirty-thousand-pound brick, headed not for a stripe on the deck but for *me*—and with a horrible *smash!* it hits the skillet, and with a blur of momentum as big as a freight train's it hurtles toward the far end of the deck—another blinding storm!—another roar as the pilot pushes the throttle up to full military power and another smear of rubber screams out over the skillet—and this is nominal!—quite okay!—for a wire stretched across the deck has grabbed the hook on the end of the plane as it hit the deck tail down, and the smash was the rest of the fifteen-ton brute slamming onto the deck, as it tripped up, so that it is now straining against the wire at full throttle, in case it hadn't held and the plane had "boltered" off the end of the deck and had to struggle up into the air again. ❖
>
> *(pp. 20–22)*

Here are some of the conventional essay-making rules Wolfe breaks:

Avoid run-on sentences.
Avoid long paragraphs.
Have a thesis statement.
Avoid redundancy.
Avoid exclamation points.
Avoid parentheses.

Now here's a rule-breaking essay by Steven Rubenstein:

## THE PEOPLE VERSUS

It was 3:02 P.M. The trial was nearly over. The jurors filed into a small room and the bailiff locked the door behind them. The defendant and his family got up and walked down the stairs and across the street into the bar.

They didn't say anything. The family—the defendant, his parents, and his brother—sat down. The defendant ordered a soda water and everyone else ordered beers. When the drinks arrived, they drank them. It was 3:18 P.M.

There wasn't anything to talk about, really. The only thing to talk about happened three months earlier. The 21-year-old defendant, with his best buddy beside him, drove off the road and into a tree. The buddy was killed and the defendant, as he would do for weeks afterward, cried.

The jury had something to talk about, because they had to decide whether the defendant was guilty of manslaughter. But the defendant and his family didn't have to decide anything. All they had to do was wait.

It was 3:27 P.M. The waitress asked the defendant if he wanted another glass of soda water. He said no.

The father left to go to the store and returned with a bag of licorice. He offered it around the table. The defendant didn't feel like any licorice. What he felt like doing was looking at the clock again. It said 3:56 P.M.

Somebody got up and punched a number on the jukebox. The Everly Brothers sang, "Bye Bye, Love" but it didn't take very long. When they were through, it was 4:01 P.M.

"I wonder," said the brother, "if they picked a foreman yet."

The bartender was polishing a large jar of pickled hard-boiled eggs that sat on the bar. Everybody watched him do it. The father asked if anyone wanted a pickled egg. Nobody wanted one.

A copy of the newspaper was lying on the next table. The father picked it up and turned to the horoscopes and read the one for Sagittarius out loud. His son was a Sagittarius.

"You make a dazzling comeback after an error. All is forgiven."

The defendant tried to smile.

The prosecutor stood on the courthouse lawn and talked to the defense lawyer. He lit a cigarette and said he didn't expect to win and that, if he did win, he wasn't going to feel very good about it. But the law says if you drive your car too fast and it goes off the road and into a tree and your best friend dies, you can be sent to jail for a year. The number of the law is 192(3)(b).

The defense lawyer and the prosecutor watched the cars cruise down State Street. It was about 5:00 P.M., which would have been rush hour if Ukiah had one.

At 8:59 P.M., the foreman of the jury rang the buzzer. The family settled into their seats and the judge put on his robe. The defendant tucked in his blue cowboy shirt but none of the jurors saw him do it because, as they filed into the courtroom, they all looked the other way.

The foreman handed the verdict to the bailiff and the bailiff handed it to the judge.

"We, the jury, find the defendant guilty . . . "

The jurors, as they left the courtroom, told the defense lawyer how sad they were and how they talked for six hours and how, in the end, there was nothing else they could do if the law says you are guilty if you drive your car too fast and it goes off the road and into a tree and your best friend dies. ❖

*(The San Francisco Chronicle, Nov. 20, 1982)*

Here are some of the essay-making rules Rubenstein breaks:

Avoid redundancy.
Avoid run-on sentences.
Add short sentences together to avoid choppiness.
Reveal topic, thesis, and purpose in the opener.

Wolfe and Rubenstein break the rules because breaking the rules "works." Wolfe wants to overload the reader and make her slightly hysterical, to re-create the pilot's sensation of nightmare bewilderment. Rubenstein wants to be repetitive and boring, because he seeks the horror of tedious time-filling against a backdrop of unthinkable nightmare.

The rest of this book will offer you scads of rules for good writing. They're good rules, and your writing will usually get better if you follow them. But trying to write well by following the rules is the long, hard road, and I'll keep encouraging you to take the shortcut: Ask, "What works?" And there is no answer to that question until you imagine what you write *doing something to somebody.*

# WRITER'S WORKSHOP

## The Reader's Dialogue

Readers typically keep their reactions to themselves as they read, but if we ask them to speak those reactions out loud, they will. I let my class read the first few sentences of a student essay one sentence at a time and asked them to say out loud everything they were thinking after each sentence. Here's the passage, beginning with the title, with some of their reactions in italics.

## Writing Outside Oneself: A Lesson Plan

*What does "writing outside oneself" mean?*
*Must be some kind of teacher's manual.*
*Is there "inside" and "outside" writing?*

In order to make beginning writing students feel comfortable about their writing, we encourage essays that are very egocentric.

*This isn't for me—I'm not going to be a teacher.*
*What does "egocentric" mean?*
*I'm not sure what an egocentric essay is—got any examples?*
*Isn't "egocentric" a bad thing to be? It has very negative connotations for me.*

We ask them to write about their own lives, to describe a favorite place or best friend, to write about a favorite holiday, or to tell a story about something that happened to them.

*I know what he means by "egocentric" now.*
*That's "inside writing" I suppose—so "outside writing" must be nonpersonal, objective writing?*
*Is he in favor of doing this or against it?*
*Why do "we" do this?*

These essays allow the students to loosen up.

*He's telling us why now.*
*He thinks it's a good thing.*

*How does egocentric writing make people "loose"?*
*I thought the problem with most writing was it was TOO loose.*

They write more freely and with greater confidence when they discover that it's OK to write about themselves.

*He's giving us more reasons for doing it.*
*I've been writing personal essays since kindergarten—I'm sick of it.*
*Why is he telling us this? What does he want?*

When one of their fellow students laughs at their funny story about getting caught toilet-papering a friend's house, they know that they can write this way and have an effect on someone.

*More examples of how personal writing does good things.*
*I bet he's going to say there's a problem with doing it that way.*
*He's going to say "but" sooner or later.*

Helping writers understand this, however, can be both a blessing and a curse.

*There's the "but."*
*I knew it—he's going to say there's something wrong with doing that.*
*He's told us about the blessing; what's the curse?*
*He's either going to tell us not to do personal writing or he's going to suggest a way to keep the virtues of personal writing and avoid the "curse."*

As you can see, readers in a crowd are busy folk, generating a messy blizzard of responses. From that blizzard, Bob, the writer, has to choose which responses to address. He can't address them all, and he wouldn't want to. He decides to talk only to writing teachers who are interested in teaching personal writing; to everyone else in the world he says, "Goodbye." And he can't please all tastes: Some readers will be scared off by words like *egocentric;* some will be repulsed by the mention of toilet paper. And he can't respond to all legitimate demands at once. While some readers are saying, "What does that mean?" others are saying, "Like what, for example?" and others are asking, "Why?" Bob can only answer one at a time and put the other questioners on hold. So Bob defines his chosen audience and imagines a likely scenario, a set of responses the bulk of his chosen audience is likely to share, whatever additional personal axes they may be grinding. Here's the text again, with the single audience response Bob chose to imagine after each sentence.

## Writing Outside Oneself: A Lesson Plan

*What does "writing outside oneself" mean?*

In order to make beginning writing students feel comfortable about their writing, we encourage essays that are very egocentric.

*What's an "egocentric" essay?*

We ask them to write about their own lives, to describe a favorite place or best friend, to write about a favorite holiday, or to tell a story about something that happened to them.

*Why do teachers do this?*

These essays allow the students to loosen up.

*Why is that?*

They write more freely and with greater confidence when they discover that it's OK to write about themselves.

*Got any examples?*

When one of their fellow students laughs at their funny story about getting caught toilet-papering a friend's house, they know that they can write this way and have an effect on someone.

*So what's the problem?*

Helping writers understand this, however, can be both a blessing and a curse.

*What's the curse?*

Bob has in fact composed a *dialogue* between himself and the reader. He's composed both parts, but he's printed out only one—his own lines—and expects the reader to know her part and speak hers.

Bob's dialogue helps us solve one of the great mysteries of writing: *What makes one thing follow another?* Why do we read one sequence of sentences and say, "That flows" or "That has transition," and we read another and say, "That's choppy"? The flowing text shows awareness of the invisible dialogue; the choppy text doesn't. See Chapter 7 for more on that.

**Now it's your turn.** Here are the opening lines of an essay. Cover them with a piece of paper and pull the paper down slowly to reveal one line at a time. (If you read the whole text at once, this game doesn't work.) After exposing each line, write down one or two responses you have to the line—questions you want to ask, feelings you want to express, desires you want met. When you've gone through the text, look it over and write a half-page about how successfully the author predicted and dealt with your responses—was she hearing you?

> *I keep hearing one line from women, over and over, a line that causes my heart to sink:*
>
> *"I'll just have . . . a salad."*
>
> *Oh, no, I think, not again.*
>
> *Then I look around. At table after table men are downing pasta, gorging on shellfish, lustily wrenching apart Cornish hens.*
>
> *And there next to them are women, nibbling on radicchio.*
>
> *Maybe taking "just a bite of yours."*
>
> *Nice dinner.*
>
> *Okay—obviously food is complicated and symbolic and our society stresses thinness and youth and many women feel pressure to look like the women in fashion magazines and some women do in fact have a weight problem or diet problems or . . .*
>
> *Enough. It's time to eat.*
>
> *Let me put it another way. If men are the reason you're avoiding food . . . eat. Because, as far as men are concerned, women who eat food are much more attractive than women who avoid it.*
>
> *I swear to you.* ❖
>
> (Warren Leight, "Real Women Do Eat Food," *Mademoiselle,* Aug. 1989)

## EXERCISES

1. Do The Reader's Dialogue with the title and first six or seven sentences of a piece of your own. Don't forget the half-page discussion at the end.

2. Do Exercise 1 using a classmate as audience. Reveal your essay opening one sentence at a time and have him write his reactions down after each. Then look at the dialogue and write a half-page essay that assesses how successfully you predicted his responses.

3. Take one of the following essay first sentences and discuss what kinds of reactions the author should expect and why he might want those reactions and use them to his advantage.

   a. Once upon a time, a little boy loved a stuffed animal whose name was Old Rabbit.

      *(Tom Junod, writing about Mr. Rogers, Esquire, Nov. 1998)*

   b. A thought-provoking dispute has emerged in the homosexual-rights community in the wake of the controversial "Jenny Jones Show" verdict.

      *(Clarence Page)*

   c. I recently read the opinion column in the campus newspaper.

   d. When Bruno Bettelheim committed suicide last March at the age of 86, the eulogies were uniformly reverent.

      *(Newsweek, Sept. 10, 1990, p. 59)*

4. Write a thesis statement for one of your essays. Write three different likely responses readers might have to it.

5. Write three different likely responses readers might have to the opening sentence of one of your essays.

6. Write an essay you'd love to read out loud to the class. Then read it out loud to them with as much drama and "performance" as you can manage.

7. Find an essay in print, in *The Writer's Way* or elsewhere, that "breaks the rules" in a way you like. Write a half-page essay discussing what rules are being broken and why, and explain why the rule-breaking works. Hand in your essay with a photocopy of the rule-breaking essay attached.

# Part Two

## PLANNING AND DRAFTING

# Chapter 3

# FINDING SOMETHING TO WRITE ABOUT

The next eleven chapters imagine that you'll be going through a series of steps called the writing process: prewriting, drafting, structuring, style polishing, mechanical editing, and publishing. The step-by-step approach can be helpful because it reminds you that you don't have to do everything at once. But there's a danger to steps: They suggest that the writing process is a lot neater and more regimented than it really is.

Most writers don't do one step, then the other; instead, they do them all, all the time. The mind's a messy place, and it's happiest when multitasking: It will leap from note-taking to paragraph writing to outlining to rewriting. While you're writing page 7, it will be rewriting page 5 and thinking up great lines for page 10 or another essay. You must let your brain go about its messy business. *Take what comes, whenever it comes*. Whenever I write, I have a notepad at my elbow—it's there right now—to catch all the stuff my mind is churning out that isn't about the task at hand.

## Where Do Good Essays Come From?

Some people have no trouble finding things to write. For others, it's the hardest part of writing. If you're in the second group, this chapter's for you.

In a sense, we know we all have lots to say because we all talk effortlessly and endlessly with our buddies. So "having nothing to write about" can only mean *that we define writing in some unhealthy way* that gives us writer's block. And we'll solve the problem by *redefining writing to be more like talking to our buddies*.

Let's explore that. First, we know that writing isn't about having a rare moment of inspiration or a unique experience, because we know we don't talk to our buddies only when we've had a stroke of genius or have just gotten back from Nepal. We talk all the time, about everything. And writers write about everything. Writing essays is like being funny. A comic isn't a person who happens to have funny things happen to him; he's a person who sees humor in whatever happens. Similarly, an essayist lives a life like yours; he just sees the potential essay in what he experiences. Here's the essayist John Gregory Dunne explaining how it works:

> My house was burgled twice and the two resulting pieces netted me a lot more than the burglars got. I can recall one columnist who eked three columns out of his house burning down: one on the fire, a second on the unsung dignity of fire fighting, and a third on his insurance adjuster and a long view on the charred artifacts of a lifetime. So avid for material is your average columnist that once, when my daughter caught my wife and me *flagrante delicto,* I seriously wondered if there was a column in it. (As it turned out, only a column mention.)

Once you catch on to the trick, essay topics will jump out of the bushes.

Second, the difference between talking to buddies and writing is not one of *content* but of *audience.* It's not that you have nothing to say; it's that you have nothing to say that *you think your imaginary essay audience wants to hear.* You're trying to write to instructors, bosses, or other authority figures, and you're telling yourself they only want to read somcthing that's never been said before and is brilliant. But most writers don't write to those audiences, and you don't have to either. Most writers write to peers or novices (people like themselves or people who know less than they do) and they only ask themselves to say something their peers will find touching or interesting, or something the novices can learn from. Once you think this way, you realize that everything you know or have experienced is of use to someone, because people who haven't experienced it can profit from your knowledge and people who have will appreciate knowing they're not alone:

> If you've ever been anywhere, you can tell people who haven't been there what it's like.
>
> If you've ever done anything, you can show how to do it to people who don't know.
>
> If you've ever read a book, seen a movie, or eaten in a restaurant, you can review it and tell potential customers whether it's worth the money.
>
> If you've ever suffered, you can assume others are suffering the same way, and you can assure them what they're going through is normal.
>
> If anything ever happened to you that was funny, touching, or infuriating, you can share the feeling with others.

You don't even have to be smart, because humans are happy to hear you talk about your ignorance, confusion, and doubt. Write about how bewildering it is to be a freshman on campus, how hilariously confusing it was the time you tried to program your VCR guided only by the instructions in Japanese English, or how you're of two minds about getting married.

To convince yourself that most good writing springs from minds and lives like yours, consider these essay theses from my students' recent work:

> I went home for vacation and had to listen to my father tell me one more time how he disapproves of my life.
>
> Mornings with my two-year-old are a joyous, comical circus.
>
> I wonder if this semester I'll finally get organized and actually get something out of school.
>
> Why are men genetically unable to clean bathrooms?
>
> The last time I got panhandled I said no. I felt guilty, but I'm not sure I should have.
>
> My mother never listens.
>
> I may have finally found a car mechanic I can trust.

There's nothing new or dazzling there, but they all made good essays. And for my final bit of evidence, here's a splendid essay about the most trivial of subjects:

## THE EGG AND I REVISITED

KRIS TACHMIER

Kids can be finicky eaters. My own three-year-old son will put up determined resistance if he sees one Brussels sprout on his plate. One hour after dinner that singular Brussels sprout will still be on his plate, undisturbed. Similarly, my seventeen-month-old daughter cringes at the sight of a carrot and immediately clamps her jaws shut, making passage into her mouth by a fork laden with the vegetable impossible. But I really have no right to single out my children when their own mother is the classic persnicketist: I cannot and will not eat eggs.

Ever since I can remember, I have hated eggs. I'm not really certain why—maybe it's their texture, or maybe it's the notion that they're really hen ova, or maybe it's the idea that eggs can assume so many disguises. A Brussels sprout will always remain a Brussels sprout; a carrot remains a carrot; but an egg will scramble, fry, poach, coddle, benedict, and devil in the twinkling of an eye. I simply cannot trust eggs.

For a while, my childhood breakfasts included some sort of egg concoction, but the minute my mother stepped out of the kitchen I would sneak over to the sink, tilt my plate upside down, and watch the shimmering yellow creation slip down into the darkened cavity of the drain. This bit of cunning was a great success until one fateful morning. I must have left a few damning fragments of eggy evidence. I was interrogated by my mother: how long, how often, how come? The next morning a glorious bowl of Cheerios was awaiting me. The egg and I were finally separated.

In the years following, my mother learned to keep eggs out of my path, but all her efforts were not enough. During lunch at high school I would invariably sit next to someone who would pull a hardboiled egg out of his sack (together with one of those miniature salt shakers) and sit there happily sprinkling and munching on it. Too bad he never stopped long enough to notice me turning green on his left . . . I might have spoiled his appetite. And there was always some inconsiderate friend who ordered egg salad sandwiches at restaurants. The mixture would always be thick and runny, and globs of it were forever dripping out of all sides of the sandwich.

With marriage, I realized that my attitude toward eggs was a little ridiculous. I decided to give the egg a second chance. I can remember the event clearly: the morning sun was shining, the smell of fresh-perked coffee filled the kitchen, and there, flattened out in submission on my plate, was one fried egg, barely distinguishable for all the salt and pepper I had poured over it. I resolutely picked up my fork, stabbed a section of the egg, thrust it into my mouth, gulped it down, felt it rumbling its way toward my stomach, and blanched as I realized it was rocketing out of my mouth. So much for a second crack at the egg.

Today I still keep my mouth empty of eggs, but my refrigerator is full of them. For the last year or so I've been raising chickens. Every day I march out to the coop and gather a half-dozen freshly laid eggs. As soon as I have several dozen I call up friends to check if they want any eggs free of cost. I think the operation a stroke of genius: I have cleverly combined charity with penitence. ❖

Assuming you hate at least one kind of food, I'll rest my case. Now let's look at some practical ways to encourage those potential essays to make themselves known to us.

## Five Principles for Getting Good Ideas

We need some labels. We'll call the spark in you from which an essay grows a *seed.* And we'll call the thing that causes that spark (the newspaper article you read, the conversation you overhear in the grocery store, the ad you see on TV) a *prompt.* The prompt happens to you; the seed is your first reaction to it. Brains that find seeds easily follow five principles:

> Don't begin with a topic.
> Think all the time.
> To get something out, put something in.
> Go from little, concrete things to big, abstract ones.
> Connect.

Since getting ideas and learning are similar processes, many of these are revisitings of principles in the Guide to Studying (p. P-2). We'll talk about each in turn.

**Don't begin with a topic.** A topic is the thing you're writing about, the subject: abortion, recent advances in weight training, your first date, how to apply a tourniquet. Anything that fits in the following blank is a topic: "This essay is about __________." Yet topics are always nouns, and nouns are useless (p. P-10), so we've done next to nothing when we've found one. If a topic could start an essay, we could open the dictionary and point.

Good seeds come in many forms:

**Questions:** "Is there any real difference between the Republicans and the Democrats anymore?" "Why is Ralph so mad at me?"

**Problems:** "I'm always behind in my work." "Violent crimes against women are on the increase."

**Intentions:** "I want to tell people about what's really going on in this class." "I want to let people know about alternatives to the phone company."

**Theses:** "There are cheaper alternatives to the phone company." "Old people are the victims of silent injustice in our culture."

**Feelings:** "I was furious when the instructor suddenly announced there would be a term paper no one knew about due in three weeks." "I was surprised to see my father crying."

**Think all the time.** We talked about this earlier (p. P-3). If you have a sense of humor, you know that the surest way to prevent yourself from being funny is to have someone demand that you be funny *now.* Instead, mull on the essay with a part of your brain all the time as you go through your days.

**To get something out, put something in.** One popular, poisonous metaphor for thinking is the light bulb clicking on over our head—the notion that ideas spring from within us, caused by nothing. To become good thinkers, we have to replace that metaphor with another: Think of thoughts as billiard balls on a pool table, idle until other balls—external stimuli—slam into them and set them in motion. Seeds are *re*-actions—we have them in response to prompts. Many of us have learned to separate input and output modes: We are either putting information into our brains or asking our brains to put out thoughts, but we don't do the two jobs at the same timc. But when things are going in is the best time to try to get things out. Children do this naturally; try reading a book to a three-year-old, and listen to her react to everything she hears or sees, or take her to a movie and watch her struggle not to talk back to the screen.

Are you a reactor? Answer the following questions:

Do you find yourself silently talking back to the newspaper when you read it?
Do you write in the margins of books you read?
Are at least 25 percent of the notes you take during course lectures your own thoughts, questions, doubts, and reactions?
As you meet up with life's outrages, do you find yourself complaining to imaginary audiences in your head?
After a movie, do you feel like you're going to burst until you find someone to talk with about it?
When you listen to a speaker or a teacher, do you find yourself itching to get to the question-and-answer period?

If you said no to these questions, you're going to have to practice your reacting skills.

Any external stimulus can be a prompt, but the best writer's prompt is another piece of writing. So if you're looking for something to write, *go read something.* You can do this in two different ways:

**Content prompts:** Writing can move you to write by saying something that makes you want to say something back. I handed out to my class an essay by Jerry Jesness called "Why Johnny Can't Fail" (*Harper's* magazine, Sept. 1999), in which Jesness, a career teacher, blasts the public school system for what he calls "the floating standard," by which all students are allowed to pass and standards are habitually lowered when students can't meet them. My student Nancy Guinta was moved to comment:

## LONG LIVE THE FLOATING STANDARD

He's a beautiful child, kind-hearted, personable. He loves people and they love him. Last winter he worked at a ski resort in the mountains, and they loved him for his enthusiasm and his energy. He even won the Employee of the Month award. His dream was to be allowed to run the snow plow. He's now working his way through the local community college while toying with several dreams: being a professional snowboarder and being a brewmaster are just two.

High school was difficult for him. Science and chemistry lured him, math tormented him, English often baffled him. He was triumphant at high school graduation, and it never would have happened if a host of sympathetic teachers hadn't given him the extra credit assignments and art projects that allowed him to pass. I thank them—those teachers with the floating standards. Without them, my son would be without a diploma, unable to go on to college, branded a failure . . . and who would have gained?

Kids the schools fail—what happens to them? Homeless people, criminals, welfare recipients, drunks—people who have been rejected by society, and who take it out on themselves and us for the rest of their lives. If we let them pass, we just prolong the time they have to find themselves and choose to become productive and not live off you and me. And how much does it really matter if they don't do the science experiment very well or their insight into *To Kill a Mockingbird* isn't sufficiently deep? Failing them just makes sure they're cut off from the real lessons of school: how to be a member of the team, how to work with other people, how to communicate, how to love learning. My son is a perfect example. The essays may have had a lot of spelling errors, but he came through the system looking at life and saying, "I can do this."

Anyway, floating standards don't end at the high school's parking lot. They're in every college, every company, on every job site. In any university you can find classes where the assignments are few and the grading is easy. Yet every study shows that going to college benefits those who go. The system is always set up to let those who can't perform slide by. By letting them slide, we let them learn.

Eventually, each individual decides what standards to set for himself in this life. I hope my son sets high ones for himself. He seems to be doing that. And I believe he is doing that largely because the System kept telling him "You're still one of us" until the maturity had time to kick in. ❖

**Models:** You can use your reading to inspire you to explore new techniques. You read the piece and say, "Wow! I like the way she did that. I'd never have thought to do it that way. Maybe I could do something sort of like it." That's called *modeling*—also known as imitation, mimicking, copying, and stealing. You can use any technical feature as a model: the structure, the opener, the tone, the use of dialogue or narrative, the use of the ellipsis or the dash—anything you never tried before. Here's an inspiring model, a description by the poet e. e. cummings of his father:

> My father . . . was a New Hampshire man, 6 foot 2, a crack shot & a famous flyfisherman & a firstrate sailor (his sloop was named The Actress) & a woodsman who could find his way through forests primeval without a compass & a canoeist who'd still-paddle you up to a deer without ruffling the surface of a pond & an ornithologist & taxidermist & (when he gave up hunting) an expert photographer (the best I've ever seen) & an actor who portrayed Julius Caesar in Sanders Theatre & a painter (both in oils & watercolors) & a better carpenter than any professional & an architect who designed his own houses before building them & (when he liked) a plumber who just for the fun of it installed all his own waterworks & (while at Harvard) a teacher with small use for professors . . . & my father had the first telephone in Cambridge & (long before any Model T Ford) he piloted an Orient Buckboard with Friction Drive produced by the Waltham watch company & . . . my father's voice was so magnificent that he was called on to impersonate God speaking from Beacon Hill (he was heard all over the common) & my father gave me Plato's metaphor of the cave with my mother's milk.

Here are two essays that students were inspired by e.e. cummings's model to write:

> Dave's porch has everything you ever wanted in a porch and more & it is located right next to the freshman dorms & you sit there in the sunshine & you can meet tons of people and most of those people are girls & they like to drink beer & we are always drinking beer on the porch & that way we can meet girls & we like the porch because it has a big chair on it and it's comfortable and the porch is made of redwood and Dave and Phil built it (with Dave's dad's wood) & it's sturdy & it's small but it's fine & you get to see all the people drive by & I can't think of where I'd rather be than on Dave's porch.
>
> *(Jeff Ochs)*

> My ex-boyfriend was a baby-faced, wavy-haired blonde with blue eyes that could be warm as a smile while his thoughts would be as cold as ice scraping against raw metal and he could charm anyone like an alligator and you couldn't get away because he would find you and follow you silently and he would watch and find out every

move you made and he would just wait and wait until you made a wrong move and then he would pounce with words like claws and he was a better liar than anyone I ever knew and he would look at you with those alligator eyes and you would freeze like a deer caught in headlights because he knew you were scared and he wanted you to be scared because he let you know that he would hurt you if you ever crossed him because he collected guns and throwing stars that he would throw, embedding them deep into wood, and he would always carry two knives on his belt, one visible and one hidden, and you knew they were there and he knew that you knew and that's what he wanted and he would manipulate anyone like a chess piece (not that he ever learned to play chess, it was a sissy game) and he would do whatever he could to whoever he could to get what he wanted with that alligator smile that was like someone walking over your grave and he wants to be a politician.

*(Kathleen Siemont)*

**Go from little, concrete things to big, abstract ones.** Since ideas come most easily in reaction to life's incoming billiard balls, the best thinking follows a predictable course: from little, concrete bits of experience to large, abstract implications. You see an ad on TV, start thinking about it, and it leads you to speculations on American consumerism, media manipulation, and the marketing of women's bodies. Or you see a parent disciplining a child in a grocery store aisle just for being alive, and it makes you think, "Why are people without training or talent allowed to do this all-important job called child raising?" or "Parents need time off too."

Here's the path my mind traveled from a little particular to a big issue. I was sitting doing nothing one day when my eyes fell on a box of Girl Scout cookies. The box had on it a picture of a girl and the slogan, "I'm not like anyone else." I reacted. I thought, "Gosh, that sounds lonely." And I valued the reaction enough to notice it and think about it. It led me to a big issue: How does American love of individuality affect Americans' ability to be members of a culture? And I formulated a thesis: Americans love their individuality so much they'll cut themselves off from everything and everyone to get it. Being "unlike everyone else" is a curse because it means you're cut off from other human beings by your differentness. I was raised a proud individualist, and I've only recently realized that the reward for being unique is loneliness.

Many of the essays in this book model this progress from a minor personal experience to a big issue. In "Why I Never Cared for the Civil War" (pp. 391–392), Shawni Allred studied a muddy pool of water in the fifth grade and used the experience to discuss what's wrong with traditional classroom teaching styles. In "Given the Chance" (pp. 276–277), Melissa Schatz met Stacey, and her experience with Stacey led her to question the entire state drug rehabilitation program.

**Connect.** We talked about connecting before (p. P-9). A lot of thinking begins by noticing that two things are related. Here's an example. One day I was sitting in an English Department faculty meeting, and we were discussing an administrative change. A colleague said, "We couldn't do that until we were sure our people would be protected." I thought momentarily, "I wonder how he knows who 'his people' are?" Months later, I was vacationing in a small mountain town and picked up the local newspaper. On the front page was an article about the firing of a group of nonunion construction workers. The boss had asked the union for workers, but there were none available, so he trained out-of-work mill workers. Later the union rep showed up, announced that union workers were now available, and insisted that the others be fired. Something clicked, and I had an essay. My colleague's attitude and the union rep's were the same: "I'll watch out for my people, and everyone else can watch out for himself." I wanted to talk about why people think that way and how they learn to rise above it.

It's hard to say how those connections get made, but we know two things: 1) the more we tell our brain that we want it to do that kind of thing, the more it does it; and 2) it isn't *work*—when something "clicks" in memory, we haven't "worked" at all.

The more *un*-like two things are and the less obvious the connection, the more fresh and stimulating is the connection when you make it. This is the Head Principle. Mr. Head was an aviation engineer who got interested in downhill skiing. Apparently no one had ever connected aircraft technology and skiing before; Mr. Head took a few runs down the hill and realized that he could make a better ski if he simply made it with the principles and materials used in making airplane wings. He invented the Head ski, the first metal ski, and made millions of dollars. He then did the same thing to tennis, inventing the Prince racket. Apparently aircraft engineers didn't play tennis either.

The Head Principle says you can't predict what will connect with what. So you can't tell yourself what information to seek. You can only amass experience and information voraciously and stir it all up together. If I had been formally researching stupid faculty remarks, I'd never have thought to read up on Northern California construction workers. If you're writing about Charles Dickens and you read only about Charles Dickens, you're just making sure you won't make any connections except those other Dickens critics have already made. Instead, go read *Psychology Today,* read Hillary Clinton's memoirs, see a movie, watch a documentary on insect societies, or visit a mortuary.

*Most of us do the exact opposite of these five idea-getting principles.* We set aside a block of time for thinking, cut ourselves off from the outside world by locking ourselves in a stimulus-free study room and look within ourselves for a large, abstract topic to write on. If you're doing any of that, your seed-finding regimen needs overhauling.

## Writing from Rage

If the due date is near and you still can't find something to write about, there's an almost sure-fire out: *Write from rage.* I once had a composition student who wrote one dead essay after another, each full of flat clichés and careless mechanics. I tried every trick in the book to get her to write something that mattered to her. Nothing worked. She got a D in the course. Two weeks after the end of the term I got a letter from her—a beautiful letter, full of fine, lethal irony. She cursed me up one side and down the other. The letter was beautifully punctuated and typed, too. She finally had found something important to say. I only wished she had found something to make her mad sooner.

We ignore our anger when we're trying to write because we think essays have to be cool. They don't. The other day a student came to me to discuss an argument she was beginning to plan. "What are you going to write on?" I said. She said something so abstract my nose started to bleed. I said, "Has anything made you mad recently?" She said, "Sure." "What?" "Well, I just got done with a production in the Music Department, and they schedule the rehearsals in such a way that now I'm weeks behind in all my classes. They, in effect, force students who want to be in the productions to shaft all their other courses." "A perfect essay thesis!" I cried. "Write on that."

There are two places in this book that continue this conversation about finding things to write about: Chapter 15 talks about finding informative seeds (p. 236), and Chapter 16 talks about finding argumentative ones (p. 249).

# Writer's Workshop

## Finding Essays in Your Life

I asked my class for a volunteer who "had nothing to say," someone whose life had been "nothing special." The volunteer (Sally) and I talked for twenty minutes. Then Sally and I looked at what she had said, looking for essay seeds. Here's our conversation, with all the seeds we found in parentheses.

JR: Tell me about yourself. What do you do?

S: I'm a student. I work in a restaurant, and I enjoy sports.

JR: What kind of sports do you do?

S: I used to compete in track, but now it's for my own enjoyment. (*Compare being athletic in formal competition with being athletic just for fun, arguing that athletics outside of organized competition is healthier, more fun, less stressful.*) I run, play basketball, do cross-country skiing, downhill. I play a little bit of volleyball, swim, play softball. I've only just started cross-country skiing. I really like it because of the solitude; there's more physical exercise. Downhill I like because of the speed and getting accuracy down. (*Write to downhillers, arguing that cross-country skiing is less crowded, cheaper, better for your body, and better for your spirit.*)

JR: What did you do in track?

S: Shot put and half mile. I had a lot of strength from weight lifting.

JR: Did you ever take any flak for doing something that was as "unfeminine" as putting the shot?

S: Sure. We were considered jocks. There was a lot of stereotyping. . . . (*Write to large, strong girls, sharing your experience pursuing a "manly" sport and encouraging them not to be intimidated; or defend the thesis: Even after the women's movement, female athletes still face prejudice.*) I was used as a guinea pig for a program. Since I was a good athlete, they wanted to see how strong they could really make me. But I ended up getting injured. They didn't provide the equipment I needed—belts and stuff like that. I strained my back. From trying to squat too much. (*Write to beginning women weight trainers, offering training tips and cautioning them about the dangers.*)

JR: Tell me about your past. What was your childhood like?

S: We grew up fairly poor. My mom divorced when I was seven, so it was just the girls in the house: my two sisters, Mom, and me.

JR: What was it like when your parents divorced?

S: I was happy about it. I was scared to death of my father. He hit us a lot. The way I look on it now, that was the only way he had to communicate. That's the way he was raised. I was scared to death of him and anyone who was ever going to raise a hand to me. It caused many problems with our relationship. To the point where I didn't know him—though he doesn't live very far from my hometown. (*Write to children of divorce, sharing your feelings and the insights you've gained from the experience; or write to children physically abused by their parents, sharing your experiences and your feelings; or defend the thesis: Sometimes divorce is good for the children of the marriage.*)

JR: How did your father's treatment of you affect you?

S: It made it hard to be affectionate with people—I'm beginning to outgrow that. Also I felt like I was a bad person, but that's also because he would tell me bad things about myself. I wanted to be a lawyer all my life, but he always told me, "Nope, you'll never be good at that, you'll never be good at that." And he told me that so many times, I tell myself that. He wanted a boy. (*Write about what it's like growing up with parents who tell you you're bound to fail; or write about what it's like being a girl in a family where a parent wanted a boy.*)

JR: Did you always live in the same place when you were growing up?

S: No, in high school we moved and I had to change schools. My mom thought I was a little too radical and the neighborhood was a bad influence on me.

JR: Do you agree?

S: No. There was definitely a better grade of education in the new place, but the new high school was in a richer neighborhood and was really into cocaine. The girls were all daddy's little girls, they got everything they wanted, they didn't have to work for anything; the guys all thought they were cowboys, which I thought was funny, since they probably never had been near a horse. (*Write a satire laughing at the foolishness of parents who move to upper-middle-class neighborhoods in the mistaken belief that they're escaping the problems of poverty or the city; or defend the thesis: "Better neighborhoods" aren't always better.*)

JR: Were you doing drugs?

S: I drank a lot, but never when I was playing any sport, because it would screw me up. (*Defend the thesis: We should fight drug abuse by helping kids find something they love so much they won't risk losing it.*)

JR: How did you ever survive long enough to make it to college?

S: I had the influence of my mother, which was very positive, very striving. She works in a field where very few women do, general contracting: multimillion-dollar buildings. She doesn't have a college degree, so she doesn't have a title, but she travels all over the country, part engineer work, part administration; she heads a marketing team. . . . She's a super-intelligent lady, and the kind of person who, when something isn't supposed to be possible, can get it done. (*Write about your mother and your relationship with her, showing the ways she helped you survive your youth.*)

JR: It sounds like your mom was a very good influence.

S: Almost too much so. I'm in awe. And I have a stepfather who's a doctor and very successful, who's also very intelligent. (*Write about the pluses and minuses of having a stepparent; or write about the pluses and minuses of having parents who are superheroes.*)

JR: What are your plans?

S: I intend to go overseas and teach. That's what I'd like. Teach English for a while. (*Write to English majors, defending the thesis: You should consider teaching English overseas for a year or two.*)

That's sixteen essays in twenty minutes from what Sally was convinced was a "nothing" life—and we never even talked about basketball, swimming, or softball! Of course, Sally's life turned out to be anything but ordinary, but the funny thing is that the same thing happens with every life, including yours, when you start looking at it this way.

**Now it's your turn.** With a classmate, do Sally-type interviews of each other. Have her interview you for fifteen minutes; then you interview her. Together, find as many essay seeds in each interview as you can. Try to find personal essays, informative essays, and arguments. Make sure that none of the seeds is a topic (a noun or a noun phrase).

## EXERCISES

1. For two days, record (in a notebook or journal) all the striking prompts you encounter: fragments of conversation overheard in the grocery store, startling ads on TV, unusual moments in class. Take two and recast them as essay seeds, a sentence to a short paragraph each, the way we did with the grocery store anecdote on p. 43.

2. Make a list of things that have made you mad recently. Take one and make an essay seed from it.

3. On p. 36 is a list of five ways to find seeds. Find one seed in your life via each item in the list. For example, for the first item, pick some place you've been and describe it to someone in a couple of sentences.

4. On p. 39 is a list of five forms a seed can take. Make one seed in each form: e.g., make a seed that's a question.

5. Write a one-page essay like the egg essay on pp. 37–38: an essay about something utterly trivial, like the contents of your purse or your secret fondness for going to the laundromat.

6. Find an essay, in *The Writer's Way* or elsewhere, that sparks thoughtful response in you. Turn that response into an essay.

7. Find an essay, in *The Writer's Way* or elsewhere, that has a technical feature you like but have never tried. Using the essay as a model, write a short essay mimicking that feature. At the bottom of the page, identify the feature you're mimicking: e.g., "I'm mimicking the use of dialogue."

# Chapter 4

# FROM FIRST THOUGHTS TO DRAFTS

In this chapter we'll take that set of good intentions we fleshed out in Chapter 3 and turn it into a bunch of pages of text (called a draft) that's crying out for rethinking, reshaping, and resaying (called revision). This stage should be playful, messy, and meandering. Writing teachers call it "prewriting" or "brainstorming," but you can call it scribbling or noodling if you want.

Many people, without saying so, have decided that this kicking-around stage shouldn't have to happen and that if it does, something's wrong. Once I asked my students to write an essay stating where they stood on censorship in the public schools. A student came into my office on the verge of tears and furious with herself; she said, "I can't write this paper; I've tried, but I just can't." I said, "How come?" She said, "Because I keep going round and round. First I thought, 'Well, I'd censor books that had explicit sex,' but then I thought, 'Maybe it's good for children to know that sex exists, and maybe it's wrong to make sex a big mysterious deal.' And at one time I figured I'd say that I'd censor stuff I personally found distasteful, but then I thought, 'What if everyone censored everything they didn't like?' So that didn't seem to work. I tried to make a list of works I thought should be censored, but when I tried to make arguments for why they should be censored, I couldn't explain what was wrong about them except I just didn't like them. What is censorship, anyway? I've decided I don't even know what the word means. Like is it censorship when an advertiser on TV tells a network it won't buy advertising time if the network runs a special on abortion? I just don't know what I'm doing, so I can't write the paper. What's wrong with me? I could always write before."

To all that, I responded, "But everything you've said *is* the paper! All that lovely, messy, fragmented mind-changing and wandering and re-examining and tripping over things is what's *supposed* to happen. Hooray! Your brain is on the move."

Drafting should be as easy as talking, and we all talk without effort. But it isn't, and the only difference is fear. When we write, we feel there's a lot on the line, and it ties us up. That feeling of constriction is called writer's block. *Our only goal in drafting is to make writer's block go away so the words keep coming.* If we keep the words coming, we'll write our way to good stuff.

Writer's block is another name for stage fright. Every writer feels some fear, just as every actor feels some stage fright, because writing is a big deal, like starring in the school play. If you're one of the lucky ones, the fear adrenalizes you, pumps you up for the performance. If you're not, the fear makes you stiff, tentative, a dull shadow of your usual fascinating self.

People get writer's block because they define writing and their relationship to it in terms opposite to the ones we practiced in Chapter 1. They don't feel like writers. So they try to be someone they're not when they write; they try to fake it. They write to people they aren't comfortable talking to. They equate their writing with their self-worth: "If I write a bad essay, I'm a bad person." So they ask too much of themselves, try too hard, and write to avoid failure. We have to replace those attitudes with healthy alternatives. Here are seventeen ways to cultivate them.

## Defeating Writer's Block

**1. Give yourself a lot of time.** How obvious. Yet no rule of writing is broken more often. We wait until the last minute before a paper is due, conning ourselves into believing that we write better under pressure. But we don't. Time pressure always heightens fear. So instead of trying to force out a draft the night before it's due, set a part of your mind nibbling at the project from the moment the assignment is made, and keep nibbling off and on throughout the day, every day, catching your thoughts as they fall in a pocket notebook.

**2. To get stuff out, keep putting stuff in.** Don't cut off the input just because you're now on output mode. Fear grows when you think, "This is all I have, and it's not much." To curb the fear, keep reading new stuff and talking with friends so what you hear can spark new stuff in you.

**3. Don't "work" at thinking, and don't think by rules.** Thinking is like making language: It's too complex, too subtle, too unconscious to do by the numbers. If you try to control the process and fail, you'll become afraid. You must *let* it happen. If you ask people to describe how they think, the good thinkers say they don't know, and it's not wise to try to find out.

Every writing day teaches me that truth. I write from nine to five, thinking hard. At the end of the day, I pack up and point my weary brain toward home. During the fifteen-minute walk, I let my mind go . . .

and the best ideas of the day begin popping into my head. I hit the front door running and reach for the notebook to catch them before they slip away.

**4. Don't demand that you know where you're going.** Geniuses have something in common: a talent for working without rigidly defined goals. They're willing to let the investigation work itself out and discover where they'll end up when they've gotten there. Less creative minds want to know exactly where they're going before they start. The genius wisely says, "How can I know I'm going to invent the laser or discover the theory of relativity when no one knows such a thing exists yet?"

Sometimes school teaches you the reverse, by telling you that you need discipline and structure and requiring you to use outlines, thesis statements, and other tools that force those skills. If someone tells you that, learn to say, "Those tools are nice when I'm revising, but NOT NOW!"

**5. Call yourself a writer.** We talked in the Guide to Studying about how important this is (p. P-5). If you've been putting it off, now's the time. You can't play good tennis telling yourself over and over, "I'm not really a tennis player; I'm not really a tennis player."

**6. Write as yourself.** The less you have to disavow yourself when you write, the less writer's block will touch you. Writer's block comes from fear of being found out. If you write to convince the reader you're someone you're not, the risk of being found out increases. Mark Twain said the great advantage of telling the truth is that you don't need a good memory. Similarly, if you're your true self, no one can expose you. The draft you produce this way may not be ready to hand in, but you'll have the draft, and that's what matters.

**7. Don't write; talk.** Since most of us are used to being ourselves when we talk, if we talk on the page we'll feel that it's the real us writing. We're also better at talking because we've done so much more of it, so we'll be more successful writing talk. Again, a first draft you've *spoken* may not be ready to hand in, but you can fix that later.

The basic way to write like you talk is to imagine yourself talking and write down what you hear. But if that isn't enough, you can make the talk real. You can talk to yourself, out loud—when you get stuck, stop typing and speak aloud to the air what you're trying to say. Or find a listener: Rush out of the room, grab the nearest victim, and dump what you're trying to write into her astonished ear.

Or you can go all the way and literally dictate your text into a tape recorder and then type a transcript. Once I was asked to edit the narrative for a film on conservation. The author of the text said it didn't sound like a person talking, and he asked me to fix it. Instead of rewriting the text, I turned on my tape recorder, read the first paragraph of the text to see what it said, and tried to *speak* the content—without looking at the written text—into the recorder. I worked my way through the text in this way, and the product was the same text, now in the language of a human speaker, not a stiff and artificial writer.

**8. Use contractions.** Remind yourself to use your talking language by using contractions: *can't, it's, I'm*. Every time you write *cannot* or *it is,* you remind yourself that you're not allowed to be you when you write; every time you write *can't* or *it's,* you'll remind yourself that's not so.

**9. Write to your favorite audience.** People get tense when they try to talk to strangers. You'll make it easier on yourself if you write to someone you can talk freely to.

Most people choose to write to one of the three toughest audiences in the world: no one, the instructor, or the whole world. No one is hard because you know the writing is pointless. The instructor is hard because she knows more than you, and she's judging (grading) you instead of reading you. (I know that in reality you *are* writing to the instructor and writing for a grade, but there are some realities it's wise to forget, and this is one of them.) Writing to the whole world is hard because there is little you can say that the whole world wants to hear.

The audience that's easiest to write to is small and homogeneous: It's made of people with the same interests, values, level of sophistication, and education. It knows less than you on the subject. It wants what you have to offer. It doesn't threaten you; it's not made up of people who are richer than you, higher class than you, academically more advanced than you, or whatever makes you feel at a disadvantage. This audience is pulling for you: friends, family, pen pals, classmates. As always, the draft you produce this way may not be ready to hand in, but you'll have the draft, and that's the important thing.

**10. Take your ego out of the loop.** We get stage fright because we feel our ego is on the line: If we fail, we've proved we're bad, inept people. The essay *is us,* and we crash if it crashes. To escape that fate, we have to unlearn the ego identification. *You are not the essay.* If it crashes, you can still be a worthy person who occasionally writes essays that don't work.

The first step in this unlearning is to realize that we choose to equate our egos with things, and can choose not to. I can go out and play soccer badly and not grieve, because I am not my soccer game, but if I write badly I must hate myself, because I am my writing. But there is nothing inherent in soccer or writing that makes me assign those values to them—I choose it. I have the power to move writing over to the "It's not a big deal" category any time I want.

Second, realize that the result of assigning such import to an action is destructive. I may tell myself that I'm helping myself write well by caring so much, but in fact the only result is that I can play soccer without fear (and therefore boldly, joyfully, and well), but I dare not write—there's too much to lose.

Third, understand how audiences read. *You* think the essay is you, but *they* don't. I learned this lesson when I observed a master class for classical guitar. A student played with extreme stage fright. The master said, "You fear because you think the audience listens to *you.* They do not. They listen to Bach, or Villa-Lobos. You are merely a messenger. You are nothing. They don't hear you. Remember this, and you'll disappear. Then there is no reason to be afraid."

**11. Purposely do what frightens you.** If you're hobbled by fear of screwing up, one way of handling it is to screw up on purpose and notice you didn't die. Make a list of what you're afraid of doing wrong when you write. Breaking grammatical rules? Misspelling words? Looking stupid? Sounding infantile? Being wordy and clumsy? Once you have the list, go do, abundantly and gleefully, all the things on it. Break every grammatical rule you can think of. Purposely misspell words—mutilate the English spelling system (doesn't it deserve it, after all it's done to you?). Say some dumb things. Write in baby talk. Take half a page to say one sentence worth of thought.

The more precisely you define your personal writing demons, the more precisely you can plot their overthrow. Once upon a time a blocked writer discovered he was telling himself as he began, "I'll die if this turns out to be mediocre." So his writing guru ordered him to *strive to write a mediocre essay,* and he found that not only could he write without the old constriction, but when he strove for mediocrity he surpassed his expectations.

**12. Thumb your nose at failure.** You can go beyond merely doing the thing you fear—you can mock it. If you write a lousy paragraph, write, "Boy, was that a lousy paragraph, and I don't care" right after it. If you feel the weight of the teacher's expectations looming over you, write a caricature of him, or a parody of professorial style. If you feel constrained to be dignified when you write, tell dirty jokes and relate comic misadventures from your wild youth. If clean pages intimidate you, take a page of your writing and scribble all over it, in ink. It helps if you cackle while doing these things.

**13. Lower your standards.** We're talking about the damage done by *feeling obligated.* A football player who chokes because he's anticipating getting clobbered is said to "hear footsteps." Most people write hearing footsteps: the footsteps of their own critical selves, coming to clobber them for not measuring up.

Most writers are burdened with obligations: obligations to the English language, to the spelling system, to the rules of grammar, to the noble art of composition, or to their parents, who are paying for their college education, to instructors, to the demands of the five-paragraph format. All those obligations instill fear and make it harder to write. To silence them, *lower your standards,* fool around, and indulge yourself at every turn. Ask as little of yourself as possible.

It works. Here's how Lewis Thomas, a modern master of the essay, discovered the benefits of not trying hard when he turned from writing medical research and tried his hand at essay writing for the first time:

> The chance to . . . try the essay form raised my spirits, but at the same time worried me. I tried outlining some ideas for essays, making lists of items I'd like to cover in each piece, organizing my thoughts in orderly sequences, and wrote several dreadful essays which I could not bring myself to reread, and decided to give up being orderly. I changed the method to no method at all, picked out some suitable times late at night, usually on the weekend two days after I'd already passed the deadline, and wrote without outline or planning in advance, as fast as I could. This worked better, or at least was more fun, and I was able to get started.
>
> *(Lewis Thomas, The Youngest Science)*

Three years after that beginning, those essays won the National Book Award.

If your guilt reflex tries to tell you that excellence lies in sweating the details, assure it there will be ample time for that during the polishing stages. Write the last draft to suit others, and write everything else to suit yourself. After all, when in the writing process do you owe other people (audiences, bosses, teachers, grammarians) anything? Not till the moment you hand the essay in. Writing's one great advantage is that none of it "counts" until you say it does. Don't throw this advantage away by insisting you write well from the first page of the first draft. What do you care how good the first draft of *Harry Potter and the Sorcerer's Stone* was?

Once you know your internal voice of self-criticism is active, you can set up a writing regimen that denies it an opportunity to speak. Forbid yourself to reread what you write until you are at the end of the draft. Or use the voice's input to your advantage. Make a rule that you never cross out anything. When the voice says that something you wrote isn't good enough, leave it and write onward, saying it all over again better or discussing what you didn't like about it. That way the voice of criticism becomes a force for *more* writing, not less.

Sheer speed helps, because it prevents you from thinking too much about what you're doing. Good early-stage writers write fast. Your normal composing pace should be as fast as your fingers will move.

**14. Quit when you're hot, persist when you're not.** Writer's block is worst when you're starting up, so we need a trick for that special moment. Every time you stop writing, whether it's for five minutes or five months, you run the risk of finding out you're blocked when you come back. Get around the problem by quitting when you're hot. Take a break on a winning note, not a losing one. Stop writing when things are going well, when you feel strong and know where you're going next. When you're at a loss, don't let yourself quit; stick with it until the block dissolves, words come, and you've triumphed momentarily.

The principle behind this is basic behavior modification. If you quit when you're stuck, you're in fact rewarding your failure: You're learning that if you get stuck you get the reward of getting to eat, to stretch, to escape. If you stick it out, wait until the words come, and then quit, you reward success. At first it seems contrary to logic: Why stop when the words are flowing? The answer is only apparent when you try it: If you quit when you feel good about the writing, you feel good all during the break and come back to the typewriter feeling strong. If you quit when you're stuck, your break is filled with dread and worry, and the return to the word processor feels like the climb to the scaffold.

The longer the break, the more important it is to quit knowing what you'll do next. When I break for five minutes, I want to know what sentence I'm going to write when I come back; when I break for the day, I typically finish with a sketchy paragraph summary of where the discussion is going in the next few passages—a map of tomorrow's journey.

**15. Write on a word processor.** Word processors reduce writer's block in lots of ways. They're *fast,* and speed dissipates fear all by itself and helps you *write like you talk* by letting your fingers almost keep up with the speaking voice in your head. They're quiet and physically effortless, so the technology disappears and you seem almost to think directly onto the page. They're fun, so they turn writing into play. The page you're working on is endless, so you lose sight of how much you've written and get over your Fear of the Page Limit. Revision is almost a video game, so the fear of Having to Do It Right the First Time goes away. If you can't afford to buy a word processor, your university has a word processing lab somewhere.

If you're a hand-writer, you probably believe that typing will make your prose cold and mechanical. It may, for a while, but you'll get over it soon, and from then on the advantages of typing are enormous.

**16. Sidestep the thing that blocks you.** Identify the thing that stops you from writing, and figure out a way to go around it. This is the opposite of suggestion 11. It sounds simple, but it isn't. A friend of mine was once telling me about a brilliant friend of hers who had writer's block—literally hadn't written anything in years. "Why?" I asked. "Because," my friend said, "every time she wrote a paragraph she read it, found it disappointing, and quit." "That's easy to fix," I said; "Just don't read what you've written." "Obviously," said my friend, "but you only say that because you don't have writer's block." *Moral:* Blocked writers feel compelled to do the thing that prevents writing.

It's easy to say you don't do that, but most of us do, at least a little. Do you ever refuse to begin the essay until you sweat out a title? Do you ever refuse to write the body of an essay until you've ground out an opening paragraph that refuses to come? Do you ever write and rewrite a sticky passage, refusing to go on until it's just right? Do you ever interrupt the steady flow of words to check a spelling in the dictionary? All these behaviors may be excuses to stop writing.

There are an infinite number of ways to stop yourself, but three are so common we'll name them.

**Fear of page one.** A colleague of mine, Dwight Culler, said he used to roll the paper into the typewriter and stare at page 1 in blank terror. Then he got an idea: He rolled the paper into the typewriter, typed "page 10" at the top . . . and found he could write with relative ease. Today he's a renowned literary scholar.

**Fear of the page limit.** This is where you are assigned a ten-page paper and are terrified you'll never find enough to say to fill ten pages. Attack this in two ways. First, fill pages quickly: double-space, use large margins, and ramble—be as wordy and redundant as you please. Pile up text until you're well past the page limit. Now the problem is no longer how to stretch to fill the assigned space, but how to cut down to fit into it. It may all be an illusion, but you'll feel better nonetheless. Second, don't let yourself know how many pages you've written.

**Fear of the essay.** This is perhaps the most common source of writer's block. Most of us write lots of things more easily than we write essays—so don't write essays, until the last draft. Instead . . .

**17. Write un-essays.** Here are seven ways to get writing out of yourself that have friendlier names:

**Reactive reading.** This is an old friend—we talked about it in Chapter 2 and Chapter 3. You read something stimulating on your chosen issue and jot down all the stuff pouring from you in response. Follow three rules. 1) *Write your reactions down as you read*—don't read, then write down your thoughts, because by then they'll be gone. 2) *Don't write on the prompt,* like in the margins; write on a notepad. Don't tell yourself you'll transcribe the notes later—you won't. 3) *Don't take notes on what the text says;* record the reactions you're having to it. If this is hard for you, force yourself by drawing a vertical line down the middle of the note page and writing text content on the left side of the page and your reactions on the right. Force yourself to fill the right side as well as the left.

**Brainstorming.** Brainstorming is messy chatting with colleagues accompanied by note-taking. Brainstorming differs from the conversations we hold with friends every day in four ways: 1) Brainstorming is done as fast as possible. 2) Brainstorming is unstructured—you try to spit out single words and phrases as well as sentences or whole thoughts, and you take whatever comes, however fragmented, however ill-phrased, however apparently irrelevant. 3) You have no standards. And 4) you record everything people say.

**Mapping.** Mapping is my students' favorite prewriting tool. You can use it to find a seed (Chapter 3), but it's usually used when you've found one. Write the seed in the center of a piece of paper and circle it. You don't need a thesis or a great idea—you can start with a word, a suggestive phrase, a visual image, a picture. Now begin brainstorming or free-associating connections between the seed and other thoughts. Let the other bits be whatever they are—words, sensations, questions. As each bit comes, write it down on the paper somewhere, circle it, and draw a line from it to the bit on the page it seems somehow connected to. Work out from the seed in all directions, letting bits cluster as they will. Try to connect everything in the map to something else in the map, so you're making a spider web, or highway system, or whatever you want to think of it as. On page 60 is the map of the essay about the sinister boyfriend on pp. 42–43.

If a bit doesn't seem related to any other bit, don't worry about it; just write it anywhere and circle it. Don't demand that you know what the bits or connections mean. If you momentarily run dry, keep doodling or retrace the spider web, so your hand keeps moving and invites your brain to contribute.

If, as you're mapping, you catch glimpses of essay structure, record them somewhere. If you notice, for instance, that many of your bits concerning industrial pollution are about the history of the problem, many are about public opinion on the issue, and many are about the federal government's role in the problem and its solution, you can

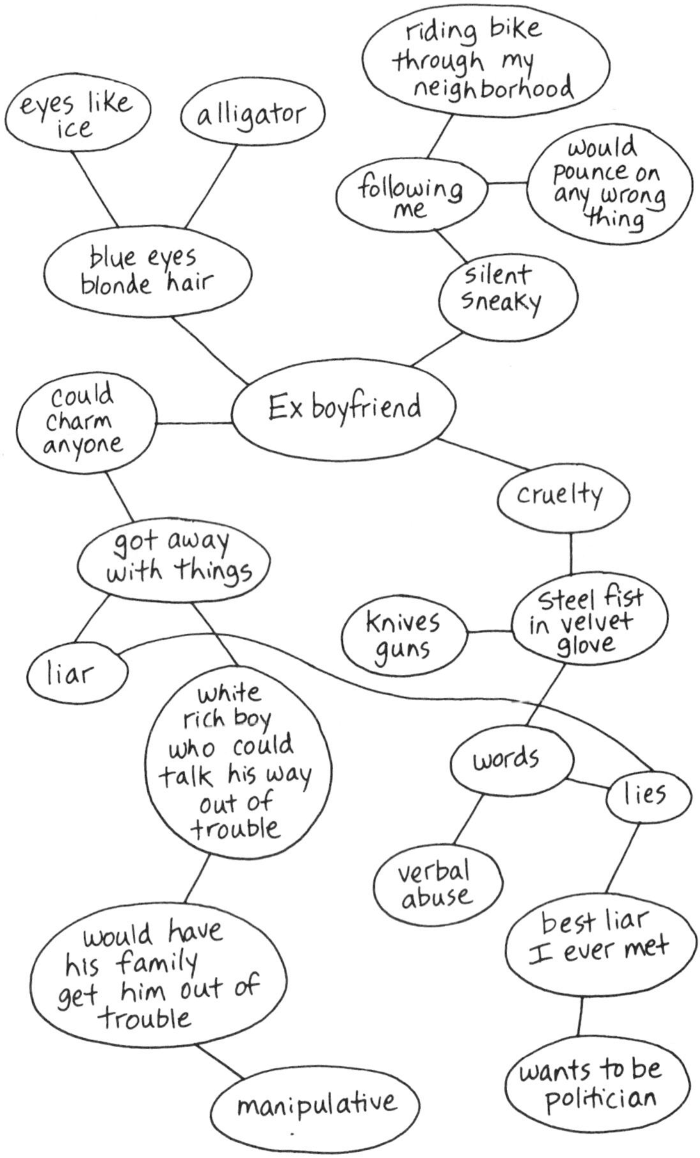


try to cluster the bits around three main arteries in the map, respectively labeled "history," "John Q. Public," and "Feds." But you needn't do any of that now. You're *generating;* you can sort, label, sequence, and analyze later.

As you map, keep reminding yourself:

*Don't map only nouns.* Map everything—nouns, verbs, adjectives, adverbs, phrases, sentences, pictures, questions. . . .

*Circle everything.* Connect every circle to something via a line. Use circles, not boxes—boxes are prisons.
*Don't be linear*—use all 360 degrees of the circle. Wander.

Don't think you're now committed to writing an essay that follows the map. You don't owe a map, or any other prewriting tool, anything. If you have to prove this to yourself, take a part of the map that you like, move it to the center of a new piece of paper, and map around it.

**Journals.** A journal is a notebook or binder where you dump everything you think, feel, or observe. It's written to and for you, and you write in it every day or nearly every day—not just when a good idea strikes. It's the only one of the prewriting tools that you use on schedule, so it gives you a lot of writing practice. But there's more to it than that: It teaches you to monitor your mind and heart constantly, as a part of life, and to value what's pouring out of them. We're always moving, breathing, thinking, and feeling; if we're writers, we observe and record what we think and feel. Most good writers keep journals, at least for a year or so until the monitoring habit is firmly established.

People who don't keep journals can't figure out what people who do keep journals find to put in them, so here are some entries from the journal of my student Susan Wooldridge, who journaled for more than twenty years and then was ready to publish a wonderful book I recommend to you called *Poemcrazy:*

> Happy morning.
> Tiniest sprouts in our herb garden. Sunlight on our plants.
>
> Aristophanes—
> "Who's there?"
> "An ill-starred man."
> "Then keep it to yourself."
>
> Perhaps the heaviness will leave soon. Perhaps I can will it away, perhaps it will just lift. All right, why is it here. Heavy dreams. Kent interested in someone else, though not truly, I knew that in the dream. Heavy weather. Anger at myself for having a job so basically useless to the world and to me. Every day. Morning energy lost on it.
>
> André Malraux said of Goya:
> "He discovered his genius the day he dared to give up pleasing others."
>
> I urge Smokey into the large field, recently plowed, we trot, canter, turn, figure 8, etc. I watch our shadow galloping across the field and try to convince myself that this, truly, is my childhood dream come true. Me galloping through a green field with my own beautiful horse.

Sometimes it feels right. Sometimes I feel guilt. Self-indulgence! Bad Sue. You should be out in the ghettoes carrying bundles of food to the starving and poor.

Doing office work. Typing like an automaton. Breathing stale smoke smells guardedly through my nose, occasionally flailing a broken fly swatter at a spiraling bumpy fly that refuses to land except on fragile typewriter parts.

Cows in the fog, dumb and heavy. Vague clumps of cows, a hog and sows in pale rows in a bog of weeds and grass and cows vacant as glass in the fog.

Words. Reasons, worries, flight.
Birds. Nested birds.

Think, when I have worked on a poem for a certain time, if it isn't getting better, if it doesn't intrigue me, it's not going to be any good.

Opened the dictionary to "fipple flute" while looking up "apposite," and found a lovely reproduction of fingerprints on this post-Halloween morning.

We went, with the rent, for another chat with Clarence and Grace. Good folk in their way. Clarence like a big cumbersome child, devilish. Grace somewhat shy, somewhat sly. Real country folk. She had pet pigs once. Cows. Clarence delivered milk during the depression. Real Illinois farmers. Clarence has been to 4 funerals this week, friends.

There will be snow tonight. And perhaps tomorrow I shall speed, skate, spin on thick ice.

Our tree is lying frozen outside. I just got the strange idea that at some level, the tree had consciousness, awareness of dying, even an ability, at an unheard level, to call to us, to appeal. But I am making this up.

And oh, this curse of words, endless rumination, introspection and self exposure. Here it is: I am a writer I am a writer I write I write I am a person who writes I am a woman I am a woman who likes to write, who chooses to write. I am a writer. No more fudging on this one, Susan, this drive will not be submerged, this is a need, a want. So follow it. Do it. Hell. Hello. Hell, Hello.

There are two things worth noting here. First, in conventional terms *nothing has happened* in Susan's life. She sees cows. She looks a word up in the dictionary. Nothing more. As always, it's the watchful eye and heart of the writer that makes things worth saying, not the experiences themselves. Second, these entries aren't mini-essays or proto-essays. They're written for the journal-keeper—an audience of one. Writing to others is different.

**Letter writing.** Most of us write well when we write letters, because we're writing as ourselves to a real audience we feel we can talk to. Write about the events of the day if that's all you feel up to; if you want to ask more of yourself, write, "I've been mulling over this thing for this essay I'm writing for a class. It's about . . . ," and block out the essay for your reader.

**Discovery drafts.** A discovery draft is a first draft that's purely exploratory; you just keep saying things and see where they lead you. You ask nothing, but you hope that by the time you're done, you will have written yourself to a sense of what you're going to do.

In a discovery draft, you're doing what Ken Macrorie, the writing teacher, calls *free writing*—brainstorming in running sentences. In its most extreme form, you write for a predetermined period of time and keep writing sentences no matter what happens. If you have nothing to say, write, "I have nothing to say" over and over until you find something else to say. Write song lyrics, gibberish, "The quick brown fox jumps over the lazy dog," or whatever, but keep writing.

**Abstracts.** Abstracts can be intimidating, but they can also be liberating if you have been mulling the essay over, your head is full of what you want to say, and you just try to dash the abstract off, like a cartoon before the detailed drawing. Chapter 7 is about how to write abstracts.

**Don't outline.** Outlining isn't an un-essay because it's an organizing discipline, not a prewriting tool. It's rigid, mechanical, structured—the opposite of everything we want at this stage. It closes you down instead of opening you up. Map or write an abstract instead.

One last word. You can always devise strategies to overcome writer's block if you can define precisely what frightens you and if you really want the block to go away. The reward for having writer's block is enormous: It means you don't have to write. Writing's a risky thing. I've suggested ways to minimize the risk, but if in the final analysis you'd rather be paralyzed and safe, no tip, no book, no teacher can make you do what you don't want to do.

## EXERCISES

1. Find a seed (Chapter 3). Then do the following things with it:

   a. Make a map from it.
   b. Brainstorm it with a classmate for ten minutes.
   c. Write a real letter to a real friend of yours in which you say something like, "I've been thinking about this essay I'm writing for my comp class. It's about . . ." Then tell your reader the essay, keeping him interested.
   d. Talk the essay into a tape recorder; then transcribe the tape. Rewrite it into an essay. Write a paragraph discussing what changes the spoken text needed.
   e. Via the Internet or elsewhere, find a piece of writing that addresses your essay's issues. React to the piece, and rewrite your essay to include the new thoughts generated by the reading.

2. Write a half-page essay in which you identify precisely what you're afraid of having happen when you write. Then go do a discovery draft in which you try to make those frightening things happen.

3. Write a half-page essay in which you identify precisely what gives you writer's block. Then write another essay in which you plot ways to sidestep the blocker—ways you can write so it comes up never or later.

4. Keep a journal for a week. Write in it at least once a day. Then take two entries and rewrite them as essay seeds.

# Part Three

## REVISING AND EDITING

# Chapter 5

# THESIS, PURPOSE, AUDIENCE, AND TONE

## The Spirit of Revising

Now that you've produced a draft, it's time to rewrite it. No other step in the writing process is so badly done by so many writers as rewriting. Shake a tree and a dozen good first-draft writers will fall out, but you're lucky if you get one good rewriter.

Most of us give ourselves rewriter's block by buying into one or more of several bad arguments. Many writers argue that since they rewrite badly, rewriting must be useless: "My rewrites are always worse than my first drafts," they boast. Other writers define rewriting in least helpful terms and equate it with mechanics: Rewriting is proofreading, checking grammar and spelling, and replacing words with better words. Others define rewriting in negative terms: Rewriting is looking for errors and blemishes and eliminating them.

As long as you hold any of these beliefs, rewriting will be an unproductive pain. Instead, adopt a new mindset:

Rewriting is rethinking, experimentation, adventure, boldly going where no first draft has gone before.

Rewriting is positive, not negative: You're enriching and expanding, not correcting; instead of deleting, you add.

Rewriting, like writing, fries the biggest fish first. You give first priority to the big deals—Do I really believe this? What else does my reader need from me?—and last priority to cosmetics like spelling and grammar rules.

The next eight chapters will show you the way. And Chapter 4 has mentioned something you can do to make it all easier: write on a word processor. Word processors destroy the whole idea of separate drafts—you're constantly composing and adding and deleting and polishing and tinkering and rethinking and resaying, in one seamless process of writing/rewriting. Word processors remove the labor penalty from revision—to revise, you just select, type, and save. And finally, rewriting on a word processor *feels good,* like playing a video game.

## How to Feel About Rules

Before we start revising, let's clear something up. The next eight chapters will offer you a few thousand rules of revision. How much allegiance do you owe them? Do you *have to* follow them? Is a rule ever wrong?

There are two extreme attitudes that don't help. The first says, "I am a student; I must obey." The second says, "Hey, writing is creative—I'm above rules." The first reduces you to marionette status, the second means no one will hire you.

What works is something in between. First, writing consists of two large stages: the creative stage (composing) and the corrective stage (editing and polishing). Your attitude toward rules differs for each. In the creative stage (from first thoughts through brainstorming, free writing, drafting, and revising), follow these principles:

Do what works.
Something "works" if it gets you the results you want.
Break a rule when breaking a rule gets you the results you want.
Break a rule when you have a good reason for breaking a rule.
When you break a rule, know you're breaking it.
Follow rules unless there's a good reason not to.
If you're not sure what to do, try following the rule—it might help.

In other words, a rule is a tool. Use it the way you use a crowbar—when it helps you out of a jam. But that means you must know what your *purpose* is. If you find yourself saying, "Hmmm—should I use a hammer or a sewing machine here?" you've lost sight of what you're trying to accomplish.

In the corrective/editing stage (spelling, grammar, formatting, following the boss's instructions), think another way. Here, follow rules slavishly. It makes no sense to say, "I am an *artiste*—I am above indenting paragraphs or spelling 'accommodate' correctly." If you don't see why, the next time you go driving try saying, "I am a creative driver—I will drive on the right side of the road" and see where it gets you.

## Revision Tools

Revision is hard because we don't know how to reduce it to concrete steps. We need a recipe ("First, combine all dry ingredients in a large bowl . . ."), and we need tools—concrete gizmos like measuring cups and sifters we can hold in our hand and do the steps with. Part Three of this book is a loose sort of recipe, and it will offer you a series of such tools. All craftsmen know you can never have enough tools, so I'm going to give you the whole hardware store. When we're done, our toolbox will consist of thesis, purpose, audience, and tone (all in Chapter 5), maps and outlines (Chapter 6), abstracts (Chapter 7), openers, closers, and titles (Chapter 8), tools for shortening and lengthening drafts (Chapter 9), peer feedback (Chapter 10), and style analysis (Chapter 11).

What do we know about tools?

**1. Each tool does a specific job.** A hammer hammers, a drill drills. You can't make one tool do the job of another, so since you need "the right tool for the right job," you need lots of tools. Peer editing won't do what a thesis statement does, and a thesis statement won't do what an outline does.

**2. Tools are for you, not the customer.** When you sell the chair you made, you don't sell the saw and drill along with it. So don't write the outline for the reader or attach the thesis statement to the essay.

**3. The purpose in using a tool is never simply to use the tool.** Nobody ever said, "I think I'll go run my sewing machine for an hour." You run the sewing machine to make a dress. So if you outline just to make an outline or peer edit just to have a peer-editing experience, you've lost sight of your real purpose. With revision tools, your purpose is always *to produce a better draft,* and if you don't end up with that you wasted your tool time. This is a version of our old friend, "Doing something teaches you nothing" (p. P-2).

Rule 3 may sound obvious, but in fact writers make this mistake all the time. They'll take a draft, outline it, maybe even learn some interesting things from the outline, leave the draft largely unchanged, and say, "See, Teacher, I outlined," as if the act were a blessing in itself.

**4. Using a tool takes skill, which comes with practice.** Even a hammer takes years to learn to handle well, as anyone who has watched a master carpenter can tell you. So we have to expect to put in some time learning to use a thesis statement or peer-editing session.

**5. Tools don't make the project good by themselves.** Even if I'm the world's greatest user of a sewing machine, the machine by itself can't make the dress beautiful. Tools just make the work easier—it's hard to sew cloth or shape wood with your bare hands. So a thesis statement will help you make a great essay, but it won't make the essay great. You still need talent, inspiration, passion, and the like.

## Diagnostic Tools

Some of the tools we're going to master belong to a special category of tools called diagnostics: tools that provide you with data you use to draw conclusions—the way tape measures, thermometers, CAT scans, and blood tests do. A thermometer tells you if you have a fever. An abstract tells you if a draft has any transition problems.

We know lots of interesting things about diagnostic tools:

1. **Diagnostic tools see things we can't see.** CAT scans see inside your brain. Outlines see inside your essay.

2. **The diagnostic tool concretizes the problem,** so we can figure out what to do about it. It changes "I don't feel well" into "I have mononucleosis." It changes "This draft seems choppy" into "The sentences are too short."

3. **Diagnostic tools always must be *read*,** and the reading requires training. First our dad has to show us how to read the thermometer; then we have to know that 98.6 equals normal. Reading writers' tools means answering questions like, What can I learn from this outline? What is the thesis statement telling me about the draft? And that takes practice.

4. **Flawed diagnostic tools are worse than no tools,** because they give false results. It's better to have no information than false information, better to just put your hand on your forehead than to be guided by an erroneous thermometer. So if you use flawed outlines or flawed Latinate percentiles, you're worse off than if you use no revision tools at all. And there's no way to use a malfunctioning tool *so carefully* that you overcome its flaws ("This tape measure is not to scale, so I'll just measure this board very carefully . . .").

5. **Diagnostic tools don't tell you what to do.** A tape measure tells you how long the board is; it can't tell you how long the board should be. A thesis statement or an outline will let you see what's going on in the draft. That's its only job. It's your job to take that insight and decide what, if anything, you should do about it. Stylistic analysis will tell you your sentences are short. Only you can decide if you should make them longer. But you need to know the sentences are short before you can make that decision.

## Making Your Own Tools

Writers' tools differ from shop tools in one important way: Shop tools are made by Black and Decker; writers' tools you make yourself. You build the thesis statement or the outline. Then you use it, by learning from it and applying what you learned when you revise. This two-step model contains three vital implications:

1. We have to build the tool correctly, or all the information the tool gives us will be unreliable (see item 4, p. 70).

2. We have to do *both* steps. Making the saw is merely a preamble to the real work of making the chair. It's easy to do just Step 1 and quit—"See, Teacher, I made the outline! Am I done now?" Doing something teaches you nothing (p. P-2).

3. A problem can crop up in Step 1, in Step 2, or in the draft. You need to know in which one of the three the problem lies. If the problem lies in Step 1, you fix it by repairing the tool (rewriting the thesis statement, for instance). If the problem lies in Step 2, you fix it by learning to interpret the data better. And if the problem lies in the draft, you fix it by revising.

Rule 3 is usually obvious in life. If you take your temperature and the thermometer reads 103 degrees, you don't blame the thermometer for reading so high, since the tool is just doing its job and the problem lies in your body. But in writing, we love to blame our tools for revealing problems in our drafts. For instance, if I ask my students to outline their essays and then to critique the outline, they'll often say, "This outline is terrible, because it's choppy and confusing and boring." But probably the outline is doing its job, which is to reveal things about the draft, and it's the draft that is choppy, confusing, and boring.

## Revision in Five Giant Steps

Revision is a messy process, so we're going to reduce it to five large steps. Step 1: Trouble-shoot thesis, purpose, audience, and tone (this chapter). Step 2: Trouble-shoot organization (Chapters 6–8). Step 3: Get peer feedback (Chapter 10). Step 4: Polish style (Chapter 11). Step 5: Edit for grammar and mechanics (Chapter 12). We'll discuss each in turn.

## Thesis, Purpose, Audience, and Tone

The four most powerful diagnostic tools at a reviser's disposal are the thesis statement ("What am I saying?"), the purpose statement ("Why am I saying it?"), the definition of audience ("Who am I talking to?"), and the definition of tone ("What mood is this essay in?"). These are what the hammer and saw are to the carpenter. You'll use them every day of your writing life.

Of course, you've been working with your thesis, purpose, audience, and tone, at least unconsciously, since the essay project quickened in your brain. Now it's time to *re*-consider them. Most writers have a sense of these things when they begin writing, but they never lock them in, and when better ones come along they welcome them. Staying committed to your first thesis is like marrying the first person you go out with—it would be a miracle if you ended up with the best one for you. And demanding that you have a big important message before you start writing is a great way to give yourself writer's block.

How soon you arrive at firm answers to the four questions depends a lot on what kind of writing you're doing. Technical or scientific writing often is sure of purpose, audience, and tone long before the writing begins, when the experiment or project is first being designed. Argumentative writing or writing in the humanities may not discover the final version of the answers until a very late draft. If you write down your thesis when you start and promise to stick to it through thick and thin, you're just promising to *not learn anything* during the drafting and revising. "How can I know what I think until I see what I've written?" writing teacher James Britten says.

One day someone mentioned in class that the opening pages of *The Catcher in the Rye* and *Huckleberry Finn* were strikingly similar. I was intrigued and decided to write an analysis of the two authors' styles. That sense of purpose (without thesis, at that point) led to another, and I found myself comparing the way Holden Caulfield and Huck used language. That led me to compare their characters generally, and that led me to talk about Holden's concept of phoniness, which led me to the hypocrisy of American phony-hating and (to my great surprise) Holden's fear of death and Americans' inability to confront death. There I stayed. And in the process, I had gone from siding with Holden to disliking him to hating him to loving him. At each stage in the writing, I knew to the best of my present knowledge what my purpose and thesis were, and at each new stage I let the old knowledge go and embraced a new purpose and thesis. When I started, Americans' relationship with death was the farthest thing from my mind.

## Topic

**Making the tool.** We talked about topics on p. 39. Of course your essay will have a topic—it's impossible to write without writing about *something*—but since nouns are useless (p. P-10), topic is next to worthless as a revision tool. The only slight value in topic making comes from *narrowing the topic* by adding detail. Here, more is better. Begin with a topic label for your essay: "Education." Now add detail: "Problems in education." Keep adding detail, making the topic statement longer, until you can add no more: "How to make public education interesting to a generation of children raised on adrenaline movies and video games."

**Using the Tool.** Since the topic statement is next to useless, make it useful by turning it into a *thesis sentence:* Just add a verb:

| **Noun/Topic** | → | **Thesis Sentence** |
|---|---|---|
| Affirmative Action | → | Affirmative Action is a cancer on American society. |
| Rudeness of young people | → | Young people are no ruder today than they were in the past. |

## Thesis

The revision tool with the biggest bang for your buck is the thesis statement. Always begin your revision work with it. Your thesis is the statement at the heart of the essay—the topic sentence, the core, the point, the lesson, the moral, the content in a flash, the *one* thing you have to say. Here are theses for three of the essays in this book:

> "Given the Chance" (p. 276): The State of California's commitment to drug rehabilitation programs is so minimal that it's impossible for social service people to help those who need it.
>
> "Why?" (p. 277): Getting sickeningly drunk to celebrate your twenty-first birthday makes no sense, but we keep doing it.
>
> "Why I Never Cared for the Civil War" (p. 391): Traditional ways of teaching school are boring and don't work, but there are powerful, exciting alternatives.

**Making the tool.** Since the thesis statement has a great gift for pointing out when we aren't really saying anything, there is a temptation to build it wrong so we can escape its frightening revelations. Obey the following tool-making rules strictly:

1. *A thesis is one complete sentence and only one.* Not a noun phrase, however large, and not two sentences, because writing a thesis is the moment when you demand to know what's at the *center,* and there can be only one center.

2. *A thesis is a declarative sentence*—not a question, since theses are *answers.*

3. *A thesis must fit well into the following template:* "In this essay I say, '__________.'" Thus the sentence "This essay explains how to change the oil in your car" isn't a thesis.

4. *A thesis should contain the word "because"*—to force you to have at least one reason.

5. *A thesis should contain the word "should"*—to force you to think about what you're trying to *do,* not just *say,* with the essay.

6. *A thesis must summarize the* entire *essay*—all parts of the essay must serve to support it.

7. *The thesis is almost never present as a sentence in the essay.* Don't pick whichever sentence in the draft is closest to your thesis and call it your thesis, and don't feel obligated to declare your thesis somewhere in the essay. Compose the thesis in your head, and then use it in the essay in whatever way works.

Occasionally, a writer will write out the thesis in a sentence or two and hand it to the reader. In George Orwell's "Shooting an Elephant," he tells how he, as a minor British official in India, was forced by the pressure of an expectant mob to shoot an elephant that had gotten loose from its owner. He tells you exactly what the lesson of the story is:

> And it was at this moment, as I stood there with the rifle in my hands, that I first grasped the hollowness, the futility of the white man's dominion in the East. Here was I, the white man with his gun, standing in front of the unarmed native crowd—seemingly the leading actor of the piece; but in reality I was only an absurd puppet pushed to and fro by the will of those yellow faces behind. I perceived in this moment that *when the white man turns tyrant it is his own freedom that he destroys.* (I italicized the thesis-JR).

But you can spread the thesis throughout a couple of paragraphs, imply it indirectly, or keep it to yourself—see "Dear Governor Deukmejian" (p. 278), "Why?" (p. 277), and "Dad" (p. 219) for examples. Similarly, you can put the thesis in the first sentence of the essay, the last, or nowhere. You're the boss. The only place you're obliged to have the thesis is *in your head.*

Some audiences and purposes demand an explicit statement of thesis, and others don't. Scientific and technical writing always states its thesis up front; fiction rarely states it at all.

8. *Every essay has a thesis, including informative essays.* In an informative essay, the thesis may not be the heart and soul of the piece, but it's there, however quietly. Here are theses for two of the informative essays in this book:

> "The Last Stop for America's Buses" (p. 387): If you understand how Mexico's bus system works, your vacation will be less expensive, more exciting, and a lot more educational.

"Why Falling in Love Feels So Good" (p. 389): With a little knowledge about your own body chemistry, you can pick a mate wisely and avoid a lifetime of unhappiness or a messy divorce.

**Using the tool.** Once your thesis is well made, you employ it by asking it questions and answering the questions. The place to begin is at the beginning: *"Did I say anything?"* If the answer is yes, go on to questions like

Did I say anything interesting?
Anything useful?
Anything risky?
Anything new?
Anything important to the reader?
Anything important to me?

But don't limit yourself to a set list of specific questions; instead, as with all diagnostic tools, try to look at the thesis and learn from it whatever it can teach you. Ask, What's going on? What can I see here? What is this telling me about the draft? What seems to be going well and what's going badly?

Remember, a diagnostic tool can't tell you what to do (p. 70), so don't assume there are universally right answers to your questions. Not all great essays have earth-shaking theses (the "I hate eggs" essay on p. 37 doesn't). Not all great essays have "shoulds" in their theses (the ones on p. 73 don't). Not all great essays have theses that can be stated simply in words ("Dad" on p. 219). Not all great essays have theses at all ("how to" essays often don't).

## Purpose

Our second diagnostic tool, the purpose statement, answers questions like

Why am I writing this?
What do I hope to accomplish?
What do I want?
What do I want the reader to do?

Like the thesis statement, it's small but mighty, and since it is terrifically revealing, writers will often go to great lengths to escape its lessons.

When we start thinking about why we write, most of our purposes are unhelpful ones:

To complete the assignment
To get a good grade

To write a good essay
To learn about the topic
To practice researching, thinking, and writing
To tell the reader something

The problem with all these purposes is *they don't tell you what to do.* A writer is constantly faced with decisions: How should I say this? Should I put this piece of information in or not? Should I do X, then Y, or the other way around? *The clearer a purpose is, the more it answers such writer's questions.* If I say, "My purpose is to write a great essay," that purpose answers no questions at all. If I say, "I want to make the reader sad," that purpose helps a little. If I say, "I want to capture the essence of my friend Sally," I can start answering specific questions about what to do. And if I say, "I want to capture Sally's ambivalence: She talks like a feminist and acts like a sex object, so I want to use her as an example to argue that her dilemma is typical of the women's movement, which has always found it easier to talk liberated than act liberated," I've got a purpose that will tell me exactly what to do.

**Making the tool.** Here are five rules to follow to ensure you're making the purpose statement right.

1. *Make the purpose statement an infinitive verb*: "My purpose is *to expose* the contemptible cowardice of the campus newspaper staff." You can start the sentence many ways: "I wrote in order to . . . ," "My goal was to . . ,": "I want to . . . ," "I intend to . . . ," "I'm going to . . ." Any of these phrases will lead you to end with a verb, which is what you want.

2. *Don't quote the topic or thesis in your purpose statement.* Your purpose and your thesis are never the same thing, nor are your purpose and your topic ever the same thing. Your thesis is what you say, your topic is what you say it about, your purpose is why you say it. You say things about things in order to accomplish things. The most common way to go wrong when stating purpose is to quote the topic or the thesis:

My purpose is to explain *why I'm dropping out of school.*
I intend to show the reader *how to change a flat tire.*
I want to illustrate *the vast differences between boys and girls.*
I'm going to convince the reader that *the Electoral College must be eliminated.*
My goal is to help people realize *they should become vegetarians.*

All the italicized phrases you just read are quoted topics or theses. A quoted topic or thesis results in a purpose statement that is true but worthless—all it does is reproduce the information we learned when we made the topic or thesis statement in the first place. In order to learn something new, follow Rule 3 until the topic or thesis disappears.

3. *Ask "Why?" and keep asking "Why?"* Purposes come in series. The result you hope to cause by writing will cause something else, which in turn will cause something else: My purpose is to convince the reader to vote Republican in the next presidential election, *so that* the Republican candidate will win, *so that* she will increase defense spending, *so that* America will have a strong defense, *so that* we will remain safe from the threat of military attack, *so that* I don't end up in some concentration camp, *so that* I don't have to eat rats to stay alive . . ." Keep asking "Why?" and getting answers until you hit a "Why?" that is unanswerable.

4. *Have at least two purposes:* to get something for yourself and to give the reader something he wants or should want. Humans are selfish; if there isn't something in it for you, you won't write, and if there isn't something in it for the reader, he won't read. Ask yourself how each of you is going to profit.

5. *Make sure your purpose is a version of the universal writer's purpose: to do something to the reader.*

**Using the tool.** Once you've written a well-formed purpose statement, the hard work is behind you. First, check one last time to make sure you didn't quote the topic or the thesis. Then ask the central question: "Am I clear on what I'm trying to accomplish?" Then move on to questions like

Is my purpose constant throughout the essay?
Does it account for everything in the draft?
Is it important to me?
Will it be important to the reader?

## Audience

A purpose is always an intent to do something *to someone*. The clearer you are about who it is, the better you'll write. Chapter 2 talked about this. Let's take it further.

**Making the tool.** A definition of audience is a paragraph or so detailing everything you know about who you're writing to. It sounds simple-minded, but don't sell it short. The audience definition is more powerful than it at first appears. And it's harder to produce than you'd think. The first time you try it, you usually end up saying something useless like "I'm writing to anyone who would like to read this essay."

We're audience-unconscious because a sense of audience in our *reading* is like air: it's always there, so we take it for granted. But the instant a writer fails to take us into consideration or assumes we're someone we're not, the significance of audience becomes deafeningly clear. Here is the opening of an essay that doesn't know who we are:

> Dance forms are characterized by the use of particular movements. The various forms of dance require differing degrees of body mathematics usage, strength, endurance, practiced ability, innate ability, and mental concentration.
>
> Butoh dance movement requires all of the above. The precision of body placement, the strength needed for sustained positions, the endurance necessary to sustain positions, the repetitive exercises to build strength and endurance, the natural ability to execute movement, and the high level of concentration are the components of the body and mind for the Butoh dancer. The development of these enable the dancer to tap inner and outer spheres of energy movement. The physical body is the initiator, receptor, and giver of these energy realms.

Our first question may be, What does this mean? But another question must be answered first: Who is this for, and how is she supposed to use it? Once the essay declares an audience and purpose, meaning becomes a handleable problem:

> **Your First Butoh Concert**
> If you're a long-time lover of dance, you probably think you've seen it all. But the first time you attend a concert of Butoh, the new, exciting blend of Eastern philosophy and Western modern-dance technique, your immediate response may be, "But they're not *dancing* at all!" Well, they really are, but they aren't doing anything you're used to calling dance. Butoh looks odd, because it thinks a different way about movement than other schools of dance do, but once I walk you through it you may find it's something you want to see again and again—and perhaps try yourself.

Here's the first paragraph of another essay, titled "Make Them Pay," that forgot to think about audience:

> There are many people in this world that are against the death penalty. They think it is wrong, inhumane, cruel, and unusual, etc. They feel that no one has the right to take someone else's life. But what about the life that was taken by the criminal in question? What gave them the right to take an innocent life? I feel that the death penalty is sufficient punishment for violent crimes such as murder and rape. Crimes like these are repulsive and should be considered crimes against humanity. Those who commit them should pay with their lives, not only as punishment for their sick mistakes,

but also as a lesson to others that such offenses will not be tolerated in this society.

Since I oppose the death penalty, this argument is addressed to me, but it misunderstands me so completely that I just find myself digging in and becoming more and more resistant. The writer thinks, for instance, that if she can convince me that the crimes are heinous I will grant her thesis; but we all know the crimes are heinous, and I don't oppose the death penalty because I think rape is no big deal—my opposition is on other grounds entirely. Once she knows me better, she'll realize that this argument isn't working.

So our first challenge is to convince ourselves that every piece of writing—even the telephone book—has an audience that is real and specific and that good communicators filter everything they say through a sense of who's listening. If you doubt this, think about how we talk to children. We immediately screen everything we say to kids, asking ourselves questions like "Do they know these words?" "Will this disturb them?" "Can they follow this?" "Am I going too fast?" "What things are they interested in?" Just remember that you must ask similar questions for *all* audiences.

**Making the tool.** Now that you're a believer, follow these guidelines as you write your audience definition:

1. *The audience is never you.* However much you may feel that you're writing to educate yourself or writing to figure out what you think or writing to get something off your chest, as soon as you give it to someone else to read, you're saying, "I think this will profit *you*." And then you need to know who that someone is.

2. *Audience must always be chosen.* There is no such thing as the only or the right or the inevitable audience for a piece of writing. You choose audience the way you choose thesis.

Let's assume that the trustees of your state university have just decided to raise the tuition . . . again. As one of the students, you decide to write an essay decrying this. Your purpose is clear: to stop the fee hike. Now, who should you write to? There are many groups who have a say in the matter: students, parents, college administrators, state legislators (since they control the state university's purse strings), teachers, and citizens (since they elect the legislators). Within these groups are smaller groups. Within the student body, for instance, there's a group of students who think it's OK for rising costs to be borne in part by the students; there's a group that's vehemently opposed; there's a group that doesn't care; there's a group that hasn't heard about the issue; and there's a group that's on the fence.

Each audience has to be talked to in a different way. The students who are vehemently opposed to fee hikes need to be preached to like brothers; those who think the hike's a good idea need to be persuaded they're wrong; administrators need to be shown alternative ways to pay the university's bills; citizens need to be convinced that it's ultimately to the benefit of society that bright kids can afford to go to college. Writing to all these audiences at once is nearly impossible. So choose. And be especially careful to avoid those circular audience definitions that appear to define audience but really say nothing, like "I'm writing to anyone interested in what I'm writing about."

3. *Smaller means easier.* The narrower your audience, the easier it is to write to, because writing is about controlling the reader—and the smaller the group, the easier it is to predict how they will react. Your easiest audience is the smallest: your best friend. As the audience enlarges, the diversity of experience, tastes, values, and beliefs grows, the reactions become more unpredictable, and the challenge of controlling the audience grows. The hardest audience is "everyone," since "everyone" is almost totally unpredictable; but oddly, that's the one students are drawn to.

There is a kind of writing whose audience is defined no more clearly than "every American citizen interested in social issues." It's what we see in *Newsweek* and *Time*. And since we see such writing all the time, we're in danger of concluding that most writing is to such audiences. But most writing isn't. For every *Newsweek*, there are a hundred specialized magazines that are just for Mac owners, or dirt bike aficionados, or scuba divers. For every national magazine, there are a thousand local club newsletters. For every newsletter, there are a thousand letters to friends. So the vast bulk of writing in our world is to narrowly specified audiences. And the essayists in *Time* and *Newsweek* are the best writers in the country. They have to be, because writing to "everyone" is that tough.

4. *Make the writing easy by choosing an audience like yourself, or make it useful by choosing an audience unlike yourself.* The more like you the audience is, the easier it is to write, because the easier it is to guess how they'll respond. Most writers know this and instinctively write as if all readers are exactly like them—thus the number of essays I get about how much fun it was to get bombed last weekend. The problem is that people just like us can't profit much from our writing, because it has nowhere new to take them—they're already where we are (see p. 271). Remember, when you're learning, the teacher who *isn't like you* has the most to offer (p. P-6). If we're writing against tuition hikes, the administrators are the hardest to write to because they're least like you, but that means there's more to be gained by winning them over.

5. *Go beyond the simple label.* Most writers, when they first start trying to describe audiences, stop at noun labels: "My audience is college students"; "My audience is working mothers." Since nouns are useless, that won't tell us enough, so push past by asking questions about the label—what do you know about college students or working mothers? Questions about audiences sound like

What gender are they?
How old are they?
How much money do they have?
How much formal education do they have?
Do they have a sense of humor?
How sophisticated are their English language skills?
How do they feel about seeing the word "asshole" in print?
How conservative or liberal are they?
What is their value system?
How close- or open-minded are they about the issue in question?
How interested are they in this issue?
How well informed about it are they?
What do they need to know from me?
What do they want from me?
How are they going to perceive me?
How will they react to what I'm saying?

We always know much more about our audiences than we at first can say. John Mercer's audience in "The Last Stop for America's Busses" (p. 387) isn't just "people traveling to Mexico." They're people who haven't been to Mexico but would like to go, who know nothing about Mexican public transportation, who are shy about going because they're worried about being out of their depth, but who like adventure and aren't looking for luxury and security. They're probably young or middle-aged, and they travel to encounter the culture. They know very little about the Mexican national character. They have a sense of humor about the little disasters of traveling. And so on.

There's one question you can't avoid answering: How much does your audience already know? Because every time you tell the reader something, you're assuming she doesn't already know it, and every time you *don't* tell her something, you're assuming she does. If I say, "Next, remove the tire's lug nuts with a tire iron," I must either explain or not explain what lug nuts and tire irons are, and either choice requires a decision about my audience's prior knowledge.

6. *More is better.* Since we want to know as much about our audience as we can, the longer a definition of audience gets, the better it must be. So keep adding detail to your definition as long as you can.

**Using the tool.** Reread the draft, keeping what you now know about your audience in mind—imagine *saying* everything to them as you read, and imagine their reaction: "How will they react when I say *this?*" You can judge the quality of the draft by the clarity of your answers: If you know exactly what the reader would say in response to every line, exactly how he would feel, the draft is sound.

## Tone

Tone is the emotional mood of the writing and is described by the same *adjectives* we use to describe people's moods or personalities: angry, sweet, frustrated, formal, snide, silly, cold, melancholy, professorial, stuffy, hip, and so on.

In school we tend to be deaf to tone. Why, I don't know, since in life mood is the first thing we notice. Yet my students tend to notice tone last, if at all, when they read. They'll discourse on an essay's content for hours, but I have to remind them to notice it's funny. And of the four big issues—thesis, purpose, audience, and tone—tone is the one my students have typically not thought about on any level. So train yourself to be tone-sensitive when you read and when you write. You already know how to "do" tone—you know how to sound angry or sad. It's just a matter of giving yourself permission.

How important is tone? It's more than garnish—often it's more important than content. People often care more about how others "feel" to them than about what they say. Every time there's a presidential debate, we see that Americans care more about how a candidate's personality comes across (does he seem warm? does he seem trustworthy?) than about his political platform.

Mastering tone begins with the realization that *you can't not have one,* any more than a person can be in *no* mood. If you ask someone how he feels and he says, "I feel nothing," you know he's in denial—and so are you if you say your writing has no tone. Any set of words will create a tone, just as any set of clothes will make some impression, so your only choices are to control tone or be out of control. Don't strive for blandness unless the boss orders you to. Few people seek to feel nothing, few people say beige is their favorite color, few love Pablum above all other foods, and few people read to feel nothing. So don't strive for tonal neutrality unless you're sure your purposes call for it—as in legal depositions and medical research. For most of us, emotion is good. The most common problem with writing is that it's too flat, so *push toward the brighter colors*—outrage, impishness, absurdity, fright, joy.

Once we grant that tone exists, we like to escape responsibility for choosing the tone of our writing, saying, "My tone is forced on me by my subject matter (or my thesis)." Never. *Tone is chosen,* just like audience (p. 79). Any subject matter and any message can be presented in any tone. You can do stand-up comedy about being burned alive (as Richard Pryor has done), write a sober, scholarly disquisition on rap (as many scholars are now doing), or be terminally silly about passengers facing their impending death in an airline crash (as *Airplane!* has done).

Cultivate a large vocabulary of tones. Tones are tools, and the more tools we have, the more powerful we are. Writing everything in the same tone is as impractical as hitting every golf shot with the same club and as boring as always wearing khakis. Anyway, tone is where the fun is. Imagine writing a letter to your bank telling them they've once again fouled up your checking account. Try several different tones:

> **Sarcastic:** I have to hand it to you guys—I never thought you'd find a new way to foul things up, but you have.
>
> **Sympathetic:** We all make mistakes—I know, I make them myself all day long. I appreciate the load of work you guys are under. I realize how it can happen, but you seem to have gotten my account confused with someone else's.
>
> **Indignant:** I have never in my twenty-five years as a businessman witnessed anything like the level of administrative incompetence that is the daily norm in your bank . . .
>
> **Suppliant:** I don't want to make a nuisance of myself, but might I ask that you re-examine your records for my account? There seems to be a mistake somewhere, and I know it's probably mine, but . . .

Chose the tone that works—which always means the tone that gets the reaction you want from your reader. In other words, tone is dictated by purpose. Sometimes anger works for you; sometimes it works against you. Only a clear sense of purpose (and of audience) will tell you which situation applies in a particular essay. If you're trying to jolt the audience out of its complacency, you may want to be obnoxious, offensive, and profane, like Sinead O'Connor tearing up the picture of the Pope on television. If you're trying to soothe a patient just before his open-heart surgery, clinical objectivity is probably called for, since you want the patient as numb as possible.

Let's watch a master writer adapting tone to his purpose and his audience. Here Anthony Burgess tries to answer the question "What makes a word a word?"

> For the moment—but only for the moment—it will be safe to assume that we all know what is meant by the word "word." I may even consider that my typing fingers know it, defining a word (in a whimsical conceit) as what comes between two

> spaces. The Greeks saw the word as the minimal unit of speech; to them, too, the atom was the minimal unit of matter. Our own age has learnt to split the atom and also the word. If atoms are divisible into protons, electrons, and neutrons, what are words divisible into?
>
> *(Anthony Burgess, "Words," in* Language Made Plain*)*

What's the tone here? It's playful—the second sentence is a joke, and the phrase "the word 'word'" is meant to tickle. It's personal—it uses *I* and recognizes the reader via the *we's.* It's informal—it uses dashes, for instance. It concretizes—it talks about Burgess's fingers. Yet the tone is also academic: The phrase "whimsical conceit" is sophisticated, and "conceit" is used in its classical sense, meaning not "vanity" but "bit of cleverness."

Burgess's simile—words are like atoms—is carefully chosen for its tone. He's trying to say, "Linguistics is as exciting as atomic physics." That may not work for you, but in 1964 when the paragraph was written, every red-blooded American bookworm wanted to be an atomic scientist when he grew up. Imagine Burgess saying, "Linguistics is as exciting as working with Steven Spielberg on a sequel to *E.T.*," and you'll feel what he wanted you to feel.

How do all these tonal choices support Burgess's purpose? He's writing a book on language for laymen. He knows that linguistics is traditionally dry for nonacademics, so he works hard to keep things lightweight and human. He tries to make it easy reading, yet he wants the reader to think, so the jokes and the occasional hard word make you work. Finally the simile says, "This is exciting stuff!" in an attempt to whip up some reader interest.

**Making the tool.** A statement of tone often starts with a single adjective: "This essay feels __________ " —informal, formal, informative, educational, personal, funny, comic, angry. But a tone is the mirror of a personality talking, and personalities can be very complex. So push beyond the single generic word. As with topic and audience, more is better (pp. 72, 81). If your tone is "funny," ask, "What kind of funny?" Perhaps it's "slightly sarcastic, gently teasing, a little grumpy but basically good-humored and ultimately sympathetic." Look at how much there was to say about Burgess's tone.

**Using the Tool.** Using a definition of tone comes down to asking two questions. First, "Is this tone intriguing/touching/powerful?" If it isn't, you may need to rewrite the essay in some color other than beige. Second, "How does this tone serve my purpose?" Your answer must be in terms of audience response: "This tone will make my reader react *thus*, and that's the reaction I want." If you struggle in answering, the problem may be in your purpose—if you aren't sure what you're trying to do, you can't tell if the tone will help or not.

Tone is closely allied with style, so read Chapter 11 if you want to continue working with tone.

## Purpose and Audience Tell You How to Write

Thesis, purpose, audience, and tone are not created equal. Nor is thesis most important, though we tend to think so. In fact, *purpose and audience are most important*, because they determine what we say and the tone we say it in. They tell us how to structure, how to begin, how to end, how long the sentences should be, whether to use slang or not . . . in short, everything. Writing is a constant series of "What should I do now?" questions: Should I state my thesis? Should I begin a sentence with "but"? Should I explain what I just said? Should I summarize in my conclusion? *Purpose and audience answer all such questions, and only purpose and audience can answer them.*

***Example 1: Should you use slang, like "home" for "buddy" or "whack" for "bad"?***

It depends on who you're writing to and why. Slang is fleeting. A few years ago every young person I knew was saying everything was "hella cool" and "hella bad." Now no one says "hella." So if you want what you write to have a long shelf life, avoid slang because it will soon be out of date. Slang also marks you as a member of a certain group. If you're talking to members of that group, using slang may earn you instant acceptance. If you're talking to outsiders, using insider slang may advertise the fact that you're not one of them. You may or may not want to do that. In the sixties many black activists methodically used black slang when talking to white audiences, in effect saying, "I don't have to speak your dialect to be worth listening to."

***Example 2: How should you structure the essay?***

It depends on who you're writing to and why. How-to essays usually go through a process step by step, because the reader is trying to go through the process herself with the essay as a guide. Technical reports usually begin with summary, conclusion, or recommendations, because they're read by bosses who don't have time to read the whole thing and want *an answer* where they can see it at a glance. Newspaper articles always put their most important information first and their least important information last, because newspaper readers skim the openings of articles, pick the ones worth reading, read until their interest flags, and quit. Arguments often start by declaring that there's something that needs fixing in the world but hold off telling the reader what the thesis is. The idea is to win the reader's attention but to give the writer time to talk him into agreeing with her. In each of these cases, organization is dictated by what you're trying to do to the reader and what he's reading you for.

### *Example 3: How much information should you give, and what style should you write in?*

It depends on who you're writing to and why. A few years ago, I was given the job of rewriting our university's course catalog. At that time, course descriptions read like this:

> **Structure of the English Language:** Basic study of English morphology and syntax, making use of the practical contributions of traditional, structural, generative-transformational grammars and other approaches to analysis of English structure.

I said to myself, "This is useless—no student can understand it, so how can it help him choose his courses?" I rewrote the descriptions in this way:

> **Structure of the English Language:** How words are made and how words are added together to make sentences.

I thought this was a great improvement. But my new descriptions were all thrown out and the old ones kept. The argument for doing so went like this: I was wrong about who read the catalog and why. Catalogs aren't read by students; they're read by faculty advisors and admissions officers at other schools. They need to know exactly what topics a course covers, so they can decide when to give transfer credit, for instance, and they aren't troubled by weighty terms like "morphology." My revision of the catalog made it useful to a new audience and useless to its old one.

### *Example 4: When should you reveal the essay's topic?*

It depends on who you're writing to and why. I once read an essay called "The Greatest Game Fish in the World." It was a three-page narrative, describing in mouth-watering detail the excitement of angling for and catching a wonderful game fish the author neglected to identify by name. At the end of the narrative was one short paragraph: "Do you want to know what it is? It's carp." End of essay. Magnificent. You see, the writer knew that his readers (subscribers to a fish and game magazine) despised carp as garbage, so he hooked them with the story, stunned them with the punch line, and stopped.

# WRITER'S WORKSHOP

## Revising for Thesis, Audience, and Purpose

Here's a first draft that's full of interesting stuff but that hasn't yet tried to answer the four big questions.

### NO TITLE WORTHY

ALBERT PIERCE

I think I got the date right. There isn't much else worth remembering. Oh, my thesis! A little advice for all you folks out there who still fall into the category defined by that all too oft-quoted song which I believe says something about those who have not yet accumulated enough scar tissue and believe that they still fit the category label "young at heart" (an interesting little concept when one stops to ponder its complexities): Boys and girls, marriage is for the birds. I could easily use stronger language, but, believe it or not, I'm turning this in as a representation of my consummate skill at argumentative articulation.

And you wonder what revelatory message I could possibly relate that would have any significance to your life? Frankly, I'm not sure that I give a damn if you read this or not.

Perhaps I should explain that it is quickly approaching two in the morning and that I didn't get any sleep last night either. I am perusing the bottom of a bottle of Jack Daniel's (I should have bought two) and my grammar, as well as my sense of good taste, are at a state so low as to not have been experienced before in my lifetime. No doubt, having read this far, you concur.

As to the matter at hand, my wife left me twenty-nine days ago, upon the date of my 37th birthday. So why, I hear you cry, are you still so damn depressed? Because marriages spanning twelve years just don't end that easily. First you have to go through two years of hell while you're still living together but don't know you're going through hell. Then your lady informs you that it's over. Naturally you don't believe it, and in your vain attempt to sway the opinion of your soon-to-be-estranged mate, discover all kinds of things which she never told you about. Excuse me a minute while I pour myself another drink.

At any rate, during the week that it takes you to find an apartment, she discovers that she has made a terrible mistake. And so begins the reconciliation. Now you are totally enamored of each other. You talk incessantly. You have sex in the kitchen. This lasts about two weeks.

After this period begins the stage in which she doubts that the two of you can really make it after all. Wednesday after the Sunday upon which she professed undying love, she tells you she "needs some space" and she hopes you will "always be her friend." This is followed by the Thursday when she won't talk to you except to say that she doesn't want to talk to you. You buy a bottle.

Excuse me, I need more ice.

This last event is quite predictable. It happens within three days prior to the due date of at least three large school projects. No problem!

And now for the first time in your life you discover real pain. I just wrote another poem and put it under her windshield wiper. I will probably never know if she reads it. I will never see her laugh, cry, complain. Twelve years. It wasn't worth it. Don't get married. It's three A.M. I'm going to bed now. ❖

The horsepower is great, but Albert knows he hasn't a clue about who it's talking to or what it hopes to do to the reader. So far it's just personal therapy.

Albert and I discussed possible audiences and purposes until he decided to write to his brother John, who was just getting married, and by implication all other newlyweds. His purpose would be to prepare them for the inevitable agony of divorce. Choosing an audience and purpose led to choosing a structure: The essay would be a letter and a list of tips. Here's how the next draft came out:

**BEST-LAID PLANS**

Dear John:

I loved your wedding. The flowers were lovely, and the bride looked radiant.

I'm writing to offer you the benefit of my experience as you start out on this new phase of your life. Marriage is a big step. It requires planning and foresight. You should be receiving this about two weeks after the ceremony, so the first flush of love is past and it's time to start planning for your divorce.

You may think I'm being a little hasty, but consider. More than half the people who get married these days get divorced. That means the odds are against you. Wouldn't it be wise to take some precautions? Having some practical experience in this area of the human experience, I will be your mentor.

First off, accept the coming divorce as an inevitability. Begin thinking of your spouse as "your future ex-wife." The agony of divorce is largely in the surprise.

Second, accept the fact that the person you're living with isn't the person you'll have to deal with during the divorce. Your loving spouse will overnight become a ruthless enemy bent on domination. You will be amazed at the similarities between dealing with an ex-wife and a gigantic corporation planning a hostile takeover of your company.

In fact, accept the fact that your spouse isn't the person you think she is *right now.* During the divorce proceedings, she will cheerfully tell you that everything you thought you knew about her was a lie: she never liked you, she always thought your jokes were lame, she really hated sex with you and just did it out of a sense of duty, etc., etc.

Now that you have the right attitude, what practical steps can you take? Prepare for the divorce in a businesslike manner. Do exactly what you would do in a business relationship with a shifty partner. Trust no one. Make sure you have at least seven bank accounts, so when her lawyers find three or four of them you'll be left with something. Make sure everything you own of value is heavily mortgaged. Have no significant liquid assets, except whiskey, which will be tax deductible after the divorce as a medical expense. Don't count on your premarital agreement saving you—all legal contracts can be broken. Most important of all, fight for your own interests. Let the other guy look out for the other guy; she will, I assure you.

Lay plans to handle the sense of worthlessness. Start seeing a therapist *now,* to get a head start. And don't make the novice spouse's mistake of severing all ties with members of the opposite sex. I'm not advising having affairs, but when the break comes you'll need women friends to pat you on the head, say you've still got what it takes, and listen as you say loathsome things about your ex.

Know the traditional behavior of the divorcing spouse and expect it. For instance, there is the False Reconciliation. She discovers that she has made a terrible mistake. Now you are totally enamored of each other. You talk incessantly. You have sex in the kitchen. This lasts about a week. Wednesday after the Monday when she professed undying love, she tells you she "needs some space" and she hopes you will "always be her friend." This is followed by the Friday when she won't talk to you except to say that she doesn't want to talk to you. You go into shock. This will always happen three days prior to the due date of at least three large school projects. Plan ahead!

If you take this advice, divorce, like thermonuclear war, can become an unpleasant but survivable disaster. And incidentally, since these realities have nothing to do with the personalities involved, I'm sending a copy of this letter to your wife, with suitable pronoun changes, to be fair. After all, after the divorce I'm hoping to stay friends with both of you. ❖

**Now it's your turn.** Here's a first draft of an essay that hasn't yet committed itself to a thesis, audience, or purpose. Write out one possible audience, thesis, and purpose and write an opening paragraph of an essay for that audience, thesis, and purpose.

## UNTOUCHABLES

DUNCAN THOMSON

Women! Can't live with them, can't get near them, drink another beer. Sweet dreams. Is it in the eyes of the beholder? I think not. You see them every day on campus, do they acknowledge you? Maybe, maybe not. They say that love comes from the heart, for a guy, I think it comes from his zipper most of the time. For a gorgeous girl, I think it comes from her attitude. Maybe you truly just have to know someone until you can truly judge them.

She was my *Cosmo* woman, my runway girl, I still think about her and miss what we once had. I feel so stupid for letting her get away to pursue her modeling career. It's over now but for the longest time I couldn't even think about another woman. Life really didn't seem worth living. Will I ever meet her again? I'm looking and she's out there, I just don't know who she is. Is this her?

It's Friday night and you're ready to hit the town. If you're under twenty-one it's a piece of cake, but if you're over twenty-one that means a night at the bars. Why we go, man, I'll never know. You're getting ready. You pick what you think will make you the most attractive person on the face of this earth. Now I feel like a million bucks. There is so much confidence in this bathroom as I stare into the mirror. You see, Mike's is to many of us guys the ultimate place to meet women. From 9 P.M. till 1, the place is completely packed with both sexes.

This is it, the time to find my Christy Brinkley, Elle McPherson. Anything is possible. This is the place where confidence becomes reality: dance, rate the pairs in the room, buy her a drink, throw some one-liners, anything to strike up a conversation. "Those are the most beautiful eyes I've ever seen." It may be corny but it does lead to an interesting conversation.

I'm all fired up as I wait in line to get in. We're going out to get drunk and meet women. Is this paradise or am I just stupid? The fellas and I head for the bar. "Two pitchers and three shots please." No, why oh why did I order shots? Oh well, here we go again.

There she is, oh god, just look at her. Blonde hair, blue eyes, but that's not where my eyes are wandering. What curves! The complete package. I can feel my body start to shake. "Hey bartender, one more shot please." I feel sick, I start talking to myself: Relax, jerkface, you haven't even talked to her yet. I still have this really nervous feeling inside but on the outside I still have that confident 90210 look.

I'm really starting to feel good from the alcohol. That other girl who didn't look so hot earlier is all of a sudden looking good. So many women! Blondes, brunettes, tall, short, skinny, voluptuous, and of course the total packages. Most other women call them sluts but I think they got it so they flaunt it. Why are they so hard to meet? I'm a nice, attractive person with a lot going for me. I stumble over to talk to one. "Do you want to dance?" I say. "Maybe next song," she replies. I turn to say hello to a friend and the snooty little bitch is gone. She was just another untouchable.

Some of these girls are so incredible, most men don't even have a chance with them. You have got to have either money, some kind of title, or something that makes you desirable. Everything you try is wrong. I know I'm probably not going to meet this woman in a bar but it's a good place to start.

Let me tell you, when you get to date one of these women just once, your whole world is great. Each day is bright, the sun is shining. Everyone looks at you with this girl, the other guys are thinking, "What? That little dork with such a hot woman?" The world is your oyster. Your dreams become reality. I know, no woman has enough power to do that. Wrong! An untouchable woman is the best thing in the world.

Then that day will come, she's gone. No heart, no soul,

worthless. It crushes you for at least six months. Eventually you get over it. Is that why I'm still in this bar?

I'm heading home, with nothing but a piece of pizza in my hand. I get home and grab that little black book and dial for a girl until I pass out. Women! Can't live with them, can't get near them, drink another beer.

God life is great. ❖

## EXERCISES

1. Write an essay describing your typical revision process and your personal definition of revision. Compare it with the ideal in the chapter. Write a list of changes you need to make.

2. Write down five topics. Then translate the five into thesis statements.

3. Convert the following topics into thesis statements:

   a. Organic food
   b. SUV's
   c. The image of African-American athletes in the United States
   d. The rising cost of a university education
   e. The effect of TV on children

4. Narrow the following topics. Example: Shakespeare → Shakespeare's mixed feelings about civil disorder.

   a. SUV's
   b. TV
   c. Education
   d. Child-raising
   e. Race in America

5. How well does each of the following obey the eight tool-making rules for theses beginning on p. 73? Are there one or more rules it fails to obey? If necessary, rewrite it as a perfect thesis.

   a. You can't legislate morality.
   b. This culture is so racist!

c. My thesis is that boxing is brutal. It's incredible to me that in a society that bans cock fighting and bear baiting, we permit the same sort of thing with human beings.
d. But I need at least a B—my parents will kill me if you give me a C.
e. What do you mean, you won't loan me your car? I loaned you ten dollars last week.
f. Why do we let TV corrupt our children?
g. Why World War II was unnecessary.
h. I love the new Ben and Jerry's flavor, Purple Haze.
i. Three reasons why everyone should exercise regularly.
j. He started it!

6. For each of the theses you revised in Exercise 5, write answers to the six tool-using questions on p. 75. Add any other good questions you can think of. Then write a critique of the imagined draft, including suggestions for improvement.

7. Take each of the revised theses from Exercise 5 and write a purpose statement for its essay. How well do the statements obey the five tool-making rules beginning on p. 76? Which rules do they fail to obey? If necessary, rewrite them to satisfy all five.

8. For each of the purpose statements in Exercise 7, write answers to the five tool-using questions on p. 77, plus any other good questions you can think of. Then write a critique of the imagined draft, offering suggestions for improvement.

9. For each revised purpose in Exercise 7, write a detailed description of a possible audience.

10. For each purpose in Exercise 7, write a detailed description of a tone that suits that purpose and its corresponding audience in Exercise 9. Explain how and why the tone suits the purpose.

11. For each of the broad audiences following, write a half-page detailing everything you know about them. When you don't know something, narrow the audience by choosing an audience within the audience. Example: I'm writing to readers of restaurant reviews → I'm writing to readers of restaurant reviews, readers who live in the Boston area, are poor, are on vegan diets, and are fighting high cholesterol.

a. Registered Nurses
b. Working mothers
c. College professors
d. Republican voters
e. Readers of movie reviews

12. For each of the following tones, describe a more precise tone by adding detail.

a. Sad
b. Formal
c. Informative
d. Angry

13. Pick any essay in the Treasury of Essays (p. 368) and answer the following questions about it:

a. What's the topic?
b. What's the thesis?
c. Where, if anywhere, in the essay is the thesis?
d. What's the purpose?
e. What's the audience?
f. What's the tone?
g. How does the tone suit the purpose?

14. Do Exercise 13 with an essay of your own.

15. Critique your answers to Exercise 13 by doing Exercises 5, 6, 7, and 8 with them.

16. Do Exercise 15 using your answers to Exercise 14.

17. For each of the following opening paragraphs, write descriptions of the work's thesis, purpose, audience, and tone. How does the tone suit the purpose?

a. The Brookfield Unified School District maintains an educational program which provides special learning opportunities for pupils who, after consideration of all pertinent data, evidence exceptional intellectual capacity. Recently your child was identified as having demonstrated a significant number of characteristics of intellectual giftedness. Therefore, he/she was nominated to participate in the identification process for possible inclusion in the program.
b. I GIVE UP. I have finally decided that Miss/Ms. Right isn't going to walk through the door. Never would I have thought that I would end up resorting to a public appeal such as this. I've been to bars, churches, the YWCA, the YMCA (was that a mistake), NOW, and every possible spot this wonderful mystery woman might be, all to no avail. This is my last resort. If you desire to help a frustrated and very nice guy, read on.
c. After hunting for a parking space, wading through a crowded registration line, and forking out $375, I expect to be entertained. That's why I decided to sign up

for a film class. Besides, I needed three General Ed. units, and English 37, seriously titled "American Film as Literature," seemed to fit the bill (no pun intended).

At the first class meeting, I watched twenty graduating seniors from Signa Phi Nothing attempting to add and wondered why. Was the course an easy A, as the Greek connection implied? Or was there more to it?

# Chapter 6

# ORGANIZATION, PART 1: MAPPING AND OUTLINING

Once you have a general sense of what you're saying, why you're saying it, and to whom, you need to ask the next large question: "What shape should all this stuff be in?" In the next two chapters we're going to practice making and using three tools that will help answer that question—mapping, outlining, and abstracting. But first let's walk through the process to see what reorganizing looks like and to see in action some of the tools we'll be working with. Here's a brainstormed first draft describing a student's friend:

> Tony can fill a room with excitement. He's very handsome. He used to have a mustache, but he shaved it off. He tells marvelous lies. He wants to be a professional actor. His eyes mist over when he talks about emotional things. He can talk well on almost any subject. Women melt before him. Tony has worked very hard at karate. He's as graceful as a panther. When he fights, his eyes burn with a passionate wildness. Onstage, he acts with unpolished, startling energy. He sweats when he acts. Last week he told me that he wasn't happy. He said he was burned out. An old back injury had suddenly recurred. He said he feared he was going insane. Today I saw him walking down the street, wearing the latest fashions and beautifully tanned. He smiled a hard plastic smile. He talked excitedly about a potential job and hurried off without a backward glance. He's twenty years old. He lives at home with both his parents. He has no job and doesn't want to go to college. He stays out and parties heavily until two or three o'clock in the morning. His mother always waits up for him.

That's twenty-five items—too many to see at a glance. Let's reduce by summarizing the twenty-five to five:

> Tony is energetic and attractive.
> He's an eager conversationalist.
> He's an expert at karate.
> Last week, he said he was miserable and acted rushed and insecure.
> He's twenty and has no prospects.

Now we can see that these five items are really two: 1) Tony has a lot of gifts and 2) his life is a mess. We can now express this as a thesis sentence: *Tony is wasting his great talents.* Now we can see how all the twenty-five original parts have jobs in that large design. Tony has power (social, sexual, physical) but can't find anything to do with it. Karate gave him a bit of an outlet, and acting a bit, but acting is only professional faking, and Tony does too much of that already. With all his gifts, he's burned out and directionless—he's wasting his time in pointless partying, and he can't get it together enough to leave his parents. Now we can *outline* the draft:

I. Tony has power and talent to burn.
   A. Sexual: Women swoon over him.
   B. Social: He can walk into a room and every eye will turn to him.
   C. Physical: He's a panther at karate.
   D. Psychic: He's a dominating force on the stage.
II. But he can't seem to do anything with his power.
   A. He's burned out.
   B. He wears slick duds but looks dead inside.
   C. His body's failing him.
III. He's twenty years old but still living like a child.
   A. He just goes partying every night.
   B. His mother still waits up for him.

And we can *abstract* the outline:

> Tony is so attractive he can walk into any party and fascinate everyone there in five minutes. He has so much natural energy that he's an expert at karate and a stirring actor. Yet he tells me he's burned out and miserable, and he seems empty, in a hurry but with nowhere to go. He's twenty years old, but without a future; he spends his time going from one meaningless party to another, with his mom always waiting up for him.

## The Organizing Attitude

Before we pick up a tool, let's make sure we have the right attitude:

**1. Organizing begins with making a model.** To organize anything, you have to see the entire design at a glance, and that means making a miniature version of it—just like the models of buildings or golf courses architects make before the bulldozers go to work. Maps, outlines, and abstracts are just three different kinds of models.

Reorganizing a draft is like rearranging the furniture in a room. The novice moves couches and bookshelves around the room, sweating and swearing, until finally she gets an idea: She makes a diagram of the room on a piece of cardboard, cuts out little paper figures for all the pieces of furniture, and pushes the figures around the diagram until everything fits. The model allows her to try a dozen arrangements in minutes without flexing a muscle, and the miniature size of the model lets her see how successful each floor plan is at a glance.

We know how big the model should be initially, thanks to the Magic Number Seven (p. P-7): seven or fewer standard sentences. You usually don't need seven; here's an essay in condensed form, shrunk to just three:

> I "did well" in school but was bored and learned little, because school was boring and irrelevant. But it doesn't have to be that way—there are ways to make classrooms exciting and useful. And they work: I still remember about paramecia because of the time my class took a field trip to the pond. ("Why I Never Cared for the Civil War," p. 391)

As soon as you understand your structure on this basic level, you can start adding details, making the model more complex. When we're completely lost we want a map of extreme simplicity, but the better we know the territory, the more map detail we can handle.

**2. Organize after you draft.** It's hard to arrange the furniture in a room when you don't have any furniture. You need to produce stuff before you can ask, "What shape should this stuff be in?" In the sciences, you're often required to use an organizational template, so you break this rule there, but in essay writing the structure is something you *discover*.

**3. Word processors make organizing harder.** Since you can only see twenty lines or so of the text at any one time, you can't see the big picture. So do your *drafting* on a word processor, but *organize* on a sheet of paper, with a pencil or pen.

**4. Doing something teaches you nothing (p. P-2).** A lot of writers outline and pay no attention at all, as if the ritual act of outlining appeased the wrathful god of organization. Reflect on the outline or abstract until the reflection leads to concrete revision strategies: "I think I'll start the essay with the old paragraph 3."

**5. Learn to organize by reading for the craft.** Essay organization is hard in part because we never get much practice in it. A lifetime of talking leaves us unprepared to organize essays, because talk is just one thing tacked onto another. So practice observing structure when you read: Ask yourself, How is this put together? How did the author get it started? How did she end? And remember, only essays can model for you how to structure essays.

We'll practice three diagnostic tools for organizing: mapping, outlining, and abstracting. Each gives us different data.

## Mapping

### Making the Tool

We talked about making maps in Chapter 4 (p. 59). It's primarily a brainstorming tool, but it will also serve you well here, after drafting.

Mapping is looser and messier than outlining and abstracting, so you want to use it when you want to break completely free from the first draft. It's like taking the pieces of the essay and tossing them into the air. It's freer in four ways. First, you can map in all 360 degrees of the circle, and you can connect anything on the page to anything else on the page via a line, as opposed to outlining and abstracting, which limit you to linear thinking. Second, a map has no starting and ending points and no sequence—there's no order to the spokes on a wheel—so mapping forces you to rethink sequence. Third, you can map anything—fragments, words, pictures—whereas outlines and abstracts work with whole sentences. Fourth, maps have *centers*, but outlines and abstracts don't, so use mapping when you're still tinkering with the essay core.

### Using the Tool

With all three of our organizing tools, the art is in the interpretation of the data. After you make the map, what does it tell you about the draft? Only practice will teach you how to answer that question. On the facing page is the author's map for "Legalize Hemp" (p. 153). What does it suggest Todd should think about in the revision? I hear it calling my attention to six things. First, Bubble A logically should be an offshoot of Bubble B. Second, Bubble B promises solutions to "political" problems, but the map never shows us any. Third, items in the map are mentioned more than once in the draft—Bubble D, for instance. Fourth, Bubble E hangs alone and unexplained, and it shows up in the draft in the last paragraph without explanation. Fifth, Bubble F seems to be from a different essay. Sixth, Bubbles F, G, and H are all together in the map but spread throughout the draft. Diagnostic tools never tell you what to do (p. 70), so Todd has six decisions to make. Is there a problem here? What should he do about it?

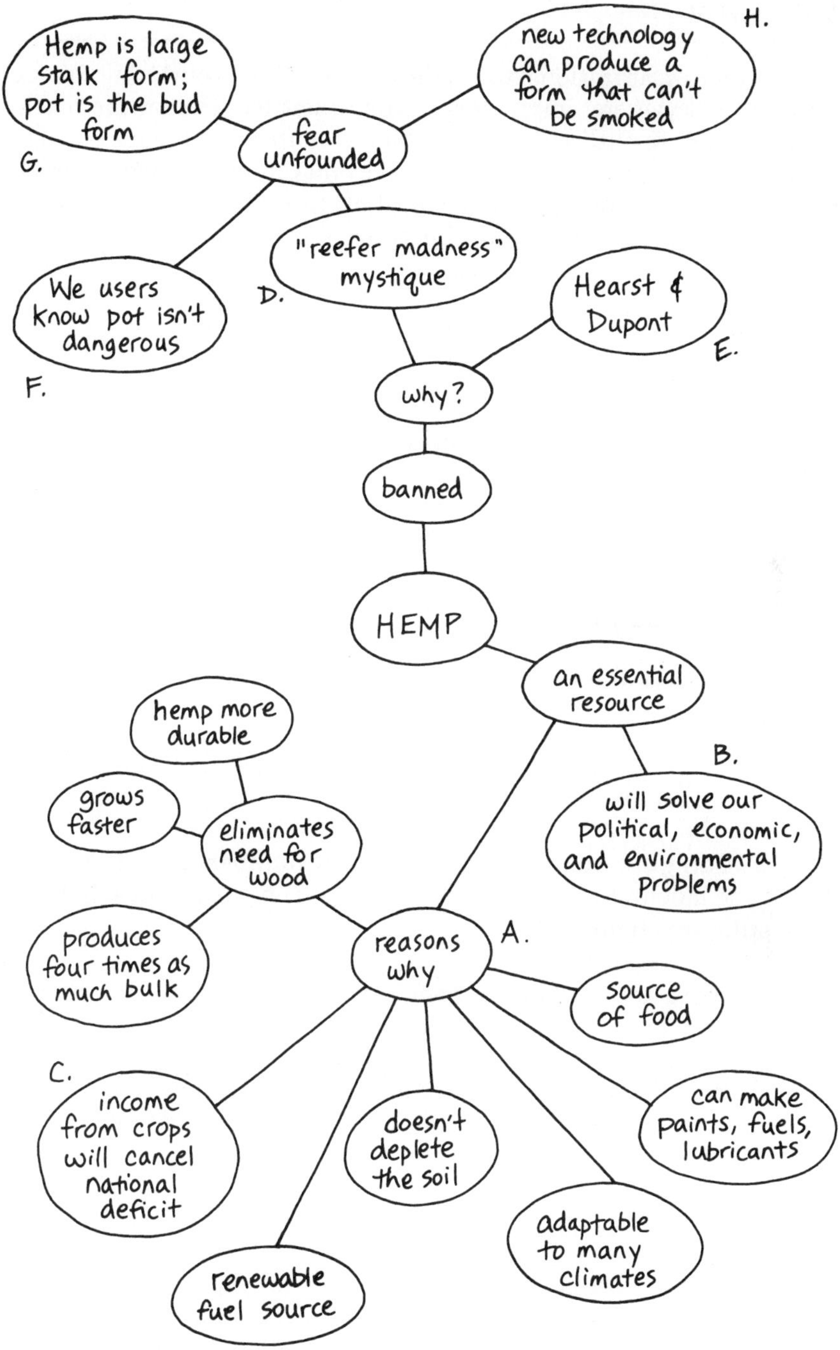
H.
new technology can produce a form that can't be smoked
Hemp is large stalk form; pot is the bud form
G.
fear unfounded
"reefer madness" mystique
D.
Hearst & Dupont
E.
We users know pot isn't dangerous
F.
why?
banned
HEMP
an essential resource
B.
will solve our political, economic, and environmental problems
hemp more durable
grows faster
eliminates need for wood
produces four times as much bulk
reasons why
A.
source of food
C.
income from crops will cancel national deficit
doesn't deplete the soil
can make paints, fuels, lubricants
adaptable to many climates
renewable fuel source

## Outlining

Of our three organizational tools, the most popular is outlining. We see outlines everywhere: Instructors outline their lectures on the blackboard, books are outlined in their tables of contents, religious services often hand out programs that outline events in chronological order, and so on. To outline, you reduce the draft to a series of sentences and list them in a vertical column. There are sample outlines on pp. 353 and v.

### Making the Tool

Outlines are wonderfully revealing diagnostic tools, but they don't work unless they're flawless. Outline making can go wrong in lots of ways, so here are a number of guidelines. To begin, since outlines are rigid, intimidating things that have a tendency to freeze a writer's blood, stay loose by following these four rules:

**1. Outline in three to five parts only.** According to the Magic Number Seven, we could have a few more, but outlining is so rigid that we want to keep things very simple.

**2. Outline in a flash.** Write the entire outline in a minute or less. Don't labor over it—try to grasp how the whole essay works in three or four steps and write them down.

**3. Don't use Roman numerals, or any numbers or letters at all.** Don't use indentations and subsections and sub-subsections. All that stuff stiffens you up.

**4. Write the outline by hand.** It loosens you up and reminds you that this is sketching, scribbling, playing.

Some people flatly refuse to do those four things. They like to labor over an outline and make it gleam with Roman numerals and lots of subsections. The finished outline looks very impressive, but the writer has turned into a slab of ice.

Now that we're loose, follow these additional rules:

**5. Don't describe; summarize.** Don't tell the reader what you did or are going to do; instead, speak the essay, in reduced form. Don't say, "I list the causes of the Civil War"; say, "The causes of the Civil War weren't racial; they were economic." You know you're doing it right when a reader can read the outline and feel he has the essay itself in short form—not a promise of an essay.

**6. Preserve the sequencing of the draft.** Don't rearrange the essay content, because then the outline can't diagnose structural problems. Make sure the first item in the outline is the first large thing the draft says, and the last item is the last large thing the essay says.

**7. Don't quote sentences from the draft.** As with thesis sentence writing, it's rare that the best sentences for the outline can be plucked as is from the draft (p. 74). Don't *select* sentences for the outline; *compose* them.

**8. Outline whole sentences only.** If you don't outline sentences you'll outline nouns, and nouns are useless (p. P-10). I can outline nouns all day without learning anything about the essay behind them. Here's a nice-looking outline I wrote in one minute on a topic I know nothing about and have nothing to say about:

I. Weapons of mass destruction: the present crisis

II. Historical causes

  A. The fall of the Soviet Union

  B. The Mideast conflict

  C. Cold-war mentality

III. Proposed solutions

  A. American proposals

  B. Israeli proposals

  C. Proposals of other nations

  D. Why they don't work

IV. My solution

Looks great, doesn't it? And it's a complete smokescreen.

Outlining what the draft *says* turns out to show only half of what we want to know, and the less important half. Remember, we're not in the business of *saying things*; we're in the business of saying things *to do things to readers*. So we need to make two outlines simultaneously, a *content* outline and a *function* outline. The content outline is the kind we just made. We'll write it on the left side of the page. The function outline will run down the right side of the page. For each item in the content outline, there will be a matching item in the function outline, explaining what *job* the sentence in the content outline is doing. Here's a dual outline for the essay called "Given the Chance" (p. 276).

| Content | Function |
|---|---|
| 1. I met Stacey, a likable drug addict, when I was working at our Group Home. | 1. Win reader's sympathy for Stacey. |
| 2. She needs a rehab program, but she can't get into one. | 2. State the problem. |
| 3. The State refuses to pay for it. | 3. State the source of the problem. |
| 4. The State isn't giving Stacey and me a chance. | 4. State thesis. |

Function outlining is a continuation of our work with purpose in Chapter 5—now we're just asking ourselves what the purpose of each essay *section* is. Follow these seven rules while making function outlines:

**9. Use your favorite synonym.** If the word "function" isn't to your taste, you can call those things "purposes," "intentions," "jobs," or "chores."

**10. Make the function statements verb phrases.** All purpose statements are inherently verbal. You can use imperatives ("Hook the reader"), infinitives ("To hook the reader"), or participles ("Hooking the reader")—it doesn't matter.

**11. Use the words "the reader."** To remind yourself that all purposes are intentions to do something *to the reader,* include those two words in the function statement: Hook *the reader's* interest, convince *the reader* with factual evidence, tell *the reader* what the problem is.

**12. Keep function statements short and familiar.** Most of the time the function of a passage is something short, simple, and well known, because when you get right down to it there are only a few functions writing can have. You can state a thesis, you can defend it, you can hook the reader with personal narrative, you can marshal facts in support of your argument, you can refute counterarguments, you can consider the consequences of taking action, and so on. Look back at the sample function outline: The four functions are all short, all ordinary. And that's good. If your function statements get complicated and strange, suspect that your intentions are really simpler than you realize.

**13. Don't reproduce content.** This is a version of the point we made about purpose statements (p. 76). If you write function statements like "Say what's wrong with affirmative action," "Tell the story about the car accident," or "Describe her parents," you're really just reproducing the stuff from the content side of the outline in altered form. If you do that, the function statements can't teach you anything new. To avoid the trap, do what we did on p. 77: *Ask yourself "Why?"* Why are you saying what's wrong? Why are you telling the story? Why are you describing the parents?

**14. Avoid universal function labels** like "introduction" and "conclusion." Such labels don't lie, but they're so broad they won't teach you anything. Since they'll work for any essay, they can't be insightful about what *this* essay is doing. To avoid the trap, *ask yourself "How?"* How does this essay introduce? How does this essay conclude?

**15. Troubleshoot by asking questions.** If you have trouble grasping the function of a sentence in the outline, ask yourself, "Why is it there?" You can rephrase the question in a number of helpful ways: What job would go undone if you didn't include that sentence? What were you trying to accomplish by including it? What are you trying to do to the reader by including it?

## Using the Tool

The first and largest question to ask of an outline is "Does this structure work?" It's a huge and slippery question, but you will probably know the answer. Beyond that, an outline can teach you a host of interesting things about a draft, so many that I can't list them for you. Each outline will teach its own lessons. So let's practice listening to outlines and seeing what they reveal. Here are three outlines, all of film reviews, to practice on. The outlines aren't perfect, so sometimes the lessons offered are about tool making and sometimes they're about revising the draft:

### Outline A

| Content | Function |
|---|---|
| 1. *Kids* is a dramatic film about adolescence. | 1. State thesis. |
| 2. A great script and young actors add to the reality of this film. | 2. Support thesis. |
| 3. There is a complex and dangerous relationship between youths and their social environments today. | 3. State problem. |

| | |
|---|---|
| 4. We must acknowledge the hell our kids are living in. | 4. State solution. |

What do I see that looks good? The outline is about something important—our kids are living in hell. And the essay moves from the small, particular thing (the movie) to larger issues—a good strategy. What do I see that needs work? Content 1 is safe and doesn't say very much, so I'd look for a way to begin the essay with more energy, more risk. I see no logical connection between Contents 2 and 3; I'm sure there is one, but I'd try to make it clear to the reader. And I don't know what Content 3 really means—what is the "complex relationship between youths and their social environments"? I'd make sure I spelled out in the draft what the complexity and danger are. Finally, the function statements don't really let us know what the essay's thesis is. We've got a "thesis," a "problem," and a "solution" . . . which one is the real thesis?

**Outline B**

| **Content** | **Function** |
|---|---|
| 1. The movie *Crouching Tiger, Hidden Dragon* is a wonderful movie. | 1. Introduce the reader to the topic. |
| 2. Although the movie seems to combine tactics from previous movies, it's a refreshing change from the average movie. | 2. Catch the reader's attention. |
| 3. All your feelings and emotions will be experienced during this film. | 3. Convince the reader to see the movie. |
| 4. Future movies have a new standard to live up to. | 4. Conclude. |

What do I see here that's good? The outline is willing to take a stand; it doesn't sit on the fence. Content 4 has a nice punch-line ring to it. And the outline language is straight and clear. What do I see that needs work? Content 1 is the weakest of the four, so I wouldn't start with it—I probably don't have to say it at all. Function 1 acknowledges this by admitting that not a lot is going on here. Content 2 seems to contain a contradiction—the movie is simultaneously innovative and familiar—so I'd want to make clear in the draft how that could be true. Function 2 sounds like the job of an opening, so I'd want to find a clearer sense of Content 2's job or move it to the front of the draft. When the outline ends, I've been told three times in four sentences that the movie is really good, but I don't have much in the way of a reason. In fact, I really have no idea what the movie is like or even what it's about. Content 3 is a step in that direction, but not enough—I'd shore up my evidence by doing a lot more describing. Function 4 tells me nothing, so I'd ask "How?" until I knew how the conclusion was working.

**Outline C**

| **Content** | **Function** |
|---|---|
| 1. "The Blair Witch Project" is a terrible movie. | 1. Inform my readers of my opinion. |
| 2. The movie failed in its efforts to be scary; it was more comical than anything. | 2. Give reasons. |
| 3. The first few minutes introduced the characters and what they were doing. | 3. Tell audience about the characters. |
| 4. The movie felt like it dragged on forever, wasn't scary, and never made any sense. | 4. List faults of the movie. |
| 5. Although the movie is terrible, I would still recommend it just so you can form your own opinion. | 5. Recommend the movie even though it's bad. |

What do I see here that's good? An opinion is stated clearly, without hedging (the movie's terrible), and three solid reasons are given (it's slow, not scary, and incomprehensible). What do I see that needs work? Content 1 has no sense of "hook" (p. 124)—I'd try to find some. Content 3 seems to add nothing to the argument, and it also seems to float alone, out of sequence; I'd try to figure out what job it's doing. Function 3 alerts me to this—it's a repetition of content (p. 104), so it obscures the function instead of revealing it. Content 4 repeats Content 2, and Function 4 is a rewording of Function 2, so I'd check to see if I've repeated myself. If I have, I'll decide where to say it best and say it once. Content 5 takes the wind out of my sails and makes me wonder why I read the outline at all. The author's just bailing out. I'd take the risk and stand by my judgment: The movie stinks. Function 5 repeats content, so I'd keep asking, "Why say that?" until I got an answer.

# EXERCISES

1. Critique the following map: Which of the map-making rules laid down in Chapters 4 and 6 does it follow, and which does it break?

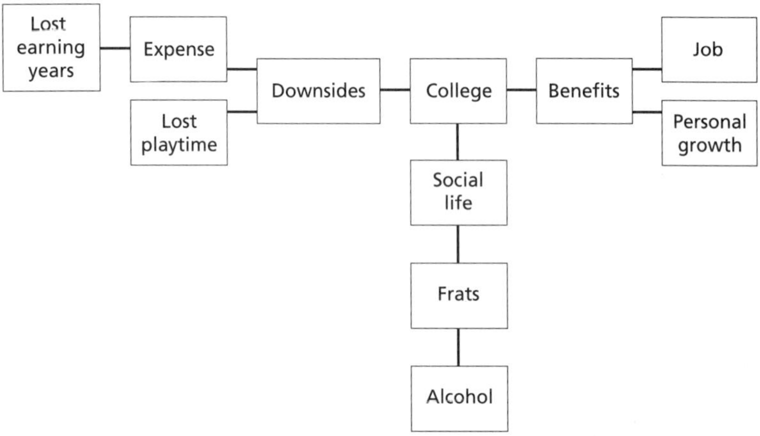


2. Pick an essay from the Treasury of Essays (p. 368) and map it. Write a critique of your map: Does it obey the tool-making rules in Chapter 4 and Chapter 6? If not, revise the map.

3. Pick an essay from the Writer's Treasury and outline it. Write a critique of your outline: Does it obey the tool-making rules in Chapter 6? If not, revise the outline.

4. Do Exercise 2 with one of your own drafts.

5. Write a diagnosis of the draft in Exercise 4, basing it on the map, as we did on p. 100: What does the map suggest is going well in the draft? What needs work? List specific revision plans, such as "Paragraph 2 should come earlier."

6. Do Exercise 3 with one of your own drafts.

7. Write a diagnosis of the draft in Exercise 6, basing it on the outline, as we did on pp. 105–107. What does the outline suggest is going well in the draft? What needs work? List specific revision plans, such as "Paragraph 2 should come earlier."

8. Write a critique of each of the following outlines, in two stages: First, describe how well it follows the fifteen outline-making rules of Chapter 6. Second, rewrite the outline to elimi-

nate any problems. Third, make a list of everything the outline tells you about the draft. Fourth, make a list of concrete suggestions for revision.

**Outline A**

| Content | Function |
|---|---|
| 1. Small-breed dogs aren't real canines; big dogs are. | 1. To put different dogs in different categories and explain why some dogs aren't considered dogs. |
| 2. Rocket dogs are Weimaraners, and the author used to have one. | 2. To explain what a rocket dog is and her own experience with owning one. |
| 3. Some friends own a black Lab the author hangs out with now. | 3. To contrast a Lab owned by her friends with her old dog. |

**Outline B**

| Content | Function |
|---|---|
| 1. The institution of marriage has been tarnished in my eyes because of my roommate. | 1. Make the reader laugh. |
| 2. Since my roommate got married, he has dropped out of school and become haggard. | 2. Win the reader's support for my stance on marriage. |
| 3. Marriage has lost all importance in America. | 3. Suggest to reader that marriage is a sham. |

**Outline C**

| Content | Function |
|---|---|
| 1. Darwin changed his mind about his own theories. | 1. Evolution is not sound science. |
| 2. Scientists hang on to Darwin's original theories. | 2. State the problem. |
| 3. Science only knows what it knows. | 3. State the source of the problem. |
| 4. It takes just as much faith to believe in evolution as in creation. | 4. State thesis. |

# Chapter 7

# ORGANIZATION, PART 2: ABSTRACTING

Once you've outlined and the outline says the draft looks good, you are *not* done, because writing isn't a list. There's something else, something *between* the items in your outline, that gets you from one to the next. Outlining won't help you get it—in fact, outlining often makes problems in this area worse instead of better. Students usually don't know what to call it, but they know what to call writing that doesn't have it: *choppy*. Choppy writing sounds like this:

> I think requiring deposits on soda bottles is unfair. I clean up my own litter. How much is a clean roadside worth to Americans? Glass is not something we're likely to run out of soon. Why should people be forced to do something they don't want to do?

Missing from that passage is what writing teachers call *transition* (or *transitions*). An outline encourages you not to think about the matter, by reducing the writing to a stack of parts. So we need an organizational tool that focuses on transition, and the *abstract* is it.

What exactly is transition? There are lots of ways to describe how it *feels*. In transitionless writing, the separate bits feel isolated, like shy strangers at a party. When you read it, you feel like you're constantly starting and stopping, like a badly tuned car trying to get across an intersection. It feels like it jumps around. Nothing feels finished. It feels choppy, jerky, rough. Transition-rich writing *flows*. We read *through* the sentences with lots of forward momentum. We never really stop. One thing follows another. Clear enough—but what is it, and how do we get it?

## Transition and Readers

Writing turns out to feel rich in transitions when both the writer and the reader agree that the next thing the text says is the next appropriate thing to do. We can describe this in two ways. One way is in terms of the reader's dialogue we tracked in Chapter 2 (p. 27). The writer writes something; the reader reacts with a question, a want, a feeling, a request for clarification; and the writer responds by addressing the want. That response prompts another reaction from the reader, and the back-and-forth continues to the end of the essay. If we try to carry on such an exchange with the author of the piece on recycling, we see the problem—she's not listening to us:

AUTHOR: I think requiring deposits on soda bottles is unfair.
READER: *Why?*

AUTHOR: I clean up my own litter.
READER: *So what?*

AUTHOR: How much is a clean roadside worth to Americans?
READER: *I don't know—what's the answer? Why does it matter?*

AUTHOR: Glass is not something we're likely to run out of soon.
READER: *So what?*

AUTHOR: Why should people be forced to do something they don't want to do?
READER: *Because people aren't naturally given to doing what's best for society? HELLO!!? ARE YOU LISTENING TO ME!!?*

Writing with transition is a back-and-forth between attentive equals. Here's Sheridan Baker discussing paragraph structure:

> Now, that paragraph turned out a little different from what I anticipated. I overshot my original thesis, discovering, as I wrote, a thesis one step farther—an underlying cause—about coming to friendly terms with oneself. But it illustrates the funnel, from the broad and general to the one particular point that will be your essay's main idea, your thesis.
>
> *(Sheridan Baker,* The Practical Stylist*)*

And here's the dialogue between Baker and the reader:

Now, that paragraph turned out a little different from what I anticipated.
*In what way was it different?*

I overshot my original thesis.
*Why did you do that?*

Because I discovered, as I wrote, a thesis one step farther.
*What kind of thesis?*

An underlying cause.
*What was it about?*

About coming to terms with oneself.
*So your previous claim was wrong?*

No, the paragraph still illustrates the funnel.
*In what ways?*

It still goes from the broad and general to the one particular point that will be your essay's main idea.
*What's that idea called?*

Your thesis.

Obviously, this approach only works if you *do something to the reader,* from the very first sentence; if you don't provoke a response, the reader is mute, and you have no reason to keep writing.

## Transition and Connectors

The second way to think about this notion of "the appropriate next thing to say" is to focus on *connectors*. Connectors are devices that link one clause to another. They look like this:

| | | |
|---|---|---|
| and | so | but |
| still | yet | first, second, etc. |
| because | thus | even though |
| since | for instance | therefore |
| furthermore | nevertheless | moreover |
| however | finally | instead |
| although | rather than | too |
| also | in fact | for example |
| consequently | in other words | on the other hand |
| while | that | as a result |

Connectors express logical relationships between sentences—they say, "I'm putting this sentence after that one for a reason, and here's what the reason is." *But* means "I'm going to qualify what I just said or disagree with it in some way." *So* means "I'm going to draw a conclusion from what I just said." *Instead* means "I'm going to offer an alternative."

The most familiar connectors are conjunctions (*and, but, so, if*), but some adverbs connect (*therefore, however*), and some punctuation marks do. The punctuation marks that end sentences (question marks, periods, exclamation points) *don't* connect, because they only tell us about what just happened, not how it relates to what's coming. Commas *don't* connect because they give us no specific relationship information. But the semicolon and the colon are highly specific connectors. The semicolon means "The next sentence is the second half of the idea started in the previous sentence." The colon means "Now I'm going to enumerate or list examples of what I just said." The typical connector is one word long, but connectors can be large blocks of text, like "Despite all that, . . ."

Now we have two ways to diagnose the quality of the transitions in any piece of writing in front of us. Writing has transitions 1) if we can write out the reader's half of the dialogue between the sentences, and the product sounds like a smooth conversation, or 2) if we can put connectors between all the clauses, the connectors make sense, and the text reads well. Armed with this knowledge, we're ready to abstract the draft.

## Abstracting

An abstract is a one-paragraph summary of the essay. You can make one by taking your outline and simply writing all the sentences in it one after the other across the page instead of in a column. Or you can look at the essay, say, "What does this say, briefly?", and spew it out. Here are abstracts for three of the essays in this book:

> **"Avoiding Therapy" (pp. 379–381):**
> The first time my daughter tried to get married, I failed miserably as mother of the bride, but now I've learned the three rules that help a mother survive the experience and preserve the mother-daughter relationship. First, give a fixed amount of money up front (that means you have to trust your daughter). Second, let go of all your fantasies about how the wedding "should" go. Finally, accept your role as "gofer" and play it cheerfully. You may feel like all this means you're failing to fulfill your responsibilities as a parent, but it really means you're expecting your daughter to fulfill her responsibilities as an adult, so in the end it's good for both of you.
>
> **"Top Chicken" (pp. 368–369):**
> It's recess and we all rush to the monkey bars. I check out my next opponent—she's a pushover. Now it's my turn. I attack. She counterattacks, but I escape her grasp and start to take her down. The crowd is screaming. Her grip loosens and she falls to the turf and hobbles off, humiliated. I strut back to the end of the line, pick at a callus, and check out my next opponent.
>
> **"The Good Mother" (pp. 394–396):**
> If you're raising a child and it's going beautifully, you may be doing a great job, or there may be another explanation. When I raised my first child, he was an angel and I got rave reviews from myself and other parents. I assumed I was different from those other moms, who screamed and spanked. Then I had my second child, who was difficult. I tried all the right parenting responses, but they didn't work, and he turned me into the cranky, spanking mom of my nightmares. From this experience I learned that children aren't created by grown-ups, and that people (including me) aren't as simple as they think they are. This knowledge will come in handy when I'm a teacher and it comes in handy now in my relationships with my

peers and family—I'm more tolerant, more willing to listen, less sure I'm right.

Abstracting asks more of you than mapping or outlining, but it also tells you more. It's the greatest diagnostic tool an essay organizer has. And since abstracting will do everything outlining can do and more, once you master abstracting you can skip the outlining stage altogether.

## Making the Tool

As you abstract, follow these rules, many of which are versions of our rules for outlining in Chapter 6:

**1. Summarize; don't describe** (p. 102). With abstracting even more than outlining, the temptation is to dodge all the hard work by telling the reader what you *did* instead of saying what you *said.* Such abstracts, called *descriptive abstracts* by tech writers, usually begin like this:

I'm going to . . .
This essay is a description of . . .
How to . . .
In this essay I said . . .
An introduction to . . .

Descriptive abstracts have their uses for *readers*, but they tell the *writer* nothing. Prove it to yourself by writing a descriptive abstract for an essay you can't write: "This essay solves the problem of world overpopulation, suggests a workable cure for cancer, and proves that Elvis is really alive." If you find yourself irresistibly sucked into describing, write, "Next in this essay I say . . . ," finish the sentence, and then delete those first six words.

**2. Preserve the essay's sequencing** (p. 103).

**3. Don't quote from the draft** (p. 103).

**4. Use the voice, tone, and point of view the essay uses.** If the essay is in first person, make the abstract in first person. If the essay is funny, the abstract should be funny.

**5. Write in a flash** (p. 102). The abstract, like the outline, will gain if you don't ponder before writing it.

**6. Write the abstract in one paragraph only.** The abstract is primarily good for diagnosing flow. A paragraph break is a big interruption in the flow, so it will obscure any transition problems and taint the diagnosis.

**7. Make the abstract about 100 words long.** It's possible to abstract to any length (see p. 135 for proof), and each length will teach you something useful. But for most people the abstract is most productive if it's 70–150 words, ¼ to ⅓ of a single-spaced typed page, about seven normal-length sentences. Don't make the abstract longer just because the draft is longer—the Magic Number Seven never changes, and every map in your glove compartment probably is the same size whether it's for your town or your state.

## Using the Tool

As with the thesis statement and outline, begin using the abstract by asking any and all large questions about what's going on: Did you say anything? Is it interesting? Did you take any risks? and so on. But since abstracts are primarily good at diagnosing transition, focus on transition issues: Does the abstract flow? Does it read well? Do you feel *pulled through* the abstract as you read?

Let's practice reading the following three abstracts critically:

> ***Abstract A*** Mark Twain is the best writer in American literature, because he could do things Cooper and Whitman couldn't do. Cooper's works were inconsistent and unrealistic. Whitman was also very influential, and liberated American literature from taboos about sex and free verse. Twain tackled taboos more successfully. In summation, American literature was shaped by Twain, Cooper, and Whitman. Twain was unique in his tact, the vividness of his descriptions, and his frank honesty. He died penniless and mad, cursing the human race. Hemingway said that all modern American literature comes from *Huckleberry Finn.* ❖

*What's going well?* The abstract has a lot to say and seems excited by it. The voice seems direct and forceful—not boring. The abstract starts right off with a meaty first sentence that wastes no time and gives itself a worthy task to perform. *What needs work?* The sequencing is shaky. We can get specific about where the problem manifests itself:

1. Sentence 3 seems to contradict sentence 1.
2. The *also* of sentence 3 implies this is the *second* of something, but we can't see the first.
3. *In summation* comes in the middle of things, and it doesn't summarize, since it tells us something new.
4. We can't see how "He died penniless and mad" is logically connected to anything.
5. The last sentence doesn't seem to end anything.

We can fix all these problems by resequencing:

> ***The Rewrite*** Hemingway said all of modern American literature sprang from *Huckleberry Finn.* Why would he say that? What's so special about Twain among the other great nineteenth-

century American writers? Two things: he did what greats like Cooper and Whitman did, only better—like break social and artistic taboos; and he had things they didn't have, like tact, descriptive accuracy, and, most of all, a willingness to look at the dark side of human nature. That willingness was so uncompromising that it drove him mad and left him penniless. ❖

***Abstract B*** A favorite way to spend Friday night for many people is to watch hardball. My nephew plays and is talented and confident. I wonder if my five-year-old son will have the chance to build his confidence. Some kids make it through without getting hit by the ball. Many parents oppose the use of the standard hardball because it's dangerous. Cost and tradition are the biggest reasons for not changing over to the ragball. The Little League Association needs to adopt the use of the ragball in this beginning league; it works just as well. Why should a potentially dangerous ball be used when technology has produced a good and safe alternative? ❖

*What's going well?* The abstract has a strong thesis, a clear sense of purpose, and a passion. *What needs work?* We need to declare the problem earlier, telegraph the transitions, and make only one sequencing change: put the refutation of the opposition's argument ("cost and tradition are the biggest reasons . . .") *after* the declaration of thesis. You can't address the rebuttal before you've stated your case:

***The Rewrite*** A favorite way for my family to spend Friday night is to watch hardball. My nephew plays with confidence, but sometimes I wonder if my five-year-old son will have the chance to build his confidence. Not all beginners get hit by the ball, but many do, and those who do often are injured and quit in fear. But there's a way to avoid that: switch from the conventional hardball to the ragball. It works just as well as the hardball without the danger. Why should a potentially dangerous ball be used when technology has produced a good and safe alternative? The only arguments against it are cost and tradition, but certainly the added expense is worth it and tradition isn't worth the cost in frightened children and injuries. ❖

***Abstract C*** The search for a golden tan is an annual quest for many white students. Tan skin is risking skin cancer, premature aging, and wrinkles. A tan is a status symbol, but it doesn't necessarily make you a better person. I'm pale and have heard all the pale jokes, but I still don't think a tan is important. The stereotypes applied to pale people are just as bad as those applied to tan people. A tan may be nice now, but it can create wrinkles that will last a lifetime. I may never be tan, but I'll have smooth skin when I'm old. ❖

*What's going well?* The thesis is clear, the author knows what she wants, she's alive, and she has arguments to support her thesis. *What needs work?* Every sentence seems unconnected to the sentences before and after. A clue is the lack of connectors: only four, and all *but*'s. Let's up the number from four to ten (two are colons):

> ***The Rewrite*** The search for a golden tan is an annual quest for many students, *but* tanners don't realize what danger they're in: tanning is risking skin cancer, premature aging, and wrinkles. A tan may make you look great now, *but* it can create wrinkles that will last a lifetime. *Of course,* a tan is a status symbol, *so* not having one means you have to put up with a certain amount of guff. *I know*—I'm pale and have heard all the pale jokes and the stereotypes. *But* you can learn to live with it. *And* there are payoffs later: I may never be tan, *but* I'll have smooth skin when I'm old. ❖

## Diagnosing Transition by the Numbers

Often you can just *feel* transition or its lack—and that's all you need to know to fix the problem. But if you want to quantify transition, here's a by-the-numbers diagnostic program:

1. Highlight all connectors in your abstract. We're only interested in the connectors *between clauses*—ignore connectors joining just words or phrases.
2. Identify every place where there is no connector between clauses. Add a connector in each of these places, if possible.
3. Identify any *empty connectors*—connectors that tell you nothing about the logical relationship between what precedes and what follows (*and, then, furthermore, moreover, which, so* unless it means "therefore," the dash). You don't need to remove the empty connectors, since they aren't hurting you, but do add an informative connector to each.
4. Identify all *false connectors*—connectors that promise logical relationships that aren't there. When you start trying to add connectors to your abstracts, there's a huge temptation to make all transition problems seem to disappear by filling your abstract with snappy-looking but dishonest connectors. They sound like this:

   > You have to have respect and then you'll be OK; *for example,* when you're a veteran nobody messes with you.
   >
   > I was struck by a careless driver who ran a stop sign. I was able to survive; *consequently* the accident resulted in complete damage to my car.

   Wherever possible, replace all false connectors with honest ones:

   > I was unhurt, *but* my car was totaled.

5. (This is the key step.) Any place where good connectors wouldn't go easily is a structural trouble spot. What can you do to solve the problem? How can you resequence the abstract to make the transitions smoother?
6. Check to see if the sentences are combining and thus becoming fewer and longer. If they are, transition is getting better. That's what connectors do—they combine short sentences into longer ones. If you do your transition work perfectly, you'll end up with an abstract that is one huge, complex, but clear sentence. But remember, ungrammatical sentences, empty connectors, and false connectors don't count.

## Structural Templates

We've talked about organization as if a writer always starts with a draft and, through tools like abstracting, seeks the essay's own unique, ideal structure. And it often works like that. But there's another way. There are only so many ways to organize thought, so essays usually turn out to be versions of conventional essay *templates,* archetypal structures writers have been recycling for centuries. You could approach organization by picking a template and fitting your draft to it:

*For a restaurant review:* Follow the customer through the stages of the meal. First discuss the ambiance, then the service, then the menu, then the salad, the soup, the main course, the dessert, and the bill.

*For an investigative essay:* Pose a fascinating question. Gather data toward an answer. Answer the question, and discuss the implications of your answer.

*For an argumentative essay:* Declare a thesis. Marshal arguments, supportive evidence, and examples to prove it. Finally, discuss the implications of the thesis.

*For a lab report:* Summarize the experiment and its findings in the introduction, describe what was done in the experiment in the methods section, reproduce the data gathered in the results section, and discuss your findings in a discussion.

This approach works, and it's a lot simpler than what we've been doing for the last two chapters, but it isn't much fun and may doom you to a certain mediocrity.

## Paragraphing

Now that we know about transitions, we can answer a favorite writer's question: How do you know where to put the paragraph breaks? If paragraphing just happens for you, let it. Don't think about it unless you know it's a problem for you.

If it is a problem, deal with it with what we've learned. Good writing isn't a list—it's a logical or emotional process. Thus there are no real "stops" along the way—one thing always leads to another. So if your paragraphs are all short, it can only mean that you haven't found the strong sequencing that allows the reader to keep moving down the road. Use outlining and abstracting to get it. If your paragraphs are too long, it probably means that you just don't like to take breaks. That's a healthy sign, but you need to learn to take pity on the reader, who needs them. Just look at your page-long paragraph and ask yourself, "Where's the best place to take a breather in here?" And put the paragraph break there. Make one about every quarter or third of a single-spaced page, unless you want a special effect: short paragraphs for jerky, explosive effects, long paragraphs for tension-building. Here's George Orwell doing the first in his essay "Marrakech," where the first paragraph is one sentence long:

> As the corpse went past, the flies left the restaurant table in a cloud and rushed after it, but they came back a few minutes later.

Tom Wolfe does the latter on p. 24.

## EXERCISES

1. Write a critique of the following abstract: Which rules for abstract making does it follow, and which does it break?

> I describe the parking problem at the University. How the problem came into existence. The Administration is responsible for the problem.
>
> Possible solutions. Riding bikes. So we could build a parking garage for students.

Read the following three abstracts. Then follow the instructions in Exercises 2–9.

> **A.** Because information learned in conjunction with music is retained accurately and for a long time, music can be considered an effective learning tool. Rating a child's musical abilities can cause egotism, self-doubt, or total rejection of music. While providing educational benefits, music also promotes creativity and reveals the beauty surround-

ing knowledge—an essential in the learning process. Music when incorporated into the school curriculum must not be performance oriented or stressful in any way.

**B.** Most articles on surviving in the back country tell how to live off the land, but I think they ignore prevention. Real survival is knowing how to avoid the dangerous situation in the first place. One survival article showed how a guy snowed in on a deer hunt couldn't start a fire, couldn't retrace his steps, etc. With a little forethought, none of this would have happened. An important factor in survival is keeping your head. Once I went goose hunting without my pack, got lost, panicked, and spent a cold night out. I learned my lesson. To survive, you don't need to know how to live off the land—just take the right equipment and keep your head.

**C.** Advertising is making all of us hate the way we look. Every company offers products to improve our bodies. We're sicker and fatter now as a result. Bulimia and anorexia nervosa are two diseases commonly suffered by young women and sometimes men. Last summer I got to know my sister's friends. Iris admitted she was bulimic. Iris's problem wouldn't go away. Advertising has made fat one of our ultimate taboos. At an interview I was told to lose fifteen pounds. I wasn't fat then. Have we gone too far? Maybe we should reduce advertising until we become accustomed to imperfect people again.

2. Write a critique of each abstract asking if it obeyed the seven rules for abstract making beginning on p. 115. Rewrite the abstract so that it does.

3. For each abstract, go through the six-step diagnostic program beginning on p. 118.

4. For each abstract, write a paragraph critiquing it as we did on pp. 116–118. Make a list of concrete suggestions for revising the draft, such as "Move the anecdote about the wedding to the front." Rewrite the abstract so that it follows your suggestions.

5. Write an abstract for an essay in the Treasury of Essays (p. 368). Do Exercise 2 with it.

6. Do Exercise 3 with the abstract in Exercise 5.

7. Write an abstract of one of your own drafts. Then a) do Exercise 2 with it, b) do Exercise 3 with it, and c) do Exercise 4 with it.

8. Write descriptions of the structural template (p. 119) used in any three essays in the Treasury.

9. Write an essay using a structural template you like, whether in *The Writer's Way* or not. Add to the essay a brief description of the template.

# Chapter 8

# BEGINNING, ENDING, AND TITLING

**B**eginnings, endings, and titles are worth special attention. They're key moments of contact with your reader, and they're superb diagnostic tools. Essays that begin well, end well, and are titled well are usually good through and through.

## Beginnings

### Making the Tool

The draft's first sentence is a popular place for writer's block. We've all had the experience of staring at the blank page, knowing pretty much what we want to say once that hurdle has been overcome, but not being able to budge. For help with that problem, follow these four rules:

**1. Write the title last.** Or rather, be on the lookout for a good title from the moment you start the project. Expect it to come late, and grab it and hold on to it when it comes.

**2. If you can't find a good opener, have none.** No introduction at all is better than an empty, formulaic one like this:

> After reading Frank Smith's book *Reading Without Nonsense* you could tell that the author has very definite views on how to teach people to read. He lets the reader know exactly how he feels about different techniques of teaching children to read.

That's just killing time.

**3. Cut everything that precedes the first good thing you write.** Instead of trying to write a great opener right off the bat, just freewrite. Then read your draft until you find a sentence that really starts something, and throw away everything above it. Assume that your first few paragraphs will be a warm-up and should be trashed. Essays don't need to gather momentum—just plunge in. Here's an opener that gets on with it:

> Frank Smith feels that reading via food labels, street signs, and board games is a good way to learn to read, because to learn to read, children need to relate the words to something that makes sense.

**4. Use a stock opener.** If you're still stuck, fall back on one of four basic strategies writers have been using for centuries:

*The thesis statement.* You declare up front (usually at the end of the first paragraph) the heart of what you have to say. Beginning writers and teachers like this one because it's easy, and bosses and other people in a hurry often like it because they can grasp the gist of a piece of writing in a minute. But it's unexciting unless the thesis is startling and provocative, like the newspaper article a while back that began, "Americans apparently like reading the newspaper more than sex," and it gives away the punch line up front, so the rest of the essay loses energy. However, scientific and technical writing usually demands thesis openers; there, you should use them.

*The question.* A question opener has three virtues. It forces you to be clear about your purpose, it's dramatic (it turns the essay into a detective story), and it shows you what to do with the rest of the essay: answer the question. There's an example on p. 127.

*The hook.* Also known as the grabber or the angle, the hook is the eye-catcher that sucks a reader into the essay like a vacuum cleaner: "The next time you are in Florida, you would do well to remember that it is illegal to have sex with a porcupine in that state" (*Charles McCabe*).

There are countless ways to hook a reader. You can start with a paradox, an idea that seems self-contradictory and therefore demands explanation—like "Americans are getting more liberal and more conservative all the time." You can tease the reader with a promise of excitement to come: "No one noticed that the world changed on August 7, 1994." You can drop the reader into the middle of things so she'll read on to find out how she got there—what Latin poets called beginning *in medias res:* "The President looked unamused as he wiped the pie filling off his face." Newspaper sports sections love hooks:

> A World Series involving the New York Yankees would not be official without a controversy. The 75th Series was stamped as the real thing yesterday at Yankee Stadium.
>
> Westside High's Cougars did what they had to and nothing more to hand Central a 24–15 defeat Saturday night.

Don't promise what you can't deliver. Don't hook dishonestly: "Free beer!!! Now that I've gotten your attention, I'm going to talk about brands of tennis shoes."

*The narrative.* Narrative openers—stories—work because they concretize and humanize right off the bat: "In the middle of the worst depression in our nation's history, one woman decided to leave her comfortable home and head west looking for a better life." "Given the Chance" (p. 276) and "The Last Stop for America's Busses" (p. 387) have narrative openers.

One subtype of the narrative opener always works as a last resort: the "how I came to write this essay" opener. Explain what started you thinking about the subject: "I was reading the newspaper the other day and noticed an article about the Federal Government taking over the Coca-Cola Company. I couldn't help thinking . . ."

Once you've got an opener, make sure it performs the following three tasks.

**5. Reveal the topic.** This is easy, so do it fast. A whole sentence is too much because it invariably sounds like "In this essay I'm going to talk about . . ." Reveal topic as you're doing more important things:

> If you're an average, somewhat chubby individual wanting to get some healthy, not overly strenuous exercise, you should consider bicycling.
>
> When you start working as a pizza delivery person, you're going to get a new view of life.
>
> Most of us, if we're honest with ourselves, will admit we've thought about committing suicide.

**6. Reveal the purpose.** Every reader begins with some basic questions: Why are you writing to me? How can I use this? Why does this matter? Begin answering these questions from the outset.

**7. Say, "Read me, read me!"** An opener is like a free sample of salsa at the grocery store—it says, "Here's a typical example of the way I write; once you sample it, you'll want to read more." Just write a first sentence you'd like to read:

> In late July 1982, presidential Press Secretary James Brady sued the gun company that made the pistol used by John Hinckley.
>
> Grandpa drank too much beer the day he jumped into the pool wearing his boxer shorts.
>
> Most Americans do not get to experience the excitement and discomfort of train travel very often.
>
> If you'd like to murder somebody but receive a penance of one year's probation and a small fine, try this: Get yourself

> blind, staggering, out-of-control drunk some night and just run over some guy as he walks across his own lawn to pick up his newspaper.
>
> Many gun control advocates believe in the commonsense argument that fewer guns should result in fewer killings. But it may not be that simple.

The following openers make you want to stop reading:

> Handguns are of major concern to many people in the United States.
>
> Driving under the influence of alcohol is a serious problem in the United States today.
>
> Bilingual ballots have been in the spotlight for many years.

You don't have to shout; you can say "Read me!" with dignity and class too. My favorite first sentence is the famous beginning of George Orwell's "Shooting an Elephant":

> In Moulmein, in Lower Burma, I was hated by large numbers of people—the only time in my life that I have been important enough for this to happen to me.

You can't say "Read me" more quietly or more powerfully than that.

Different kinds of writing value the three tasks differently. Scientific and technical writing values "Read me" hardly at all. As a result, few people read scientific and technical writing for fun. Academic writing values thesis highly but doesn't think about purpose very much—who knows *why* you write an essay about sickness metaphors in *Hamlet*? Entertainment journalism values "Read me" above all and often has no purpose beyond momentary titillation.

## Using the Tool

Begin by asking the central question: "Does this beginning make me want to keep reading?" Next, ask if the other two tasks were accomplished: revealing topic and revealing purpose. If you can't find a sense of purpose, make sure the draft has one and that you know what it is.

Let's practice on two professional openers. How well do the following beginnings do their jobs? Here is the opening paragraph of C. S. Lewis's *A Preface to Paradise Lost:*

> The first qualification for judging a piece of workmanship, from a corkscrew to a cathedral, is to know *what* it is—what it was intended to do and how it is meant to be used. After that has been discovered, the temperance reformer may decide that the corkscrew was made for a bad purpose, and the communist may think the same about the cathedral. But such questions come later. The first thing is to understand the object before you: as long as you think the

> corkscrew was meant for opening tins or the cathedral for entertaining tourists, you can say nothing to the purpose about them. The first thing the reader needs to know about *Paradise Lost* is what Milton meant it to be.

We know Lewis's subject: How did Milton mean for *Paradise Lost* to be used? We know his purpose: to tell us how Milton intended his poem to be used so that we may judge it truly. We know that this should matter to us: Until we have what Lewis offers us, he implies, we are doomed to misconstrue Milton's poem.

Does Lewis say "Read me"? That depends on who we are. You can't write to everyone, and Lewis doesn't try. He's writing to college literature students primarily, so he speaks in a voice that is learned—to win our respect—but also personal ("you") and mildly witty (corkscrews and cathedrals) and forceful ("know *what* it is"). I think he does well.

The second sample is by Robert Schadewald, writing in *The TWA Ambassador,* TWA's in-flight magazine. The essay is called "How Do It Know?"

> What is the most remarkable device in the world? The electron microscope? Perhaps it's the brain scanner? Or the side-looking radar?
>
> No, it's something that has no electronic circuits, not even any moving parts. According to a joke that made the rounds a few years back, the most remarkable device, in the opinion of one gentleman, is the Thermos bottle, for it keeps hot things hot and cold things cold. Asked what's so remarkable about that, the man replied in awe, "How do it know?"
>
> How indeed.
>
> It used to be that an educated person could keep up with things, could understand how things work . . . Today's space-age technology leaves the layman out in the cold; the technical specialist is hard-pressed to keep up with developments in his very own narrow field.
>
> Before technology runs away with us all, we've prepared this "uncomplicated" guide for you, explaining how things work. We've chosen six modern-day wonders most of us encounter every day. . . . We consulted experts in each of the various fields, and asked them that simple question, "How do it know?"

Schadewald's topic is clear: how six common modern devices work. His purpose, too, is clear: to explain to the reader how the machines around him work. We have no reason to read except mild curiosity—we don't need to know how a telephone works—so Schadewald invents a need. Technology is running away from us, he says; we're "left out in the cold." Fight back, Schadewald says.

Does Schadewald's introduction say, "Read me"? That depends on who you are and what you want. Schadewald is obviously trying to sell the essay as light entertainment. The essay tells jokes, it's chatty and clever and easy-going—just the thing for killing thirty minutes of flight time.

## Conclusions

### Making the Tool

Conclusions are almost as good at breeding writer's block as beginnings. Anyone who's ever found himself stuck on the porch looking for the right last words after a first date knows that. That's why we've invented lots of get-me-out-of-this formulas for concluding: "Last but not least, I'd just like to thank . . ."; "And so, without further ado . . ."; "Thank you very much for your attention to this matter"; "I'll call ya."

Concluding is surrounded by lots of toxic myths, so let's begin by clearing them out. Here are some rules for what *not* to do:

**1. Don't summarize the essay or repeat the thesis.** This is a shock to lots of people, but the fact is that unless the piece is a manual, a summary conclusion is a waste of time, a deadly bore, and an insult to your reader. Only do it if your teacher tells you to.

**2. Don't seek the last word.** If you write a paper on the national economy, you're *not* going to end all discussion of the national economy. Yet the conclusion must say, "Here we can stop for now"—like a campsite on a walking tour, a home for the night. To ask more of yourself is to guarantee writer's block.

**3. Don't feel obliged to have a conclusion.** It's OK to say the last thing you have to say and simply stop. Essays without conclusions actually read well—and a lot better than essays with a last paragraph of filler or needless repetition for conclusion's sake. The essay called "Dad" (p. 219) is an example.

The list of things to *do* is frighteningly short:

**4. Study concluding by reading for the craft.** (p. 5.) As you read essays throughout your life, read with an eye on how each one solves the dilemma of ending.

**5. Plan your conclusion from the get-go,** as a part of the whole-essay design. The conclusion is the place your structure has been taking you all along. If you ask a question, you're committed to giving the reader an answer. If you're writing a lab report, you're committed to discussing the significance of what you learned. If you begin with a human interest story, you're committed to returning to the people in it so the reader isn't left wondering what happened to them. If you begin by stating a problem, you're committed to offering a solution (or confessing you have none).

Here's how it looks. A student reviewed a local taco stand. His thesis was that it was all right, but that it couldn't compare to the Mexican food he was used to back home in L.A. Here's an abstract of his essay, with his concluding sentence intact:

> When I was young, I learned to love the great Mexican food in L.A., but now that I'm here in the sticks I keep seeking a restaurant that comes up to that high standard. In that search I tried Alfredo's. It was pretty good, but hardly spectacular, and the search continues. Now, if you want real Mexican food, I know a little place not far from Hollywood and Vine . . .

And here's an abstract of a review of a local counterculture restaurant, titled "Lily's Restaurant . . . And More":

> Lily's has a wide range of sandwiches, all tasty and reasonably priced—and more. Lily's has a clientele ranging from student hippie to lumberjack—and more. It has soups, vegetarian meals, and friendly, casual service—and more. It's also got cockroaches, so, no thanks, I'm not going back.

**6. Use a stock closer.** Conclusions, like introductions, fall into types. If you can't find a conclusion, do one of the following standards, but remember: Each one commits you to an essay structure that sets it up, so you can't paste it on as an afterthought.

*The answer.* "Given the Chance" (p. 276) and "Exactly How We Want It" (p. 275) do this. If you begin by addressing a problem, you naturally end by deciding what's to be done about it. If you begin by asking a question, you end by answering it.

*The full circle.* A full-circle conclusion ends by returning to where it started, to the very first thing the essay said. A student began a paper on a quiche restaurant by referring to the author of the best-seller *Real Men Don't Eat Quiche,* saying "Bruce Feirstein has obviously not been to Quiche Heaven," and he returned to that in his concluding line: "I don't care what Bruce Feirstein thinks; he doesn't know what he's been missing." If you begin with a *person,* return to that person: "Perhaps, if these changes are enacted, no one will suffer the way Alice suffered again." The essay on the Mexican restaurant does this, beginning with the author's beloved L.A. haunts and returning to them, as does "Scratch that Itch" (p. 381). But notice that coming full circle is *not* summarizing or repeating a thesis.

*Taking the long view.* After you've arrived at your destination, you explore the long-term implications of your discovery, consider the larger issues, or raise the next question (pp. 140–142). If you've argued that women are getting more into weight lifting, talk about the long-term implications for women's self-image, standards of female attractiveness in our culture, and sexism. This can work with personal writing, too. The long-view conclusion is just about the only way to conclude a thesis-opener essay without summarizing or restating. "A Moral Victory?" (p. 393) and "Why I Never Cared for the Civil War" (p. 391) have brief long-view conclusions.

*The punch line.* If no better conclusion has come to you, you can usually end with your best line. "Eradicat"and "How to Audition for a Play" both have punch-line endings.

### Using the Tool

There is no fancy diagnostic program for conclusions. Just read the conclusion and ask yourself if it works. If you think it does, it does. If it doesn't, assume that the problem is a symptom of a problem in the draft's overall design, and go back to abstracting.

## Titles

The title is the drive-thru of revision, the quickest diagnostic tool a writer has. In about two seconds you can tell if the essay is good or not.

### Making the Tool

I don't really need to tell you how to write titles, because most people can write great titles the moment they *ask themselves to*. But if you want a method, follow these five rules:

**1. Have one.** The biggest problem with titles in school is a lack of one.

**2. Do the same three jobs you did in your introduction:** Declare the topic, imply a thesis, a purpose, or a task to accomplish, and say "Read me, read me!" Any title does at least one of these three; the trick is to do all three.

Some titles just state topic:

Prayer in School
Friendship

Some titles do topic and purpose without much "Read me!":

The Joys of Racquetball
Mark Twain: America's Finest Author

Fad Diets Don't Work

Some do a lot of "Read me!" and no topic:

Give me *Massive* Doses!
Killing Bambi

What we're striving for is the title that does all three:

Tube Addiction
Yes, Virginia, Leisure Is a Good Thing
Anatomy of the Myopic Introvert

**3. Don't have your title state the thesis,** because it's wordy and dull. It's enough to imply or suggest it:

| Title | Implied thesis |
|---|---|
| A Gamble for Better Education | We should have a state lottery. |
| China Syndrome | The food at Ho Chin's is poison. |
| In the Long Run | Jogging is good for you. |

**4. Use a stock format.** If you shy away from suggesting your thesis in your titles, you can force yourself to by using any of three title formats:

*The question*: "School Music: Fundamental or Thrill?"; "What Is Pornography?"
*The "why" title*: "Why I Hate Advertising"
*The declarative sentence*: "Breast Feeding Is Best"

Yes, that last one breaks Rule 3—see rule breaking, p. 68.

**5. Use a colon title.** We've just said that a good title should declare a topic, imply a thesis, purpose, or task, and say "Read me!" But most titles are two or three words long, and doing all three tasks in such a small space is hard. One way around that is to stick two titles together with a colon. Write a title that does two of the three tasks, put in a colon, and then add a title that does the third. Colon titles are a bit stuffy, but they work. Sometimes you do the topic, put a colon, then do thesis and "Read me!": "Television: The Glamour Medium." Sometimes you do it the other way around: "Rotten in Denmark: Images of Disease in *Hamlet*."

## Using the Tool

As with the introduction, ask of the title, "Does this work? Does it make the reader want to read the essay?" You'll know the answer.

Next, ask, "Does it do the three tasks of a perfect title?" If the title is faulty, blame the draft: If you can't find a hint of thesis, it's probably because the draft doesn't have one; if you can't find signs of life, it's probably because the draft doesn't have any.

## EXERCISES

1. Write a one-page essay describing how successfully each of the following openers does the three tasks of an opener discussed on p. 125:

a. The horror of those seconds will forever haunt Cindy Ferguson. She was driving her three sons—the identical twins Tommy and Tony and her baby, Lee—to a party, when suddenly her Vega was smashed from behind. A tremendous explosion hurled her, Tony, and Lee onto the street. Cindy raced back to the car and pulled Tommy's burning body from the wreck, throwing herself on him to smother the flames. . . . As Cindy lay there on top of her son, the other driver approached her. But when she pleaded for help, he staggered away.

(*"The War Against Drunk Drivers,"* Newsweek)

b. Early in Campaign '82, supporters of the statewide initiative requiring deposits for soft drinks, beer, and mineral water sold in bottles and cans had every reason to expect success. In late August, Mervyn Field's California Polls showed Proposition 11 favored by a 2–1 margin. In early October, the measure was still ahead 20 points . . . But the early signs of support came before opponents of the measure—the bottle and can industry, brewers and soft drink makers, most labor unions and supermarket chains—unleashed the full force of their war chest.

(*Alan Cline, "The Life and Death of Prop. 11,"* Chico News and Review)

2. Do Exercise 1 with an essay from the Treasury of Essays (p. 368).

3. Do Exercise 1 with an essay of your own. Rewrite the opener to include any task you find missing.

4. Pages 124–125 list four stock openers. Write an opener of each type for one of your essays.

5. Write an opening for one of your essays using the "how I came to write this essay" device (p. 125).

6. Pages 129–130 list four stock conclusions. Write four abstracts for one of your essays, using one of the four in each.

7. Write critiques of the conclusions in three essays in the Treasury of Essays: How do they work? Do they use any of the four stock conclusions on pp. 129–130? How does the essay design plan for the conclusion?

8. Do Exercise 7 with one of your own essays.

9. Here's a list of titles from essays on censorship. For each title, answer the question "Which of a title's three tasks does it do?" Rewrite any titles that don't do all three so that they do—make up content if you need to. Example: "Eating" → "Tomorrow We Diet: My Life as an Overeater."

   a. Why Is Censorship Needed?
   b. Who's to Judge?
   c. From a Child's Point of View
   d. You Want to Read *What?*
   e. Censorship: The Deterioration of the First Amendment
   f. Censorship

10. Write four titles for one of your essays, one in each of the four stock formats on p. 131.

11. Write colon titles for three of the essays in the Treasury of Essays.

12. Write a colon title for one of your essays.

13. Write a one-paragraph critique of the title of one of your essays: Does it do the three tasks of a perfect title (p. 130)? If it doesn't, rewrite it so that it does.

# Chapter 9

# MAKING THE DRAFT LONGER OR SHORTER

It's time to practice the writer's art of writing to the assigned length.

Beginning writers usually think an essay should be as long as it takes to do the task at hand—you write till you've said it all. That almost never works, because in life there's almost always a length limit. Once I wrote a 2,000-word essay for a national news magazine. The editor said, "I like it, but we have a 1,050-word maximum." I said OK, and sent her a cut version that was 1,100 words. She said, "I like it—but you have to cut fifty words." I said OK, and did. Two days later, she called and said, "We're seven words too long—which seven words would you like to cut?"

In the beginning of your career, the problem is usually that the draft is too short. But after you've been writing for a few years, the problem reverses itself and the draft is almost always too long. So we'll talk about making drafts longer and shorter, and if you don't need both skills now, you might later.

Begin by drafting everything you have in you—don't think about length at all. Then look at the boss's length limit and cut or expand to suit.

## Making It Shorter

You make a text shorter in one of two ways: Say it all, faster, or say less.

To say it faster, we need only notice that Chapter 5 reduced essays to single sentences (thesis statements), Chapter 6 reduced them to three to five sentences (outlines), and Chapter 7 reduced them to paragraphs (abstracts), so any coherent text can be reduced to any size. Just to prove it, here are successively shrunk versions of "A Moral Victory?" (in its full 500-word form on pp. 393–394):

The half-size version:

> In 1984, some white male police officers sued San Francisco, claiming they were the victims of reverse discrimination because

> they had been passed over for promotion in favor of less qualified minority officers. The U.S. Supreme Court has refused to hear their case. This may seem to be a victory for minorities, but isn't it really a loss for us all?
>
> I'm married to a white male, and I've seen a lot through his eyes. He's an engineering professor who has worked in industry for thirteen years. Unfortunately, reverse discrimination is for him a fact of life. Employers are forced by federal quotas to give preference to Hispanics, blacks, and women.
>
> My sister is also an engineering professor in the same system, but basically what she wants she gets, because the quota system makes her a sought-after commodity. It took my sister a long time to appreciate the injustice of this.
>
> Right now her department is interviewing for a new instructor. The department doesn't actually have an open position, but the university has funding for a certain number of faculty who meet "specific criteria." The candidate is black, so of course she's irresistible!
>
> We feel an awful sense of collective guilt in this country for what we've done to women and minorities, and we should. But can we really right past wrongs by creating new ones? I don't propose that we forget our past, but I think it's time to forgive ourselves and move on. ❖

The quarter-size version:

> The U.S. Supreme Court has refused to hear a reverse discrimination case concerning San Francisco policemen. Is this a victory for minorities or a loss for us all? My husband is an engineering professor. Unfortunately, reverse discrimination is for him a fact of life. Employers are forced by federal quotas to give preference to Hispanics, blacks, and women.
>
> My sister is also an engineering professor, but basically what she wants she gets, because the quota system makes her a sought-after commodity. Right now her department has a job that's open only to people who meet "specific criteria"—being black, for instance.
>
> Americans feel guilty for past racism and sexism, and we should. But it's time to forgive ourselves, and move on. ❖

The eighth-size version:

> Reverse discrimination isn't a victory for minorities, it's a loss for us all. For my husband, reverse discrimination is a fact of life. But my sister gets anything she wants, since she's female, and her department has a job that's open only to minorities. We should feel guilty about our past, but it's time to forgive ourselves and move on. ❖

The sixteenth-size version:

> Reverse discrimination is a loss for us all. My husband suffers from reverse discrimination daily, but my sister gets anything she wants, since she's female. Guilt is good, but let's forgive ourselves and move on. ❖

On the head of a pin:

> Reverse discrimination is a loss for us all; let's forgive ourselves and move on. ❖

To say less, you think differently. You reduce the essay to a short list, and you pick from the list. You think, "I'd like to talk about the San Francisco discrimination case and my husband's experiences with reverse discrimination and my sister's change of heart and the hiring her department is doing, but I just don't have the time, so instead I'll focus on my sister's change of heart and leave everything else for another day." You can do this on paper, by mapping or outlining and choosing a chunk.

## Making It Longer

Making a text shorter is pretty easy compared to the harder problem you face when the teacher says "Give me five pages" and you've run dry after two paragraphs.

We practice solving this problem throughout this book. In Chapter 4 we brainstormed and free wrote to expand a seed into a draft. In Chapter 10 we'll use peer editing to show us how the draft could become something bigger and better. In Chapter 16 we'll use a thesis statement as a springboard to an endless conversation. All of these activities are based on the idea that a draft is just a starting place.

You can expand in three ways: filling in, expanding the canvas, and asking the next question.

## Making It Longer by Filling In

Saying it in more detail does *not* mean saying exactly the same thing in twice as many words. It means filling in blanks and providing background detail. An essay is like a painted portrait. The one-paragraph version is like a happy face—nothing but a circle for the head, a curved line for the mouth, two circles for eyes. Now we're going to go in and start adding details—lips, ears, irises, pupils. Then we can add details to the details—chapped skin on the lips, ear hair, bloodshot eyes. We can keep adding details forever, like sharpening the resolution on a TV screen by increasing the number of pixels. Imagine a passage from an essay on changing a flat tire, in various degrees of detail:

*Short version:* Remove the hubcap.

*Longer version:* Remove the hubcap with the tire iron.

*Still longer:* Find the tire iron. It's a long iron bar. Stick one end under the lip of the hubcap and pry until the hubcap comes off.

*Even longer:* Find the tire iron. It's a long iron bar and is probably alongside your jack, either in the trunk or under the hood. Stick one end under the lip of the hubcap anywhere along the circumference and pry until the hubcap comes off.

*Longest so far:* Check to see if you have a hubcap—a Frisbee of shiny metal covering your lug nuts. If you do, you have to remove it. Find the tire iron. It's a long iron bar and is probably alongside your jack, either in the trunk or under the hood. If you want to stay clean, be careful—it, like the jack, is likely to be pretty yucky if it's been used before. Grasping the iron in your left hand (if you're right-handed), stick the end that is flattened and slightly canted under the lip of the hubcap anywhere along the circumference and push hard on the other end with the flat of your right hand. The hubcap should pop off. If it doesn't work, push harder. Don't worry—you can't hurt the iron or the hubcap. Keep prying until the hubcap comes off, whatever it takes. If it's stuck, try different spots around the lip. Above all, DON'T wrap your right hand around the bar when you're prying—if you do, when the hubcap comes loose, your fingers will be crushed between the iron and the tire or fender.

To make the point that text is infinitely expandable, I asked my students to write narratives of recent experiences; then I asked them to take a small portion of the narrative and rewrite it as full of detail as possible. Here's the original story Mark Wilpolt told:

> Yesterday the rain stopped and the sun came out. I had been doing homework all day, so I jumped on my bike to experience the drying streets. Along the way I decided to turn the bike ride into a trip to the gym. I arrived at the gym and worked out on the Nordic Track for fifteen minutes. On the way home, I took the scenic route along the creek, enjoying the fall colors, the clear sky, and the foothills, with their new patches of snow, in the background. Who says exercise isn't fun? ❖

And here is Mark's expansion of five of his original words, "I arrived at the gym," into an essay:

> The entrance to the Sports Club is its own little world. As I walk through the lobby, the day care is on the right. A dozen kids are running around the plastic playground as perfect smiling employees in their twenties look on—a Norman Rockwell scene for the 90's. The beauty salon is next: women with big hairdos and long, fluorescent fingernails giving their customers that extra little something they can't get from the workout floor. Then the big-screen TV, surrounded by comfy sofas, and the snack bar, tempting you to just skip the exercise and vedge.
>
> I hand my card to the girl at the front counter. Whoever is on duty, it's always the same: a bubbly smile and a musical "Hello, how are you today?, have a nice workout" as she zips my card through the computer, like she's been waiting all day for me to show up and make her shift. They must major in Smiling, the people who get hired for that position. Tough job.
>
> Next I must negotiate my way past the aerobics room. Why they make that whole wall one giant window of glass I'll never know. Is it so women can see the class going on inside and feel

guilty because THEY don't look like that, or so men can watch the proceedings and get their heart rate up in anticipation of their workout? Whichever the case, there's a bench right there in the hall inviting everyone to sit and stare. As I pass, I want to sit and ogle the women of all shapes and sizes who are jumping and twisting and sweating in their Spandex. Of course they'd probably revoke my membership.

In the Big Room, a dozen machines, none of which I know the name of, for shoulders, thighs, chest, back, quads, biceps, even a machine to exercise your NECK for heaven's sake. A ten-thousand-dollar machine to exercise your NECK? Also there's a fleet of Stairmasters, a bank of treadmills, a rank of stationary bicycles, a squadron of rowing machines—and the Nordic Track. None of them going anywhere, but some of them being driven pretty hard. The humorless faces of the exercisers say, "This is serious business."

All the machines call to me, "Me, do me first. No, work on your arms first," but it's hard to hear them because a dozen TV sets suspended in rows where the wall meets the ceiling are blaring, "Watch ME instead!" No way to avoid it—you work out and you watch TV. "Wheel of Fortune" is on. I'm trapped. I get on the Nordic Track and stare. The clue is "Person," five words. The champ has the wheel.

"I'd like an S, please."

"Yes, two of them!" DING, DING. "Spin again!"

"I'd like an R, please?"

"Yes, there are FIVE R's!" DING, DING, DING, DING, DING.

The champ buys a couple of vowels. ❖

The tricky part is realizing that arguments or thought processes can be expanded just like information can. Shawni, the author of "Why I Never Cared for the Civil War" (p. 391) could easily expand it to book length by researching the degree to which American schools use the lecture-and-test approach to teaching, citing successful classroom alternatives to it, and detailing how they work and why they succeed.

## Expanding the Canvas

Another way to lengthen is to ask, "What's the larger issue?" If the first way of lengthening was like adding details to a painting, this way of lengthening is like pasting the original work in the middle of a much larger canvas and painting the surroundings.

Seeing the larger issue depends on realizing that all issues are specific versions of larger issues:

| **Specific Issue** | **Larger Issues** |
|---|---|
| Why I deserve an A in English 1 | How grades are determined; what grades mean; how are students evaluated? |
| My father was a brute, and I couldn't do anything about it. | Psychological effects of bad parenting on children; why do people have children? children's rights |
| Why I don't vote anymore | What's wrong with American politics? America's apathy crisis |

## Asking the Next Question

Asking the next question means exactly what it says: When you finish the draft, you ask yourself, "What's the next question to be asked and answered? What's the next task that needs to be done?" No argument ends the debate, no task completed means the work is over. In writing as in science, answers only generate more questions, and there's always a next thing to learn or do. For instance, if you write an essay successfully arguing that the U.S. shouldn't explore for oil in the Alaskan tundra, the next question might be, "OK, what *should* we do to solve our growing energy problem, then?"

These three ways of expansion can be visualized if you place your thesis in the middle of a conventional outline, like so:

I. ____________________

  A. ____________________

  B. ____________________

II. ____________________

  A. Your thesis

    1. ____________________

    2. ____________________

  B. ____________________

III. ____________________

  A. ____________________

  B. ____________________

Now you can *see* where the potential for expansion lies. To expand by filling in, add material to the sections of the outline *indented under* the thesis—sections IIA1 and following. To add by expanding the canvas, *move to the left*—instead of using the thesis at IIA, use the one at II. And to ask the next question, do the task *below* the thesis—section IIB—then the one below that, then the one below that.

# WRITER'S WORKSHOP

## Expanding Essays

To practice the three ways of expansion, let's take two short student drafts and list some ways to fill them in, raise larger issues, and ask next questions:

### SEX AND TV

MARJORIE CROW

Do you hate turning on the TV and all you see are people touching each other sexually and some taking off their clothes? Well, I'm tired of it. There is much more to human relationships than sex. Yes, some people would agree that sex has a lot to do with a relationship, but sex on TV is what I'm most annoyed with. Sex is enticing and sex does make products sell, but the question is, should sex be thrown around like it's yesterday's lunch? I feel that something has to be done. It would be great if the media would monitor the shows that we see, but in reality they want to broadcast what will sell, and sex sells. ❖

**Questions for Marjorie**

1. *Filling in:*

What are some examples of how sex is portrayed on TV?
*How* does TV use sex to sell things?
What exactly are the messages we're being sent about sex by TV?

2. *The larger canvas:*

How our culture treats sex
How TV influences our values and beliefs
Our culture's portrayal of women

3. *The next question:*

How can we stop the marketing of sex?
Who is ultimately responsible?
What other ways are there that TV cheapens our lives?

## TYRANT!

TRICIA IRELAND

Christopher Columbus should not be regarded as a national hero. He was a terrible man who worked only for selfishness and greed. He was not the first on his expedition to spot land; a man named Roderigo was. But according to his own journal, Columbus took credit because the first to spot land was to receive a yearly pension for life.

When Columbus landed in the Bahamas, he took the natives by force and made them his slaves. Hundreds he sent back to Spain; others were held captive in their own country. He made them bring him a monthly quota of gold, and when they did they received a copper coin necklace. If they were found without a necklace, their hands were cut off and they were left to bleed to death.

I don't know why we teach our children to admire and respect Columbus. There exists a terrible amount of ignorance regarding the truth around him. It's time to teach the truth. Columbus Day shouldn't be celebrated, and Columbus himself shouldn't be seen as anything but the cruel tyrant he was. ❖

### Questions for Tricia

1. *Filling in:*

What else did Columbus do, good and bad?—tote up his virtues and vices.
What's the rest of his story? How did he get the idea to go exploring? How did he die? And so on.
How did the Columbus myth get started?

2. *The larger canvas:*

What's a hero?
Tradition vs. truth in history
The European bias in our view of history

3. *The next question:*

What about other heroes like George Washington—are they fables too? Should we also expose them?
Why does this matter, since it's ancient history?
How can we change the way we teach history so it isn't so biased?

**Now it's your turn.** For each of the following essays, write out ways to expand the draft by a) filling in, b) writing on the larger canvas, and c) asking the next question.

## OPEN THE DOOR

PAULA BONKOFSKY

College-level students shouldn't be punished, or worse, locked out of classes if they arrive late. Certainly if it becomes habit the teacher should speak with the student and affect their grade accordingly. But on occasion, students who are never regularly late are late because of circumstances that were out of their control. These students should be allowed to come in and participate with their class. Yes, it really is their class because they paid for it. ❖

## SEX, LIES, AND POLITICAL BASHING

KERI BOYLES

Lately, it seems as if you can't turn on the TV without seeing some political campaign commercial blasting the opposition. Instead of telling us what they stand for and what they plan to do in office if they get elected, they spend the majority of their time smearing their opponent. These commercials are exactly the reason why a lot of people are presently disgusted with politicians. Not only are they insulting to the voter, but they skirt the issues as well, focusing on their opponent's flaws instead of informing the voter on what their actual policies are and how they plan to "clean up" the messes that politicians (unlike themselves, of course!) have gotten this country into.

It's time to say enough is enough. These distasteful commercials shouldn't be allowed. Candidates should only be able to state what their beliefs and policies are, without smearing their opponent. Voters would then be able to make logical, rational decisions without being bombarded with all the other pointless garbage they are all subjected to when watching their favorite TV shows. Personally, I don't care if Clinton inhaled or not! ❖

## EXERCISES

1. Pick an essay from the Treasury of Essays (p. 368) and rewrite it to half its length in two ways:

    a. Say it all, but twice as fast, as we did on pp. 135–136.
    b. Cut the essay's scope in half, as we did on p. 137.

2. Do Exercise 1 with an essay of your own.
3. Do Mark's assignment on pp. 139–140. Describe in one paragraph a recent personal experience; then retell it in two pages, adding as much detail as you can but without changing the scope.
4. Write a one-paragraph argument. Then write answers to the three questions from this chapter: How can this be filled out? What is the larger canvas? What is the next task? Be sure to deal with each of the three. Then rewrite the argument to 1–2 pages, using the material generated by the questions.
5. Write a one-paragraph argument. Read it to the class and ask them to respond to it, not as English majors but as thinkers. Rewrite the argument to 1–2 pages, using the material generated by the conversation.

# Chapter 10

# PEER FEEDBACK

Peer feedback (also called "peer editing") is the writing teacher's term for giving your work to a reader and asking, "What do you think?" We've been practicing for this since Chapter 2. Over and over we've imagined the reader responding to us and practiced using that response to tell us if what we're writing works. Now it's time to give the manuscript to a breathing human being and see if our guesses were right. This is the one step in the revision process you can't do alone, because you can't read your own writing—you're always reading what you intended to do, not what you did.

Peer feedback is the most powerful step in the rewriting process. Ten minutes of conversation with a thoughtful reader will open doors you don't even plan to knock on. And in a sense it's the easiest step in the process, because the reader does the work, not you. But ironically, in practice, peer editing often turns out to be worse than useless—the writer ends up overwhelmed and resentful, and the reader ends up frustrated and unheard. To make this revision tool pay off, you have to build it right by following the many rules you're about to see in this chapter.

## Rules for Readers

**1. Don't focus on what's wrong or list mistakes.** Doing so is devastating for the writer, it's not how people learn, and there's no such thing as right and wrong in writing. Instead,

**2. Tell the writer how the text reads to you.** Say things like, "This paragraph confused me," or "I wanted to know more here," or "The title made me laugh." This is the one thing the writer can't do for himself. The writer hits the golf ball, but only you can tell him where it lands. You can't be "wrong," since you're just declaring what you experienced while reading. The writer can't argue with you, for the same reason.

If you do this one job, you'll have served your writer well, but there's much more help you can offer:

**3. Identify the source of your reactions.** Find what in the text is causing you to feel the way you do. You help a little if you say, "This essay feels cold," but you help a lot if you add, "I think it's because of all the academic jargon."

**4. Suggest possible revision strategies.** Show the writer possible ways to work with the essay features you're observing. You help a little if you say, "The opening paragraph seems lifeless," but you help a lot if you add, "Why not start the essay with the personal narrative in paragraph 4?"

Rule 4 runs a lot of risks. You must remember that it's not your job to tell the writer how to write, and the writer must remember that she doesn't have to follow your suggestions—she decides what to do, because she's the writer. But if you can both stay in your proper roles, "You could do this . . ." suggestions can be golden.

**5. Generalize and note patterns.** Make broad statements that apply to the essay as a whole. Note when the same sort of thing happens over and over. Every time you make an observation about a place in the text, ask yourself, "Are there other places where similar things occur?" If you don't do this, feedback tends to be an overwhelming flood of unrelated suggestions.

**6. Fry the biggest fish first.** Address the thing that will help the essay the most first and the thing that will help it the least last. Don't polish the brass on the Titanic by picking at comma placement or a single word choice if there are matters of purpose, tone, large-scale organization, and logic to discuss. Prepare by asking yourself, "What are the three comments that would help the essay the most?"

**7. Give yeas as well as nays.** Give as much energy to pointing out what pleased you as to what didn't. "Keep doing this, this, and this" teaches at least as well as "Dump that, that, and that." And it feels a lot better. Psychologists who study marriages say that in healthy ones affirmations outnumber criticisms by about five to one. You may not be able to maintain that ratio, but you can embrace the spirit of it.

**8. Help the writer see alternatives and possibilities.** Think about what the essay could be that it isn't yet. Ask, Where can this draft go from here? What else could it be doing? What related issues does this open up?

*This is the most precious gift you can give the writer, because it's the one thing she's least likely to be able to do herself.* To do it you have to stop staring at the draft and asking "What needs fixing?", step back, and think outside the box. Ironically, this is the easiest part of the feedback process for the reader, because all you have to do is *share your thoughts on what the draft says.* Since you didn't write it, you'll have things to say about it the writer will never think of, and those thoughts will open doors and make new essays possible.

To do this last task well, both the writer and the reader must remember that the purpose behind peer editing is not to rid the draft of errors but to remake the draft into the best possible essay. That usually means replacing the essay with another. Looking for errors to fix creates a tunnel vision that prevents that large-scale growth.

**9. End by prioritizing.** Since a good peer-editing session touches on a dizzying range of issues, avoid overload by ending with a highlighting of the two or three suggestions that have the biggest potential for gain: "Of all the things we've talked about, I think those two ideas about opening with the story about you and your mother and dropping the tirade about rude telemarketers are the best."

## Rules for Writers

Most writers respond to criticism in one of two calamitous ways: the Defensive Response and the Submissive Response. In the Defensive Response, the writer fights off everything the reader says and tries to argue the reader out of her reaction, trying to "win" by preserving the draft against the threat of change. In the Submissive Response, the writer assumes that anything the reader says is "right" and slavishly agrees to follow any and all suggestions. Neither response will help you write.

If you're given to the Defensive Response, use the following tools to change your attitude:

**10. Write to do something to your reader,** not to please yourself. Then you'll want to know if the draft worked, and you'll realize only the reader can tell you. It's like hitting a golf ball: It's not a matter of how much you enjoyed the swing, it's a matter of where the ball went.

**11. Ask for peer feedback before you're "done."** If you wait until the project feels finished, you'll fight off advice as a parent fights off criticism of his children. The earlier you ask for feedback from readers, the better.

**12. Show that you know the reader is doing you a favor.** Peer editing is real work, good peer editors are precious and rare, and you need them. Express gratitude before, during, and after the session. An occasional "Thanks, that's a good idea, I can use that" reminds both parties of why you're doing this.

**13. Begin the conversation by asking your reader questions.** Good writers never just hand over the manuscript and say, "Please make it better" or "What do you think?" They ask specific questions about whether decisions they made actually worked: Did you think the title was funny? Is the tone too impersonal? Was the purpose of paragraph 5 clear? Asking questions forces you into the role of the supplicant, the person who wants something. You're needy; the reader is kind enough to meet your need.

**14. Prod your reader to follow the rules for readers listed above.** Ask how the text reads, not what's wrong. Steer the reader away from errors and corrections—and toward virtues and additions. Ask, "What's the biggest fish we have to fry?" Focus on patterns instead of individual glitches. All these strategies will lower your resentment level.

**15. When it's over, say "Thank you."** Remind your editors and yourself that they were doing you a favor.

**16. Wait two days before making any revision decisions.** However saintly we are, it hurts to be told our writing isn't perfect. In time the pain eases, and we're open to learning.

**17. If you're firmly in the grip of the Defensive Response, *forbid yourself to speak.*** Don't argue, explain, or justify what you've written—those are all ways of telling the reader to stifle her feedback. Instead, listen, say "Thank you," let some time pass, and decide what you want to do.

If you're given to the Submissive Response, use the following tools to change your attitude:

**18. Understand why it doesn't work.** The Submissive Response looks "nicer" than the Defensive Response, but it's just as deadly, because it means you're writing for the wrong reasons. You don't write to do what other people want; you write to do something to them you've chosen to do. Thus no one can tell you what to do, since they don't know what you're trying to get by writing. That's why writing is fun. You're in charge. The reader says, "These paragraphs are really choppy," and you say, "Good. Choppiness is just the feeling I wanted."

**19. Memorize the following truism:** *In any critiquing session someone will pick out the best thing in your essay and tell you to get rid of it.* That's because really good bits are unexpected, and some readers dislike anything that disturbs their tranquil slumber.

**20. Wait two days before deciding to follow someone's advice,** and ask yourself, "I know that Sal wants me to do this, but do *I* want to do this?"

**21. Have your work read by several readers.** Each one will want you to "fix" the essay in a different way, and you'll either go mad trying to make them all happy or you'll realize that pleasing readers isn't what writing is about.

## Peer Editing in Groups

Peer editing in groups, like in classes, tends to chaos and fragmentation, so you need some additional guidelines to maintain order:

**22. Raise one issue at a time.** Good students violate this rule with the best of intentions. They come to class with their ducks in a row and want to get on with it, so they start the discussion with a list: "I've got four things I want to say about the draft: First, the thesis is unclear; second, . . ." When the lecture is finished, if you're lucky, someone will address one of the issues on the list and everything else will be forgotten.

**23. Stick to an issue once it's raised.** If someone raises a question about structure, discuss structure until all comments on structure have been heard.

**24.** To make sure this guideline is followed, **make sure that what you say connects with what the previous speaker said.**

**25. Stay with an issue until clarity is reached.** This doesn't mean grind down all opposition until everyone in the room thinks the same thing. It means talk about it until the group figures out where it stands. If there are different opinions in the room, get clear on what they are, who's on what side, and why they feel that way. If the class can't make up its mind, be clear that it can't make up its mind.

During a peer-editing session in one of my classes, one student pointed to a paragraph in the draft and said, "I'd cut that—it doesn't seem to fit." Someone else cried, "No—I thought that was the best part of the essay!" People immediately lined up behind both speakers. Everyone saw the same thing: The paragraph stood out from the rest of the essay as a thing unto itself, and it was interesting, provocative. Half the class wanted to remove it so the essay could go on about its business; the other half wanted to abandon the draft and write a new essay that pursued the richer possibilities in the outsider paragraph. Both solutions were good ones, and the class did a fine job of clarifying the writer's choices for her. Now the writer can decide what she wants to do.

**26. When you agree, say "I agree"; when you disagree, say, "I disagree."** It's easy to talk yourself out of this, because "I agree" seems unnecessary and "I disagree" seems unkind. But it's vital. The writer doesn't really care how *one reader* reacts to the draft; he cares how *readers as a group* react. Nothing is more damaging to a writer than when one quirky reader offers an off-the-wall suggestion and all the sane readers silently scream "No!" but no one says anything. Make a special effort to voice your *disagreement,* since silence implies consent.

**27. Use our organizing tools.** Since group editing is much more fragmented and chaotic than editing one-on-one, you have to work even harder to organize the chaos by doing the things we've already talked about: look for patterns, connect, generalize, and prioritize. Keep saying things like

I think what Will is saying ties in with what Eunice said a few minutes ago.
In different ways, we keep coming back to structural issues.
I'd like to get back to the question of purpose and audience—that seems crucial to me.
So it sounds to me like some of us like the tone and some of us think it's too folksy.

### The Writer's Role in Group Editing

A group needs a leader, and since the writer has the most at stake and knows what he wants, he may as well be it.

This role is fraught with peril. If you can't lead without being defensive, then ask a couple of questions to start things off and say nothing else. But if you have the necessary self-control, you can do yourself a lot of good by following one rule:

**28. Remind the group to follow the rules.** Keep saying things like

How many others agree with Nell?—a show of hands, please.
As long as we're talking about structure, what other structural comments do you have?
So what do you think I should do about it?
Are there other places where that sort of thing happens?
How big a problem is that?
So what does the essay need the most?

## Peer Editing for Mechanics and Grammar

Mechanics and grammar—comma placement, sentence structure, spelling—are legitimate topics in peer editing, but most conversations on those topics turn into useless nitpicking and wrangling that helps the writer hardly at all. So before you bring those topics up, be sure you're practicing some of the chapter's now-familiar rules:

**29. Keep frying the biggest fish first.** Discuss mechanics only in those rare cases where mechanical problems are the overriding issue.

**30. Discuss grammar and mechanics only in general terms.** If the problem isn't habitual, ignore it.

**31. Prioritize all mechanical advice.** Tell the writer how serious the problem is. Are you saying, "Since we've taken care of everything that really matters, we'll tinker with spelling," or are you saying, "My God, we've got to do something about the spelling before we do anything else!"?

# WRITER'S WORKSHOP

## Peer Editing a Peer-Editing Session

Doing something teaches you nothing (p. P-2), so in order to learn from peer editing we need to reflect on what we did.

Let's practice critiquing a critiquing session. Here's a draft. After it I've written out the peer-editing conversation my class had about it. In the margins I've noted when rules were being followed or broken.

### LEGALIZE HEMP: AN ESSENTIAL RESOURCE FOR THE FUTURE

TODD BURKS

Hemp, falsley known to many as marijuana, is an essential resource for the future of the planet. In todays age of environmental awareness is seems silly that we are not taking advantage of such a valuable commodity. Not only would the legalization of hemp save our forests, but it would stimulate the presently ailing economy.

Although both marijuana and hemp are derived from cannabis sativa, you can't get "stoaned" from hemp. You see, hemp is the large stock form while marijuana is the small "budding" form. Unfortunately, negative stigmas have been placed on hemp since marijuana became a popular street drug back in the late thirties. "The flower was said to be the most violent inducing drug in the history of mankind." Those of us who have experimented with the marijuana form Know this to be false.

The legalization of hemp (marijuana) for personnal use does not concern me. However, the legalization of hemp as a valuable resource would alleviate many political, economic, and environmental ills that plague the world.

To begin, hemp legalization would virtually eliminate the need for wood in paper products. Four times the amount of hemp can be grown on an acre of land than wood. The hemp takes only four months until harvesting, compared to nearly ten years for trees. Furthrmore, hemp paper is more durable than wood paper, lasting four times as long, and it's cheaper to produce.

The adaptibility of hemp to many soils and climates would allow for extensive growth worldwide. Unlike many rotation crops that degrade the soil, hemp roots actually permeate the soil, allowing for more productivity.

Hemp seeds could also develop into daily diets around the world. "The hemp seed is the second most complete vegetable protein, second only to soybeans. However, hemp seeds are more easily synthesized by humans due to the high content of enzymes, endistins, and essential amino acids." The seeds can also be used to make margarine and a tofu-like substance.

Almost one-third of the hemp seed is oil. Hemp oil can be used in paints and varnishes, eliminating the need for petrochemical oils. The biodegradeable hemp seed can also be used for diesel fuel and lubricant, causing less environmental pollution.

Finally, the rapid growth rate of hemp makes it the number-one renewable biomass resource in the world. "Biomass is fuel, whether it be petroleum, coal, or hemp." Therefore, hemp can be used in place of fossil fuels. Rather than carbon monoxide hemp gives off carbon dioxide which is naturally synthesized by our atmosphere.

It is obvious that hemp has gotten a bad rap due to the popularity of marijuana as a street drug. Not to mention the false propaganda headed by Hearst and DuPont early in the twentieth cent. However, with todays technology in genetic engineering, we can produce a plant that is purely stalk and is not possible to smoke. Finally, with government regulation and taxation we could virtually wipe out the trillion-dollar deficit hanging over our heads. ❖

Here's the classroom conversation. "Remember to . . ." in the margin indicates the rule is being broken.

*Remember to begin with the writer's questions.*

It seemed like you jumped right into your argument, and you could hold off on that a little more—like in your introduction, explain what hemp is, what you're going to use it for, then start saying, "But this is the reason why it's not being used . . ." *Fry the biggest fish first.*

There was one sentence I'd take out: "Those of us who have experimented with the marijuana form know this to be false." That could weaken your case, because we could say, "Oh, it's a pot smoker, he just wants it legal so he can smoke it." *Remember to stick with an issue once it's raised.*

He says legalization for personal use doesn't concern him, but I think it does concern him, because I don't see how you can start reforesting the fields of hemp for commercial use without some people doing it for personal use too. *Remember to stick with an issue once it's raised.*

He needs to make more of how he just wants to legalize the genetically engineered plants. *Remember to stick with an issue once it's raised.*

A couple of things I thought when I read it: If we have all this hemp, what do we do with the pot? Do we legalize that as well? And this fossil fuel thing: I've heard there's about fifty or so alternatives to replace fossil fuel; the only problem is it's really expensive to do so. *Remember to raise one issue at a time.*

Maybe you could argue, "The fossil fuels are limited, this is replaceable . . ."

That gets around the cost issue.

It ends up you can still grow it in Mexico for a tenth the cost. There's no way we can compete with Third World countries where it grows wild along the road.

As far as throwing out the "those of us" sentence, I don't know. Because obviously in the back of the reader's mind they're saying, "Wait a minute—some people have experimented with it, and I'm sure they have something to say about it." But I think that could be a potentially strong argument.

*Connect with previous comments. If you disagree, say so.*

Everyone seems to agree that the essay should either drop that aside about personal use or develop it more. Let's get a show of hands: How many think it should be dropped? And how many want to develop it? *(Rawlins)* (The vote is to drop it.)

*Stay till consensus is reached.*

Todd, didn't you tell me that it's just the stalk that makes the paper and stuff, so there's no reason to even worry about it being misused as pot?

You can certainly breed out the THC content—they've been intensifying it for twenty years, so I'm sure you can reduce it by the same genetic engineering.

I'm sure if I'm a farmer I'm going to grow hemp when I can grow pot for twenty times the money.

I'm confused about whether hemp and marijuana are the same thing, because in the first sentence you say "hemp, falsely known as marijuana," and in the third paragraph you say "hemp (marijuana)."

*Tell the writer how the text reads to you.*

Well, they're both *Cannabis sativa,* but one is the long stalk form and the other is the flower form. *(Author)*

*Remember not to explain or defend yourself.*

So they're from the same family but two separate plants?

Same plant, different breeding. *(Author)*

That issue seems to be an important one. Does the group agree that that issue needs to be clarified? *(Rawlins)* (Signs of agreement throughout the room)

*Connect, generalize, prioritize.*

I don't understand that bit about Hearst's false propaganda.

*Tell the writer how the text reads to you.*

Don't you remember the "killer weed" business in the fifties?

What's that got to do with Hearst and Du Pont?

At the time hemp was the second biggest crop after cotton, and they were going to use it as an alternative to paper products. Hearst and Du Pont rallied against it, because Du Pont has the patent on sulfuric acid, which breaks down wood into pulp, and Hearst had huge tracts of forest land, so they didn't want hemp to hurt the wood paper market. That's when they started all this reefer madness thing. *(Author)*

That all sounds like great stuff—I'd put it right into the essay. *(Rawlins)*

*Suggest revision strategies.*

I'd just prefer "cent." to be turned into "century."

*Remember to fry the biggest fish first.*

Me, too.

*Say, "I agree."*

How do you spell "stoned"? "S-t-o-n-e-d"?

Is spelling a problem in the essay? *(Rawlins)*

*Prioritize mechanical issues.*

Yes. *(Several voices)*

Like what? *(Rawlins)*

"Falsley." "Personnal." "Furthrmore." *(Several voices)*

Also there are two "finally's." When I hear the word "finally" I think, you know, "finally," so when I hear it again I go "Whoa . . ." I just deleted the last "finally."

You could say "sorta finally" and "really finally."

Before we turn to grammar and mechanics, are there any larger issues anyone wanted to talk about? *(Rawlins)*

*Fry the biggest fish first.*

In the last paragraph when you say "bad rap" I could tell it was your voice. The essay seemed so technical, when I got to "bad rap" I thought, "Gee, it's not so technical anymore."

Are you saying you *like* "bad rap" and want more of it, or that you *don't* and suggest Todd take it out? *(Rawlins)*

*Turn comments into concrete revision suggestions.*

It just seems like a contradiction—it sticks out.

So you'd like the tone to be more consistent. *(Rawlins)*

One question that I have: There are three large quotes in the paper and you don't say where they come from or who said them or anything. They're just kind of there, so . . .

On the first page you talk about "political, economic, and environmental" benefits of hemp. You talk mostly about environmental, and you mention economics at the end, but I really didn't see much about political.

*Remember to stick with an issue once it's raised.*

Is that the thesis of the essay there? Because I thought the end of paragraph 1 was the thesis.

You know, you talk about "negative stigmas" twice, in paragraph 2 and the last paragraph. I wonder if you need to do that.

*Remember to generalize and connect. Several of the comments address structure.*

Should this be two sentences?: "Not to mention the false propaganda headed by Hearst and Du Pont . . ." Maybe it should be a comma.

*Remember to fry the biggest fish first.*

Is punctuation a problem in the essay? *(Rawlins)*

*Prioritize.*

No. *(Several voices)*

You say it can be used for diesel fuel and lubricant . . . I'm sorry, I just don't get that. I don't work on cars.

*Tell the writer how it reads for you.*

I need to know more about hemp roots penetrating the soil. It's not that I don't agree—I'm just not going to buy it until I know what it all means.

I hear several of these comments addressing the same issue: You'd like *more information*—what exactly the roots do to the soil, how exactly hemp and marijuana are different, how hemp can be used for diesel fuel. *(Rawlins)*

*Generalize and connect.*

I've been playing with this sentence in paragraph 2: "You see, hemp is the large stock form, while marijuana is the small 'budding' form." I tried, "While hemp is the large stock form of *Cannabis sativa,* marijuana is the small budding form."

*Remember to fry the biggest fish first.*

You could just cross out "you see," couldn't you?

The only sentence I had trouble with was "The flower was said to be the most violent inducing drug in the history of mankind." I'm not sure what a "violent inducing drug" is.

That's a quote from a book. *(Author)*

*Remember not to defend.*

I still don't understand it.

I think it should be "violence-inducing drug."

Okay, we're nearing the end. What are your biggest and most important suggestions to Todd? *(Rawlins)*

*Generalize and prioritize.*

Explain yourself more—like the roots and the soil.

Make it clearer what the difference between pot and hemp is, and how you can grow one without running the risk of growing the other.

Tell us more about Hearst and Du Pont—that was interesting.

You know, many of your comments relate to structure. For instance, the way the essay talks about stigmas twice, and the two "finally's," and the two thesis sentences, and the way it promises to discuss politics in paragraph 3 but never does. If we were going to restructure, I thought the very first comment of the day gave us a good design: First list the virtues of hemp, then explain why we're prohibited from using it, relate the history, and *then* argue that the ban should be lifted. That suckers the reader into agreeing before he knows what he's in for. (*Rawlins*)

*Connect, generalize.*

**Now it's your turn.** Have a classmate distribute copies of his draft to the class. Peer edit the draft as a group, in the manner of Chapter 10. Then individually write a one-page essay in which you critique the group's performance by answering the following two questions: Which of the chapter's thirty-one rules did the group and the author follow? Which did they break? Then write down two resolutions: What two things are you personally going to do differently the next time you peer edit?

# Chapter 11

# REWRITING FOR STYLE

Now that we've said something and given it shape, it's time to think about style.

Style in writing means exactly what it means in the rest of your life: It's the *how* instead of the *what,* your way of doing things, your manner, your way of expressing yourself. In writing as in life, it's easy to care too much about style and too little about substance—we all sometimes fall into the error of thinking that how our hair looks is the most important thing in the world. So we need to keep style in its place, which is here, after the more important matters of saying something and organizing it have been addressed.

## Style as Clothing

Writing style is like clothing—the decorative covering we put over the content. This tells us everything we need to know about it:

**Style is independent of content.** You can say any message in any style, just as you can put any sort of clothing on any body. Anyone can wear a tutu or a wetsuit or a belly-dancing costume. You may get laughed at or run from, but that's a different issue.

This is the most important lesson about style to learn, because writers defend bad writing by insisting that what they say determines how they say it. "I have to be stuffy and pretentious, because I'm talking about this very serious issue," they say. Never.

**Style is chosen.** You decide what style to use, the way you decide what clothes to wear. Even if you got dressed this morning without thinking about it, you decided. You could have worn something else. You're responsible for the choice.

**You can't *not* choose.** You can't write without style, any more than you can dress in no way at all. Whatever language you use will have a certain sentence length, be passive or active, use Latinate words or avoid them. Doing what's "in" or what everyone else is doing is still a choice. Since you can't not choose, you want to control your choosing.

**Style sends a message.** Some believe it shouldn't be that way, but it's true: the way you use language, like the way you dress, is heard as a message by everyone who sees it. Style, someone famously once said, is the subtlest level of meaning. If you wear your baseball cap backwards, people will assume you're telling them something. If you wear a business suit, people will assume you're telling them something. You can't stop the process, so you want to control it.

**Choose your style for the effect it has on the reader.** There is no good or right style, only styles that produce the response you want in the reader and those that don't. Every day, I decide to dress in the way that I guess will produce the response in my students that I want. I wear a tie, because I guess that they'll see it and say, "This guy is serious and professional about what we're doing." It has nothing to do with my personal taste—I hate wearing ties.

Remember, controlling effect never equals doing what the reader wants. You *may* want to please, but you don't *have to*. You can wear a clown suit, or nothing, to class if you're willing to take the predictable reaction.

**Alternatives equal power.** The more ways I can dress, the more places I can go and the more things I can do. If I can only wear a T-shirt and jeans, I can't go to the ball. If I don't own a wetsuit, I can't go scuba diving. Similarly, the more ways I can write, the more responses I can provoke and the more things I can do with my writing.

**Most of us choose by habit.** We write the way we dress—the way we always do, without thinking about it much. This is giving up our power to choose and thus control our audience.

**Style is where the fun is.** Trying out different words and sentence structures should feel just like playing dress-up or trying on clothes at the mall: it's a game. Try on the clown suit, sample a few wigs, slip into the slinky cocktail dress . . .

## How to Master a Style: Three Steps

Style is a series of *choices:* Do you make the sentences long or short? Do you write in first person or third person? To control a stylistic choice, you have to do three things:

**Believe you have the choice.** Obviously, if you don't know the choice is available to you, you can't make it, so first we must become *style conscious.*

Consciousness comes in two stages. The first stage is realizing that English offers you the options. Sometimes this stage is easy. Everyone knows that English will let you write long sentences or short ones, for instance. Sometimes it isn't so obvious. Not all of us realize that English will let you write passive sentences or active sentences, and almost no one outside the academy realizes that English will let you write Latinate words, Romance words, or Germanic words.

Once you realize that the language offers you the option, Stage Two consists of realizing that you still have the option whatever you're writing about and whatever you're saying. Many writers say, "Sure, I know that English makes it possible to write in concrete language and short sentences, but I can't do it here—I'm writing about serious, sophisticated stuff, so I *need* abstract language and long, complex sentence structure." Any time you tell yourself that your topic or your message dictates your style choice, you're wrong. You can say anything about anything in any style.

**Understand the effect of your choices.** You must know what happens if you do it a certain way. If you make your sentences short, how will readers react? If you make them long, how will they react?

As with all predicting of human behavior, this is an inexact science. If you wear your baseball cap backwards, some people will react with "Oooh, he's cool" and some with "What a doofus." If I wear a tie to work, some students will react with "He's a competent professional" and some with "He's stuffy and boring." As always, expect readers' responses to be a lot like your own: How do *you* feel when you read a lot of short sentences?

**Master the technique.** It's not enough to own the bicycle; you have to learn to ride it.

Let's practice the three steps, using three elements of style: sentence length, Latinate diction, and concretion.

## Sentence Length

**Believe you have the choice.** First we must believe that sentence length is something we can control independent of content. We can prove this to ourselves either by taking a passage of very long sentences and dividing them up (that's easy) or by taking a passage of very short sentences and combining them (that's harder). Here's a passage from a student essay about Buddy Bolden, the legendary blues man, in various sentence lengths from short to very long:

> ***Short*** There are some things historians agree on. Bolden played cornet. No one could play like him. His fellow band members said so. Even Jelly Roll Morton said so. Morton was egocentric. Bolden worked as a barber. He had his own business. By noon, he was working on his second bottle of whiskey. You had to go to him before noon if you wanted a decent hair cut. He gradually went insane. He was committed to a state mental hospital. That was in Louisiana. He was committed in 1907. He died there twenty-four years later. (15 sentences)
>
> ***Medium*** There are some things historians agree on. Bolden played cornet like no one before or after him could do, for one thing. His fellow band members said so. Even Jelly Roll Morton said so, and he was egocentric. Bolden worked as a barber and had his own business. By noon, he was working on his second bottle of whiskey, so you had to go to him before noon if you wanted a decent hair cut. He gradually went insane and was committed to the East Louisiana State Hospital. He was committed in 1907 and died there twenty-four years later. (8 sentences)
>
> ***One sentence*** (which is how the student wrote it) Historians agree that Bolden played the cornet as no one before or after him was able to do (accounts of everyone from fellow band members to the egocentric Jelly Roll Morton confirm this), that he was self-employed as a barber (one to whom—if a decent haircut was important—you went before noon, by which time he was usually working on his second bottle of whiskey), and that he gradually went insane and was committed in 1907 to East Louisiana State Hospital, where he died twenty-four years later.

**Understand the effect of your choices.** Short sentences "feel" lots of different ways: earthy, plain, solid, masculine, childlike, simple-minded, choppy, wise, primitive, honest, blunt. Long sentences "feel" the opposite of all those: sophisticated, intelligent, intellectual, scholarly, clinical, educated, fluid, suave, subtle, deceptive, pretentious. Mid-length sentences feel in the middle. Armed with this knowledge, you can decide how you want to be "felt" and choose a length to produce that feeling.

**Master the technique.** We can all break long sentences into shorter ones, but how do you combine short sentences to make longer ones? Consider a simple pair of sentences:

> I went jogging yesterday. I saw a dead deer.

How many tools does English give us for combining these into one? The best-known is the *conjunction*:

> I went jogging yesterday, *and* I saw a dead deer.

But conjunctions are just the beginning. Consider these possibilities:

> *When* I went jogging yesterday, I saw a dead deer. (dependent clause)
>
> *Jogging* yesterday, I saw a dead deer. (participial phrase)
>
> *During my run* yesterday, I saw a dead deer. (prepositional phrase)
>
> I went jogging yesterday; I saw a dead deer. (semicolon)
>
> I went jogging yesterday, saw a dead deer, and . . . (compound verb)
>
> The dead deer *that I saw* while jogging . . . (relative clause)

Any of these can be combined with any others:

> *When* I saw a dead deer *during* my run yesterday . . . (dependent clause and prepositional phrase)

Now it's just a matter of forcing yourself to use the tools you aren't practiced with. Think like a skater in training: Spend some time practicing axels, then some time practicing figure-eights. Work on turning sentences into participial phrases, then into dependent clauses, and so on.

## Latinate Diction

**Believe you have the choice.** This is the hardest step with this aspect of style, because few people have ever heard of Latinate diction, but it's perhaps the stylistic choice that packs the biggest wallop for readers.

To understand the choice you've been making unconsciously all your life, a brief history lesson: English is a Germanic language, which means it is descended from an ancient parent language spoken in Germany perhaps six thousand years ago. As a result, the ancient root of the vocabulary—words like *good, foot, dirt, water, mother,* and *eat*—are all Germanic and have been in the language from the beginning. These are the words that you learned first when you were growing up, the words you use most often and know the best. Centuries after that Germanic beginning, mostly between 1150 and 1800, English borrowed a lot of words from French and Latin. The French words were brought into English largely by contact with French high culture, so the French vocabulary in English tends to feel arty or genteel: *banquet, dine, fashion, genteel, cuisine, honor, virtue,* and *chef.* Our Latin vocabulary was brought into English by scholars and scientists, who were all reading books in Latin and trying to reform the English vocabulary so it would be as much like what they saw there as possible, so it feels scholarly, scientific, and clinical: *condition, instinctual, relativity, procedure, effective, factor, element, consideration, criterion,* and *process.*

You can say anything in any one of these three vocabularies, Germanic, French, or Latinate. Again, the way to prove this to yourself is to take passages using one of them and rewrite them in another:

> *Germanic:* I saw the guy who I think did it leave the place with two other white guys—I don't know who they were.
> *Latinate:* The alleged perpetrator was observed to exit the premises in the company of two unidentified male Caucasian individuals.
>
> *Latinate:* Violation of any of these statutes will result in immediate and permanent expulsion.
> *Germanic:* If you break any of these rules, we'll kick you out.

**Understand the effect of your choices.** The effect of using French vocabulary turns out to be so minimal that we'll ignore it. But the effect of Latinate and Germanic vocabulary hits readers like a sledge hammer. Since we all learn Germanic vocabulary before we're seven years old, it remains associated with "the basics." Germanic writing feels earthy, strong, honest, childlike, male, "real"—all the things we said about short sentences, in fact. Since we learn our Latinate vocabulary primarily in school, and especially in college, it always feels professorial, intellectual, professionally competent, and fake. In addition, Latinate words are simply *harder* for us to understand, since we learn them later in life, so the more of them you use the harder a reader will have to work to understand you. If we use enough Latinate words, the difficulty of the style out-shouts the content, the same way a wild bow tie distracts us from what someone is saying, and readers end up dazzled and baffled.

This is a very dangerous thing and an omnipresent cancer in our society. The disease goes by many names: BS, bureaucratic English, bureaucratese, political English, Engfish, Pentagonese. Not surprisingly, the people with the most to hide and the greatest need to impress—the government, the military, advertising, the police, politicians, and all bureaucracies, including your college—use it the most.

And we all fall for it. Here's a highly Latinate passage. See how impressed you are by it, and how unimpressive its Germanic revision is?

> *Latinate:* Studies of a significant number of choice situations in the main conclude that when faced with an alternative between an object (either material or abstract) of lesser value and a high degree of certainty of attainment and an object of greater value and a low de-

gree of certainty of attainment, the certainty of the former object renders the object a greater value than the potentially obtainable object. In fact, it has been shown that in cases where the value of the potentially obtainable object exceeded the value of the certainly obtainable object by a factor of two, the uncertainty of attainment still rendered the less valuable object the more profitable choice.

*Germanic:* A bird in the hand is worth two in the bush.

So in the case of this stylistic feature, we can talk about how much is too much. The typical Latinate level of American newspapers is 20%, which means one of every five words on the page is from Latin. Significantly less—10% or lower—will feel earthy or simple when we read it. Significantly more—30% or higher—will feel intellectually impressive and begin to impair our ability to understand. Forty percent Latinity (four of every ten words) is incomprehensible to most of us. So unless you're engaged in an intentional snow job, keep your Latinate level below 30%. But don't strive for a percentile below 10% either, unless you want to sound like a child or a Hollywood Indian.

**Master the technique.** To control your Latinity, you need a way to spot Latinate words when you use them. Here's how it's done:

1. Latinate words are marked by distinctive affixes (prefixes or suffixes). Assume a word is Latinate if it begins or ends with any of the following:
   *Prefixes: a-* (for example, amoral), *ab-, ac-, ad-, ante-, anti-, co-, com-, con-, de-, di-, dis-, e-* (eject), *em-, en-, ex-, il-, im-, in-, ir-, ob-, op-, per-, pre-, pro-, re-, sub-, super-.*
   *Suffixes: -age, -al, -ance, -ant, -ar, -ate, -ence, -ent, -ible, -ic, -id, -ile, -ion, -ite, -ity, -ive, -or, -ous, -tion,* and nouns with *-a* (data), *-is* (crisis), *-ude* (decrepitude), *-um* (datum), *-us* (campus), and *-y* (contingency).
2. Any word whose root can take any of these affixes is also Latinate. So *use* is Latinate because you can add *-al* (*usual*), *close* is Latinate because you can add *dis-*, and *muse* is Latinate because you can add *-ic.*
3. Assume that any word that can't take any of these affixes is Germanic.
4. Make sure the "affix" you're looking at is truly an affix. To do this you must make an informed guess about what part of the word is the *root* (the core or center) and what part is *added to the root* fore or aft. For example, *illogical* is a root *log-* plus the prefix *il-* and the suffixes *-ic* and *-al,* so *illogical*

is Latinate, but *ill* isn't Latinate because *-l** isn't a root. *Dive* isn't Latinate, even though *-ive* is in our list, because *d-** isn't a root. Guessing what's a root and what's an affix comes with experience. Roots are usually syllables and are often words by themselves, but not always.

5. Be suspicious of words using *re-* and *ex-*, because those prefixes can now be stuck on any verb or noun, as in *re-throw* or *ex-husband. Re-* and *ex-* words can only be assumed to be Latinate if the *re- doesn't* mean "again" and the *ex- doesn't* mean "used to be," as in Latinate words *excuse* and *relation.*
6. Ignore any affix that isn't in our list, since it tells us nothing: *-ly, -ing, -ed, -s.*
7. Reduce a word to its simplest form—it makes the categorizing task easier:

| **If you find . . .** | **Simplify it to . . .** |
|---|---|
| swam | swim |
| collects | collect |
| men | man |
| running | run |
| abstractly | abstract |

8. Don't worry about individual problem words. We're only interested in your *habits* here, and one word won't alter the data.
9. You can check any word you're puzzled over by looking in a *etymological dictionary,* a dictionary that gives you word histories, but you don't have to, thanks to Rule 8.

Now we need a way to calculate the level of Latinity in our writing. It's called a *Latinate percentile.* Choose any passage of one hundred consecutive words in your writing. Highlight each and every Latinate word in the passage. Make a column list of all highlighted words. List the words in the order in which they occur in the passage, first Latinate word at the top and last at the bottom. List each word every time it appears—if you use the word "institution" ten times, list it ten times. After each word in the list, put in parenthesis the evidence that made you put it there, like this:

illogical (il-, -ic, -al)

Count the number of words in the column, and write the number below the column, like a total in math. Compare the number to our norms: 10% is low, 20% is normal, 30% high, 45% and above astronomical.

## Concretion

**Believe you have the choice.** Concretions are things you can perceive with the five senses—tastes, smells, sights, sounds, touches. The opposite of concretions are *abstractions:* thoughts, opinions, feelings, ideas, concepts. By extension, in language concretions are words or passages that *evoke* sensation—they make you feel like you're smelling, seeing, and so on, when you read them; abstractions don't. Concretions and abstractions can be nouns, verbs, adjectives, or adverbs.

*Concretions:* swim, jump, door, shoe, nose, crash, prickly, wet, slowly, saunter, trumpet, Hollandaise sauce, CD
*Abstractions:* idea, think, love, wonder, consideration, problem, anger, threaten, perversely, extreme, honest

As with all style features, we begin by convincing ourselves that any message can be said either in concretions or in abstractions. Most writers think that certain writing tasks are inherently concrete, like describing a car crash or showing how to bake a cake, and certain tasks are inherently abstract, like discussing philosophy or religion. To break down that prejudice, take "inherently" concrete or abstract statements and translate them into the opposite style:

*Abstract:* Modern society suffers from alienation.
*Concrete:* All of us walk through this world rubbing shoulders but never really touching.

*Concrete:* The car skidded off the slick macadam, rolled twice, and folded itself around a three-foot-thick oak.
*Abstract:* A terrible accident occurred.

*Abstract:* Gun ownership can lead to the possibility of serious injury.
*Concrete:* If you buy a gun, there's a good chance you'll shoot your foot off.

*Concrete:* His eyes were twitching, his hands were trembling, his brow was coated with sweat, and he kept pacing back and forth mumbling to himself.
*Abstract:* He was nervous.

**Understand the effect of your choices.** Concrete language, because it involves the senses, is *emotionally intense*—it makes us feel. It's *easier to understand,* because humans are primarily feelers, secondarily thinkers. It's *compelling*—we believe it—because we feel like we're getting the facts, the actual evidence, instead of just the opinion. And finally, concretions are *fun,* because feeling is fun.

So where would you ever want to write abstractly? In school, where teachers are trying to get you to master abstract thought. In places where you want to remain rational and concretions would reduce the conversation to an emotional brawl, as in discussions of volatile issues like race or abortion. In places where clinical objectivity is a must, as in medical writing or reporting on scientific experiments. When you're applying for government grants, and you want to appear as professorial as possible. So as always you need both styles.

**Master the technique.** To control our concretion level, we first must be sure we can distinguish between concrete and abstract on the page. Begin by asking if you can perceive it with your senses. Be careful: we tend to say things like "I could *see* she was angry," but in fact you can't—you can hear that someone is shouting, see she's red in the face, and feel she's beating you with her fists, so those are all concretions, but anger is a *conclusion* you draw from the concrete data, so anger is an abstraction. And don't assume that if the word makes you feel, then it's concrete—lots of abstract ideas, like *racism* or *Christianity,* evoke strong feelings.

There are other measuring sticks:

Most concretions are visual, so ask yourself if you can *draw* the word—if so, it's concrete.

Ask yourself, "How do I know?" If you say, "The door is red" and ask yourself how you know, the only possible answers are "Because I looked" or "Because I have eyes." When you find the "How do I know?" question producing only obvious or silly answers like this, you're dealing with a concretion. But if I say, "America is becoming more uncivil" and ask myself how I know, I realize I need *evidence* to back that up, and that's a sign that I've got an abstraction.

Imagine you're serving on a jury and a witness makes a statement under oath. If the attorney can ask the witness to back up the statement with evidence or proof, it's an abstraction; if not, it's a concretion.

Once you know for sure whether a passage is concrete or not, how do you make it concrete if it isn't? Here are eleven ways.

**1. Ask, "What's my evidence? How do I know?"** and write down the answers. You write, "He loves me," ask how you know, and write down, "He leaves little love notes on Post-Its in secret places, like in my physics class notebook, so I discover them when I'm in class."

**2. Ask, "Who's doing what to whom?"** Talk in terms of *people.* Almost everything you write is about humans doing things—express it in those terms. "Practice charity" becomes "Hand the next homeless person you see ten dollars." "The usage of a dictionary is encouraged" becomes "I encourage teachers to use a dictionary."

J. M. Barrie, who wrote *Peter Pan,* knew the power of people, so *Peter Pan* begins with this note:

> Do you know that this book is part of the J. M. Barrie "Peter Pan Request"? This means that J. M. Barrie's royalty on this book goes to help the doctors and nurses to cure the children who are lying ill in the Great Ormond Street Hospital for Sick Children in London.

People appear in those two sentences eight times: you, J. M. Barrie, Peter Pan, J. M. Barrie, doctors, nurses, children, and sick children. Take the people out, and the loss hits you like a chill wind:

> All royalties from the sale of this book are donated to further medical research in pediatrics and to help defer the cost of indigent pediatric medical care.

**3. Use "I" and "you."** You and the reader are the two concretions you've always got.

**4. Let people talk.** All quotations are concrete, because they're *heard*. Quote the speech of the people you mention, even if you have to invent it.

**5. Concretize your verbs.** Verbs are the parts of speech most likely to go abstract, so we want to focus on them and force them to concretize. Abstract verbs are like *is, are, continue, accomplish, effect, involve, proceed, utilize, initiate, remain,* and *constitute.* Concrete verbs run, jump, smell, fall, shrink, and fly.

**6. Particularize your concretions.** Some concretions are better than others—more emotive, more colorful. *Move* is colorless; *slither* is colorful. The difference is one of *particularity*. To particularize a word, ask yourself, "In what way did it happen?" or "What kind of thing was it?"

| Less lively | More lively |
|---|---|
| move | slither, slink, sashay, saunter, crawl, skip |
| car | ragtop, four-door, SUV, lowrider |
| horse | pinto, Clydesdale, swayback plow horse |
| hairdo | mullet, cornrows |

Particulars have an amazing persuasiveness, as every good salesperson knows: The more particulars, the more we're *sold* on what we read. When I read an ad for a powerboat that says,

> Kurtis Kraft 10-inch runner bottom, blown injected, 1/4-inch Velasco crank, Childs and Albert rods, Lenco clutch, Casale 871 Little Field blower, Enderle injection,

I don't know what any of that means, but I can't help thinking, "It must be a great boat!"

**7. Tell stories.** Narratives encourage concretion, because they're usually about things *people did*.

**8. Use the active voice.** Passive constructions make the people disappear. In an *active* sentence, the doer is the subject: "George broke the chair." A *passive* construction—a form of *to be* plus a past participle—doesn't need to mention the doer at all: "The chair was broken."

There is one large exception to this rule. In scientific and technical writing, if you are describing a process—a step-by-step series of events—then *what was done* is all that matters and *who did it* is a distraction, so use the passive voice. Write, "The surface liquid was drained off and the residue transferred to a sterile petri dish"; don't write, "One of my lab assistants, Pippi Carboy, drained off the surface liquid and Lance Credance, a post-doctoral fellow who shares the lab, transferred the residue to a sterile petri dish."

**9. Use metaphors.** A metaphor is an implied comparison. Instead of stating an abstraction, you state a concretion the abstraction is *like*. That sounds intimidating, but in fact you use metaphors ten thousand times a day. Instead of saying to your roommate, "Your living habits are filthy and revolting," you say, "You're a pig." You can't articulate clearly on a sleepy Monday morning, and instead of saying, "My mental processes are impaired," you say, "I can't jumpstart my brain." Instead of saying, "That rock band is out of date," you say, "They're dinosaurs."

Everyday English is stiff with metaphors. In the world of sports, for instance, teams lock horns, fold, choke, run out of gas, get snakebit, and look over their shoulder. Players press too hard, go flat, carry teams, get swelled heads, rest on their laurels, and coast. Quarterbacks pick defenses apart and have to eat the ball, and pitchers throw smoke, pull the string, and nibble at the corners. But the best metaphors are the ones you make up yourself. An interviewer once asked Charlton Heston what Cecil B. DeMille, the legendary Hollywood director, was like, and Heston replied, "He cut a very large hole in the air." It hit me like a brisk breeze in the face.

To make up a metaphor, you just take the abstraction and ask yourself, "What physical process is this like? What do I see when I try to visualize it? How does it feel in the body? How would I draw it?"

Having your boyfriend terminate your relationship feels like getting your heart ripped out and handed to you; you imagine him booting you out the door and you landing on your butt on the pavement; and so on.

**10. Use similes.** A simile (pronounced "SIMMalee") is a metaphor with the comparison spelled out with the word *like* or *as:*

> Writing unrhymed poetry is *like playing tennis without a net.*
>
> *(Robert Frost)*

> While her mind had wandered, her eyes had gone on reading, dutifully moving from word to word *like well-trained horses through a haylot.*
>
> *(John Gardiner)*

Students are more comfortable with similes than with metaphors because they're easier to spot.

**11. Substitute examples.** When you find an abstraction, ask yourself, "What's a concrete example of that?", and replace the abstraction with the example. On a TV show I heard Stanley Kramer, the movie director, talking about how he financed his first movie. Straight out of the army, knowing no one and nothing about getting financial backing, he walked into a bank and asked for the money. Kramer wanted to say, "I'd never been in a bank before except to conduct minor personal financial transactions." But being an entertainer, he knew how dull that would sound, so he said, "I'd never been in a bank before except to *take out twenty dollars.*" He was really saying something like, "I'd never been in a bank before except to (do things like, for example,) take out twenty dollars."

When Robin Lee Graham, who sailed around the world when he was sixteen and wrote a book about it, explains why he loved sailing, he might have said, "Sailing was a chance to escape from all the meaningless busywork of my life." Instead he says,

> It was the chance to escape from blackboards and the smell of disinfectant in the school toilet, from addition and subtraction sums that were never the same as the teacher's answers, from spelling words like "seize" and "fulfill" and from little league baseball.

The Bible loves to illustrate abstract lessons with concrete examples. It won't say, "Be generous with others"; it will say, "Take your bread and divide it in half and give half to a stranger."

We've mastered three stylistic features, but we're just getting started. We can use the same three steps to master dozens or hundreds of others that remain. For instance:

Do you use adjectives rarely or often?
Do you ever use dashes? Semicolons? Parentheses?
Do you use the active voice or the passive voice?
Which carry the weight, your nouns or your verbs?
Do you use the first person, "I," or the third person?
Do you use contractions (*can't*) or full forms (*can not*)?
Do you use slang or Standard English?

The world of style is all before you. Have fun exploring.

## EXERCISES

1. Rewrite the following passages into shorter sentences without changing content. Then rewrite them into the longest clear, grammatical sentences you can make. Keep the word total roughly the same.

   a. I got mostly A's and a few B's all through high school and have managed, for the most part, to do the same in college. I'm sure that most people, when they hear that, are thinking, "That means she's really smart." Well, I'm not stupid, but I don't know nearly as much as people think I know. I just learned how to pass tests. I got an A in history, but I couldn't tell you where the first battle of the Civil War was fought. I got an A in geometry, but I couldn't in a million years tell you the area of a circle. There are many things I "learned" that have vanished from my memory, thanks to some flaws in the teaching system.
   b. Ryan changed every concept that I held about myself as a mother and a person. He changed my views about parenthood, children, and personality. He showed me that children are not simply empty slates awaiting impression; they are active participants in their environment, making their own imprints on the world, evoking response from their caregivers. I have had to redefine my goals as a parent, and recognize that infants are born with distinct personalities intact. My job is to guide what is there by nature, not create the perfect person with my superior nurturing skills. I have less power than I thought. All those simple absolutes about who I am—

I'm not a spanker, for instance—now seem open to debate and dependent on context.

2. Analyze the long-sentence version you wrote in Exercise 1 to see how you did it: List all the *devices* you used to add sentences together (p. 167).

3. Combine each pair of sentences in as many different ways as possible. After each, write which grammatical device you used—e.g., "conjunction" (see p. 167).

a. I am studying to become a parent. The issue of discipline has suddenly become very important to me.
b. I was determined to do my best. I read books on the subject.
c. I couldn't ride my bike. The tire was flat.
d. Teachers should use interviews to measure how much students learn. They shouldn't use multiple-choice tests.
e. The air was filled with smoke. It blistered my lungs.

4. Here are two passages:

**Passage A.** Academic excellence has been achieved through a distinguished faculty whose primary responsibility is superior instruction. While each campus has its own unique geographic and curricular character, all campuses, as multipurpose institutions, offer undergraduate and graduate instruction for professional and occupational goals as well as broad liberal education.

**Passage B.** The center's major objective is the construction of effective theories that will result in significant conceptual and practical impact on composition pedagogy as well as stimulation of further research.

Do the following things to each passage:

a. Calculate its Latinate percentile.
b. Rewrite the passage in as low a Latinate percentile as you can.
c. Calculate the Latinate percentile of your rewrite passage.

5. Write a parody of one of these old saws in as Latinate a style as you can, like we did on pp. 168–169:

a. Don't count your chickens before they're hatched.
b. Too many cooks spoil the broth.

6. For each of the words below, decide if it's Latinate or not. If it's Latinate, give as many proofs as possible for your decision.

a. act
b. consider

c. real
d. understand
e. three
f. use
g. door
h. city

7. Concretize the following sentences by using the eleven concretizing tools beginning on p. 172:

a. Drunk driving needs to become less socially acceptable.
b. The drug traffic should be ignored, so law enforcement can concentrate on more important matters.
c. Graduation from high school is almost mandatory for avoiding menial labor jobs in later life.
d. The potential of large underdeveloped lands and the intensification of farming areas currently being cultivated are the sources of multiplying the output of the world's food supply.

8. Replace the following concretions with more *particular* concretions (p. 173):

a. dog
b. car
c. walk
d. talk
e. red

9. Identify the following as concrete or abstract:

a. beekeeper
b. air
c. university
d. presentation
e. anger
f. three
g. one o'clock
h. sore
i. family

10. Highlight all the concretions on a single page from one of your essays. Take the paragraph with the fewest concretions and rewrite it as concretely as possible.

11. Write an essay in which you go through the three steps of mastering a stylistic feature with one of the following features:

a. contractions
b. colorful verbs

12. Write a short essay describing your own writing style. How do you usually write? Do you have more than one style? If so, where do you use each? Consider sentence length, Latinity, contractions, concretions, energetic vs. dull verbs, fragments, and slang, but don't limit yourself to these elements.

# Chapter 12

## EDITING

Finally, it's time to go over the text line by line looking for rule-following problems. This isn't just more of Chapter 11. There, we tried to make our sentences *effective;* here we're trying to make them *legal.*

## Getting the Editing Attitude

The trickiest part of editing is doing it for the right reasons. To do that, embrace the following six principles:

**1. Editing is not writing.** Many people believe that if you follow all the mechanical rules, you're writing well. That's like believing that if you're never off-sides, you must be a great football player.

In fact, writing is the original multitasking activity, which is why it's challenging. To write, you must have thoughts, express them, organize them, polish your language, clarify your thesis, be aware of your audience, and follow mechanical rules. In this corporation, you do all the jobs, from executive to mailroom.

**2. Editing is different from creating.** A writer's tasks fall into two groups, creative tasks and obedience tasks. Everything we've done so far in Chapters 1–11 is creative, and rules have been something we've chosen to follow or not (p. 68). Now we have to become obedient little rule-followers. That means we literally have to shift into a different part of our brains.

If you don't make that shift, you can't edit. If you try to create and correct at the same time or try to edit out of your creative brain, all that will happen is that the creative brain will rule and you won't edit. That's why every publishing house employs line-editors, people who do nothing but line-edit and who aren't allowed to tinker with the creative side. So follow their lead, and create a step in the writing process when you redefine yourself as a line-editor and then *edit, and only edit*. Obviously this line-editing step must come dead last, since if you do anything else afterward you'll have to line-edit again.

**3. Editing is screen cleaning.** Most of us line-edit for the wrong reasons: 1) so readers won't misunderstand us; 2) so editors will read us; 3) so readers won't think we're fools; and 4) to show respect for the English language. Of these, the first is not true, the second begs the question, and the last two make us write out of fear and timidity. The healthy answer, the only one that makes us stronger, is *edit to make the TV screen disappear*. Think of the printed page as a TV screen. Your message is the TV show behind the tube. You want all the viewer's attention going to the show, and none to the glass screen itself. You want the screen to *disappear,* so that the viewer looks *through* it to what's behind it. Now imagine the screen is dirty and covered with specks and streaks. The viewer's eyes will be snared by the mess and distracted from the image behind it. That's what you're trying to prevent. Misspelled words, invented punctuation, or never-before-seen sentence structure call attention to themselves. You want 100 percent of the reader's attention on what you're saying. Trai reed-ign tHis, sentecne and yew'l see wut ii; meat. Every mechanical oddity is a tiny tug on the reader's sleeve pulling her focus away from your content.

That's why rule-following gets you no credit by itself—if you do your work well no one notices. No TV producer can become famous simply for cleaning the glass on the TV screen, and no writer ever got rich off his splendid spelling. Yet that's also why mechanics are vital: If the viewer can't see through the screen, it doesn't matter how creative your TV show is.

This model helps us stay clear of all the emotional and ego-centered issues surrounding rule-following. It isn't about knuckling under to the Man, or being judged, or jumping through hoops, or not looking stupid. It's just about eliminating distractions and keeping the force of your message undiluted.

**4. Mechanics are learned by exposure and feedback.** Chapter 1 says you're not going to learn mechanics by reading a book, listening to a lecture, or having someone circle all your mistakes. Instead, use exposure and feedback—in other words, read a lot and find a tutor. But only one kind of feedback helps. It must be on your own writing, it must be in language you understand, and it must help you accomplish something you value. So sit down with a mentor (probably your instructor) and an essay of yours you really want others to read, and talk through each mechanical correction, with you explaining why you did what you did and the mentor explaining a new way to think about it. Most people need about three hour-long sessions.

**5. Stripping to the skeleton makes mechanics easy(er).** Most of us write problematic sentences, not because we don't know the rules, but because when the sentences get complex we can't see how the rules apply. Nobody would write *"It's a problem for I," but lots of people do write *"It's an ongoing problem for my husband Andy and I." The problem is simple busy-ness, and you fix it by simplifying the sentence until you can see what is basically going on. Strip the sentence down to its skeleton—its basic framework—and ask if the skeleton looks good by the rules you already know. If *"It's a problem for I" is illegal, then *"It's an ongoing problem for my husband Andy and I" is illegal, and we fix both sentences the same way, by changing *I* to *me.* (The asterisk in front of the sentence, which you'll see throughout this chapter, means the sentence is illegal.)

To strip to the skeleton, toss out all the unnecessary parts of the sentence: prepositional phrases, all adjectives, all adverbs, all introductory phrases. Reduce compound verbs to simple verbs. Keep tossing until you see if the core is solid or not:

> *I'm not so knowledgeable about computers that when problems are presented to me that I instantly find solutions.
>
> Skeleton: *I'm not so knowledgeable that that I find solutions.
>
> Rewrite: *I'm not so knowledgeable about computers that when problems are presented to me I instantly find solutions.*

> *Spearguns come in two forms: the kind that you cock and fire by pulling the trigger (this kind has better range). The other kind is called a Hawaiian Sling, which doesn't fire by a trigger and is usually cheaper and more simple.
>
> Skeleton: *Spearguns come in two forms: the kind you cock and fire.
>
> Rewrite: *Spearguns come in two forms: the kind you cock and fire by pulling the trigger (this kind has better range) and the kind called a Hawaiian Sling, which has no trigger and is usually cheaper and simpler.*

*Which* problems frequently need this sort of work, and they need an extra step. Take the *which* clause by itself, replace the *which* with a personal pronoun, and reorder the words to make a sentence:

> *The Board has set two ground rules which only one must be followed by manufacturers.
>
> Skeleton of the *which* clause: *Only one they must be followed by manufacturers.
>
> Rewrite: *The board has set two ground rules, only one of which must be followed by manufacturers.*

*Children aren't familiar with print and it becomes a challenge to them, a problem in which they can and must make sense of.

Skeleton of the *which* clause: *They can make sense of in it.

Rewrite: *Children aren't familiar with print and it becomes a challenge to them, a problem they can and must make sense of.*

**6. Ultimately, mechanics can't be explained.** The rules are more complex than words can say. Consider the commas in these two pairs of examples:

A tall, handsome, unmarried stranger

A typical pushy American tourist

Why commas in the first sentence and none in the second? It's almost impossible to put into words, so *all handbook rules lie by oversimplification*, including the ones in this chapter. In the end, the only thing that will steer you right is a sense of how English "goes," and *that* you get from years of reading.

## "Grammar"

The rules we call "grammar" combine at least three different sets of rules: conventions, rules of logic, and rules of clarity. It's helpful to keep the three separate, since we master each in a different way.

### Conventions

Language is conventional. Conventions are rules that can't be figured out or explained—they're just "the way it's done." Unless you're learning English for the first time, you already know at least one set of English conventions—the set used by your parents or peer group—and the only question is whether you need to learn additional ones. Any convention is as good as any other as long as everyone in the group agrees to abide by it, so there's nothing wrong with the ones you know or better about the ones you're trying to learn.

Most of us know the conventions of Colloquial English (CE), but the conventions of formal Essay English (EE) are occasionally different:

CE: Everybody has to bring *their* own pencil and paper.
EE: Everybody has to bring *his* own pencil and paper.

CE: Try *and* get some rest before the big game.
EE: Try *to* get some rest before the big game.

CE: *Can* I go now?
EE: *May* I go now?

CE: *Who* is this intended *for*?
EE: *For whom* is this intended?

Since no one can explain conventions to us, the only way to learn them is by hanging out with the group. If you want to learn the conventions of Essay English, read a lot of essays. There is no alternative.

### Rules of Logic

Some people think that all grammar is logical. We now know better, because conventions have no logic, but there is a small pocket of grammar that is logic-based.

All of the following examples are illogical.

*Q: Do you mind if I sit here? A: Sure.

*That's a very unique sweater.

*He won't do nothing about it.

*I could care less if he quits.

*I need alot of attention right now.

Here are the logic problems:

"Sure" must logically mean "I do mind!"

*Unique* means "unlike everything else," so it's logically impossible to be *very* unlike something—either it's unlike or it isn't.

If he won't do nothing, then logically he must do something.

If you could care less, then logically you must care some.

*Lot* is a noun and *a* its article, so there must be a space between them.

The heart of language logic is consistency, which grammar calls *parallelism:* Once you start doing it one way, you must keep doing it that way:

If you're making a list and the first item in the list is a verb, make all the items in the list verbs; if it's a participle, make all the items participles. The same goes for nouns, adjectives, full sentences—anything.

If you start telling a story in the past tense, stay in the past tense.

If you start talking about *parents* in the plural, stay in the plural.

If you start referring to a hypothetical person as *her/him,* continue calling her/him *her/him.*

The four most common parallelism problems are unparallel lists, tense changes, subject–verb agreement problems, and noun–pronoun agreement problems.

**Unparallel lists.**

*I gained organization and speaking skills, along with thinking quick.

The first item in the list is "skills," which are things you possess; the second item is "thinking," which is an action. Things you *have* aren't parallel with things you *do*. You could fix it in several ways:

Rewrite: *I gained organization and speaking skills, along with the ability to think quickly,*

or

*I gained the ability to organize, speak well, and think quickly,*

or

*I got good at organizing, speaking, and thinking quickly.*

**Tense changes.** The law of parallelism says, Stay in the same verb tense unless your meaning has shifted tense too.

*A spelling game *may* excite the children and make learning fun. The class *will be* split in half. The first half *will* continue reading and writing while the second half *plays* the game. The group playing the game *would* line up across the room. Each child *is* given a chance to roll a set of dice.

Here's a revision in present tense:

Rewrite: *A spelling game can excite the children and make learning fun. Split the class in half. The first half continues reading and writing while the second half plays the game. The group playing the game lines up across the room. Each child is given a chance to roll a set of dice.*

**Subject–verb agreement.** Subjects and verbs are supposed to agree in number—they should both be singular or both be plural. Most agreement problems occur when the subject and verb get separated by distracting business in between:

*If a child is made to write on a topic of little interest to him, the *chances* of his learning anything from the experience *is* slim.

Rewrite: *If a child is made to write on a topic of little interest to him, the chances of his learning anything from the experience are slim.*

*The price of letter-quality printers have fallen dramatically.

Rewrite: *The price of letter-quality printers has fallen dramatically.*

**Pronoun agreement.** Pronouns *refer to* nouns: In "George said he could," *he* refers to "George." A pronoun has to follow four rules. The noun it refers to must be physically present on the page. The noun must *precede* the pronoun. The noun must be the *first* noun you reach, reading back from the pronoun, that can logically be the pronoun's referent. And the pronoun and noun must *agree in number:* They must both be singular or plural. Colloquial English violates the fourth rule in two cases:

1. Pronouns like *anyone, anybody, everybody, no one,* and *nobody* are logically singular, so possessive pronouns that refer to them must also be singular:

   *Everybody has to bring *their* own juice.

   Rewrite: *Everybody has to bring her own juice.*

2. Anonymous single people ("a student," "a parent") need singular pronouns:

   *The key to writing success is choosing subject matter *the child* is familiar with and a vocabulary level *they* are familiar with.

   Rewrite: *The key to writing success is choosing subject matter the child is familiar with and a vocabulary level he is familiar with.*

**The limits of logic.** The only problem with approaching language logically is that it often doesn't work—logic will talk you into error almost as often as it will help you out of it. Here are two examples.

1. Essay English disapproves of *"A crowd of people are outside," because *crowd* is a singular noun and requires a singular verb: We should write "A crowd of people *is* outside." But if that's so, then, since *lot* is also a singular noun, it too should take a singular verb, so we must write *"A lot of people *is* outside," which is nobody's English.
2. "It's raining" violates the first three rules of pronoun usage above, but everyone agrees it's good English.

So remember, *convention always trumps logic*—if the two are in conflict, be guided by convention.

## Rules of Clarity

**Pronoun reference.** Some language rules try to prevent confusion and misreading. We've already mentioned one set: the rules governing pronoun use above, which are designed to prevent confusion like this:

> *I placed my order at a counter *that* looks like a regular fast-food restaurant. (The counter looks like a restaurant?) *It* is partially blocked off so *it* didn't bother me while I was eating. (The restaurant is blocked off? What didn't bother you?) After I ordered and paid for *it,* I sat down. (What did you pay for?)
>
> Rewrite: *I placed my order at a counter that looks like the counter in any fast-food restaurant. It's partially blocked off so I wasn't bothered by sights of food cooking while I was eating. After I ordered and paid for my food, I sat down.*

**Misplaced modifiers.** A *modifier* is any word, phrase, or clause that modifies (roughly, "tells you something about") a noun or verb. When words modify other words, make sure the reader is in no doubt about which words modify what. Most of the time it's obvious and there's no problem: If I say "As the sun was sinking in the west, the tall Texan slowly lowered himself onto the stool," *tall* modifies *Texan,* and *slowly, onto the stool,* and *as the sun was sinking in the west* all modify the verb *lowered.* But modifiers get unclear in two positions.

First, when a modifier ends a sentence, it can be hard to tell which preceding noun or verb the modifier refers to:

> *County Sheriff Wayne Hamilton this morning discussed the problems of lodging in the jail unconscious people suspected of being drunk with the Jefferson County Commissioners.

"With the Jefferson County Commissioners" modifies some verb, but we can't tell which one, so the sentence ends up implying that people are getting drunk with the Commissioners. To solve the problem, *move the modifier*:

> Rewrite: *County Sheriff Wayne Hamilton this morning discussed with the Jefferson County Commissioners the problems of lodging in the jail unconscious people suspected of being drunk.*

Second, when a modifier begins a sentence, it's often unclear what part of the sentence it refers to, so Essay English lays down a rule that it must always refer to the subject of the sentence. If the modifier refers to some other word in the sentence, the problem is called a *misplaced modifier,* and you have to *move the thing being modified to the subject position*:

*As a future teacher, censorship seems to me to be an overblown issue.

Rewrite: *As a future teacher, I think censorship is an overblown issue.*

But if the thing being modified is nowhere on the page, it's a *dangling modifier* and you have to *add the implied subject:*

*Despite having spent $1.3 billion since 1992 on county jails, the need for more jail cells is still strong.

Rewrite: *Despite having spent $1.3 billion since 1992 on county jails, we still need more jail cells.*

## Punctuation

People often think of punctuation as a guide to reading *rhythm*—a set of instructions about where and how long to pause. There's some truth in that. Consider the following four sentences, all correct, all read a little differently:

George the gardener was arrested yesterday.

George, the gardener, was arrested yesterday.

George—the gardener—was arrested yesterday.

George (the gardener) was arrested yesterday.

But punctuation is a guide to pausing only about 10 percent of the time; otherwise it's a guide to *syntax*—a set of instructions about the grammatical structure. The capital letter beginning every sentence is saying, "New sentence begins here." The colon is saying, "We just finished an independent clause and are about to start a list." The dread consequence of this is that in order to see where the squiggles go, you must understand how your sentence is put together—you must know when you're ending one independent clause and beginning another, for instance. Sorry about that.

### The Comma

The comma is the all-purpose mark that says, "An infinitesimal interruption or pause goes here." It's the most common punctuation mark, it does the most jobs, and it's the most loosely defined, so it's also the hardest to master. Ninety percent of all punctuation errors are comma placement errors. To confuse things further, commas are often optional:

After working all day we'd all pile into George's old pickup.

After working all day, we'd all pile into George's old pickup.

Commas do four main chores:

**The introductory comma.** Commas mark when a long introduction is over and the main clause begins:

After the town had been battered by high winds for seven straight days, the rains came.

If the introductory bit is short, the reader probably won't need the comma's guidance, and you can leave it out:

After dinner I went to bed.

**The conjunctive comma.** Commas mark when one independent clause ends and a conjunction begins another:

The rage swept through him like the angel of death, and he stooped and picked up the knife.

The loss of Flanagan will certainly hurt our offense, but we've devised some trick plays to make up for that.

As with the introductory comma, this comma can be dropped if the clauses are short and the reader is unlikely to get lost:

The rage swept through him and he picked up the knife.

**Parenthetical commas.** Commas *surround* parentheticals—that is, phrases or clauses that interrupt the flow of the sentence. They come *in pairs,* like parentheses:

He stood over Ragnalf, sword drawn, and exulted.

I backed the old Rolls, inch by inch, into the narrow parking space.

My friend, my best friend, just lied to me.

Parentheticals have to be *felt*—there is no hard rule about what's parenthetical and what isn't:

Sometime after 3:00 A.M. he staggered slowly across the lawn.

Sometime after 3:00 A.M. he staggered, vomiting, across the lawn.

Lots of little things are conventionally treated as interruptions even though they don't feel very interruptive, and you should just memorize the fact that they're surrounded by commas: names in direct address, states or countries after cities, years after days, exclamations:

Bill, will you tell Harry that, uh, that guy out in Cleveland, Ohio, needs that stuff by March 13, 2004, or we're in trouble. Oh, damn, I already told him.

**Series commas.** Commas punctuating a series of *three or more* go between each pair, including the last one:

He turned slowly, sensually, and seductively.

Generations of students were taught to leave that last comma out, and newspapers may not include it, but formal essays put it in.

### Things Commas *Don't* Do

Beyond putting commas where they belong, you have to make sure you don't put them where they don't belong.

First, commas do not go between a subject and its verb, even if the subject is huge:

*The reason why I didn't tell you about cracking up the car and having to spend the night in jail, is that I simply forgot.

Rewrite: *The reason why I didn't tell you about cracking up the car and having to spend the night in jail is that I simply forgot.*

Second, commas do not go between conjunctions and their following clauses:

*I never showed up because, my parents wouldn't let me have the car.

Rewrite: *I never showed up because my parents wouldn't let me have the car.*

Third, commas do not go between two sentences with no conjunction:

*The teacher cannot teach children to read or write, this can only be learned through doing it yourself.

Rewrite: *The teacher cannot teach children to read or write; this can only be learned through doing it yourself.*

*Go to the top row and carefully remove the plug wire, the little cap just pulls off if you put enough effort into it.

Rewrite: *Go to the top row and carefully remove the plug wire—the little cap just pulls off if you put enough effort into it.*

That no-no is called a *comma splice*—the splicing together of two sentences with only a comma. It gets a huge amount of attention in school and from some readers outside school, so it's worth learning to avoid. Say to yourself, "A comma isn't big enough to join sentences by itself;

I need more." *Don't reword the sentence*; replace the comma with a semicolon, colon, or dash, or keep the comma and add a conjunction.

A popular comma splice is the *however* comma splice:

> *I'd really like to come, however my scheduling just won't allow it.
>
> Rewrite: *I'd really like to come; however, my scheduling just won't allow it.*

*However* (and words like it—*nevertheless, therefore*) is really an *adverb*. Since it's not a conjunction, it and a comma can't join independent clauses. You need a semicolon.

Fourth, commas do not go between *pairs* joined by conjunctions, except pairs of sentences:

> *He stooped with an air of graceful insouciance, and picked up something shiny from the gutter.
>
> Rewrite: *He stooped with an air of graceful insouciance and picked up something shiny from the gutter.*

Fifth, commas do not surround "anything that can be taken out of the sentence." Use your oral reading sense to tell you where there's a sense of interruption or turning aside:

> The Boston Red Sox, who are my favorite team, seem determined to break my heart.
>
> The Boston Red Sox who trashed that reporter's car should be heavily fined.

Finally, commas don't go "where you breathe." Sometimes they do, but it's a rule that will lead you astray as often as it pays off.

## The Semicolon

The semicolon does three things:

**The antithetical semicolon.** This semicolon joins sentences that are halves of a balanced pair—an *antithesis*. It says, "Don't think the thought is over just because the sentence is over. Keep reading; you're really only half done":

> Personal writing isn't trying to sell you anything; it's just trying to share a part of the writer's life.
>
> If it's above 70 degrees, he's too hot; if it's below 70 degrees, he's too cold.

You'll know the semicolon is right *if a comma feels right, but you realize that would produce a comma splice.*

**The series semicolon.** Semicolons join a series of short sentences that have this same feeling of "read me all at once":

> Nobody came. George was too tired; Suzy was held up at the office; Leroy forgot.

**The postcolon semicolon.** Semicolons show up in lists following colons, when the items in the list get so large that they have punctuation of their own:

> They arrested three of our boys: Bill, Lars, and Sven.
>
> They captured three of our boys: Bill, whose leg wound had started to bleed again; Lars, the one with the eye patch; and, worst of all, Sven.

### Things Semicolons *Don't* Do

Semicolons do not join sentences and following fragments—use a colon or dash instead:

> *There is only one reason why the new sex education program will never succeed; parental objections.
>
> Rewrite: *There is only one reason why the new sex education program will never succeed: parental objections.*

### The Colon

The colon comes *after a sentence* and announces that what follows will list or enumerate something the sentence *promised* but didn't specify:

> Every time we try to make the relationship work, we run up against the same two obstacles: my personality and her personality.
>
> There are three secrets to a successful business: location, location, and location.

Many people say a colon precedes a list, which is OK as long as you remember that it can be a list of one:

> She knew what she needed: chocolate.
>
> He suddenly had a wonderful idea: Why not hold the show right here?

### Things Colons *Don't* Do

Colons do not follow sentence fragments. When you feel the urge to do that, either use no punctuation or rewrite the opening so it's a sentence:

> *The three main problems facing the Middle East today are: poverty, Iraq, and religious fanaticism.

Rewrite: *The three main problems facing the Middle East today are poverty, Iraq, and religious fanaticism.*

or

*The Middle East today faces three main problems: poverty, Iraq, and religious fanaticism.*

## The Dash

The dash is the most loosely defined punctuation mark there is, so lots of teachers don't want you to use it at all. It's nothing more than a big pause. Use it when you come to a halt in the midst of a sentence and neither a semicolon nor a colon fits.

Most dashes come in two places. The first is between a sentence and a following fragment:

> He either had to say yes or tell her why not—a hopeless situation.
>
> It's already raining outside—pouring, in fact.

The second use of dashes is to surround a drastic interruption in the middle of a sentence:

> Suddenly there was a noise—it sounded more like a cannon than anything else—and the south wall disappeared.
>
> It was Shakespeare—or was it Madonna?—who once said, "All the world's a stage."

Almost everyone mistypes dashes. Type a dash with no spaces before or after, like so: "word—word." The dash is not a hyphen, so if your computer can't print dashes, type two hyphens, like so: "word--word."

## Parentheses

Everybody knows that parentheses indicate a whispered aside, but punctuating around them can get confusing. Punctuate the sentence without the parentheses; then put the parentheses in, leaving all other punctuation untouched:

> He was tall and mean-looking.
>
> He was tall (very tall, in fact) and mean-looking.
>
> He was tall, but his legs were short.
>
> He was tall (very tall, in fact), but his legs were short.

## Question Marks

Put a question mark after any sentence that is syntactically a question, whether it "feels" like a question or not:

Why don't you come over tonight and we'll order pizza?

Will you be kind enough to reply as soon as possible?

### The Hyphen

The hyphen is a word-making tool. It lets us combine words and affixes to make three kinds of words:

**The compound adjective hyphen.** The hyphen adds words together so they can be used as adjectives.

five ten-gallon hats
a nine-to-five job
a soon-to-be-fired-for-his-incompetence employee

In practice it's hard to tell if a familiar two-word adjective should be written as two words, a hyphenated word, or simply one word: is it *red hot, red-hot*, or *redhot*? Just look it up in a dictionary. If it isn't there, hyphenate.

**The verb-phrase noun hyphen.** This hyphen adds a verb and its following adverb together so they can be *used as a noun*:

We were on a stake-out.

The car needed a little touch-up.

Both of these hyphens say, "Take this group of words and think of it as a single word." The key is that *the phrases have been moved from their natural position*. In their natural positions, they have no hyphens:

The hat held ten gallons.

I worked from nine to five.

The employee was soon to be fired for his incompetence.

We were going to stake out the house.

I asked him to touch up the paint on the car.

**The prefix hyphen.** Hyphens join prefixes to words if the joining is an awkward one:

ex-husband vs. extinction

pro-choice vs. productive

### The Apostrophe

There are three kinds of apostrophes:

**The contraction apostrophe.** This apostrophe marks places where letters have been dropped out in contractions and reductions:

could not → couldn't

I will → I'll

I expect he is swimming about now. → I 'spect he's swimmin' 'bout now.

The apostrophe goes exactly where the letter dropped out, and you need one for each place where a letter or letters used to be:

Write *doesn't,* not **does'nt.*

Write *rock 'n' roll,* not **rock 'n roll.*

**The possessive apostrophe.** This apostrophe marks possession, which is a loose kind of ownership:

The pitcher's absence forced the cancellation of the game.

The men's room is locked.

The book's disappearance remained a mystery.

The rules for positioning the apostrophe are inflexible:

1. If the noun is singular, add *-'s*:

   one dog's collar

   Do this even if the noun ends in *-s* already:

   one dress's hemline

2. If the noun is plural and is pluralized with an *-s*, add the apostrophe after the *-s* that's already there:

   some dogs' collars

   some dresses' hemlines

3. If the noun is an irregular plural, add *-'s*:

   the men's department

   the octopi's mittens

4. If the word showing ownership is a *pronoun,* use no apostrophe at all: *his, hers, theirs, yours, ours,* and especially *its.* Memorize it: *Its* means "belonging to it"; *it's* means "it is."
5. If the noun is singular and ends in *-s,* sometimes the possessive looks or sounds funny, in which case some people give you permission to drop the second *-s:*

Ted Williams's batting average
or
Ted Williams' batting average

**The odd plural apostrophe.** This apostrophe separates a plural noun from its pluralizing *-s only if* it would be confusing to the eye to use a normal plural form:

I love the Oakland A's.

Give me two 10's.

How many *e*'s are there in *separate?*

## Quotation Marks

Quotation marks do four things.

**They surround someone else's exact words when you quote them:**

> I can still hear Monique saying, "But I didn't *mean* it!"
>
> Her exact words were that she "hadn't a clue" about his whereabouts.

Use quotation marks even if the speaker or speech is imaginary:

> I can just imagine what my father would say: "How are you going to pay for that?"
>
> Nobody ever said, "Have a lousy day."

**They create ironic distance**—the punctuational equivalent of a wink. They surround language you use but want to disown—language representative of the way *someone else* talks:

> Doctors never like to talk about pain. When I'm sick, I don't "feel discomfort"—I *hurt*!
>
> Unions are always talking about "parity."
>
> I don't want to meet your "special friend."

**They surround minor titles:** titles of little things or parts of things, like chapters from books, songs, essays, short stories, or newspaper articles. The titles for the big, whole things (books, anthologies, newspapers) are *italicized* or underlined.

> "The Telltale Heart" vs. The Collected Works of Edgar Allan Poe
>
> "Man Bites Dog" vs. the *New York Times*

**They surround words as words:**

How do you spell "necessary"?

I hate the phrase "special education."

Sometimes italics do this job.

### Things Quotation Marks *Don't* Do

Quotation marks don't surround your own title at the head of your essay. They don't give emphasis to words or suggest heightened drama:

*Win a free trip to "Paris"!

*"Special" today, broccoli 35 cents/lb.

### Spacing and Positioning

Follow periods and all sentence-ending punctuation marks with two spaces.

Follow all commas and semicolons with one space.

Follow colons with one space, unless what follows the colon is a complete sentence, in which case you can use two spaces.

Parentheses surround words without internal spacing (like this) (*but not like this ).

Dashes and hyphens have no spaces around them—like this—but not — oops! — like that.

Quotation marks always come outside commas and periods; they come inside colons and semicolons; and question marks and exclamation points go wherever the sense dictates: If the question or exclamation is a part of the quotation, put it inside (He said, "Why?"); if the question or exclamation is the whole sentence, put it outside (Why did he say "ragmop"?).

Incidentally, you can't really learn spacing by looking at books, because typers think differently than typesetters do.

## Spelling

I have bad news. First, the world has decided that spelling matters enormously. If you can't spell, most readers will conclude you're illiterate, stupid, or both. Second, the world's spelling standards are very high. Two misspellings per typed page is considered poor. Third, spelling English is fiendishly hard, and nothing can make it easy. Fourth, spell-checker computer programs won't save you, because a misspelled English word often looks just like another word (*their/there, planning/planing*). The only good news is that spelling is one of the world's most fascinating games.

The four most common ways people try to learn to spell don't work. Let's rule them out now:

**Don't try to spell by rule.** There are a few rules that help you spell (on p. 200), but each will only solve one problem in a hundred.

**Don't try to spell phonetically,** by sounding words out. Most of the words you use a lot don't follow the rules.

**Don't spell by mnemonic devices.** A mnemonic device is a trick, jingle, or story to help you remember something: "the princi*pal* is your *pal*"; "I shot *par* on two se*par*ate golf courses." Mnemonic devices work, but they're slow and cumbersome. I learned to spell *receive* via the famous mnemonic "*I* before *E* except after *C*," and thirty years later I still have to stop and recite the jingle every time I write the word.

**Don't try to learn to spell by reading.** Good readers are often terrible spellers, because reading well depends on *not* focusing on the letters.

So much for what doesn't work; here are seven techniques that do:

**Spell for fun.** Fall in love with language and words and become fascinated by how they work. Read books about words. Trace interesting etymologies in the dictionary. Play spelling games like Scrabble, Boggle, Password, and Perquacky; do crossword puzzles.

**Spell by recognition.** You can train yourself to recognize correctly spelled words the same way you remember faces or the names of movie actors. You look at *doesn't* and say "That looks right" and you look at **dosen't* and say "That looks funny." This method is effortless—you don't really work at remembering Brad Pitt's name—but it doesn't happen until you *care*.

**Spell by using the dictionary.** As my friend Steve Metzger puts it, "You spell with your arm"—the arm that reaches for the dictionary on the shelf.

**Spell morphemes, not words.** A morpheme is a piece of meaning. Words are made out of them. *Unlisted* has three: *un-* (which means "not"), *list,* and *-ed* (which means "past tense"). The vocabulary of English really isn't a million unrelated words; it's a million recombinations of a few morphemes. If you can spell the morphemes, you can spell the words. Once you learn the morpheme *syn-,* meaning "together," you've learned the tricky part of spelling *syndrome, syndicate, synchronize, syntax, synagogue,* and about 450 others. Once you learn the morpheme *par,* meaning "equal," you've learned the tricky part of spelling *parity, disparate, compare, disparage, reparation,* and dozens more.

If you're unsure of a word, break it into its morphemes and spell each morpheme:

*familiar* = *family* + *ar* (so **fimiliar* must be wrong)
*vicious* = *vice* + *ious* (so **viscious* must be wrong)
*preposition* = *pre* + *pose* + *ition* (so **prepisition* must be wrong)

**Get hints from other forms of the same word.** Often a letter we can't hear in one form of the word sounds distinctly in another:

circUit: think of *circuitous*
musCle: think of *muscular*
mouNtain: think of *mount*
condemN: think of *condemnation*
critiCize: think of *critic*
grammAr: think of *grammatical*
utIlize: think of *utility*
defInItely: think of *definition*
sentEnce: think of *sententious*
relAtive: think of *relate*
corpOration: think of *corporeal*

**Make your own list of demons.** Most of us only misspell forty or fifty words. It doesn't take long to make a list of them; then you can drill on them.

**Memorize a few rules.** A very few rules are worth learning:

1. *I* before *E* except after *C,* or when sounded like *A,* as in *neighbor* and *weigh.*
2. In stressed non-final syllables, double the consonants after short vowels; keep consonants single after long vowels. *Matting* needs two *t*'s, *mating* needs one.
3. Final *-e*'s disappear before suffixes starting with vowels; they don't disappear before suffixes starting with consonants: *manage*→*managing, management; consummate*→*consummation, consummately.*
4. Final *-y* becomes *-i* when followed by a suffix, and it never disappears: *pity*→*pitiful, rely*→*relies, controversy*→*controversial, family*→*familiar.* Exception: *-y* before *-i* or after a vowel stays *y: pity, pitying; stay, stayed.*

## The Worst That Can Happen to You

Perhaps half of my students deal with mechanical problems by avoiding any situation in which they might arise. If a word is hard to spell, they just don't use it. If they aren't sure how to use a semicolon, they don't use it at all. Once they realize that long sentences risk structure problems, they use only short, simple sentences. In a sick way, this approach works, but it's the worst thing that can happen to you, because once you start writing with the purpose of avoiding error, the logical end result is to not write at all. Writing is inherently risky, like skiing or driving a race car. That's why it's a rush. Embrace the risk, the way a race car driver looks forward eagerly to the twisting stretch of road.

## Following Format

A format is a set of rules about how an essay is laid out on the page: how big to make the margins, whether to type the title in full capitals or not, where to put the page numbers. Some students consider such matters too trivial for their attention, but editors and publishers don't. A friend of mine worked hard on an article for submission to a magazine. "Find out the magazine's format and use it," I said over and over. He had more important fish to fry. He submitted it in a format of his own invention, and they sent it back with a copy of their format sheet asking him to please use it if he wanted them to read his work.

There are no universal format rules, so the only way to know what the format is is to ask the boss. Use this format for school papers if your instructor hasn't mandated one:

1. Use only one side of standard size (8½" × 11") paper of medium weight (20 lb.) or heavier.
2. Print—never hand-write—using a quality printer with a relatively new cartridge.
3. Proofread carefully, and make all handwritten corrections or additions neatly, in black ink.
4. Keep a margin of one inch on all four sides of the page. Approximate the right margin, breaking long words with hyphens to get close to the one-inch border.
5. Center each line of your title. Don't underline it or put quotation marks around it (unless it's a quote). Don't use full capitals; capitalize the first letter only of the first word and all important words: all nouns, verbs, adjectives, adverbs, and anything over four letters long. Put more space between your title and the text than there is between the lines of text themselves: If you're double spacing the text, triple space between title and text. Don't have a title page unless you're told to or the essay is more than thirty pages long.
6. Put in the upper right-hand corner of page 1 the following information: your name, the course *number* (e.g., Anthro. 210B), and the date.
7. Connect the pages with a staple in the upper left-hand corner. Don't fold the pages or dog-ear them.

8. Use 1½ spacing if your printer has it; if not, double space.
9. Indent the first line of each paragraph five spaces. Don't put extra space between paragraphs.
10. Number all pages after page 1. Put the page numbers in any one of three places: upper right corner, top center, or bottom center.
11. Use no eye-catching fonts or letter sizes. Be simple, conventional, and understated.

## Proofreading

Proofreading is reading over the text to look for places where your fingers silpped and you typed *natino* instead of *nation.* It's the very last thing you do before printing the final copy. To get in the mood, begin by realizing four truths:

**Realize why proofreading matters.** You become a zealous proofreader the day you grasp how destructive a typo is to your reader's concentration. A single typo can undo all your hard work. How do *you* react when you read about "fist graders," "shot stories," or "censoring textbools"? Well, everybody else reacts that way too. And as a writer you'd rather be dragged naked through cactus than get that reaction.

**Realize how proofreading problems are fixed.** Spelling problems are problems of *knowledge,* and you fix them by *learning;* typos are just finger slips, and you fix them by learning to *look.*

**Realize that your word processor's spell checker won't save you.** Spell-checker programs make typo problems *worse,* because they lull you into thinking they've fixed the problem when they haven't. The program will catch all the "hte" typos, but it leaves all the ones that produce another word: "shot stories," "fist graders," and so on.

**Realize why proofreading is hard.** It's because all your life you've been practicing the art of *not looking at the letters.* Good readers read by skimming and guessing—experts estimate you're actually seeing perhaps 25 percent of a text.

To proofread well, you stop *reading* and start *staring.* Here are seven principles to guide you:

**Assume there's at least one typo.** If you don't, you'll never find any.

**Set aside a time for nothing but proofreading**—you can't do it and anything else too, since it uses your eyes and brain in a unique way.

**Ignore content.** As soon as you start listening to what the text is *saying,* you'll start seeing what you expect and not what's there.

**Read backwards,** to prevent yourself from predicting.

**Go slow.** Any attempt to hurry and you'll start guessing and skimming.

**Don't just proofread individual words;** proofread phrases and clauses. Otherwise you'll miss goofs like these:

> *I would explain that in our society there correct and incorrect forms to use.
>
> *The little cap just pulls off it you put enough effort into it.
>
> *After two weeks, it is evident that the that the consistent and continual printing errors are the result of a defective printer.

**Proofread the new text and everything surrounding it** when you revise a proofread text to make sure you haven't introduced large-scale problems like lack of parallelism (p. 185).

## EXERCISES

1. List three mechanical *facts* (not principles or attitudes) you didn't know before you read Chapter 12. Begin each with "I didn't know that . . ."
2. Line-edit a page of manuscript in class as a group. Have a volunteer distribute a double-spaced page of essay to the class. Divide the readers into teams of two. Have each team make a list of three mechanical problems in the text, each with a repair and a clear, concrete explanation for why it's a problem. Have each team identify one problem, repair it, and explain it in front of the class. Discuss each presentation to see if the group agrees.
3. Make a list of mechanical topics covered in this chapter: format, parallelism, semicolon usage, etc. Have each member of the class sign up as class expert on that topic. Line-edit a classmate's essay page as in Exercise 2, with each expert reporting on any problems in her area of expertise that appear in the draft.

# Chapter 13

# PUBLISHING

## What, Me Publish?

I know what you're thinking: Publishing is for the professionals. Publishing is what people like Stephen King and J. K. Rowling do. But you can publish, and what's more, you must.

Think of the writing process as an electric circuit. The purpose is to get juice to the end of the line. In writing, the end of the line is when the text reaches the audience. In the line are four on-off switches. They are discovering something to say, drafting, revising, and publishing. If any of the switches is open, the current stops; if they're all closed, the current can continue.

There is no way for the current to get around the switches or compensate for an open switch by working really hard at the others. If you think well, draft well, and revise well, then let the manuscript sit in a drawer, you've accomplished nothing. Publishing is what we did all the work of Chapters 1–12 for.

In a sense, publishing is the easiest step in the writing process, because everybody knows how to mail a letter. It's just terrifying. But that's only because we have a grandiose definition of publishing. Publishing in fact means nothing more than *making something public.* So publication means writing a letter to the editor of the local newspaper or writing a news article for your club's newsletter or posting a thoughtful response to someone else's posting on an electronic bulletin board.

## Ways to Go Public

Let's talk about eight ways to get into print, from easiest to hardest.

### Electronic Publishing

Distributing your email messages to mailing lists or posting comments in a chat room is publishing lite. It's so easy, people do it for relaxation. There is no quality control—everything anyone wants to say gets published—but that's good for us when we're new because we can't be rejected. The glory of e-publishing is that the feedback is instantaneous—instead of waiting months or years for your piece to be edited, printed, distributed, bought, read, and responded to, you get reader reaction in minutes.

E-communities come in two forms. The first is email distribution lists. You can make your own list with your email software, but usually you'll join one already in place by asking (via email) the person in charge of it to add you to the mailing list. Then you send an email message to all members and individual readers write back. The second is chat rooms, where you post a message on an electronic bulletin board, and anyone who logs on can see it and post a reply on that same bulletin board. These groups go by several names—chat rooms, BBS, newsgroups, conferences—and to find them you need only enter a key word in your Internet search engine and look at the Web sites it gives you—many of them will have chat rooms attached. There are chat rooms for everyone, including people who hate Barney the dinosaur and people who want to discuss Spam (the meat product, not the email).

E-publishing may not feel like "real" publishing, but you will have the basic publishing experience: seeing your work provoke response in readers. Oh boy, will you get response. E-communication is famous for it.

## Publishing in the Classroom

When you hand around copies of your writing in your composition class and ask for response, you've gone public—and for many of us, that's enough to give us dry mouth.

Next, take the work to other classrooms. Exchange essays with another writing class for feedback and criticism. Organize an anthology of best essays from all the writing sections in your department, appoint an editorial board, and submit your work.

## Publishing on Campus

There are a lot of places on campus where mere mortals can get published. On my fairly small campus there is

- a weekly student newspaper, printing informative pieces, student essays, music and movie reviews, and letters to the editor;
- a twice-yearly campus journal, printing essays about the academic life of the campus;
- a literary magazine, printing poems, book reviews, and short stories by students;
- student journals in several academic programs, printing the best work students are doing in their class writing projects;

- a magazine published by the Women's Center, addressing women's issues;
- several student-edited counterculture periodicals;
- a handbook for incoming students;
- an alumni magazine;
- and countless newsletters for individual programs, like the English Department's Writing Center newsletter.

Some of these have readerships you have things to say to, and all of them are desperate for copy.

If you want to publish every week, you can join the campus newspaper staff. They'll be delighted to have you—every newspaper is short on good help—and they won't ask you to be good right away; they'll train you.

## Community Publications

All communities offer a long list of local publishing opportunities, and, like the campus publications, community pubs typically are understaffed and the standards are not high. Most obviously, there is the daily newspaper, with its insatiable appetite for letters to the editor, travel tips, book reviews, rock concert reviews, recipes, human interest pieces on the man who built a house out of discarded CDs, and essays on issues of the day. And there is always more than one newspaper. Even in my small town there is the politically conservative daily, a politically liberal and arts-oriented weekly, an arch-conservative weekly, an ultra-liberal weekly, a holistic health weekly, a monthly devoted to area hunting and fishing, and a weekly devoted to the local rock music scene.

There are venues other than newspapers. Newsletters are probably the easiest, because they are so plentiful and so desperate for copy. I get nine newsletters in the mail: from my scuba diving club, the American Heart Association, the local yacht club, the local small-boat racing organization, the organization for owners of my particular sailboat, the in-town chapter of the Sierra Club, the regional Sierra Club office, the alumni of a personal growth seminar, and a national mountain-biking association. Someone has to fill all those pages. And it feels good to publish in such places, because newsletter readers are grateful for your efforts.

The time-honored way of breaking into publication is the letter to the editor. If you start there, be proud of it. I lovingly recall an old cartoon in which a beaming woman is on the phone saying, "We're having a few friends over—Herbert's letter made it into the *Times*."

## Desktop Publishing

Self-publication means just what it says: You publish the piece yourself. More and more, authors are circumventing the publishing rat race by making their own texts and selling them. Before computers, this was almost impossible, because anything produced this way looked amateurish, but no longer. Desktop publishing software (Pagemaker is the favorite among novices) and a good printer allow you to do everything short of the binding, with professional results. Any small print shop will be happy to bind and cover the product. Now you're ready to walk into a bookstore and talk the owner into putting your work on the shelves, or just set up a table in the Student Union. It's do-able. A friend of mine decided he didn't like the mealymouthedness of the local newspapers, so he started his own. He sells subscriptions, but mostly he just gives the paper away by putting stacks of it in busy public places. And he gets read.

This is not easy. You (or someone) needs to be good with desktop publishing software, graphic design, bookkeeping, marketing, and salesmanship, funded well enough to pay the printing costs, and—most of all—motivated enough to organize the project and see it through. A book that will help you through it is *The Publish It Yourself Handbook*.

## Magazine Articles

Yes, you can sell articles to national magazines. *Newsweek* will pay you $1000 for a 1000-word opinion essay. *Reader's Digest* will pay you $300 for a paragraph about a funny thing that happened in class, for heaven's sake. And many of the slicks will look at your work, even if you're an amateur. A glance at past issues of *Newsweek* shows guest essays by "nonwriters" such as a female orchestra leader, a merchant seaman, a truck driver, and an owner of a family winery. Many of the biggest women's magazines are 75 percent to 100 percent composed of unsolicited freelance submissions, and they pay well.

Now for the bad news. First, the competition can be fierce. Popular magazines like *Redbook* may publish only one article out of several hundred received. Second, the editorial process can be grueling. Third, you can't make a living freelancing for magazines.

To submit to national magazines, do six things:

**Buy a copy of *Writer's Market*.** This wonderful paperback, owned by every freelance writer in the world, will tell you everything you need to know about the logistics of submitting to specific magazines. You look up *Sports Illustrated;* it tells you useful things: Will they read manuscripts from people they don't know?; What's the editor's name and address?; What's the desired manuscript (MS) length?; What's their editorial philosophy?; How much do they pay?; and so on. It will tell you about publications you didn't know existed: if you want to write about your experiences snowboarding in Colorado, WM will list for you every publication interested in snow sports, snowboarding, Colorado, or Rocky Mountain recreation and tourism. If you have the money, also buy *The International Directory of Little Magazines and Small Presses,* which will tell you about markets too small or too specialized for WM to notice.

**Study the customer.** Ask yourself, "What publications print things like my piece?" Pick one, then tailor the piece to suit it perfectly. Publications don't buy what's good; they buy what fits in with their program. *Sports Illustrated* only prints *Sports Illustrated*–type articles, and if you send them something else they'll just say no.

**Send for the writer's guide.** Many magazines have manuals for submitters, greatly expanding on the information in *Writer's Market.* They're free if you write and ask for one, and they'll tell you all about what style to use, what approach they favor, how to format the text, and so on.

**Decide whether to submit a finished piece or query first.** With a very short piece, it makes sense to write it completely, then submit the finished manuscript. With longer pieces, you don't want to write the entire piece until someone buys the idea, so you send a query letter: "Would you be interested in a piece on a day in the life of the local ski patrol?"

**Concentrate on the easy markets.** Some markets are hungrier for material or friendlier to newcomers than others. *Playboy* is a brick wall. The four markets easiest to crack are:

*In-flight magazines,* the slick magazines you find in the seat flap in front of you during a commercial airline flight.

*Guest spots.* Most national magazines have reserved a spot for one outsider essay per issue. In *Newsweek,* it's "My Turn"; in *Time* it's simply called "Essay"; in *MS.* it's "Guest Room"; *in Runner's World* it's called "The Finish Line"; in *Cosmopolitan* there's one for women, "On My Mind," and one for men, "His Point of View."

*Travel and tourism.* Every newspaper has its travel section, and it counts on people like you, since it can't afford to send reporters on vacations.

*Sporting and hobby magazines.* Because their budgets are small, they rely heavily on freelance writing.

**Keep sending it out.** Freelance writers get rejected a lot, so you have to learn to take the rejection and keep pitching. You'll have the strength to do this if you remember the basic truth of publishing: your piece wasn't rejected because it was bad; it was rejected because it didn't fit that particular editor's needs today. When you find someone who needs what you're selling, she'll buy it.

### Academic Publishing

Academic publishing is done in professional journals. Every discipline has them—your campus library probably subscribes to several hundred—and usually no one outside the discipline ever sees them.

Academic publishing is difficult and unrewarding. Every professor in the country is trying to get into those same journals, so the competition is fierce. Typically, journals are booked years in advance; if you did get accepted, your piece wouldn't see the light of day until you had graduated. They won't pay you a dime. So forget about academic publishing unless your instructor specifically encourages you to submit your work.

### Books

All writers dream of writing a book. But books are the toughest way to try to get published. The time and labor commitment is enormous, the chances of getting into print are minuscule, and even if you succeed, the rewards are years away and you probably won't make any money.

## Preparing a Manuscript for Submission

The logistics of submitting a manuscript for publication are the same whether you're submitting to the campus newspaper or a national magazine. You need:

1. A professional-quality, double-spaced manuscript, immaculately line-edited and proofread and in the format of whatever market you're submitting it to;
2. A publication to submit your manuscript to—a newspaper, magazine, or newsletter that prints the sort of thing you've written;
3. An address and a name of someone at that publication—usually an editor—to send the manuscript to. Do everything in your power to get a name, not just a title. The information is often printed on the editorial page of each issue, or you can call the publication and ask who handles what you're selling. *Writer's Market,* too, can help.
4. A mailer—a 9" × 11½" envelope. Never fold a manuscript.
5. A SASE—a self-addressed, stamped envelope, the same size as your mailer—so the manuscript can be returned to you if it's rejected. Professionals paper clip the stamps to the envelope instead of licking them.
6. A cover letter—a short, uncomplicated letter in which you say what the manuscript is and what you'd like the editor to

do with it. You may also want to include other information—you might say you're willing to revise if the editor wishes—but less is more. Cover letters are often two sentences long, and one of the two may only say thank you. Don't try to sell, defend, or apologize for either the piece or yourself.

Be specific about precisely where you expect the editor to use the piece: "Please consider this for publication *in your Spring Supplement's 'Out and About' section.*"

Put a paper clip on the manuscript—don't staple—put the cover letter on top, and put them and the SASE in the mailer. Put stamps on the mailer, say a small prayer, and put the mailer in the mail.

### Business Letter Format

The cover letter doesn't say much, but it matters a lot, because it's the editor's first experience of your work, and from it she will decide whether you are a true member of the club of writers and whether you can follow directions. So slave over the letter, the way you slave over your appearance before an important job interview.

Business letter format is a long series of tiny rules and regulations, all of which you must follow to be a member of the club. Here's a template:

1012 Maiden Lane
Chico, CA 95926

October 5, 2003

Marion Haste
Associate Editor
Sports Department
Leisure Magazine
2300 Avenue of the Giants
New York, NY 10010

Dear Ms. Haste:

Please consider the enclosed manuscript, "Mountain Biking After Age Sixty," for publication in the Golden Years section of your magazine.

Thank you for your consideration.

Sincerely yours,

Jack Rawlins
jrawlins@csuchico.edu
(530) 898-6468

Things to observe about this format, from top to bottom:

1. Your address goes at the top, without your name. You can include your phone number here if you wish, or you can add it after your signature, or put it in the body of the letter.
2. Use the Post Office's standard two-letter abbreviations for states—two capital letters, no periods—and always include Zip Code numbers in addresses.
3. Spell out the month in the date. Don't use all numbers (6/23/03)—numbers are too casual.
4. Use the editor's full name, without a title—not even "Mr." or "Ms."
5. List the editor's job title on its own line, unless it's one word, in which case you *may* list it after the name: "John Smith, Editor."
6. Use the *entire* address, including all departments, subdivisions, and numbers.
7. Underline the title of the publication.
8. In the salutation, address the editor as "Mr." or "Ms." and his or her last name. Follow the salutation with a colon, not a comma.
9. Have at least two paragraphs, even if paragraph 2 is just for show.
10. Double-space between paragraphs, and don't indent the beginnings of paragraphs.
11. Use "Sincerely yours" as the complimentary close—don't invent something original or clever.
12. Sign your name. The most common error in business letter writing is to forget to do this.
13. Type your name under your signature, exactly as you sign it—if you sign "Bubba," type "Bubba."
14. Include an email address somewhere in the letter if you have one.
15. Business letter margins are bigger than essay margins, so move your tabs in a little left and right.
16. Proofread like mad—a single typo can scotch the deal before it gets off the ground.

## EXERCISES

1. Make a list of three publications on your campus. Brainstorm essays you might write for each of them.

2. Submit an essay to the guest editorial or similar column in your campus newspaper.

3. Make a list of your favorite sports, hobbies, and activities. For each, find one magazine or newsletter devoted to it. Brainstorm one essay you might write for each.

4. Find a chat room or email distribution list that discusses a topic of interest to you. Make a contribution to the conversation. Bring to class a copy of your contribution and the responses it provokes.

5. Submit a letter to the editor of the biggest newspaper in your area.

6. Use *Writer's Market* to identify two possible buyers for a piece you've written. Answer the following questions for each:

   a. Does the periodical read unsolicited manuscripts?
   b. Does the periodical want you to send a query letter before submitting?
   c. What is the name and address of the editor you would send the manuscript to?
   d. What are the length limits?
   e. How much do they pay?

7. Write a query letter to one of the two periodicals in Exercise 6.

8. Prepare a piece for publication and submit it, following the steps in Chapter 13.

# Part Four

## MODES OF WRITING

# Chapter 14

# PERSONAL WRITING

When you're doing personal writing, the basic rule is the same as for all writing everywhere: You can't do it if you haven't read a lot of it. So the easiest way to write a good personal essay is also the most pleasant: Read all the personal essays in the Treasury of Essays (p. 368) and then *write one like them.*

Personal writing doesn't teach the reader something utilitarian, like how to crochet or what to do with bored children on a rainy day. It doesn't argue the reader into buying a thesis, like "We should immediately offer economic aid to Russia." Instead, it's a sharing of the self. When Kris Tachmier wrote the wonderful personal essay about how much she hated eggs (p. 37), she wasn't trying to teach you something new about eggs that you could put to practical use, and she wasn't trying to convince you that you should hate eggs too; she was just saying, "If you know how I feel about eggs, you'll know a part of me." And we love the essay not because we've learned something useful or been persuaded, but because we feel so close to Kris.

Most personal writing is in one of three forms:

Narrative: "This happened to me . . ."

Character sketch: "I know this interesting person . . ."

Personal symbol: "This car/necklace/recipe means a lot to me . . ."

We can usually do good personal writing as soon as we know that anyone cares. I had a student who wrote perfunctory essays until I gave the assignment to write "the essay your classmates would most like to read." He dashed off this great personal symbol essay about a basketball court:

## CITRUS HOOPS

RYAN CURRY

I lace up my Chuck Taylor high tops in a New York basket weave—not the normal straight style for me. I want to stand out and show the world that they shouldn't mess with me. I pull down my socks so that they crumple atop my highs, put on my gray shorts—pull 'em down so that my jock strap is seen on my back—and slip into a T-shirt that says "In your face, I do it with grace." Ya see, I'm goin' back ta Citrus—ta Citrus—ta Citrus.

To many, Citrus is just an elementary school located at Citrus and 4th Avenue, but to many others it's the ultimate place to play roundball. The three full courts all have baskets of different heights: one at eight feet, one at eight and a half, and one at nine and a half. From dawn to dusk on weekends and from 3:00 to 8:30 on weekdays, games are played. In Chico there is no better place to hoop.

Ya see, on eight-and-a-half-foot baskets everybody can create. Pretend that you're Larry Bird, Charles Barkley, Magic Johnson, Cheryl Miller, and, of course, Michael Jordan. Anything is possible: twenty-foot fade-aways, reverse gorilla dunks, alley oops, and sweet drives down the lane. It's the place where fantasies become realities: top of the key, jab step, cross over, down the gut, split the D, rise to the occasion, double pump, 360-degree right hand "slam jam bam" as Dick Vitale would say. It's a game of fast breaks, quick shakes, pump fakes, and talking trash in your face.

But before you decide to go play at Citrus, ya gotta have an understanding. If you're new you're gonna have to prove yourself. And if people start talkin' about Sir Ronald, understand that Sir Ronald is the only man known to have completed a Double Dip. No, it's not at Baskin-Robbins. A Double Dip is when a player dunks the ball and before it hits the ground takes it out of the air and dunks it again. Understand and respect the veterans and you'll stand a chance.

I finish lacing my shoes, step through the wire fence and call "winners." Everybody looks, nobody argues. When you're a Citrus veteran no-no-noooobody will mess with ya. ❖

I later found out he was the leading scorer for the varsity basketball team. He had simply assumed I wasn't interested in hearing about any of it.

Since personal writing says "This is me," and humans are pretty unpremeditated, often personal writing has little visible sign of structure, thesis, or purpose:

## DAD

MICHAEL CLARK

I remember he used to take forever in the bathroom. Some mornings I could get up, eat breakfast, get ready for school, and leave without ever seeing him. I'd hear him, though: coughing, spitting, and gagging himself. Anyone else hearing him in the morning would probably think he was going to die. But he had always done that, and I figured it was just the way all grown men got up in the morning.

When he came home in the evenings you could tell he was glad not to be at work any more. It was always best not to ask him questions about anything or make any kind of noise. Mom would ask him a couple of things while she was fixing dinner. He'd answer her. Otherwise he'd just sit at the dining room table with his martini, reading the newspaper.

At dinner, Mom would make most of the conversation. He generally reserved his participation for when we kids got too lighthearted or proud or disrespectful or something and needed trampling.

When I played in Little League, he'd drive me. The Conservation Club was next to the park. He'd hang out there until practice was over. Once he ambled over a little early. He interrupted the coach and insisted on explaining the infield fly rule—not just once but three times. He'd have gone on like a broken record if the coach hadn't stopped him and thanked him and quickly dismissed the team.

I always hated riding home with him after he'd been at the Club. Winter was the worst. We'd take our trash to the town dump. The dump was also right next to the park, so naturally we'd stop in at the Club. We'd always stay past dark. On the way home I always wanted to tell him you shouldn't drive so fast on a day's accumulation of ice and snow, but I never did. The couple of times we slid off the road didn't convince him. He'd just rock the car out, get back on the road, and drive on as if nothing had happened.

As time went on, he'd come home later and later in the evenings. Often he'd come through the door all red-faced and walk straight into the bedroom, where we'd hear him moan a little and talk to the dog. Then he'd pass out and we wouldn't see him again until he came home the same way the next evening.

With my brother in the Army and my sister at college, I was the only one around to see that Mom was spending her nights on the living room couch. Though it didn't surprise me, the divorce came as kind of a blow.

I've seen him a couple of times since then. He's remarried. I think I called him last Thanksgiving. ❖

A little chaos just adds to the believability:

> Well, the big news is I'm pregnant. Boy, do I hate that word—PREGNANT, sounds so harsh. "With child" sounds positively smarmy. "Expecting" always makes me want to say, "Expecting what?" It's not that I'm not pleased about this—I just don't think I'm comfortable with the jargon yet. And oh boy, is there jargon! La Leche League, Bradley, Lamaze, LaBoyer, transition period, episiotomy, and baby blues. In my naive way I assumed I'd have this baby, take a week off, and then jump into student teaching. Then I read the books, became acquainted with the terminology, decided to take the whole semester off. What I'm slowly realizing is that I'm not just PREGNANT, I'm having a BABY—that books about the next twenty years. This is going to CHANGE my lifestyle! AAAGGGHHH! ❖

> Burn out. I've been doing this for too long, and it seems like everyone around me feels the same way. I want to go beyond bitching this semester, so like the last three semesters I've told myself I'm going to take it easy. This time I mean it. I really do.
>
> I can already see I'm lying. I want to audit the modern poetry class. And I want to keep tutoring. And I need to keep a few hours on the job. The money will be nice, and if I stop I'll have to start at $3.35 an hour when I go back. Then there's the newspaper. That ought to take a couple hundred hours. And I want to save time for my own writing. I've told myself I need to keep Tuesday and Thursday afternoons free. I'll probably have to tutor at one of those times, but if I'm lucky I'll be able to keep the other one free.
>
> Planning. That's the key. I've got to stop bitching and start planning. If I'm still bitching two weeks from now, I'll have to say it's hopeless. ❖

If personal writing doesn't need coherent organization or thesis, what *does* it need? First, dramatic intensity: The reader feels he's in the scene, living it along with the writer, feeling the wind in his hair and catching the tang of gunpowder in his nostrils. Second, a sought effect: The reader senses that everything in the essay adds up to one thing and takes us to the same endpoint. Let's look at ways to get each one.

## Show, Don't Tell

There's a paradox about drama: The worst way to communicate to the reader how you're feeling is to tell him. Ryan wouldn't strengthen "Citrus Hoops" by saying "I'm really proud of being one of the Citrus gang"; he would weaken it. Michael wouldn't strengthen "Dad" by saying, "My father was a pathetic drunk, and I feel like I lost out on having a father as a result"; he would weaken it. Instead, Ryan puts us on the court and lets us *feel* his pride; Michael lets us *watch* his father act out his life and witness his isolation.

Writing teachers traditionally express this insight by the ancient incantation, "Show, don't tell." These are just different words for the basic lesson of the concretion section of Chapter 11: To get life, concretize and particularize. Avoid generalized abstractions: "He was really weird"; "It was the most exciting class of my life"; "I was so scared." Replace them with concretions. Let the particulars create the feeling you want—then don't bother to explain to the reader what he's just *experienced*. Don't *describe* the movie; let the reader *watch* the movie. This passage from a first draft does it wrong:

> She was impulsive, funny, and highly irresponsible. I liked her because she did things I wouldn't do. I was reliable, down to earth, and boring. She was spontaneous. I looked up to her. In my eyes, she was a leader because she did things I was afraid to do. In many ways, she was immature. She had no concept of responsibility. I loved being with her, though, because she was fun. Being with her was like being on a vacation.

We understand perfectly, but we feel nothing. When the author rewrote to *show*, the new version began,

> "Hey, Cathy, I'm dying for an In-N-Out burger and fries and, you know me, I don't want to go alone. I'll pick you up in ten minutes."
> "But Nikki, it's . . . CLICK . . . ten o'clock at night," I respond to a dial tone.

Later in the new draft we get this:

> During the freshman initiation ceremony in high school, our friendship was born. We were dressed in costume (unwillingly) and instructed to do something totally silly and asinine in front of the entire student body. Nikki, dressed as Pinocchio, was told to tell a lie. "I love this school," she blurted out emphatically. Everybody booed.

Now we really *get it*.

More is better. "For two years she lived like a hippie" is OK; "For two years she lived in a cabin and raised goats" is better; great is "For two years she lived in a cabin with a chiropractor, slept with goats, and quoted Euell Gibbons." Here's a nice more-is-better description of an eatery:

> I was living in Laguna Beach and working at Tip's Deli. Tip's served beer and wine, chopped chicken liver, lox and bagels, pastrami on Jewish rye, and imported cheeses to a colorful clientele. Wally Tip was a short, plump, balding Jew originally from Toronto who claimed to have been a pimp in Las Vegas and made one believe in the possibilities of a Jewish Mafia. I liked him a lot. On Sunday morning he cooked breakfast himself, sweating and swearing over his tiny grill as he made his Tip's Special Omelet, which he served for a ridiculously low price to local businessmen and hippies and outsiders from Los Angeles who bitched about the fat on the pastrami, compared the place unfavorably to Ratner's, and left looking pleased. There was usually a long wait. Every time an order was turned in, Wally looked dismayed and muttered that the bastards would have to wait.

"Show, don't tell," taken all the way, produces an essay that's like a movie, where events unfold before our eyes and the writer says nothing:

## FORGET HOMEWORK

JENNIFER WISSMATH

"Jen, please!"

"Jeez, Darron, relax—I'm coming."

"I called you three times; this food has been sitting here forever!"

"I was taking an order and it hasn't been here that long. Where's the ticket for this order? I don't know where it goes."

"Table three. Hurry up . . ."

Man, he gets on my nerves. This plate is really hot. Hurry up, lady, move your stupid salad plate. "Here you go. I'll run and get you some Parmesan cheese. Do you need anything else?"

"Is our bread coming?"

"Oh, yes, it should be right out."

Okay, Parmesan, water—whoa! I almost slipped. There's a puddle in here the size of Lake Michigan. This whole station is a mess! You could never guess that there were two other waitresses who were supposed to do sidework before they left. I'm going to be here until way after 10—shoot, it's 9:45 right now. I guess my homework will just have to wait. "Here you go. Enjoy your meal—I'll be right back with your bread. Darron, I need the bread for Table 3."

"I already sent that out!"

"Well, Table 3 didn't get it. Hurry, the man on that table has been waiting forever."

There's the door—oh shoot, more people. Why are they coming in so late? I'd love to tell those jerks to leave—we could all get the hell out of here a little sooner. Let's see: Table 3—bread; Table 2—eating; Table 11—almost finished, they'll leave first; Table 8—okay; Table 16—take order.

"Hello, how are you doing this evening? Are you ready to order?"

"Yes. Honey, you go first."

"Um, okay. I think I'll get the eggplant."

"Oh, I was going to get that. Hmmm, I guess I could get lasagna and we could pull the old switcheroo."

("Jen, please!")

"But, hmmm, I'm not sure I really feel like lasagna."

Oh, God, could you please hurry up?

"Okay, she'll have the eggplant and I'll have the raviolis."

"Honey, I don't like raviolis."

"How about . . . well, I'll just stick with the lasagna."

What a revelation. Don't waste my time or anything. I don't think I'll ask them if they want salads. "Would you like any garlic bread?"

"Oh, yes—Honey, let's get it with cheese?"

"I don't like it with cheese . . ."

("Jen, please!!!")

"Will that be all for you?"

"Honey, don't forget the wine."

"Oh, yes, we would like a liter of White Zinfandel."

Oh, please, make my night longer. I don't have anything else to do. I don't really need to read those three chapters for my history quiz, and I'm sure my teacher wouldn't mind my handing in a late paper. This job is too much. If I didn't need the money so badly, I would probably get straight A's.

"JEN PLEASE!!!"

Damn. Let's see—this goes to Table 8. Oh my gosh, they don't even have their drinks. I just love getting a late rush. "Here you go—I'll be right back with your drinks. Do you need some Parmesan cheese?"

Okay—drinks, drinks, Parmesan. Then deliver food, check water, pick up plates, pour coffee, add tickets, clear tables, be civil, do sidework, fill Parm holders, fill sugars, clean station, clean salad bar, mop floor, go home, *forget homework*, go to bed. ❖

Chapter 11 gives you eleven ways to concretize an essay (pp. 172–175). But all eleven are revision strategies—they think in terms of *adding* concretions to something you've already written. Instead, build the essay up from concretions. Instead of brainstorming by asking abstract questions ("What sort of a person is he?" "How do I feel about her?"), begin by listing objects, gestures, or fragments of dialogue that capture the spirit of your subject. Ask:

How does she dress?

What are her personal catch-phrases?

What objects does she surround herself with?

What were her most revealing moments?

What is she famous among her peers for saying or doing?

How does she talk?

When you imagine her, what is she doing?

"Dad" might have begun with a list like this:

Coughing and spitting in the bathroom
Explaining the infield fly rule to coach
Talking to the dog
The Club
Sliding off the road in the car

Next, turn the items in the list into scenes, showing without telling. Once I asked a student what moment best captured the spirit of his grandmother. He said he once went with his grandmother to buy a Christmas tree at a lot. The salesman said, "You wanna stand on that?" and she climbed up and stood on the tree.

## Choosing an Effect

Once we have good concretions to work with, we need a rationale for putting them together in some way. Don't outline—it will just drive away the spontaneity we liked in the passages on p. 220. And don't begin with thesis, though thesis may emerge, because it forces you back into telling instead of showing.

Instead, think about effect: What are you trying to do to the reader? That effect may involve a thesis or a moral, but it doesn't have to. You can leave it pretty vague in the beginning: "I'm trying to capture what it feels like to play in a rec-league softball tournament"; "I want the reader to meet my father." The sought effect will become more specific as you work. Here are specific effects for some of the essays in this chapter:

"Dad": to capture the miserable alcoholic isolation my father lived with, and my inability to get near him.

"Forget Homework": to capture how hysterical, frustrating, and dehumanizing my night-time job is, and to show how infuriating it is to have it ruin my schoolwork.

"Citrus Hoops": to capture the pride and cockiness of Citrus court life; to record the style and tone of that subculture.

## Does Personal Writing Have a Thesis?

Personal writing is a sharing of the self, and teaching and sharing often don't mix. If we're chatting with a buddy and we suddenly sense that she's trying to teach us something, we'll probably feel condescended to. So personal writing usually doesn't have a sense of "The lesson to learn here is . . ." On the other hand, almost all writing has a central idea. Essays like "Forget Homework" and "Dad" don't really teach, but they do have theses. The thesis for "Dad" is "My father was cut off from the human race and his family by his alcoholism." The thesis in "Forget Homework" is something like "My wage-earning job often prevents me from being the best student I can be." And if we wanted to, we could *turn any personal essay into an argument* by drawing larger conclusions from the experience. We could use "Dad" to make the argument that our culture teaches males to deal with their emotional pain through silence and self-inflicted isolation. We could use "Forget Homework" to make the argument that it's to society's advantage to support student aid programs, so worthy students can concentrate on getting the most out of their education. Chapter 17 has two essays that use personal narrative in this way, "Given the Chance" (p. 276) and "Why?" (p. 277).

## WRITER'S WORKSHOP

### Concretizing Abstract Generalizations

Let's look at how a writer revises a very "tell-y" character sketch so that it "shows" instead.

## MY MOTHER

LORI ANN PROUST

She is understanding and always there for me. She listens and is full of positive support. I am lucky to have someone who is both a close friend *and* a mother. Not everyone has this kind of a relationship.

I could find endless words in the thesaurus to describe my mother, but the one word that stands out above the rest is "incredible." She is my sole support system. Whenever something exciting happens or there is a crisis in my life, she is the first person I turn to. I have seen many friends come and go in my life, but my mother is different. For eighteen years of my life she has always been there for me. No matter the distance in miles between us, we are always close. She understands me and knows me better than anyone else I know. She doesn't make demands nor does she pressure me with school and my future. She has complete faith and trust in me that I am doing the right thing with my life. I make her happy by letting her know I am happy and like who I am and where my life is taking me.

Every day I count my blessings and think about how grateful I am to have a mother who loves me. Not once do I take this for granted. I cannot imagine my life any differently without her. One thing is for certain: it just wouldn't be the same. ❖

Lori Ann's classmates said they simply didn't *believe* the essay—it felt like a sales pitch. They encouraged Lori Ann to start from concretions. She said, "Well, I just had a phone conversation with her that was pretty typical—maybe I could use that." She did, and this is what she got:

## MOTHERS . . . ?!!

"Hello?"

"Hi, Mom. How was your day?"

"What's wrong?"

"Nothing is wrong, Mom. I just called to tell you I found an incredible place to live next year! It's an apartment in an antique house. It has hardwood floors, high ceilings, it's close to school, has lots of potential, and the rent is *only* . . ."

"Does it have summer rent?"

"Yes."

"Forget it then."

"Fine, Mom."

"I already told you that neighborhood is dangerous and full of rapists."

"Mother, I've lived on this street for the past *three* years now."

"And what about the fraternity boys across the street? Do you know what you're in for?"

"Mother, these guys are my friends and I have also lived across the street from a fraternity house before . . ."

"Forget it."

"Fine, Mom. Would you rather pay $225 a month for me to live in a two-bedroom apartment instead of $150 a month? You'd also have to buy me a car because the only apartments available in September are five miles from campus."

"Does your friend Denice know what a slob you are? Does she know *you're* the reason why you had cockroaches in your apartment last year?"

"Mother, that's because I lived in a *dive!* I found cockroaches before I even moved in . . ."

"Oh, are you suddenly scrubbing floors now? I just don't see why you can't wait until September to find a place to live. I'm *not* paying summer rent."

"Fine, Mom. I just thought you might *appreciate* my consideration in letting you know what I am doing with my life before I sign the lease."

"Well, it sounds like you're going to do it anyway."

"Thank you for your support, Mom."

"Bye." Click.

"Good-bye, Mom; I love you too."

To think that mothers are understanding is the world's ultimate illusion. I had to sit in the bathroom as I was talking to my mom because there were thirty screaming girls in the hallway; stereos were blasting, and if this wasn't enough, the smoke alarm was going off because the cooks were burning dinner. I had to control myself from sticking the phone down the toilet and flushing it. That's how understanding she was being.

My mother can be full of positive support but not when you need to hear it the most. "I'm sure you can find something cleaner, can't you? You're such a slob—I guess it wouldn't matter anyway." Right, Mom. To my mother's dismay, I am an immaculate person—just ask any of my friends. She is practically married to the Pine Sol man. She thinks her house is as sterile as the hospital. Well, I have news for her . . .

Whenever something exciting happens in my life, my mother is usually the first person I turn to. I don't know why because she always shoots down my dreams. I sent her flowers and a poem I wrote myself for Mother's Day and what does she do? She acts irrational over the telephone. "Why can't you wait until September to find a place? I'm not paying summer rent." Right, Mom. I already told her twice I would pay summer rent myself. Anyone with common sense would realize that it's an advantage to find the best place *now.* That way you don't have to pay storage over the summer.

For eighteen years of my life she has raised me. She knows me better than anyone else I know. It just doesn't make sense why she can't be more sensitive and supportive of my dreams. All I wanted was to hear her say, "It sounds great!" But it was obviously too much to ask.

The phone rang as I was finishing this paper tonight.

"Hello?"

"Hi. I've been talking to your father about that apartment, and he said he would pay half your summer rent. That way we don't have to pay for storage." (What did I tell you, Mom . . . ) "So go ahead and sign the lease." (I didn't tell you before, but . . . I already did!)

"I'll see you soon, Mom. I love you."

My mom will never know this, but I went ahead and signed the lease yesterday, without her approval or support. I felt good about it, knowing I did the right thing. Today's phone call reassured me that I had done the right thing. Although my mother can be irrational sometimes, she is still my mother and I love her dearly. ❖

The phone conversation forced Lori Ann to come out from behind the safety of the first draft's clichés and face some complex, feisty realities. There's much more to say now, and the essay crackles with the energy of conflict.

**Now it's your turn.** Write a draft of a personal essay. Highlight every abstraction. Replace the abstractions with concretions. Then delete the abstractions.

## EXERCISES

1. List the objects, verbal expressions, and behaviors that capture the essence of someone in your life, as we did on p. 224. How does he usually dress? What are his verbal tics? What possessions matter to him? And so on. Write a paragraph showing how one item on the list reveals the heart and soul of the person.
2. Make a list of three abstract generalizations about someone in your life ("He's very generous"). Imagine how a movie would film scenes to show that the person is what you say she is. Then write an essay showing those scenes without telling.
3. Write a half-page to one-page monologue or dialogue that reveals the character of someone in your life.
4. Write an essay that, like "Citrus Hoops" (p. 218), says most clearly and loudly to the world, "This is me."
5. Use one of the personal essays in the Treasury of Essays (p. 368) as a model (see "modeling" in the index for guidance).
6. Describe a setting from your life that matters to you, like the deli on p. 222, in a paragraph or two. Then rewrite it to twice that length by doubling the specific concrete detail.

# Chapter 15

# WRITING TO INFORM

With informative writing, the basic rule is the same as for all writing everywhere: You can't do it if you haven't read a lot of it. So the easiest way to write a good informative essay is also the pleasantest: Read all the informative essays in the Treasury of Essays (p. 368) and then *write one like them.*

## What's Informative Writing?

Informative writing differs from personal writing in its purposes. In personal writing, the goal is to share a part of yourself—if the reader knows Kris Tachmier by the end of "The Egg and I Revisited" (p. 37), the essay has done its job. In informative writing, the reader is going to go out and *do* something practical with the information: plant a garden, learn to waterski, get a good deal on a used car. Most of the writing that's earning money in the real world is informative: service manuals, cookbooks, technical and scientific reports, encyclopedias, textbooks, travel guides, and 90 percent of every newspaper or magazine.

Since purposes are independent of content, the same material can be turned into any kind of essay. My student Aaron Kenedi wanted to write about his memories of watching his grandmother slaughter chickens, but he couldn't decide if he wanted to focus on his relationship with his grandmother or teach the reader the practical ins and outs of chicken slaughtering. Why not write two essays, I said, one personal and the other informative? So he did. I like both of them. Here's the personal version:

## INVITATION TO A BEHEADING

AARON KENEDI

When I was about nine, my grandmother came to visit us on our little farm in California. She was from Freeport, Long Island, and if you couldn't tell by her accent, the way she dressed would have given her away, in pleated polyester slacks and a loud plaid shirt, complete with long red nails and a sprayed coif like plaster of Paris. Thus attired, she turned to me one day and out of the blue said, "Ya neva know when ya might need to kill a chicken" and headed for the hen house. After a moment of reflection I decided she had a point, and so, partly horrified and mostly fascinated, I followed her. The chickens we raised were strictly for eggs, so it was all new to me.

She prepared herself like a Zen master—meditation, deep breathing exercises, and stretching. In her thick Hungarian/New York/Jewish accent, she told me, "Chickens aw de tastiest boid in de land when dey aw fresh. Yaw grandfathah loved de chicken in goulash, paprikash, you name it. Oy, dat he didn't have dose triple and double and God knows how many bypasses. It vas de cigars dat kilt him, lemme tell you . . ."

"Foist thing you do," she explained, "is get yourself a pair of gloves, an old shirt, a plastic bucket, a shawp ax, and some running shoes. Nikes are de best—dey got dat little swoosh on de side, makes you look fashionable. It's impawtant to always look good." When I asked her why running shoes, she looked at me blankly and said, "You ever tried to catch a chicken dat knows it's about to die?" I stepped aside and let Grandma limber up.

Next she stepped into the chicken coop, looking like some sort of lunatic surgeon—yellow gloves, black boots to her knees, and an apron reading "Party Animal." She propped a cardboard box up on a stick with a string tied to it, handed me the string, and gave chase. She was indefatigable, unyielding. It was a scene out of Monty Python, but it worked, I pulled the string, and finally the chicken clucked nervously under the box.

I brought the chicken over to the chopping block. Grandma felt the edge of the ax blade in her hands. I thought maybe I could see a slight grin on her lips when she declared it "not quite shawp enough" and proceeded to hone it with a stone until it glinted in the sunlight. She took some practice swings, saying, "Ya don't vant to botch de first try. Ya vant clean, quick cut right through de old neck. Nothing woise than a howling chicken." She didn't need to convince me.

She set aside her thick glasses and I held the bird carefully. Summoning all her might, she perfectly separated the head from the body. Before I realized it was dead, the bird got up, flapped its wings as if merely startled, and took off in circles around the wood pile. The blood spurted from its neck in thick streams, and it would convulse with each spurt like some avant garde modern dance student. "Dat's nawmul," Grandma said as she leaned on her ax and wiped her brow. "Dey usually jog around a bit afterward."

After the chicken fell in a heap in front of her, Grandma wound its feet together and hung it on an oak branch to let the rest of the blood drip out. "It's a bit like drip-drying the wash," she told me. "Only you vant to make sure the dogs and cats—or the flies—don't get at it."

We moved the operation into the house, and Grandma changed out of her bloody shirt and into an apron. She dunked the bird in a pot of boiling water, sat down on a stool on the front porch with a big garbage bag next to her, and began pulling out clumps of feathers like she was petting a shedding cat. "De hot water loosens up de hold de quills have on the feathers, just like a chuck key does a drill," she explained. Pointing to the now-naked bird, she said, "Heah's de tricky pawt. You see doze little bristles where de feathehs used to be? Vell, ve don't vant to eat dem. So ve got to singe dem off." And she pulled out a Zippo lighter, flicked it on smoother than any movie gangster, and ran the flame lightly over the skin.

The next step was harder to take. Grandma set the bird on its back on the cutting board, took a cleaver, and hacked the neck off with such force that it flew across the room. Then she put on a rubber glove, gritted her teeth, and stuck her hand down the hole where the neck used to be. It sounded like mushing a banana around in your mouth, which was bad, but the smell was horrendous, like a rotten deer carcass in the woods. She pulled out the heart, giblets, and liver and showed them to me like a Mayan priest at a sacrifice. Next came the gizzard. "Chickens swallow all sawts of crap," Grandma explained excitedly. "You never know vat you'll find in a gizzard. Once yaw great grandmother found a gold ring." We tore it open and there before our eyes were some roofing nails my dad had used to build the chicken coop, one of my Matchbox cars, and a penny.

I wanted Grandma to cut off the feet, but she insisted they were delicious to "suck on." "Now ve boil the whole damn thing and make soup—make the best chicken soup you've ever had," she said. "And tomorrow I'll show you how to make a zip gun." ❖

Here's the informative version:

### YOUR FIRST KILL

AARON KENEDI

Foster Farms no longer raises chickens. Instead, they raise large-breasted mutants so juiced on hormones they make Hulk Hogan seem normal. Armour raises its poultry in an environment so unspeakably inhumane that it makes you ashamed to be a human being when you hear about it.

You probably know all this—that's why you've decided to raise your own chickens. You're willing to do the work it takes to eat meat that's tastier, cheaper, healthier, and easier on your karma. But chickens don't come chopped up and packaged, so eventually (around the time of the summer's first barbecue) you're going to have to butcher a chicken yourself. Here's how. The method you're about to read is my grandma's, so you can rest assured it's quick and safe.

The first thing you need to know is that, unless you get emotionally attached easily, it will be easier to kill chickens than you think. Chickens aren't cuddly or adorable, and they aren't loyal—they'd do the same to you if the roles were reversed. And they can't cluck, poop, or peck when they're dead.

Roosters are okay to eat, but hens are better, because they're plumper and you'll have more of them in the coop. But before you grab your least favorite and start whacking, do some things first. Dress in old clothes you can throw away, because killing a chicken is about as dirty a job as it sounds. Wear comfortable shoes, preferably running shoes, because a chicken that senses doom is as difficult to catch as an Elvis concert. Consider laying a trap: Tie a string to a stick, use the stick to prop up a box, and chase the chicken until she chances to pass under—then pull the string.

Now comes the icky part. You can do it two ways: Either swiftly and violently twist the bird's neck until it snaps, or sharpen your trusty ax, have a friend hold the little bugger on a chopping block, and unleash a mighty whack on the bird's neck. Cut cleanly the first time, because a half-beheaded chicken makes a sound you've never heard before and will never want to hear again. Snapping is cleaner, but it takes some strength. Axing is easier, but the bird will run around for a few minutes. It's a shock at first to see a headless bird sit up and start jogging, blood spurting out of its neck causing it to shake and convulse, but you have to drain the blood anyway, so this method kills two birds with one stone (sorry).

After the chicken has exhausted itself, tie its feet together and hang it on a branch or clothesline over a bucket to let the remaining blood drip out—about two hours. Don't let dogs, cats, or flies get at it. Meanwhile, boil a large pot of water, prepare some table space, and sharpen your cleaver or largest knife. Put the carcass in the boiling water for about one minute *only*. This will loosen the quills and make picking the bird much easier. Pull out all the feathers, containing them immediately, while they're still wet, in a large trash bag or something similar.

Now you have a naked bird covered with little bristles where the feathers used to be. You can't eat them—it's like eating the rough side of those two-sided kitchen sponges—so you must burn them off. Light a gas burner or a cigarette lighter and, without cooking the chicken, carefully singe off each bristle. It's the most time-consuming step in the process, but it's essential for your gastronomic well-being.

Your chicken now looks a lot like the thing you buy in Safeway. Except on the inside. Now comes the other icky part. If you opted for the snapping method earlier, you first must chop off the head where the neck meets the body. You can also cut off the feet at this point, though Grandma swears they're the tastiest part. Now put on a rubber glove, take a cleansing breath, stick your hand down the hole where the neck used to be, and pull everything out. It's gross, it's messy, it smells like death, you'll feel like a brute, but it must be done. An alternative is to take your knife and split the carcass from the butt to the collar and pry the breast apart with your hands. This method is cleaner because you don't have to grab and squeeze any entrails, but the smell is just as bad. Once laid open, the inside of a chicken is practically designed for disemboweling—just remove everything. Throw the organs away like I do, or fry them up and eat them like Grandma does. The small thing that looks like a Hacky Sack footbag is the gizzard, where the chicken grinds to dust what she eats. If you're curious, cut it open and see what the chicken's been eating. Grandma insists her mother once found a gold ring in one.

Now rinse the bird under cold water and decide how to cook it. Chop it into pieces (that's another essay) and prepare a nice Kiev or marsala sauce, or plop it whole into a large pot, add vegetables, and make the tastiest, cheapest, healthiest chicken soup you've ever had. Grandma would be so proud. ❖

Informative writing is also different from argumentative writing. In informative writing most of what you say isn't a matter of opinion, and your relationship to the audience is different than in writing an argument. When you argue, you're trying to talk your reader into giving up her opinion and accepting yours, and she doesn't want to go along, but in informative writing the reader grants that she needs what you're offering—a new owner of a VCR doesn't need much persuading to convince him that he needs help programming the thing. Aaron's chicken-slaughtering experience could easily have been turned into an argument—perhaps making the case that Americans have lost touch with the eternal verities like birth and death and need to get their hands bloody once in a while.

## The Three Challenges

Informative writing offers the writer three challenges: 1) we don't feel knowledgeable enough, 2) it's boring, and 3) something called the COIK problem is ever-present. Let's find ways to deal with each.

### You Don't Feel Knowledgeable Enough

It feels fraudulent to set yourself up as the expert. This is entirely a problem of audience definition. You are the teacher the moment you're talking to people who know less than you. If you know how to play Solitaire or Tomb Raider and the reader doesn't, you have knowledge she wants.

You've been learning all your life. And for everything you've learned, there's someone who doesn't know it and would profit from learning it. If you've been in Mrs. Mercer's twelfth-grade English class at Holy Name High School, there's someone coming into the class blind who doesn't know how the class works and who could benefit from your expertise. If you watch football on TV, there's someone who doesn't and who would benefit if you explain what he's seeing.

To make sure you and your reader know your respective roles, lay them out in paragraph 1. Tell the reader up front that you know something he doesn't know and that he will profit from knowing it:

> OK, so your boyfriend dumped you. If your relationship was anything like mine, you probably feel like the lowest, most good-for-nothing human being on earth. Well, I'm here to tell you that you can and will survive your breakup. Here are some things you can do to speed your recovery.

> Is there central heating and air? Does the place have a dishwasher? Is the rent reasonable? Of course they're important considerations. But when looking for a place to rent, in our obsession with the inanimate, we often overlook one of the most important ques-

tions: What's the landlord like? If you're looking to rent, you should be asking yourself some key questions about your potential landlord.

**Warm up with a mock-informative essay.** If the role of teacher feels awkward, warm up by doing a teacher *parody.* Write a *mock-informative essay,* a send-up of informative essays where you take something dead simple—chewing gum or putting toothpaste on a toothbrush—and pretend it's as complicated as building a space station. Here's a masterpiece of the genre:

## ERADICAT

PETER GERRODETTE

Putting out the cat can often be an emotionally trying experience. Cat owners are for the most part uniquely susceptible to feelings of guilt, frustration, and inadequacy. These feelings are normal and do not necessarily indicate an unhealthy cat–person relationship. Rather, dilemmas of this kind are often a direct consequence of the subliminal nature of what I term cat-to-people communication lines. Frequently it is the misinterpretation of signals on this network that leads to hardships and bad feelings all around. For a serious breakdown in communication, you should consider a competent cat psychologist. For more day-to-day concerns, I would like to offer some potentially useful strategies, the effectiveness of which is entirely dependent on the integrity of the cat–person relationship.

When first faced with a cat who is reluctant to exit, it may be best to try the traditional mainstay of the cat owner, the Here Kitty Kitty strategy. One stands poised at the door, radiating a sense of anticipation and singing "Here Kitty Kitty!" or a variation thereof. It's best to use the same intonations as when feeding the cat. Occasionally it may be necessary to extend your hand, loosely clenched, indicating the possibility of a tidbit, thus luring your cat out the door; however, use the subversive strategy sparingly, because cats will soon become wise and ignore your efforts.

Another strategy is the fall-back position of owners who do not or cannot reason with their cats. This is the Brute Force approach. Any time you have to bodily move or pick up your cat, you've lost. Applying this strategy means using your size and bulk to unfair advantage, like the playground bully you knew in third grade. In a new relationship, the Brute Force approach can be especially damaging, as cats are particularly sensitive to recriminations.

A third strategy is the ultimate synthesis of man's appeal to reason. I like to term this course of action the Descartes strategy,

> in honor of the thinker who gave us "I think, therefore I am." Cats always make a point of letting you know that they exist. Rubbing your leg and kick-boxing your shoe are examples of this behavior. A cat capable of philosophizing should be reasoned with. You must convince your cat that it's in his best interest to be put out. Maggie, for instance, is a lap addict. She understands that if she doesn't abide by the house rules, she doesn't get her fix.
>
> Finally there is the Fred Flintstone strategy. At this point in your relationship you have accepted the possibility that your cat is smarter than you are and you sing to yourself, "Someday maybe Fred will win the fight! When that cat will stay out for the night!" ❖

Mock-informative essays are great fun, but they're only good as ice-breakers, because they dodge the teaching challenge. The joke lies in making simple things difficult, which is the opposite of what good informative writing tries to do.

## It's Boring

It's true that informative writing lacks the emotional wallop of personal writing and the intellectual drama of argument, which means you'll have to work harder to stay alive and keep your reader awake. Use the "showing" tools from Chapter 14 and the Concretion section of Chapter 11 to keep the energy up, and remember it's always about remaining a living person on the page and staying aware that your reader is alive as well. With that in mind, even recipes can be brought to life:

> My roommate and I are your basic health nuts. We never eat red meat or pork, and we try to stay away from sweets. Our main subsistence comes from rice cakes, fruits, and vegetables. Every once in a while, though, we break. This tremendous urge to eat something incredibly fattening seems to take over. Yes, the moment has finally arrived. It's fondue time.
>
> Cheese fondue is our favorite thing to pig out on. Not only is it delicious, it's easy to make and fairly inexpensive. The first thing to do is make sure you have all the ingredients . . .

## COIK Is a Constant Problem

Informative writing looks easy—you just tell the reader how to bake the cake or what to see in Yellowstone National Park, right? But most informative writing, even the pro stuff, *fails*—when was the last time you really learned how to do something by reading a book? So it must not be easy at all.

It's not easy because of a little problem called COIK, which stands for "Clear Only If Known." COIK writing can only be understood if you already understand it before you read it. Almost all the informative writing you see is COIK writing. You can't understand the auto manual unless you already understand auto repair; you can't understand the book on home wiring unless you already know how to do home wiring; you can't understand the chemistry text unless you're a chemist.

COIK problems are inherent in the way informative writing is made. You, the writer, know the information already—otherwise, you can't teach it. But because you know it, you can't remember what it's like to not know it. So you talk to the reader as if she already knows what you have to teach. Here's a writer having COIK problems in an essay for novices on how to change spark plugs:

> To begin, make sure that everything you need is handy. That means get out a socket that fits snugly over your spark plug, the new plugs, and a grease rag, and put them within reach. Next, open your hood and locate the old plugs.
>
> Go to the top of the first row and carefully remove the plug wire—the little cap just pulls off if you put enough effort into it. Then put your socket over the old plug and turn it to the left until the plug is removed. Then take the new plug and carefully tighten it by hand in the hole left by the old plug. When you have tightened it as much as you can by hand, put the socket on it and turn it to the right until it is extremely tight. Be very careful while tightening the plug; it's made of porcelain, which cracks very easily. The plug is worthless if it's cracked.
>
> Put the wire back on the top of the new plug. Go on to the next plug in line and repeat the same process until you run out of plugs. The process is now complete, and even this mechanically inept person could do it, so you should have no problem whatsoever.

If you've never worked on a car, the first paragraph alone will leave you with many questions:

> What is a socket?
> What is a spark plug?
> Why change spark plugs?
> Where do you get new plugs, and how do you know what kind to get?
> How do you locate the old plugs?
> How do you know when plugs need changing?

The author can't imagine anyone not knowing answers to these questions, so she assumes the knowledge, and the reader gets lost and quits reading. You have to make sure that doesn't happen. Here's how:

**Realize that COIK problems are inevitable,** so you must maintain constant vigilance against them.

**Define your audience's level of expertise precisely,** and keep it ever in mind. Constantly ask yourself, "Will my audience understand this?" "What have I assumed they know, and am I right to assume it?" Hear them asking you questions like "What does that mean?" and "How exactly do I do that?"

**Get yourself some real readers.** Spotting COIK problems is hard for you but easy for them. Ask them to tell you where they're confused or what they were left wanting to know.

## Eight Teaching Tips

Now that you feel like a teacher, here are eight teaching techniques that help people learn.

**Give an overview.** An overview is a summary, a simple map of the territory you're about to traverse. If I'm going to take you through the thirty steps of a tricky recipe, you'll appreciate knowing that overall you're going to 1) make the stuffing, 2) stuff the meat, 3) make the sauce, and 4) bake the meat in the sauce. Overviews often use lists: "First, . . . second, . . . third . . ."; "There are three things you must do . . ." The typical overview is one sentence long, so it's in essence a thesis sentence. Here's an overview of "How to Audition for a Play" (pp. 243–244):

> Scoring at the audition comes down to four things: knowing what you're getting into, doing a little homework beforehand, dressing the part, and acting confident when you're on.

Overviews are most helpful when they come early in the essay. Overviews as conclusions usually make readers feel stupid.

**Give examples.** No generalization or abstraction ever existed that isn't easier to understand with a following "for instance." Here's an abstract definition:

> A thesaurus, like a dictionary, is arranged alphabetically, but instead of definitions it lists words that are synonyms or antonyms of your source word. It offers alternatives to words you feel are used too often, are too bland, are not descriptive enough, or contain connotations that do not apply.

That would have been COIK writing if the writer hadn't gone on to give an example:

> For instance, let's say you're writing about the desert and you realize you've used the word "hot" nine hundred and thirty-two times.

Look up "hot" in the thesaurus and it will give you a list of similar adjectives: parching, toasting, simmering, scalding, scorching, and blazing.

If you need a crutch, force yourself to write *for example* and *for instance* a lot, but readers don't need these links and they can usually be cut out in the rewrite.

**Use analogies.** An analogy says that X is like Y: Writing is like playing tennis in the dark, style is like the clothing your essay is wearing, canelloni are like Italian enchiladas. Analogies are great teachers because they make what the reader is trying to learn familiar by translating it into terms she already understands. Here's an analogy for how to breathe while singing:

> To use the diaphragm correctly, you must imagine your midsection is being pumped up like a tire.

Most analogies use the words *like, as,* or *as if,* but not always: "Imagine your diaphragm is a tire being pumped up." "Canelloni are Italian enchiladas."

**Tell the reader what not to do as well as what to do.** Warn the reader away from common errors she's likely to make. List the five most popular ways to screw up, and tell the reader not to do them. Recipes almost always fail to do this, which is why I can't cook. "The Last Stop for America's Busses" (p. 387) tells you not to expect the air conditioning or bathrooms on Mexican first-class busses.

**Tell the reader why.** Once a dishwasher repairman came to fix my dishwasher. He told me three things: "Always rinse your dishes before putting them in the washer"; "Buy dishwasher soap in the smallest container you can find"; and "Run your sink water until it's as hot as it can get before running the dishes." I would have ignored all three instructions, since they sounded like he was just trying to get me to spend money, waste time, and increase my energy bill, but the repairman knew how to teach, so he told me *why* I should. Rinse the dishes, he said, because the dishwasher's drain pipe is small, so it clogs easily, and it's rubber, so it can't be cleared by drill or Drano. Once it clogs it's a major repair to clear it. Buy small boxes of soap, he said, because dishwasher soap is an unstable chemical with a short shelf life, so you want to use it up quickly. Run the water to hot, he said, because dishwasher soap is engineered to work in very hot water—less hot, and the soap doesn't dissolve. I understood; I've done as he suggested ever since.

To force yourself to say why, write "because" after every instruction, and go on to explain.

**Draw a picture.** If you're describing things you can see—how to tie a clove hitch, a typical backyard garden layout—words are clumsy. Just draw it; make what tech writers call a *graphic*. That's obvious, but students often don't because they think it's cheating to make writing easy.

**Use imperatives.** Imperatives are commands: "Do this!" "Don't do that!" Shy writers find imperatives pushy, so they avoid them with passives and other circumlocutions. Don't:

The plugs should be tightened. → *Tighten the plugs.*

A deep mixing bowl and a pair of chopsticks are needed for mixing. → *Get a deep mixing bowl and a pair of chopsticks for mixing.*

**Seek to persuade.** Informative writing is almost defined by its lack of persuasive purpose—what's persuasive about how to change your spark plugs?—but we always write better if we're trying to sell something; it gives us oomph. It only takes a slight twist to recast a purely informative intent into a persuasive one:

| Subject | Thesis |
|---|---|
| gardening | A backyard garden will provide you with cheap, healthy food, good exercise, and a tan. |
| choosing a landlord | Picking a landlord may be the most important part of renting an apartment. |

## WRITER'S WORKSHOP

### The Eight in Action

Let's read through an informative essay and note when and where the eight teaching tips are used. I've marked such places with numbers and labeled each in the right margin:

## HOW TO AUDITION FOR A PLAY

STEVE WIECKING

You're standing in the center of a room. Dozens of people surround you, watching intently your every move. You are told what to do and you do it. Sound like the Inquisition? It isn't, but some might call it a close relative: the audition.

Every few months of every year your college's drama department offers every student the chance to audition for a part in a stage production. (1) As a theater arts minor who was cast with no acting experience in a one-act play last October, I can tell you that auditioning for a play is a truly horrifying, but ultimately rewarding experience. Who wouldn't want to show their stuff up there behind the footlights? Auditioning is open to anyone, and the best way to go about it is to prepare thoroughly and go into it with a feeling of confidence.

*1. Persuasive purpose*

(2) Just as if you were going to a job interview at your local Burger King, (3) you have to know some practical information before an audition. First, what kind of an audition are you going to? If the audition announcement calls for a "cold reading," you're in for performing any given scene from the play unprepared. Well, almost unprepared—there is some accepted cheating. (4) Go to your main library or the Drama Department's script library and check out the play. (5) Find out what that Macbeth guy is up to or what's bugging Hamlet. (6) Don't try to memorize; just be happy with the head start you'll have on the material because you know what's going on.

*2. Analogy*
*3. Overview*
*4. Imperative*
*5. Example*
*6. What not to do*

Instead of a cold reading try-out, you could be going to one that calls for a monologue. (7) In that case, prepare, *memorize,* a two- to three-minute scene of a single character speaking from any play of your choice (unless instructed otherwise). This requires some hopefully obvious rules. (8) Choose a character that suits you. Be as realistic as possible concerning age, sex, and situation. (9) Freshman girls not yet over the trials of acne should not attempt the death throes of Shakespeare's King Lear. (10) Avoid overdone roles like Romeo or

*7. Imperative*
*8. Imperative*
*9. Example*
*10. What not to do*

Juliet—(11) to the directors, these have become *11. Why*
(12) like hearing "Hello, Dolly" sung without *12. Analogy*
cease. (13) And above all avoid Hamlet. (14) *13. What not to do*
Each director has his own idea of what he wants *14. Why*
Hamlet "to be or not to be," and it usually
comes in the form of Sir Laurence Olivier—
stiff competition at its worst.

Once you know where you're going and
what to expect, the proper clothing is neces-
sary. Dress subtly and comfortably in some-
thing adaptable (15) like jeans and tennis shoes. *15. Example*
(16) You have to be able to move well, and (17) *16. Why*
you don't want to be so flashy and singular *17. What not to do*
that the casting director sees only a paisley
tie or psychedelic tights instead of a possible
character. (18) I recently watched a girl audi- *18. Example*
tion in a red, white, and blue sailor suit with
spiked heels. If the directors had been casting
"Barnacle Bill Does Bloomingdale's" she would
have been a shoo-in, but otherwise it was man
overboard time on the Titanic.

(19) Once prepared, at the audition noth- *19. Overview*
ing is more important than confidence. Pre-
sent yourself well. (20) Eye the surroundings *20. Imperative*
as if to say you know where you are and have
control of the room, and greet the directors
pleasantly to show them you want to be there.
Handed an unfamiliar script? Make a quick
choice as to what you're going to do and stick
with it. (21) *Don't glue your eyes to the script.* *21. What not to do*
(22) I guarantee no one has ever been cast for *22. Why*
having a wonderful relationship with a Xerox
copy. When your turn is over, exit graciously
with a smile and a "thank you" that let people
know the chance was appreciated.

Of course, this all sounds easier than it really is, and you may say that I've left out one key requirement: talent. But talent you either have or you don't, and if you've seen many college drama productions you'll know that it isn't exactly a huge prerequisite after all. ❖

**Now it's your turn.** Do to an informative draft of your own what we did to Steve's essay: Identify in the margins any places that do any of the eight teaching tips on pp. 240–242. If there are any of the eight the draft hasn't done (and you should do most of them more than once), rewrite, adding passages that do them.

## EXERCISES

1. Do the first half of the exercise in the Writer's Workshop (p. 244) with any essay in the Treasury of Essays (p. 368). Photocopy the essay and note in the margins where it uses the tools. Then list all the tools the essay doesn't use. Don't rewrite the essay.

2. Practice adding the persuasive edge to informative topics by rewriting the following informative topics as theses, the way we did on p. 242:

   a. Shopping at garage sales
   b. How to sing
   c. How to survive divorce
   d. Where to take kids on a rainy day
   e. What is cholesterol?

3. Write a one- to two-page mock-informative essay (p. 237).

4. Prewrite an informative essay by writing a list of every possible question your reader might want answered.

5. Tell the class your informative essay topic and ask them to generate every possible question they would like answered or other readers might like answered.

6. Using the information from Exercises 4 and 5, write the essay.

7. Rewrite the following instructions so they are as unboring as possible and COIK problems have been minimized. Assume the reader is an experienced driver who has never dealt with a flat tire before:

> To change a flat tire, jack up the car on the corner where the flat is. Remove the flat with a lug wrench. Replace the flat with the spare. Remove the jack.

8. List all possible questions a reader might have after reading the following restaurant review:

> Carmelita's is a pretty good Mexican restaurant. I recommend it if you like Mexican food. I especially like the carne asada, though it may be a little picante for your taste. The prices are low and the portions are ample. My one complaint is they don't have flan, which is something I really go to Mexican restaurants hoping for.

9. Take an essay seed and write thesis and purpose statements based on it for two essays, one personal and one informative.

# Chapter 16

# WRITING AN ARGUMENT, PART 1: THINKING IT THROUGH

With argumentative writing, the basic rule is the same as for all writing everywhere: You can't do it if you haven't read a lot of it. So the easiest way to write a good argumentative essay is also the pleasantest: Read all the argumentative essays in the Treasury of Essays (p. 368) and write one like them.

## What's an Argument?

In an argumentative essay you try to move people to agree with you. That's different from personal writing, because personal writing doesn't seek agreement; we can love eggs and still connect with Kris Tachmeir's loathing of them in "The Egg and I Revisited" (p. 37). And it's different from informative writing, because informative writing allows little ground for *dis*agreement: When Andrew Roe tells us that international hostels are the cheapest decent lodgings in Europe (p. 385), if a substantial number of the readers say "I disagree," he's either factually wrong or he's arguing instead of informing.

An argument isn't just a belief or an opinion, like "I like the Beatles," because an opinion gives the reader no grounds to agree or disagree, and it doesn't urge the reader to join you. An argument is an opinion with reasons to back it up and intentions to sell itself to others. As soon as you say, "I think the Beatles are vastly overrated, and I'm going to try to get you to agree with me," you've got an argument on your hands.

An argument isn't a sermon, because a sermon preaches to the converted. Its listeners don't need persuading; instead, it *celebrates* a message the audience has already accepted, allowing them to renew their faith by agreeing all over again. Most so-called "arguments" are sermons in disguise, because they assume the reader grants exactly what they purport to be arguing for. Most arguments against gun control, for instance, assume that gun control equals gun prohibition, that the Constitution guarantees American citizens the right to own handguns, and that citizens' ownership of handguns is a deterrent to crime—exactly those things your reader *doesn't* grant and will have to be convinced of.

If you're in doubt about whether you're writing an argument, reduce it to a thesis statement (Chapter 5) and apply two tests. To avoid merely stating an opinion, use the *Should Test:* Does the thesis have the word "should" in it?

> You should buy your groceries at a local market, not at a chain store, because the owner cares about you and your money stays in town.

> You should go see Steven Spielberg's latest movie—it's marvelous.

To avoid the sermon trap, use the second test, the *Stand-Up Test:* How likely is it that a substantial number of the people in the audience will stand up after you state your thesis and say "I disagree"? If you can't imagine more than a scattered few doing it, you're preaching. Go find something that will make more people want to stand up and confront you.

## Finding an Argumentative Prompt

That's easy—arguments seek you out every minute of every day. You're being handed an argument every time

> you eat in a restaurant and like it (in which case you can argue that other people should eat there) or don't (in which case you can argue that other people shouldn't);

> a teacher or the University frustrates you or betrays you or treats you shabbily (in which case you can argue that something should be done so you and other students don't have to suffer like that anymore);

> a roommate, police officer, parent, best friend, shop clerk, or other human being does something to you that drives you crazy or makes you mad (in which case you can argue that people like that should be taught to be different).

In short, the world is constantly presenting us with evidence that Things Aren't the Way They Should Be, and we should feel moved to try to Fix the Problem by arguing those who Don't See It into doing what we think they should do about it.

## Thinking It Through vs. Selling the Case

Let's assume you've found your argument. The work that remains can be divided into two stages. Stage 1 (this chapter) is thinking it through—what teachers call critical thinking, where you try to reason your way to a position you really believe and that really holds water. Stage 2 (Chapter 17) is selling the case, where you take the thought-through position and find ways to sell it to your audience.

The main problem people have making arguments is trying to argue and think at the same time. You must think before you argue, because if you try to do the two together, the second poisons the first. Seeking the truth is a process of exploration, risk taking, and discovery. It requires openness and a willingness to look stupid and fail a lot. Convincing others is about selling and winning. People trying to sell and win stop their ears to everything that doesn't strengthen their position. If you're selling a car, any sense of the car's weaknesses makes you a weaker salesperson, so you convince yourself that the car is a treasure. Most people, however much they tell themselves they're thinking, are in fact selling an idea to themselves, shouting down all thoughts that threaten to complicate the initial close-minded position.

## Why Thinking Is Hard

We can't think well until we understand the obstacles in our way. Thinking seems to be an extremely difficult act, judging by the small number of people you and I know who do it well. How many friends do you have who impress you by how well they reason? I rest my case.

But thinking isn't hard the way juggling is hard. It's really just that we don't *want* to think, for a number of reasons, which we might as well face:

**1. Thinking is unemotional:** Emotions blind us to reason. Since we are at the core emotional creatures, forsaking our emotions feels like forsaking our very selves. In science fiction, humans are defined by their emotionality, and the alien races are always scientific, sterile, and unfeeling. *Star Trek*'s Mr. Spock is lovable only because despite all his talk about hating feelings and being glad he doesn't have any, we always know he has them and that's what makes him human. Most of us are devoting our lives to learning to honor our feelings better and getting others to respect them, so telling our emotions to take a hike feels like a step backwards.

**2. Thinking is impersonal and objective:** Objectivity means that what's true for me is true for you. Though it's easy to give lip service to that idea, we all know it isn't so. You and I are fundamentally different—I'm me and you're not. If you're late, you should apologize; if I'm late, you should learn to be less rigid. Critical thinking says we don't get to be the center of the universe anymore.

**3. Thinking is consistent:** What's right and true now is right and true tomorrow and the day after, and what's right and true in one situation is right and true in another. Thus if Country X can invade Country Y because Country Y has the potential to make weapons of mass destruction, then any country can invade any other country that has that potential, at any time. If one President should be impeached for lying, any President who lies should be impeached. We hate having to embrace consistency. We want to use whatever "rules" prove the case we want to prove at a particular moment, but we don't want to have to live by those rules when they don't get us our way. Thus a political party out of power uses underhanded tactics to block the political appointments of the party in power, then complains when the tables are turned and the other party, now out of power, does exactly the same thing. Not fair! What's sauce for the goose is sauce for the gander, as the old folks used to say.

**4. Thinking is debilitating:** It makes us weaker in a fight. Anyone who tells you that critical thinking will make you a winner is mistaken. Just look at American politics—does the better thinker win the election? No, the election is won by the person with the warmest speaking style or the best haircut or the catchiest slogan. Reagan was one of the most popular Presidents in history, and not even his staunchest fans claim he was a thinker. Any politician who makes the mistake of actually *reasoning* in a public debate watches her ratings plummet. And no scientist or academician ever won an election without disguising her background. That's because people are persuaded by emotions and affect. Critical thinking strikes them as cold and clinical—inhuman, in short. Persuading is selling, and the best sellers, used-car salesmen, don't use logic.

So if you want power over others, the ability to manipulate them or control them, critical thinking isn't your friend. As you are about to crush your opponent with the killer argument, CT will rear its ugly head to remind you that you're being inconsistent and subjective.

So why put effort into thinking? Because life isn't always a battle for power or control. Because you want to know who you are and what's going on in your head. Life is about gaining self-knowledge. Your thinking is a huge part of who you are. Thinking badly is like shooting baskets badly in your driveway by yourself—there's no worldly penalty, but it's a crime against a universal rule: Do things well.

These four principles come down to one fact: Thinking demands a subjugation of the ego. If your ego is weak, you won't want to do this chapter's work. The ego is a good thing, but it isn't the only voice running your life. Do what you must to strengthen your ego; then, when it's strong enough to step aside, give it a rest and experience the pleasures of ego-free living. Now you're ready to think. And once you really *want* to think, I promise you that if you'll follow the steps of this chapter you'll think well. (And no doubt end forever your chances of getting elected President.)

## How to Think: A Template

Thinking needs something to think *about,* so we'll begin by freewriting a draft and reducing the draft to a thesis statement, à la Chapter 5. Now we can reduce the amorphous thinking process to three operations to perform on the thesis, in this order:

1. Eliminate language problems in the thesis.
2. Examine the principles and the consequences of the thesis.
3. Perform seven cleanup tasks (I'll explain later).

### Eliminating Language Problems

Language problems in the thesis statement are anything in its wording that gets in the way of our thinking. If I say something and mean something else, or say something that can mean lots of different things, or say something that is so negatively worded that it judges the issue before I get a chance to think it through, my reasoning will be fatally corrupted before I begin. Language problems must be corrected before going on to Steps 2 and 3; otherwise, they'll keep re-infecting you, like poison-ivy infected clothing you keep putting on every morning.

We'll break the job of troubleshooting language into two steps:

a. Make a well-formed assertion.
b. Eliminate clouding language.

### Making a Well-Formed Assertion

Before we start doing hard thinking, we must make sure we've got a thesis we can work with. When we make arguments, it's dangerous to be too bold or too definite, so we make *ill-formed assertions* that take little or no risk. Behind such remarks lie hinted-at arguments, and we must bring those arguments into the light of day:

The police in England didn't even carry guns.

(*What are you implying? That not carrying guns will prevent crime? Or that the English police were fools?*)

Almost all of the world's great chefs are men.
(*What are you implying? That women are inferior to men? Or that women are discriminated against in the restaurant business?*)

Skateboarding is not a crime.
(*What are you implying? That skateboarders should be allowed to do anything they want? Or that skateboarding should be a crime?*)

The two most popular ill-formed assertions are *rhetorical questions* and *reasons*.

The *rhetorical question* asks a question and hopes the reader will take the risky step of translating it into an assertion for you:

Who are you to decide when someone should die?
(*Implied assertion:* Capital punishment should be stopped, because no one has the right to decide when someone should die.)

Why shouldn't young people be allowed to have a good time and blow off steam once in a while?
(*Implied assertion:* The police should stop trying to break up parties, because young people should be allowed to have a good time and blow off steam once in a while.)

To translate a question into an assertion, do one of two things: *answer the question*, or *turn it into a declarative sentence:*

Don't skateboarders have a right to be heard?
(*Answer:* Skateboarders have a right to be heard.)

If people are so concerned with the environment, why do they live in wooden houses?
(*Declarative sentence:* People who profess to be concerned with the environment yet live in wooden houses are hypocrites.)

The *reason* is harder to spot, because it *is* an assertion—it's just not the final assertion. It's an assertion that states a *reason* and lets the reader do the risky work of arriving at the conclusion. It's the "because" clause that follows the unstated thesis. It's a popular ploy in conversation: "Sure, you're a man" means "You don't have any understanding of what women's lives are like and aren't qualified to speak on the subject, *because* you're a man."

Verbal fights are often nothing but a series of reasons without conclusions: "But you said you'd pick me up at 3 P.M.!"; "Well, you forgot to pick me up yesterday!"; "Yeah, well, I got called to a meeting I didn't know about"; "Well, you never even tried to call me." Entire political campaigns have been waged through them: "A woman has a right to choose" is a *because* in defense of the real thesis "Abortion should be legal"; "Skateboarding isn't a crime" is a *because* in defense of the real thesis "Skateboarders should be allowed to skateboard on the sidewalks." And some people use them to avoid making decisions: "Do you want to go to the movies tonight?" gets the response "Well, we haven't been out of the house for a while . . ."

To expose a reason posing as a thesis, put the word "because" in front of it and try constructing a "should" clause that can precede it and feels more like *the thing you're really trying to get:*

> Step 1: Smokers have rights too.
> Step 2: _________ because smokers have rights too.
> Step 3: Smoking in bars should be allowed because smokers have rights too.

## Eliminating Clouding Language

Now that you have a well-formed assertion, ask yourself what it really says. Language is *ambiguous*—most words can have a dozen meanings or more, and when we combine words in sentences the possible meanings multiply. We're wonderfully blind to this; we're always pretty sure we know exactly what we mean—but we're wrong. A student writes:

> American children are really spoiled, and the schools are encouraging it.

That seems clear until we think about it for a minute. What does "spoiled" really mean? I could say that a spoiled child is one who has been treated too nicely and thus has come to ask for things he doesn't deserve. But if I think about it I have to ask: How can you be too nice to someone? How does being nice to someone harm him? Some people think it spoils a child to let him cry, listen to his complaints, or give him a voice in how a family or classroom operates. Others consider such things basic human rights and think it's unjust to deny them to children. If "spoiled" means "selfish," well, isn't everyone selfish—aren't you always doing exactly what you want to do, and isn't that a good thing? And if "spoiled" means "thinking you're something special," well, isn't it good to think you're special, and aren't you? And how much does a person deserve, and who decided that? If "spoiled" means "never learned you can't have it your own way all the time," well, some people do seem to have it their own way all the time, so are they spoiled?

The more familiar and accepted the assertion, the more likely that your meaning will go unexamined. "TV is mostly garbage" is a statement all of my students grant, but the more you think about it the harder it becomes to say what it really means. How can art or entertainment be "garbage"? Is TV supposed to be doing something and failing? What is "good" art? Is TV garbage because it's stupid (in which case, what's the intellectual level of an hour spent playing basketball or gardening?), or because it's full of ads (in which case, is all selling garbage, or just the highly manipulative selling, or what?), or because it's bad for you (in which case, how can art be good for you?)?

None of this is your fault. Language is inherently cloudy, for at least two reasons. First, *no one teaches you what words mean*—you just figure it out, by hearing others use them. Thus your sense of what a word means is quite literally your own invention, and not surprisingly, other people, who think differently and have different experiences with the word, come to different conclusions. Second, *words' meanings drift through use.* As people use words, they use them in slightly new ways, and those slight meaning shifts, multiplied through millions of uses, mean a word may mean something today it didn't mean last week or last year. There is no way to fix or stop either of these processes, no way to make language unambiguous; you can only work hard at damage control. And there is no step-by-step way to do that, beyond looking hard at language and asking "What does that really mean?" repeatedly. But there are two kinds of cloudy language we can be on the lookout for, loaded language and clichés:

**Loaded language.** Loaded language is language that contains judgment within it—it says "That's good" or "That's bad":

| **Neutral language** | **Loaded language** |
|---|---|
| women | broads |
| homosexuals | fags |
| cops | pigs |
| Southerners | rednecks |
| sexually active | promiscuous |
| sexually explicit | smut |

Like loaded dice, loaded language predetermines the outcome of the thinking process by assigning positive or negative value up front. If I say about a politician, "He conferred with his advisors," I've remained neutral; if I say, "He conferred with his *cronies*," I've damned him as a crook, and if I say, "He conferred with his *henchmen*," I've damned him as a thug.

Fixing loaded language is in theory easy: Look for any words that evoke strong "yea" or "nay" responses and replace them with neutral substitutes.

**Clichés.** A cliché is a phrase you've heard so many times you don't stop to think what it means anymore: *dead as a doornail, until hell freezes over, the bottom line, dumb as a post, you can't fight city hall, tip of the iceberg, last but not least, how are you doing?, and so in* *conclusion, in the fast-paced modern world of today, farm-fresh eggs.* Politicians don't want you to think too hard, so political positions tend to get reduced to clichés: *law and order, pro-choice, save the whales, show the politicians who's boss, new world order, compassionate conservatism, a thousand points of light.*

Clichés put your brain to sleep and prevent clear thinking by inviting a reflex response, like waving the flag at a political convention:

> College students have a *right* to *have a good time* and kick back once in a while.
>
> We must support the soldiers *fighting for our freedom* in the Near East.
>
> The University should do everything it can to encourage *diversity.*

Ambiguity increases with use—the more a word is used, the less sure its meaning becomes. So clichés, which are used constantly and everywhere, come to mean everything and nothing.

Clichés are easy to spot: If it's a word or phrase you hear everywhere, it's a cliché, and you've learned to stop thinking about it. Once you've spotted a cliché, either replace it with words of your own or ask the cliché hard questions, the way we did with "spoiled" on p. 253

Since all words are ambiguous, the task of eliminating ambiguity in an argument would be never-ending. Instead, look at your assertion and ask, "Do any of these words pose *serious* ambiguity problems?" There is a set of hugely vague, heavily loaded American buzzwords that are guaranteed to bring any argument to a standstill: words like *sexist, racist, American, equality, freedom, liberty, rights, fascist, liberal, natural, environment, diversity, feminist,* and *conservative.* If you use any of them, it is pointless to continue until you break through the fog and figure out what you're really saying.

## Examining Your Assumptions

Now that we have a well-formed assertion relatively free of cloudy language, we've got something we can think about.

Thinking about a thesis comes down to two tasks: understanding where the thesis comes from and understanding where it leads. Imagine the thesis as a step in a process or timeline: the thesis *emerges from* or *rests on* principles or assumptions, and it *leads to* consequences:

> Principles → thesis → consequences

If we accept the principles on which a thesis is based and accept the consequences of supporting it, we truly support the thesis; if we don't, we don't.

Every thesis rests on basic principles or assumptions:

Thesis: Americans should never accept public nudity, because it would rob making love of all its intimacy.
Principles: *Making love depends on intimacy; intimacy in lovemaking is good.*

Thesis: The government has no right to tell me to wear seat belts, because it's up to me if I want to kill myself.
Principles: *The government does not have the right or obligation to protect citizens from themselves; suicide is a right; my death would affect only myself.*

Thesis: Meat is good for you—that's why Nature made us carnivorous.
Principles: *Whatever is "natural" is "right." We cannot or should not alter our primitive makeup.*

Thesis: Americans have the right to own and use automatic weapons because the Constitution says so.
Principles: *The Constitution is always eternally right; the language of the Constitution is unambiguous; "arms" means "any kind of arms."*

Principles are merely larger theses, the big beliefs that justify your smaller belief: "*Since* I believe that the Bible is the literal word of God (large belief), I *therefore* believe that the universe was created in seven days (smaller belief)." All thinking goes like this, from larger beliefs to smaller ones, so until we articulate those larger beliefs and see if we really buy them, we don't know if we believe the smaller theses or not.

Principles are beliefs or values, and there is no such thing as a true or false belief. So you'll never find yourself simply agreeing or disagreeing with the principle, unless you're a zealot. Every principle begins a slippery and fascinating conversation about *when, in what situations, and to what extent* you accept it. Let's begin that conversation with each of the four theses above and their underlying principles. If clothing promotes intimacy, does a member of a nudist colony feel less intimate with other members than clothed people do? If your own death is really just your business, why buy life insurance? If we should eat meat because we ate meat a hundred thousand years ago, should we also live in caves and kill our neighbors? If the Constitution is always right, why did it condone owning slaves and prevent women from voting? All principles produce such interesting conversations. To get started critiquing a principle, ask two questions:

**"Where do I draw the line?"** Since principles are never a matter of true or false, the real question is how far will you go in supporting them, and when do you bail? Everybody is for free speech . . . up to a point. Everybody thinks protecting the environment is good . . . up to a point. Everyone thinks the Constitution is a good document . . . up to a point. Everyone thinks we should be natural . . . up to a point. The question isn't whether you believe, but where you draw the line. Take the underlying principle, make up more and more extreme applications of it, and discover when you say "Enough's enough."

> Thesis: We need special university admissions standards for minority students. After all, they didn't ask to be born into disadvantaged environments.
>
> Principle: *Standards should be proportional to a candidate's advantages.*

Where do you draw the line? Should graduate schools have higher admission requirements for graduates of "good" colleges, since they've had the advantage of a good undergraduate education? Should personnel officers have hiring criteria that rise as a job applicant's family income rises? Should disadvantaged students in your class be graded on a grading scale less rigorous than the one used on you?

**"What's the philosophical antithesis?"** Another way of discovering where you draw the line is to imagine your principle as one half of a pair of opposites—an *antithesis*—and ask yourself to what extent you believe the *other principle* as well.

All principles come in opposite pairs: "Nature knows best" vs. "We should evolve and rise above the level of beasts"; "The Constitution is a perfect document" vs. "Governments should grow and evolve as we become wiser"; "I have a right to run my own life" vs. "Society has a right to curb individual behavior for the good of all." Only zealots can pick one side of the antithesis and call it the right one; the rest of us find a working compromise, a spot on the spectrum connecting the two. We say, "I'm all for freedom of speech, but there are limits . . ." or "Sure, you have the right to live the way you want, but you have to consider your neighbors too." Like two magnets, the two ideals pull at us, and we move between them until the forces are balanced. If you don't see the merit of both sides of the antithesis, you're missing something.

Imagine concrete scenarios where the principles come into play. For instance, we all believe that customers should be responsible for their own purchasing decisions—and that companies who make and sell things should be responsible for their products. So where do you stand between those two conflicting beliefs? Who's responsible when a boater ignores storm warnings, takes a dinghy out into the ocean, and drowns? Who's responsible when a tire manufacturer makes a flawed tire, knows it, covers up the fact and continues to sell the tire anyway, and drivers are killed? Who's responsible when a customer buys a cup of very hot coffee at a drive-through and spills it on herself? Who's responsible when tobacco companies tell customers that cigarettes cause cancer, then spend millions in advertising to persuade customers to smoke, and a smoker dies of cancer?

As you work with antitheses, guard against two popular mistakes. Don't work with the antithesis of your *thesis;* instead, work with the antithesis of the *principle.* And don't equate the antithesis with the simple negative of the principle—the principle with a "not" added. Notice that in every thesis/antithesis pair in our examples, the antithesis is more than the principle with a "not."

## Examining the Consequences of the Thesis

Every time you argue for something, you have to think about what will happen if you get what you're asking for. All actions have consequences. If you can't accept the consequences of your thesis, you can't accept your thesis. If you see no consequences to your argument, you aren't arguing.

All actions have *an infinite number of* consequences, so some of those consequences must be good and some bad: AIDS reduces population pressure; recycling increases pollution from paper and plastic processing plants. If you only see one consequence to your argument, you're missing the others. If you only see good consequences to your argument, you're missing the bad ones. The question you must answer is, do the good consequences outweigh the bad or vice versa?

Weighing pros and cons is laborious, so we like to reduce our workload by pretending that actions have one and only one consequence: "Vote for A—he'll give us a strong military defense"; "Vote for C—he's a newcomer and we'll show the incumbents we're fed up." Single-issue voting is just another name for not seeing the *other* consequences of an action.

There are two kinds of consequences, logical and practical. Logical consequences are *the conclusions you are logically forced to accept if you accept your original thesis.* If an idea is true, then a host of other ideas that follow from it must also be true. For instance:

> **If** you argue that the cops shouldn't have arrested your friend Bill when he got drunk and began shooting off his shotgun at midnight because he wasn't trying to hurt anyone, **then** you are logically committed to arguing that no one should be held accountable for her actions if she doesn't intend to do harm, and **thus** the person who gets drunk and wipes out your family with his car can't be held accountable either, since he didn't mean to do it.
>
> **If** you argue that you should get a good grade in a class because you worked really hard, **then** you are logically committed to arguing that one's grade in a course should be determined by effort, and

> **thus** you must agree that you should get a lousy grade in any course where you get A's on the tests without trying hard.
>
> **If** you argue that the death penalty in America is racist because most people on death row are black, **then** you're logically committed to arguing that any system in which a group is represented beyond its demographic percentage is biased, and **thus** the NBA is racist and the death penalty is sexist against men.

*Practical consequences* are easier to grasp. They are the other events that take place if the action you're arguing for takes place:

> Thesis: Sex education is a bad idea because it undermines the authority of the nuclear family.
> (*It may have that one bad consequence, but it may also have good ones: It may help stop teen pregnancies and save people from AIDS. Are more people suffering from unwanted pregnancy or a non-authoritative family?*)
>
> Thesis: We desperately need a standardized national competency test for high school graduation, because high schools are graduating students who can't even read or spell.
> (*Such a test might mean that graduates spell better, but the other consequences might create a cure worse than the disease. More students would drop out, student fear would increase tenfold, and vast sums of money would be diverted from teaching to testing, just for starters. Overall, would we be better off or worse off?*)

## Seven Cleanup Tasks

If you crafted a well-formed assertion and thought through its underlying principles and its consequences, you've done an honest day's work. But if you have energy left, there are seven cleanup tasks you can perform.

**Ask, "How do I know?"** A belief has to come from somewhere. Ask yourself where you got yours:

> You lived through it.
> You heard it on TV.
> Your parents taught you.
> Logic led you to that conclusion.

A belief is only as sound as the soundness of its place of origin. Arguments about morality that are defended by "The Bible says so" have only as much authority as readers give the Bible, which varies from total to none.

**Ask, "What are the facts?"** For almost all arguments, facts matter, and if you don't have any you're guessing:

> Thesis: Most welfare recipients would jump at the chance to get off the dole and support themselves.
> (Research question: *What percentage of welfare recipients say they would jump at the chance if they were offered a job?*)
>
> Thesis: I don't want to wear seat belts, because I don't want to be trapped in the car if there's an accident.
> (Research question: *How many people die in car accidents because they are trapped in the car by their belts, and how many die because they aren't belted in?*)

**Ask, "Like what?"** Force yourself to concretize all abstractions and generalizations with at least one "for instance":

> Thesis: Schools should censor books that are clearly harmful to children.
> (*Make a list of those "clearly harmful" books, and ask yourself how you know they're harmful.*)
>
> Thesis: Punishment in schools is never necessary.
> (*Make a list of specific imaginary disciplinary situations in the classroom and invent nonpunishing ways of handling them.*)

**Ask, "What should be done?"** Most arguments contain a call to action: "Somebody should *do* something about this." If your thesis doesn't have one, ask yourself what you want done and who you want to do it:

> Thesis: TV is a waste of time.
> (*What do you want me to do, shoot my TV? Limit my children's TV time? Organize boycotts of advertisers who sponsor violent programs? Do you want Congress to legislate guidelines for children's TV?*)

If you are arguing *against* a course of action—"We *shouldn't* do X"—ask yourself, "OK, if we don't do X, what are we going to do *instead*?":

> Thesis: It's a crime to hand out condoms in elementary school classrooms. It just encourages the kids to have sex at that age.
> (*What are we going to do instead? Kids are having babies at age fifteen. Do you know something that will work better than handing out condoms?*)

**Ask, "How will it work?"** If you're asking that something be done, ask yourself exactly *how* it will be done:

Thesis: College professors should be hired and promoted on the basis of their teaching, not publication, because teaching is their primary job.
(*Nice idea, but in fact no one knows how to measure good teaching. Should we test students to determine how much they learn during the term? Should we ask them how much they like the instructor?*)

Thesis: Salaries should be determined by the principle of comparable worth. Jobs that demand equal skills and training should pay equal wages.
(*How do we determine the worth of a job? How does the worth of an English professor with ten years of college who writes critical articles about unknown dead poets compare with the worth of an unschooled baseball player who swings a piece of wood at a ball? And which is harder to do, write a great essay on Keats or hit a curve ball?*)

**Avoid black-or-white thinking.** When we think, we like to make things easier on ourselves by pretending there are only two possibilities, black or white, and our job is to choose one. *This is never true*; there are *always* other alternatives, shades of gray. Black-or-white thinking is also called "playing either/or" or thinking in absolutes. When you find yourself doing it, ask yourself, "What are the options I'm *not* considering?"

Sometimes the words *either* and *or* are actually used:

Thesis: We can *either* spend some money and live in a healthier environment, *or* we can let the ecosystem get worse and worse.
(*What are the other alternatives? There may be ways to help the environment that don't cost money, and there may be better ways to spend our money than this proposal.*)

Thesis: The National Parks have to charge user fees *or* they'll have to close.
(*What are the other alternatives? There are other ways for the state government to fund the parks—taxes, for instance.*)

But often the either/or is disguised and we have to learn to see the implied dichotomy:

Thesis: I had to spank her—I can't let her think it's OK to smear peanut butter on the carpet.
(The implied either/or: *You have two choices, either to spank your kids or to let them run amok. What about other forms of reacting to negative behavior, like discussing it, modeling, or rewarding good behavior?*)

**Avoid *post hoc* reasoning.** Any time you argue "X caused Y," you have to watch out for the logical fallacy called in Latin *post hoc* *ergo propter hoc,* meaning "after this therefore because of this." It means you're assuming that because event X *preceded* event Y, X necessarily *caused* Y. That's not always so. The Korean War broke out shortly after I was born, but my birth didn't make it happen. And if there is a connection, it's never easy to say what it is, because this world is a complicated place and outcomes usually have hundreds and thousands of interrelated causes. Pick any cultural event and ask "What made it happen?", and the answer will be "Lots of things." What caused the rising teenage pregnancy rate from 1950 to 1995? Teen movies, MTV, sex education or the lack of it, the lack of a social consensus on moral behavior, the automobile, working parents, the decline of the church as mentor, peer pressure, alcohol abuse, laws limiting teens' access to birth control, male machismo, anti-abortion campaigns, the social stigma attached to buying condoms, and on and on. What caused the Hippie revolution in the sixties? The Beatles, the space program, John Kennedy, increased wealth among young people, a growing distrust of Eisenhower conventionality, Elvis Presley, LSD, Leo Fender, Andy Warhol, increased percentage of young people in college, the invention of polyester, the Viet Nam war, the Civil Rights Movement, and on and on.

Sometimes *post hoc* thinking announces itself:

> Thesis: Legalizing gambling leads to crime. In the sixteen years since they legalized gambling, New Jersey's crime rate has increased 26 percent.

But sometimes it's buried deep beneath the language, and you have to dig it out:

> Thesis: Trial marriage doesn't work because statistics prove that people who live together before marriage are more likely to get divorced than people who don't.
> (The *post hoc* assumption: *Since the divorces followed the trial marriages, the trial marriages caused the divorces. The logical weakness: It's also likely that the sort of person who is willing to flout society's customs by cohabiting also gives herself permission to leave a bad marriage.*)

When you spot *post hoc* thinking, just ask yourself, "Is there a provable causal relationship?" and "What are all the *other* factors affecting the outcome?" Keep reminding yourself how hard it is to prove causation. Americans have been trying for decades to figure out if the death penalty reduces crime rates or if violence on TV causes violent behavior in children, and after thousands of studies, we can't get definitive answers to either question.

# WRITER'S WORKSHOP

## Using the Tools

Here's a thesis followed by the kind of conversation you might have with yourself about it, armed with the tools we've used in this chapter. Whenever I've used one of the tools, I've italicized it.

> Thesis: Capital punishment is wrong because we say murder is wrong and then we murder people for murdering. If we execute a criminal, we're as guilty as he is.

The first thing we need to do is reformulate the thesis to follow the principles of Chapter 5. Doing that gives us

> Capital punishment should be abolished, because murdering a murderer makes us as guilty as he is.

Now we're ready to get to work.

There's a question about *clouding language* here: What does "murder" mean? It usually means "killing I don't approve of," which only postpones the question of whether I should approve of state executions or not. If "murder" means "illegal killing," executions aren't murder because they're legal—but should they be? The language is also *loaded,* since murder is inherently bad. "Execute" isn't much better, since it's a euphemism that obscures the graphic ugliness of the act and is therefore loaded positively. Maybe "killing" is the only neutral word. The thesis is also a *cliché,* since the opinion has been expressed in these exact words a million times, so I might try to say it in fresher language or at least realize that it will be hard for me to be open-minded about language so familiar.

There are a number of *underlying assumptions:* that all killing is wrong, that all killing is murder, that killing by state decree is the same as killing in passion and for individual profit, that performing an act to punish a guilty party is morally identical to doing it to an innocent victim for personal gain. I'd better *see where I draw the line.* Let's take the first one. Almost no one really believes that all killing is wrong, and neither do I. Killing is acceptable in some circumstances and under some kinds of provocation. Some people tolerate killing in battle; some don't. Most people grant police officers the right to kill, but only under the most strictly defined circumstances—what are they? Euthanasia is often favored precisely by the people least willing to grant the state the right to kill. Few people would call killing someone who was trying to murder you murder. So where do I draw the line? What are the features of acceptable killing that separate it from unacceptable killing?

It's not easy to say. Even if I decide that individuals can take life to protect themselves from danger, how immediate and life-threatening does the danger have to be? Can I shoot someone who has just shot me and is reloading? Someone who is aiming a gun at me? Someone who is carrying a gun? Someone who has threatened to kill me? Someone who has tried to kill me, is now running away, but will probably try again?

I'm struggling here with a *philosophical antithesis* between two abstract principles: the belief that human life is sacred versus the belief that individuals and society have the right to protect themselves from grave threat. When does the threat become grave enough to justify killing the threatener? A few people say "Never" and will die without raising a hand against their killers. I'm not one of them. Some people say that individuals never have the right to take life, and that when the state takes life in war or law, that act represents the collective will and is therefore OK. That may be a moral cop-out—maybe every soldier should take personal responsibility for every death he causes. At the other extreme are totalitarian states that execute people who might someday cause the state inconvenience.

If I claim that killing is justified when innocent parties are under immediate threat, there are *other consequences* to that logic that aren't pleasant. For one thing, a state execution that takes place two years after the crime is unjustified, since no one is directly threatened. For another, it puts victims in the same quandary women face when they're told, "If you're being raped, be sure you get severely beaten up so you can show the bruises to the police." So if he's waving a knife at me I have to make him cut me?

Another *underlying principle* working here is that executing a convicted murderer is like murdering an innocent person. Do I believe that? If the criminal has committed a heinous crime, does that terminate his rights as a human being? And if he has been judged by a supposedly impartial legal system, and there is no passion or personal gain influencing the decision, doesn't that make it unlike murder? In fact, if killing a murderer is wrong, then a *logical consequence* of believing that is that we must question the entire morality of punishment: Why is it wrong to execute a murderer but OK to fine a traffic speeder or deprive a child of his dinner for mouthing off? All these principles and consequences are as open to questioning as the original thesis, of course.

If I abolish capital punishment, *what's the alternative?* I could lock murderers up for life, but is that really more humane? If killing criminals makes me no better than criminals who kill, doesn't imprisoning criminals make me no better than criminals who imprison? Lifelong imprisonment is certainly punishment, so if I convinced myself I didn't have the right to punish, I wouldn't like this any better than execution. If I resolve not to punish, what methods are left to me to deter violent crime? People talk about "rehabilitation," but that's a loaded cliché and *how will it work?* ❖

Notice how the discussion doesn't lead to final answers, but rather to more questions. That's always how it goes.

**Now it's your turn.** Pick one of the following statements and write a page of critical thinking about it, using all the tools of the chapter.

a. Prohibition proved that you can't legislate morality—if people want to do something, they'll do it.
b. Intelligence tests are racist. Blacks consistently score lower on them than whites.
c. Boxing is brutal. It's incredible to me that in a society that bans cock fighting and bear baiting, we permit the same sort of thing with human beings.
d. I didn't want to hurt him, but I had to say it or I wouldn't have been honest.
e. Twenty-five years ago the public schools abandoned sound-it-out reading approaches, and the nation's reading scores on standard tests like the SAT have been dropping ever since.
f. But I need at least a B—my parents will kill me if you give me a C.
g. What do you mean, you won't loan me your car?—I loaned you ten dollars last week.
h. Marijuana isn't so bad in itself, but it leads to heavier drugs. Most cocaine and heroin addicts started out on pot.

i. If my neighbors want peace and quiet, why do they live in a student neighborhood?
j. Female reporters have to enter male athletes' locker rooms. If they don't, they can't do their jobs.
k. Don't get mad at me—I didn't mean to do it.
l. Of course she deals drugs—how else can you make a living if you live in the projects?
m. He started it!
n. Vote for Jimenez—he's for the family!
o. You never bring me flowers anymore.

## EXERCISES

1. Using the three generic prompts for arguments on p. 248 as models, form two seeds for argumentative essays you might write.

2. Write a one-page essay exploring the ambiguities in one of the following italicized words. Don't grab at a quick, simplistic answer; explore the complexities.

a. When he never called me again, I felt *used*.
b. School libraries shouldn't include *pornography*.
c. I have the *right* to not breathe other people's smoke.
d. It's not *fair* to be graded down for being late when your car won't start.
e. I only use *natural* cosmetics.
f. The American legal system is *racist*.

3. Do the exercise in "Now it's your turn" on p. 265 with a thesis from an essay of your own.

4. Use a thesis from one of your own essays to answer the following question. What is the one step in the critical thinking process, from avoiding questions as assertions (p. 252) to avoiding *post hoc* reasoning (p. 261) that poses the greatest challenge to your thesis and promises to generate the most insight into it? Write a one-page essay applying the question to the thesis and reaping the benefits.

5. Do the following tasks with a thesis from an essay of your own:

a. List two principles it's based on.
b. Write out the antithesis of each principle. Make sure it isn't the negative of the principle (p. 258).
c. Pick one principle; describe one hypothetical situation where you support that principle and one hypothetical situation where you don't.
d. In a half-page essay, discuss where you draw the line (p. 256).
e. List two good practical consequences of accepting the thesis and two bad ones.
f. Write down one logical consequence of accepting the thesis.

# Chapter 17

# WRITING AN ARGUMENT, PART 2: SELLING THE CASE

**N**ow that you've thought through your position, it's time to think about ways of selling it to your audience. You have to do three things:

Define your objectives realistically.
Establish a positive relationship with your audience.
Find a dramatic structure.

## Define Your Objectives Realistically

Many writers, when they undertake an argument, set out to do impossible things. They try to have the last word, to say the pure truth that no one else has ever said and that ends debate forever. That only gives you writer's block.

Instead, think of arguing as making your small contribution to the ongoing debate. The contribution isn't "truth"; it's your personal view of things. It doesn't end debate; it generates it by stimulating thought in other people. It needn't even be the only opinion you have—it can be just one of the many thoughts you have on the matter.

Think of this as the Stew Theory of argumentation. Imagine a gigantic pot of Argument Stew always cooking on the Stove of Our Culture. Every citizen is responsible for contributing something to this stew. The more varied the contributions, the better the stew gets. No contribution—no individual potato or carrot—is the "true" one, the "right" one that makes all the other ingredients unnecessary. So don't try to toss in the potato that ends the stew; toss in *your* potato to enrich the mix. And it doesn't help to go up to the stew and say, "I really agree with the potato that last guy threw in," so simply agreeing with someone else's argument doesn't count. Arguing isn't voting.

You can see the stew-making process on computer network conferences. You toss in a potato by posting a thought you've had, and it may provoke a hundred thoughtful reactions in a day—all of them of value, none of them the "right" or "final" one that shuts everyone else up. For example, I gave my students a prompt on our English Department's classroom computer network and asked them to react via their keyboards and then react to each other's reactions. Here are the prompt and the first few minutes of response:

**The prompt:**

A California School Board member has suggested that schools ban homework. He has two reasons: 1) homework is interfering with the family by taking the child away from family life, and 2) homework is discriminatory, because students with PCs and other assists have an unfair advantage over students who don't. What do you think?

**The conference:**

Eric: If we can't have homework because some people have computers and some don't, how can we have anything? Lectures are obviously "unfair" because some people hear better than others.

Lindsay: I find it hard to believe that there are absolutely no resources for these children who lack computers or typewriters. If this is indeed the case, then the rules should be changed, so that assignments could be handwritten.

Jill: I baby-sit a seven-year-old whose parents are poor and don't have the money for a computer—but the kid has a Sega system and dozens and dozens of games. So is it a problem of resources or priorities?

Eric: Trying to "fix" America's family or social problems by banning homework is like trying to clean up our toxic dump problem with a toothbrush. We're always looking for the quick fix, the regulation that will make our world a healthy, happy one. No such thing.

Lindsay: I loathed homework just like any other kid. But the plain and simple fact is, homework teaches responsibility. Every child is going to have to learn this sooner or later.

Aaron: The new family structure is part of the problem. My aunt is a single parent, and she cannot say no to her son. She tells him to do his homework, he begs to play Nintendo, and she gives in. It's emotional blackmail, and lots of single parents feel it.

Adam: I can see how it is unfair if one kid turns in a paper with amazing graphics and a pretty cover page and gets an A where someone with the assignment done on a typewriter gets a B. I have seen this injustice, and it must stop!!

Joan: Stop the discrimination, sure, but stop it by stopping grading, not homework.

Aaron: If families are worried about homework interfering with their together time, why don't they help little Timmy do his homework?

Lori: Why do we assume that homework is boring and unrewarding?

We continued in this way for one and a half hours, and at the end had more to talk about than we did when we started. Nobody "won."

## Establish a Positive Relationship with Your Audience

The Chair Theory of arguing says imagine your reader sitting in a room full of chairs, each chair representing an argumentative position. She is sitting in the chair that represents her opinion. You're sitting in your own chair, some distance away. Your goal as arguer is to convince her to get out of her chair and move to the chair next to you. What makes a person willing to move toward someone? Does a person come toward you if you tell her, "You're an idiot for sitting in that chair. I can't comprehend how anyone with the intelligence God gave a dog could sit in that chair"? Does she come toward you if you tell her, "Only an evil or cruel person could sit in that chair"? Does she come toward you if you coldly and impersonally list several strictly logical reasons why she shouldn't be in that chair? No. Yet most arguers approach their reader in exactly this way, and they harden her heart against them by so doing.

Let's take another approach. Let's agree that when you argue, you want to be the kind of person people find it easy to agree with and be convinced by. To be that kind of person, you have to do three things: be human, be interesting, and empathize.

### Be Human

People aren't convinced by facts and logic; they're convinced by *people*. Every politician who makes the mistake of reciting lots of facts and figures loses the election. But most people do everything they can to hide their humanity when they argue.

A typical experience: A student of mine turned in an essay that began like this:

> Attempts to correlate murder to punishment rates have been made for a long time. Most of these studies were full of errors because they were showing the correlation between murder rates and the presence or absence of the capital punishment status, not to the actual executions, which are what really matter. Others failed to properly isolate murder rates from variables other than punishment, even when these variables are known to influence murder rates.

So it went for three pages—conventional dehumanized argument style. I asked her, "Why are you writing about the effects of incarceration anyway? What's it to you?" When she told me, I said, "Wow! Put it in the essay!", and the next draft began:

> I was in prison for four years. True, I was an officer there, but at eight hours a day, sometimes more, for forty-eight weeks a year . . . well, I put in more time than most criminals do for their serious crimes. My opinions certainly did change while I worked there.

Now we're ready to listen.

## Be Interesting

There's a myth out there that says scientists are convincing. So when we argue, we put on our imaginary lab coats and get as boring as possible. It doesn't work. Go the other way. Perform. Give the audience a good time. Instead of beginning a movie review with a thesis plop like "*Problem Child* is a hackneyed film that offers the viewer little more than a rehash of previous films in the genre," one reviewer began like this:

> *Problem Child* is the story of a misunderstood and unwanted boy who finds love from a caring adult who discovers a side of himself he didn't know as he deals with the child's painful struggle to be accepted.
>
> Vomit.

## Empathize

If you ask people what they most want from the people they argue with—their spouses, partners, boyfriends, parents—the usual answer is "I want them to understand my point of view." Instead, most of us go the other way and advertise our lack of empathy: "I can't imagine anyone thinking that way; how can you possibly believe that? You can't mean what you're saying,", and so on. A simple "I see where you're coming from" can bring down a host of defenses.

You can do this as a ploy, but it's better if you see the truth of it: The other guy really isn't a fool, and he really has valid reasons for thinking as he does—remember the Stew Theory. As long as you believe that only a moron could disagree with you, you need to do more critical thinking (Chapter 16) to break you out of your narrow-mindedness.

This is a hard truth to grasp in our culture, because our model for argument is the two-party political process, which thrives on demonizing the opposition. But that's not *arguing;* that's *fighting*. So ask yourself, Is the fact that Democrats are encouraged to think Republicans are idiots and monsters, and vice versa, really doing the country any good? If you think not, don't add to the problem by doing it yourself.

## Four Diagnostic Questions

To push yourself toward our new healthy relationship with your reader, answer the following diagnostic questions and put some form of the answer in the essay:

**What is the opposition's argument?** Express your reader's viewpoint to yourself, fully. Don't condemn, ridicule, or deflate it—just understand it. Then put your understanding in the essay—tell the reader you got it, you respect it, but you don't agree with it. Then explain to the reader why not.

**What would my reader most like to hear me acknowledge about him?** If you're writing an essay addressed to the University administration and defending the thesis that the threatened fee hike for University students is unfair and shouldn't be enacted, what would your reader (the University administrator) most like to hear you acknowledge about her? Probably that administrators aren't fiends who just like to rip off students. So you add a passage reassuring her: "I know that administering a university isn't easy, especially in these hard times. You aren't raising fees just for the fun of it. We both want the same thing: to see the University be as good as it can be. I think we can avoid student hardship *and* keep educational quality high."

**What is my reader's most likely fear in response to my argument?** You're writing an essay arguing that the Green Tortoise, a counterculture, low-rent bus line, is an attractive alternative to planes, trains, or conventional bus lines. What is your reader's most likely fear in response to your argument? Probably that the busses are full of winos and creeps and driven by drugged-out slackers who aren't safe on the road. So you add a passage reassuring her: "I know everyone's image of cheap bus travel: being sandwiched between a wino in the seat to your left and a pervert in the seat to your right. But the Green

Tortoise isn't like that. The customers are people like you and me: relatively clean, sober, normal people just trying to get somewhere without spending a fortune. Nor are the drivers and other employees your stereotypical space-case flakes, though my driver did wear a tie-dyed T-shirt; every employee I dealt with was sober, professional, and competent."

**How is the reader likely to dislike me for saying what I'm saying?** When you try to talk people out of their beliefs, they often resist by defining you in ways that justify their not hearing you. Ask yourself what form that dislike will take; then reassure them: "I'm not who you fear I am." For instance, if you're defending a thesis that says, "Formality is a dying art; people don't know how to dress up and be formal anymore," the most likely negative image your reader will get of you is that you're a snob. So you add a disclaimer: "I'm not one of those people who think Levi's or pants on women is a crime against nature. I love being casual, and I live in jeans most of the time. I'm not saying formality is better than informality; I'm saying that every once in a while knocking out a really fancy recipe, getting dolled up, and inviting friends over for grown-up time is *fun.*"

All this does not mean you should always be nice when you argue. Some of the essays in this book are deliciously nasty. Be as nasty as you want when you're attacking one group and talking to another, as in "Dear Governor Deukmejian" (p. 278), or when you decide to use confrontation as a tactic—in effect saying, "I'm going to shake things up and be a little rude on purpose," as "Social Dictators" (p. 396) does. Just remember that confrontation raises hackles, so in essence you're putting up barriers you'll have to get over somehow.

## Find a Dramatic Structure

Many arguers figure that since an argument is won by cold facts and logic, the structure should be as rigid as a scientific experimental write-up: thesis at the end of the first paragraph, supportive arguments in numbered series, and so on. That doesn't work, because arguments are won by people, so go the opposite way: Avoid stiff, logical structures at all costs, and look for dramatic alternatives. Consider the following four experiments: a parable, two kinds of narrative, and a letter. Want more inspiration? The Writer's Workshop that follows has arguments in the form of a list and a satire.

## EXACTLY HOW WE WANT IT

SCOTT THOMPSON

Marvin was almost finished. He was on his way to his final department: Body Parts and Functions. He followed the shadows into the arena. There were different lines for each piece of the human body. His first stop was Facial Features. Marvin selected two squinty eyes, a big nose with a mole on the end, a mouth with large loose lips and extreme overbite. This was perfect because it exposed the crooked teeth he carefully selected. Marvin looked in the mirror: "Ah, yes, exactly how I want it."

Next stop: Torso Department. After studying the different choices he selected Number 1: fat. Marvin looked in the mirror: "Ah, yes, exactly how I want it."

Off Marvin went to the Limbs Department. Here he chose a couple of chubby weak arms and legs. The legs he made sure were short enough to make his height under five feet, four inches. Marvin looked in the mirror: "Ah, yes, exactly how I want it."

As Marvin walked to the Externals Department, all he could think about was how perfectly everything was working out. He chose pale, mottled skin and lank, greasy hair. Marvin looked in the mirror: "Ah, yes, exactly how I want it."

Marvin was now on his way to the final department, Afflictions and Diseases. Marvin was undecided between cerebral palsy and muscular dystrophy. He figured that since he already had almost everything he wanted, he would leave the good diseases for others. He just took acne and poor eyesight.

Marvin took a good long look in the mirror: it was all exactly how he wanted it. In a few days, the paperwork was completed and he returned to his school. As he walked on campus, he was greeted with "Hi, Shrimp! Here's Dumbo! Hey, Four-Eyes, how many fingers am I holding up?" The day continued with pretty much the same treatment. Marvin came straight home from school, went to his room, lay on his bed, and, with a tear in his eye, whispered, "Ah, yes, exactly how I want it."

Doesn't make sense, does it? So why do we act as if it was true? People don't come into this world with a choice of how they look or what physical problems they have. Why treat them as if they're responsible and it's their fault? Next time, think about it and refrain from the stares, the gestures, the funny comments. ❖

## GIVEN THE CHANCE

MELISSA SCHATZ

I met Stacey three weeks ago, when she came to live at the Group Home where I work as a counselor. I liked her immediately. She's a bright, friendly, attractive sixteen-year-old. She's on probation for two years for petty thefts, and she has a two-year-old son. But her biggest problem is that she's a speed freak—she's addicted to shooting methamphetamine directly into her blood stream.

After spending a month in Juvenile Hall, where she went through withdrawals, Stacey came to the Group Home in fairly clean condition. But she has run away from here twice since then, staying out several days each time. She admits that she was "using." She says she's been an addict for several years now. Her parents are drug addicts too. Stacey wants to quit, but she needs help. She says she needs to go through a drug rehabilitation program. I believe her.

Unfortunately, I can't get Stacey into one. I've tried, but everywhere I've turned I've run into a wall. You see, drug rehabilitation programs cost big money—two to three thousand dollars for a one-month stay. And absolutely no one will pay for Stacey to go into a program.

Of course Stacey herself doesn't have any money. Nor do her parents. And addicts don't have medical insurance. This doesn't surprise me. What does surprise me is that the State, which has taken custody of Stacey, placing her in a group home in the first place, refuses to pay for drug rehabilitation. It makes me angry. I feel as if the State has said, "Here, hold on to this," and then chopped my hands off.

Now, I know that drug rehabilitation programs aren't cure-alls. It takes more to kick a drug habit and keep it kicked, especially a mainline habit. It's a day-to-day struggle. Yes, I've known addicts who make their annual trip to the drug rehab. But I have also known addicts who *did* turn their lives around on such a program. Doesn't Stacey deserve the chance? While the State has her in custody, the opportunity is perfect. We're at least obligated to try. And isn't it money well spent, if it saves us from having to support Stacey in prison in the years to come?

Given time, the Group Home could help Stacey work through her behavior problems, get through high school, and learn some social and emancipation skills. But the fact is that unless she kicks her drug habit, she probably won't stay long. Her probation officer told me the next time she runs away he'll put her back in Juvenile Hall to clean out. We both know this doesn't work. Just taking the drugs away isn't the answer. But apparently the State has decided the real answer is too expensive. They tell us to fix these kids, but won't give us the tools. They're not giving Stacey or me a chance. ❖

## WHY?

DANA MARIE VAZQUEZ

I looked forward to it for months. I began the countdown in March. Only thirty-five days, only twenty-three days, only fourteen days. As the days passed and it got closer, my excitement grew. Finally it was the night before. I counted down the hours, minutes, and even seconds. "The time is 11:59 and 50 seconds—beep—the time is 12:00 exactly," the recording said as my friends yelled, "Happy birthday" and I popped the cork on my bottle of champagne. It finally happened: I was now twenty-one years old. My friends insisted that I drink the entire bottle of champagne myself. Why? Because it was my twenty-first birthday.

As I was guzzling the champagne, my friends were encouraging me to hurry because it was already 12:15 and the bars would be closing at 2:00. Oh yeah, I just had to go to Safeway and contribute to the delinquency of minors by buying for my twenty-year-old roommate. Snapping pictures the entire time, my roommates cheered me on until I reached the finale at the check stand and the clerk ID'ed me and announced to the entire store that it was my twenty-first birthday.

After a round of applause and much cheering in Safeway, I was dragged out the door and shoved into a car. "We've got to go to Joe's," they exclaimed as we raced towards my downfall. Once inside, I was given a drink that contained every alcohol known to Man. As I sucked mine down, my roommate kept refilling it. Why? Because it was my twenty-first birthday.

"It's her twenty-first birthday," my roommate shouted to a guy across the room she knew. "Then come join our game," was his reply. This dice game was quite easy. The rolls of the dice were counted and whoever reached twenty-one drank a shot. Lucky me—I was chosen to drink a shot of vodka and a shot of a Russian apple. Did my dice roll equal twenty-one? No. Then why did I have to drink? Because it was my twenty-first birthday.

"Yeah" my roommates shouted as I barely downed the vodka. "Let's go to Riley's," they laughed as we ran down the street. "Just a beer, all I want is a beer," I pleaded as we entered. Why was I still drinking even though I didn't want anything, even a beer? Because it was my twenty-first birthday.

So we all chugged a beer and raced on to the Top Flight. "It's her twenty-first birthday," they shouted at the doorman as he checked my ID and I swayed to the pounding music.

"Go tell the bartender and you'll get whatever you want," he screamed at me. I followed his command and ordered a Long Island iced tea. This wasn't a very wise choice because it also had many different types of alcohol in it, but at that point I really wasn't thinking. They were getting ready to close the bar, so I pounded my drink and we left.

About a half hour later—BOOM—it hit me. I began removing everything I had put in my stomach in the last three days. I did this, I'm told, for close to two hours. I was so hung over the next day that all I wanted to do was crawl into a hole and die. But did I go out to the bars still? Yes. Why? Because it was my twenty-first birthday.

I've thought about my birthday a lot lately, and I don't understand the rationale I and everyone else used that night. I don't like it, but I don't think it will change. You'd think I would be the first to want to change it . . . but it was my roommate's twenty-first birthday three days ago. We took her out to the bars and made her drink and drink. She got sick at Riley's, puked at Top Flight, and vomited at Shell Cove. She could barely walk, but we still took her to the Bear's Lair. Why? Because it was her twenty-first birthday. ❖

## DEAR GOVERNOR DEUKMEJIAN

CINNAMON KERN

Yesterday when I was lured into the local Family Planning Clinic by promises of free birth control and easy sex, I was saved by your brave decision to cut their State funding.

The lobby was full of misguided souls like myself with leering faces. We oozed promiscuity like cheap perfume. We sat and watched as other brainwashed victims left, clutching their brown paper bags with lewd expressions as they hurried to cheap encounters with strangers.

When I went into the accounting office, the woman there told me in a sad voice that they would be unable to provide me with State-funded birth control and I would have to practice abstention. My dreams of romantic half-lit encounters with all those delicious young men crashed to the floor. I knew that without birth control, I couldn't have sex. With that den of iniquity shut down, people will have to stop their disgusting sexual behavior and behave in a chaste, pure manner. I know that this brave move will help generations after us lead clean lives.

Thank you so much for your faith in mankind's ability to control their fleshly urges. It saved me from a life of degradation and filthy promiscuity.

Sincerely yours,

Cinnamon Kern ❖

# WRITER'S WORKSHOP

## Using Models

Chapter 3 showed how to use models to open doors and inspire yourself to try experiments you'd otherwise never think to undertake. Nowhere is that more useful than in arguing, where our internal paradigm can be so constipated. Go read the newspaper and magazine columnists who have to hold readers' interest day after day or they don't get paid—read Alice Kahn, Russell Baker, George Will, Jonathan Alter, Molly Ivins, Mona Charin, or anyone who writes a regular column in a major newspaper. Here's an inspiring model:

### TWENTY GOOD REASONS TO CRY*

STANLEY BING

1. Your team has just lost the seventh game of the World Series.
2. Your stockbroker is arrested for insider trading, and you realize the guy never did one single unethical thing for you.
3. Your wife has run off with Marvin Hamlisch.
4. You decide to forgo your designer clip joint and have your hair cut by Rocco at the local barbershop. Six dollars and fifteen minutes later, you emerge with a kind of abrupt, vertical look currently sported only by military men and recently deinstitutionalized mental patients.

---

*Esquire, June 1987, p. 225.

5. Indoor soccer.
6. You shave off your mustache and remember that you hate your face.
7. You forget to pre-order the vegetarian meal on TWA and, famished, eat two stuffed bell peppers in marinara sauce before you realize what you've done.
8. You spend $540 on a state-of-the-art compact disc player, only to find out the next day, in the current issue of *Audiophile*, that digital tape has suddenly become the decreed format of choice.
9. Twenty-four-year-old MBA's who earn in excess of a million dollars a year and complain their lives are empty.
10. Two weeks with your parents at their geriatric enclave in Sun City, Arizona.
11. You hear from your dermatologist that the only way to save your hair is to have injections of estrogen.
12. Your wife absolutely refuses to let you buy that personal helicopter you saw in the window at Hammacher Schlemmer.
13. In the course of a schmooze with a bright and frisky young woman you thought understood you, she inquires, "Woodstock? You mean Snoopy's little dog?"
14. Fatty corned beef.
15. You find yourself actually paying attention to Dr. Ruth Westheimer.
16. You don your seersucker suit for the first time since last summer and find that, while you can still button the trousers by forcing every bit of air from your lungs, the fly flares so radically your zipper shows.
17. In New York City today, the only legal place to light your post-dinner Monte Cruz is at home with your wife or in the middle of Central Park—and you don't feel all that safe in either location.
18. You enter a room filled with intelligent, dynamic, slender women, and realize that you will never know a single one except at exorbitant personal cost.
19. You are stuck on an elevator with Siskel and Ebert.
20. Your dog, Rags, with whom you shared every confidence and crisis for more than seventeen years, can no longer control his bodily functions. You make that last, inevitable trip to the vet. Afterward, you stand on the sidewalk in the bright sunshine, alone for the first time since your youth, wondering where life goes and, in your heart, knowing. ❖

My student Lizette Strohmeyer found Bing inspirational, so she wrote this:

## SIXTEEN REASONS YOU CAN'T START YOUR ESSAY

1. You had a power failure and now your Macintosh won't work.
2. You haven't bought the footnote-and-bibliography program yet.
3. Can't find a pencil.
4. You found a pencil but it's not sharp enough and you don't have a pencil sharpener.
5. Your thesis isn't ready to talk to you yet.
6. The moon is in Scorpio, Capricorn, Aries, whatever.
7. Speaking of astrological signs, your horoscope tells you that today is the day for romantic liaisons and you need to get shopping for a new outfit.
8. You need to clean your room first and you can't do that until you do your laundry, and your boyfriend's, and since you've got the washing machine warmed up you might as well do your roommate's too.
9. The moon is full.
10. The moon isn't full.
11. Though you've never done it before, you suddenly have an urge to walk the family dog.
12. Still can't find a decent pencil.
13. You broke a nail.
14. You left your lucky writing shoes over at a friend's house.
15. Ever since you watched *Annie,* you've always held on till tomorrow.
16. You set the alarm clock for four in the morning. When it goes off in a piercing frenzy, you open one eye, look around blearily, and marvel at how dark four in the morning is. You flop one leg out from under the covers, feel the icy chill, and retreat under the down comforter. You remember that interrupting sleep cycles can cause lasting physical and psychic damage, and as a health measure you go back to sleep. ❖

**Now it's your turn.** Read the model essay below. Using it as inspiration, write an argument unlike one you'd think of yourself.

## PROTECT YOUR INALIENABLE RIGHT TO STEER TANKS*

ADAM HOCHSCHILD

Certain misguided elements in Washington are now arrogantly questioning the constitutionally guaranteed right of Americans to possess assault rifles. This outrageous attack on our liberties hits at the very foundations of everything our Founding Fathers fought for.

And it's a creeping attack as well. First the do-gooders went after the "Saturday night special." Now they're going after the assault rifle. Tomorrow they could very well be going after the tank. Surely no other example shows so clearly the dangers in this new un-American mania for banning weapons.

Tanks have an honored place in our history. Their indisputable ancestor, the horse, was enshrined in the fabric of American life even before the Constitution. If today's ban-everything liberals had had their way two hundred years ago, Paul Revere would have had to walk on his famous journey, perhaps taking days or weeks. And could the mail have been carried across the West by a Joggers' Express?

When tanks came along, it was the cavalry who sent them into battle. And just as an earlier generation of Americans in peacetime enjoyed the right to collect horses or use them for sport, so too, do we enjoy the same rights with the tank. Today, no foolish restrictions prevent law-abiding sportsmen from enjoying the thrill of target shooting with the splendid machines. Serious collectors can freely compare the technological capabilities of American tanks with historical models and German, Chinese, or Israeli imports. And all of us living in this increasingly dangerous society can rest secure in knowing that we enjoy the age-old right to defend our homes and property with a turret-mounted 105-mm cannon.

What if the ban-everything do-gooders, claiming that these weapons might fall into the hands of drug gangs, attempt to ban tanks? An American right and tradition, stretching back to the frontiersmen and beyond, would be irrevocably lost.

Most important, the do-gooders fail to understand that tanks don't destroy cities, people destroy cities.

---

**San Francisco Chronicle*, "Sunday Punch," May 7, 1989.

The drug scourge is indeed a terrible menace. But the way to deal with it is not by banning weapons that have a long and honorable history in the hands of sportsmen, collectors, and citizens defending their homes, but by getting these drug people off the streets. For good. Preventive detention is one solution. Mandatory capital punishment for all crimes is another. Capital punishment for all residents of drug-infested areas is a third.

In fact, with bold and imaginative tactics such as these, the tank itself could provide a useful tool in suppressing the drug problem once and for all.

And we who know and love these weapons would be glad to offer our services. ❖

## EXERCISES

1. Find an argumentative essay in *The Writer's Way* or elsewhere that uses an unconventional technique and use it as your model—write an argument that uses that technique. Attach a copy of the model to the essay, and at the bottom of the essay tell which technical feature you're imitating.
2. Write an argument in one of the following forms:

   a. a fable or fairy tale
   b. a dialogue
   c. a TV sitcom
   d. a TV game show

3. Write an anti-cliché—an essay that argues *against* a trendy belief people hold without thinking about it: Argue that hunting is moral, machismo is beneficial to society, or exercise is unwise. Anti-clichés appear on pp. 373, 393, and 396. *Don't make it a joke*—mean what you say.
4. Take an argument from the Treasury of Essays (p. 368) and write a one-page essay answering the four diagnostic questions on pp. 273–274. How many of them did the essay address?
5. Do Exercise 4 with an argumentative essay you found outside *The Writer's Way.*
6. Do Exercise 4 with an argumentative draft of your own. Rewrite the draft, adding passages to address any of the four diagnostic questions you didn't address.

7. Write an essay using one of the following essays from Chapter 17 as a model:

a. "Exactly How We Want It"
b. "Why?"
c. "Dear Governor Deukmejian"
d. "Twenty Good Reasons to Cry"

# Part Five

## ACADEMIC WRITING

# Chapter 18

# WRITING IN SCHOOL: AN INTRODUCTION

## What's New? Nuthin'

When you write in school, how much of what we've learned in Chapters 1–17 has to be unlearned? The great danger in academic writing is that you'll say, "Well, all that stuff about purpose and audience and writing like a human being is OK when you're writing an opinion piece for the local newspaper, but academic writing is different. I'm writing to an audience of one, a teacher who knows more about the subject than I do; I'm writing for a grade; I'm required to write, and the topic isn't of my choosing, and I know next to nothing about it. So all bets are off and everything I've learned in Chapters 1–17 doesn't apply." No, a thousand times no! The Laws of the Universe still apply. Chapters 1–17 still speak the truth. We just need to take those rules and apply them to the highly specialized set of writing circumstances that is school. Let's take some of the important principles from earlier chapters and see what they teach us about academic writing.

### 1. You need exposure to learn how to write.

Chapter 1 says you can't write something until you've been exposed to lots of models and seen "how it goes." How much academic writing have you read? Unless you're a professor, the answer is probably "None." So ask your instructor for sample essays to use as patterns, or ask her to recommend a journal or two in the field whose articles you can browse through in the library.

### 2. You need motivation.

However hard it may be to find motivation when you're overworked, out of time, and writing on a topic you aren't fond of in a course you're being forced to take, you still need it. And fear or a need for a grade won't work well. How you learn to care is largely up to you, but here are two hints. Everything in the world is intellectually interesting to a thoughtful mind, and the true performer gets up for every performance, however small or cold the audience may be.

### 3. You need time to prewrite and revise.

Writing is supposed to be a multistage process allowing you to think, reflect, rethink, and revise repeatedly. School will rarely give you the time. *The single most difficult thing about writing in school is the lack of revising time.* There is no way to create extra hours in the day, so all you can do is learn to use the little time you have well:

*Start thinking about the assignment from the moment it's assigned.* Even if you only have an evening to *write* it, you can *mull it over* for days with a part of your mind and jot down thoughts while doing work for other courses.

*Plan to do two drafts.* Nobody's first draft is all that good.

*Write an abstract before or after your first draft.* It will take five minutes and pay big dividends.

*Devote thirty minutes or an hour to peer feedback with a respected reader.* Once you've drafted, another mind will take you farther faster than yours will.

*Don't try to save time by not proofreading.* One grisly typo can shatter your reader's confidence in you.

### 4. Topics are worthless.

This is doubly true in school, where writers regularly fall into the error of thinking that if they know what they're writing *about,* they know what they're doing. Never let yourself describe a writing project by stating its subject. Always press on to the meaningful questions: What are you saying about the subject? Why are you saying it?

### 5. Have a thesis.

In school writing, thesis is absolutely key—more important than purpose, even. In my thirty years of teaching, it's been rare to find an academic paper with a thesis. Resistance to having a thesis is amazingly strong—with every essay assignment I say, "And you must have a thesis," and almost everyone ignores me.

There's a good reason for that: Having a thesis is hard when you're new to the field and time is short. In school you're asked to say something insightful about *Hamlet* or the recent presidential election, you're given perhaps a week to think about it, and it may be your first exposure to literature or political science. No wonder you're reluctant to go out on a limb. So you take the student's out: You *say a lot of stuff* about the subject, but you don't commit to a central assertion.

There is no way to make thesis making easy in school, but it helps to turn to three old friends: 1) Start thinking about the assignment from the moment it's assigned; 2) don't press for thesis too early—if you are going to arrive at an insight about *Hamlet*, it should happen near the end of your thinking process, not the beginning; and 3) ask yourself a question (What drives Hamlet mad? What is the effect of increased numbers of Hispanic voters on recent presidential elections?). A question helps you stay focused on the idea that you're seeking *an answer*. The answer will be a thesis.

The "should" (p. 74) often has little place in an academic thesis, because school writing often has little purpose beyond the accumulation of knowledge or critical analysis for its own sake. If your thesis is "Hamlet had good reasons for going mad" or "The North was no less racist than the South during the Civil War," and you can't see how you want anyone to do anything about it, that's OK.

### 6. Know your audience.

Your audience in school is unlike any you'll encounter in the outside world, but you do have one, and the game is the same: Understand how the reader thinks so you can predict her reactions and control them, in order to get what you want. In school you have a readership of one, one whose worldview is unknown and probably wildly different from yours, so predicting her responses becomes a Herculean task. But you have one advantage over the nonschool writer: The reader is standing right in front of you. So *ask her:* What does she want? What format does she like? Is word processing required? Does she want you to include a paraphrase of the reading assignment? Can the assignment be done as a list, or does it have to be in paragraphs?

And you can make some intelligent guesses. If you try to imagine how a teacher thinks, you can put together a list of things that are likely to please her and get the grade you're after. Grading papers is a chore, so if you make grading yours painless and rewarding, your teacher will love you. Thus you should do the following nine things:

a. *Answer the question,* if one was asked. State the answer boldly, so it's easy to see, and put it up front.
b. *Follow directions slavishly*. Every teacher has something specific in mind when she gives an assignment. Doing something else, no matter how well you do it, misses the point.
c. *Waste not a word*. Make sure sentence 1 jumps right to the heart of the matter.
d. *Have a strong thesis,* and show the reader where it is.
e. *Highlight structure,* so the reader sees easily what's going on. If the assignment has asked you to do three things, use headings to show the grader where you're doing each one.
f. *Follow format.* Make the essay physically easy to read and to grade by having dark, clear print, a conventional font, and neat corrections, and by including all pertinent information—your full name, the course's full identification, the date.

g. *Use a colon title (p. 131)* to let the reader know at the outset which assignment this is and that you have a point.
h. *Be interesting.* Boredom is the paper grader's biggest enemy. Your mission, should you choose to accept it, is to rouse the grader from her slumber and make her glad she read your essay. Be funny, daring, provocative, dramatic, lively.
i. *Use a boilerplate structure.* Both because the grader wants to read you fast and because time is short, you may want to fit your essay into one of two standard cookie-cutter structures:

| **Thesis and Defense** | **Problem—Solution** |
|---|---|
| 1. State your thesis. | 1. Ask a question or state a problem. |
| 2. Explain, defend, support, gather evidence. | 2. Gather evidence and reason your way toward an answer |
| 3. Discuss implications of your discovery. | 3. Arrive at an answer or solution. |

### 7. Know your purpose.

You have several purposes. The first to come to mind is getting a good grade. To accomplish this, follow Rules a–i above. Next, since your teacher usually has a very specific purpose in mind for every assignment, be sure you know exactly what it is and make it yours. Ask if you're in any doubt. Finally, school has a short list of general educational goals you can assume are yours unless the instructor tells you they aren't:

**Show you did the reading and understood it.** This is the skill at the heart of most college assignments.

**Use the course tools.** The course has been teaching you a set of skills, a methodology, a philosophy, and a body of knowledge; put them to use. If you've spent the last weeks working with feminist theory, use feminist theory in your paper. If the course has been practicing statistical analysis, use statistical analysis in your paper.

**Talk the talk.** In the Guide to Studying, we talked about the importance of joining the club (p. P-5). Write to demonstrate your membership in the club of scholars. The primary badge of membership is talking the talk—using the jargon of the course. Every course, every discipline, has its argot. Literary criticism talks about symbols, subtexts, archetypes, genres, and deconstruction, for instance. At first, using a dialect that isn't your own feels like faking, but mimicry is key to learning (p. P-6), and using the new words is the only way to ever make them your own. Also, you need the jargon—it helps you say things easily. To talk about literature without words like "symbol" and "archetype" is like talking about cars without being able to say "tire" or "transmission." If the jargon doesn't facilitate your message making, you probably aren't using the course tools.

**Walk the walk.** Comport yourself like an academic. Imagine you're playing the role of a professor in a movie:

*Depersonalize the writing (pp. 172–173).* Academic writing says, "This isn't primarily about me; it's about *Hamlet*." Avoid "I" and "you."
*Get more formal.* Avoid contractions (p. 54). Use "however" instead of "but."
*Write longer, more complex sentences.*
*Raise your Latinate percentile (p. 170).*

**Perform a research-based analytical task.** Academic writing seeks to teach you to do critical thinking and data-gathering research. So *don't* design essays where your feelings, opinions, or personal experience are the sole source: "I love my old rickety car"; "Nobody I know cares about popular music anymore"; "I'll never forget my raft trip through the Grand Canyon"; "There are no good men out there."

You can certainly use personal issues as a starting place, but redefine the task as an academic one. "My father's alcoholism tormented me when I was young" becomes "According to experts, what common psychological problems do children of alcoholic parents face?" "I think parents should stay home and take care of their small children instead of shipping them off to daycare" becomes "According to authorities in the field, how do children raised by stay-at-home parents and children raised primarily in daycare environments compare in terms of later mental health and success?" "I hate this short story—it's confusing" becomes "Why does the narrator in this story choose not to tell its events in chronological order?" Here are more such refocusings:

| **Personal essay** | **Academic essay** |
|---|---|
| Infant circumcision is sexist. | Routine infant circumcision is brutal, has no demonstrable medical or health benefit, and should be discontinued. |
| Rape is a horrifying affront to women. | What are the accepted psychological theories on why people rape? |

| | |
|---|---|
| | What cultural factors produce a rape-prone society? |
| Nobody reads anymore. | How has the schools' approach to teaching reading changed in the the last twenty years, and has it made any difference in students' reading performance? |

You'll know you have an academic task when you ask yourself, "How do I know my thesis is valid?" and the answer is *not* simply "Because that's how I feel" or "Because that's what I believe," but is also

because that's what the experts say.
because the evidence and the research say so.
because that's the logical conclusion to be drawn from the facts.

**Use citations.** Citations (which we used to call "footnotes") are those little asides where you tell the reader where you got a quote, opinion, or piece of information (p. 330). If you are having that dialogue with other writers, you'll have to tell your reader every time you use someone else's words or ideas by adding a citation. The more citations you have, the more you can rest assured that you're doing the academic thing.

Students can get cynical about citations, and nearly everyone has ponied up a faked bibliography to make an essay look more researched than it is. But if you think about it, whenever you write on an issue of interest to a discipline, your writing is making a contribution to an ongoing conversation. So wouldn't you want to hear what other contributors have been saying on the matter?

**Avoid plagiarism.** Plagiarism is using a writer's work without attribution and thus implying it's yours. You're plagiarizing if you use another's words, thoughts, facts, sequence of ideas, or anything else of value, without telling the reader where you found it. Since in the academy one's scholarship is the most valuable possession one has, and since academic writing requires constant use of other people's work, the danger of plagiarism is sky-high and the punishment Draconian: In any university with integrity, the penalty for plagiarism is expulsion.

Some plagiarism is an intentional attempt to cozen, but a lot of it is an innocent misunderstanding of the code of the academy. Those who misunderstand argue:

I only have to cite *quotations*—I don't need to cite if I use my own words.

I don't have to tell the teacher these aren't my words and thoughts because I'm just a novice and she'll assume they aren't mine.

If I cite too much the teacher will think I didn't do any original work.

None of that logic flies, especially the last statement—ironically, most instructors will be more impressed by citations, because they mean you actually did some reading. So give a citation every time you repeat something that isn't common knowledge that you didn't get out of your head, even if that means doing it after every sentence. Chapter 24 will show you exactly when and how.

The Internet has made plagiarism epidemic, for lots of reasons: The information on the Net is being given away and doesn't seem to belong to anyone; an author's name is often hard to find; it lacks the "weight" of publishing—no editing, printing, binding, or bookstore shelving—so you don't feel you owe it anything; there's no visible place of origin; traditional citation format doesn't work. The Napster generation grew up with the idea that lifting from Net sources wasn't stealing. It is, and you must cite sources for Net material, however onerous the task. See pp. 334–336 for help.

### 8. Write as a human being to human beings.

Writing as performance, writing to real people who are interested and involved in what we're saying, who need our help or want to be touched, entertained, amused—for most of us, that's where the payoff in writing is. Yet often, in school, all that seems to have little place.

There are two ways you can deal with this. First is to create an empowering fiction. Don't write to the instructor; write to an imaginary audience of real people who really want to know what you've learned and are looking forward to being entertained. They appreciate your wit. They want to be moved. Do this through the early drafts. Then, if you must, you can rewrite for school in the last draft, but you will have reaped the benefits of using the earlier approach.

But there is another solution. I once had a student whose writing was playful and personal and delightful to read. I told him, "I love this stuff, but you know you can't write like this for other professors." He said, "Odd that you say that. I've been writing like this for years, and every instructor has liked it but told me all the other professors wouldn't. I still haven't met the instructor who doesn't like my work, so I just keep doing it." If you try writing to your professor as if he were a real person reading you for pleasure, the fiction might come true—he just might shift gears, go along with you, and be grateful.

# Chapter 19

# WRITING ON LITERATURE

Why does TV's detective series "Columbo" always let you know who the murderer is up front?

7. Describe the historical, cultural, biographical, or literary background of the work. What was the political climate during Shakespeare's time, and how were his plays shaped by it? What happened to Charles Dickens in his youth that shaped his views of society and its treatment of the lower classes?
8. Interpret the work through the lens of a specific critical approach, literary theory, or individual critic: How does *Hamlet* look through the eyes of a Freudian psychologist, feminist theory, or Marxism?

## Thesis and Topic

Again, ignore topic and focus on thesis (p. 288). Literary criticism, perhaps more than any other form of writing, needs to heed this warning. If you know what your paper is *about*, you know nothing. Even if you *have a lot of things to say* about that topic, you've only just begun. Don't rest until you can finish this sentence with confidence: "In this essay I'm arguing that ________." Remember to let the thesis emerge late in the writing process (pp. 288–289).

## Critical Approaches

Most criticism doesn't just say, "I read the book and this is what I thought." Instead, it uses a *critical approach*—a methodology based on principles about how people read, how literature affects us, and how artists create. It's the equivalent of a personal philosophy in one's life, and, like a personal philosophy, it makes your work easier by organizing your thoughts and giving you a vocabulary so you can name the stuff you're working with. The popular critical approaches are formalism, cultural studies, archetypal criticism, deconstruction, feminist criticism, and psychological criticism (especially Freudian), but there are lots of other interesting ones. I can't explain the approaches to you, but your instructor may well be teaching you one right now and expecting you to use it. If not, ask her to recommend a good introductory textbook on literary criticism, like *A Handbook of Critical Approaches to Literature* (Wilfred Guerin et al., New York: Oxford, 1999).

## The Opening Paragraph

Literary papers' first paragraphs follow a strict set of conventions. Here's a model:

> In his generation, Spenser was doubly unique. Not only was he the best poet, he was, in a sense, the only poet. Other men did, of course,

write verse. But he alone presented himself to the world as a Poet, as a man who considered writing a duty rather than a distraction.

(*From "The New Poet Presents Himself: Spenser and the Idea of a Literary Career,"* PMLA, *circa 1978*)

Do what this opener does:

First, Say something interesting in sentence 1.

Second, by the end of the first paragraph, have established a thesis to be defended or a problem to solve.

Third, identify the artist and/or the work(s) you're discussing. If everyone knows the author, identify the work by title only: "In *Hamlet* . . . ," not "*In Shakespeare's *Hamlet* . . ." If the artist needs to be identified and is well known, use only the last name: "In Spenser's *Faerie Queene* . . . ," not: "*In Edmund Spenser's *Faerie Queene* . . ." Identify the genre of the work only if there is a likelihood the reader won't know it: "In the short story 'Gimpel the Fool' . . . ," but not "*In the novel *Moby Dick* . . ."

Fourth, avoid all direct statements of intention: "*In this essay I'm going to . . ."

## Quotations

All good literary criticism quotes a lot from the work, because quoting reminds you to support your claims with evidence, and because it's a way to enjoy once again the good bits, like watching the trailer for a great movie you love. If you aren't quoting several times a page, suspect that you're generalizing without supporting.

But there's a danger: Quoting is fun and easy, so there's a temptation to turn the essay into a collection of the work's greatest lines—after all, the author says it better than you can anyway. Don't do this. Remember, the essay is your words and thoughts, reinforced throughout by quotation, not a photocopy of the work. So *quote often, but quote little bits.* Pare each quote to the absolute minimum you need to make your point. Be reluctant to quote even a complete sentence:

> **Bad:** The boy's feelings for the girl are intense and confused: "Her name sprang to my lips at moments in strange prayers and praises which I myself did not understand. My eyes were often full of tears (I could not tell why) and at times a flood from my heart seemed to pour itself out into my bosom. I thought little of the future. I did not know whether I would ever speak to her or not or, if I spoke to her, how I could tell her of my confused adoration."

> **Better:** The boy's feelings for the girl are intense and confused: "Her name sprang to my lips at moments in strange prayers . . . At times a flood from my heart seemed to pour itself out into my bosom . . . I did not know . . . how I could tell her of my confused adoration."

**Best:** The boy's feelings for the girl are intense and full of "confused adoration."

If you master this kind of parsimoniousness, you can quote ten times a page or more.

## Page References

A page reference is a referral to a specific place in the work you're discussing. You write, "Hamlet says he won't kill Claudius because he wants to catch Claudius in a moment of sinfulness," and you refer the reader to the place in *Hamlet* where that happens: You add "(III iii 73–94)," which means Act 3, scene 3, lines 73–94.

References to anything but your central text will need full-blown citations in the manner of Chapter 24, but references to your central text can be done in shorthand. The *first time* you reference your primary text, provide a citation that says, "This and all subsequent references to this text are to . . ."; then give all the bibliographical information. In all subsequent references, give only the page number (or line number for poetry, or the act, scene, and line numbers for plays) in parentheses immediately following the reference—don't wait for the end of the sentence:

**A play:** Hamlet refers to "the fatness of these pursy times" (III iv 153) (or 3.4.153).

**A poem:** Browning's Duke says he "choose(s) / Never to stoop" (42–43) when explaining why he didn't ask his wife to behave.

**A novel:** When Pip fears death, he regrets most painfully losing the opportunity to apologize to his loved ones for his mistakes (432), thus demonstrating that he blames himself.

## Tense

Literary criticism adopts a curious convention regarding tense. Describe plot events and author's acts in the present tense:

Wrong: *Ishmael *decided* to sign on as a crewmember of the *Pequod*.
Right: Ishmael *decides* to sign on as a crewmember of the *Pequod*.

Wrong: *Dickens *used* a first-person narrator in *Great Expectations.*
Right: Dickens *uses* a first-person narrator in *Great Expectations.*

Break this rule only when you're talking about a writer's biography or there is an actual past tense in the fiction:

Dickens *wrote Great Expectations* when he was 48 years old.

Ishmael *is* on board the *Pequod* only because he *was* depressed and *needed* a vacation.

# Chapter 20

# WRITING IN THE SCIENCES

**F**irst, our universal reminder: You can't do something until you've seen it done, and you can't write something until you've read a few examples of it. So go read a few articles in scientific journals.

## Audience and Purpose

When you're writing in the sciences, audience and purpose are obvious. You're writing to colleagues in the field. You and they speak the same language, and you share a knowledge base and a keen interest in the discipline. You've done some sort of research or experiment that has produced some new knowledge. That knowledge is immediately useful to your readers, who are going to use what you've learned to make tomatoes more resistant to rot or improve patients' physical therapy or decide whether to use surgery or chemotherapy on a tumor. So they're eager to hear what you have to say. You don't have to persuade them or win them over or capture their attention. They aren't interested in your entertainment value; they care only about your being as clear and thorough as possible so they get it right. So the primary goal of scientific prose is to avoid ambiguity (p. 253), and to accomplish this it's willing to be unexciting and fussily detailed. Compare titles: Titles in the humanities tend to be colorful and suggestive—*Surprised by Sin*, *The Golden Bough*, and *The Raw and the Cooked* are three famous examples. Scientific titles sound like this: *The Effect of Neutron Irradiation on the Titanium Carbide Distribution in Rapidly Solidified Austenitic Stainless Steels of Varying Titanium and Carbon Content.*

Because a primary goal is to avoid COIK problems (p. 238), you'll depend on peer feedback (Chapter 10): Ask your readers, "Where are you confused? Where would you like to know more?"

In science the data is everything and the data-gatherer nothing, so remove yourself by using the passive voice (p. 174): Don't write

"*I interviewed* fifty women between the ages of 13 and 21"; write "Fifty women between the ages of 13 and 21 *were interviewed*."

## Structure: The Lab Report

Scientific writing usually is a way of saying, "Hey, I've discovered something I think you can use in your work or your studies." That discovery is usually the product of the scientific method, in which you first form a *hypothesis*, a guess that can be proved or disproved by data-gathering: "I bet that watching TV cartoons produces increased incidents of violent behavior in daycare children" or "I bet that daily doses of Baby Ruth candy bars will lower cholesterol levels in childless women." Next, you design an experiment to test the hypothesis; then you perform the experiment and gather data; then you crunch the numbers, process the data, and come to a conclusion: The hypothesis did or did not prove to be true. This experimental model dictates a four-part structure for the write-up, usually called the *lab report* structure: Introduction, Methods, Results, and Discussion.

### Part I: Introduction

Tell the reader everything he needs to know to understand the experiment he's about to witness. State the hypothesis to be tested. Explain why it matters, what led you to ask the question in the first place, and what you hope to learn. Review the history of research on the topic, so the reader knows all that was known up to the moment of your experiment.

A large part of this kind of back-filling is the *literature review*, where you survey what has been published on your topic. In a lit review, almost every sentence is a summary of the findings of some study or report: "Jones and Pendergast (1998) found that incidences of prostate cancer among white males over age 55 increased dramatically in geographical areas with overcast, damp winters." Every such summary needs a citation and an entry in the bibliography (see Chapter 24), so don't be surprised if you find yourself giving a reference for every sentence.

### Part II: Methods

Tell the reader what you did. Describe in detail how the experiment was designed and how it was carried out. Err on the side of excess information. Ideally, a fellow researcher could take your Methods section and duplicate the experiment in her own lab, as if following a recipe. Remember to use the passive voice (p. 174).

### Part III: Results

Tell the reader what the objective findings were. Summarize the data gathered and process the numbers. With most scientific work, this will involve *graphics*—tables, graphs, charts. Don't interpret or draw conclusions—save that for the next section.

### Part IV: Discussion

Tell the reader what you learned. Discuss the implications of your findings. Did the experiment work? Do your findings have any significance? Why do your findings matter, and in what way? What should we go learn next?

# Chapter 21

## ESSAY TESTS

There are two kinds of written exams in college: subject tests, which test your expertise in a field like astronomy or sociology, and literacy tests, which test how well you write. I'll talk about the universals of written test-taking first; then I'll talk about the special demands of subject tests and literacy tests.

## The Universals

The biggest problem you face in a test is shortage of time. You can't make the problem go away, but there are ways to make the problem smaller:

**Write something beforehand.** Write a letter to a friend while waiting for the test to begin. You'll come out of the starting gate at full gallop.

**Take a moment to prewrite.** Two or three minutes spent mapping (p. 59) will usually pay for themselves by giving you a sense of direction, so you don't come to the end of your time only to discover the essay you wrote isn't the essay you wish you had written.

**Get on with it.** Make sure that your first sentence jumps into the heart of things. If the test asks a question, begin by writing an answer.

**Write in your own language.** It takes time to translate your thoughts into someone else's dialect.

**Write only one draft.** You won't have time to rewrite or make a clean copy. If you write something and hate it, cross it out and keep writing.

**Watch the clock.** Doing all the assigned tasks moderately well is better than doing half of them thoroughly.

**Waste not one word.** Don't repeat the question. Don't feel obligated to write complete sentences. Most short-answer test questions can be answered in an apt word or two. Here's a bad answer and a good answer to the test question "What tragedy in Charles Dickens's youth shaped his later fiction?":

> **Bad:** The tragedy in Charles Dickens's youth that shaped his later fiction was the five months he spent working in his relative's blacking factory.
>
> **Good:** Blacking factory

**Answer the time-saving questions first.** The least time-consuming answers are the short ones and ones you know for sure. So first write the short answers you're sure of, then the long answers you're sure of, then the short answers you're not sure of, and last the long answers you're not sure of.

**Proofread for garbled meaning.** You don't have time to revise, but you can skim-read to see if you wrote the words you intended.

**Proofread for a pet mechanical problem.** You don't have time to line-edit, but if you know you write comma splices, proofread only for them.

Apart from time issues, there are two tips that will help you in all situations:

**Get excited.** You write better if you care about what you're saying. In a test this is difficult but not impossible. Remember, a car salesperson isn't excited by the car; she's excited by the selling.

**Concretize** (p. 177). The test question will probably ask you to address an abstraction: an idea, a theory, an issue. Immediately begin by asking yourself, "What's a concrete example of that?" and start writing there. If the test asks you to talk about America's cult of victimhood, start with the person who sued McDonald's because the coffee was hot. If it asks you to talk about declining moral standards, start with Enron or with Martha Stewart's insider-trading scandal. If it asks you to talk about symbols, start with the Confederate flag flying over the North Carolina state capitol.

## Subject Tests

In Chapter 18 we talked about giving the instructor what he needs to read and grade you easily (p. 289). In subject tests, where time is short and your reader is grading even faster, we need that mentality in spades.

**Do what the instructor wants.** The only way to know what that is is to ask, *before the test starts.* Are you supposed to have your own ideas, or are you supposed to repeat the lecture? Does spelling count? Are you supposed to use the jargon of the course? Is this a check to see if you've done the reading?

**Follow directions slavishly.** For instance, decide at the outset how many tasks the question poses. How many assigned tasks are there in the following exam question? "What is a metaphor? Give an example." I count two, but many students will do one and forget the other. After you've written, *reread the question* to see if you forgot to do anything. And scrutinize the language of the question: Whenever I ask on a test, "What is the *significance*" of something, half the students give me a *definition,* which is something different.

**Answer the question.**

**Telegraph your structure.** Highlight your thesis, label your sections, number any series.

**Don't dump knowledge.** It eats up your time, multiplies your chances of being wrong, and infuriates your grader. Do only what is asked of you.

## Literacy Tests

Literacy tests have a different purpose than subject tests, so you approach them differently. The purpose is to see if you can write, so you want to do everything we said leads to good writing in Chapters 1 and 2: Write to human beings, be alive and personal, say something you care about, write to do something to someone, initiate a dialogue with the reader, and so on. Doing these things may be more important than staying on the question, thinking well, structuring rigidly, or knowing anything.

Yes, mechanics count, but it's best not to focus on it, since you can't fix your mechanical problems on site and "trying hard" makes mechanical problems worse. Students who "try hard" end up writing unnatural fakery like these:

*Friendship is a need to which there can be no denying.

*It is that which brings about a similarity of Anson's view.

The people who do best on literacy tests are the ones who say, "To heck with the grade; I'm going to have fun!", or who set out to give the reader/grader the time of her life. Write something you'd love to read and you'll do fine. Here are some particular ways to help yourself do that:

**Avoid the lowest-energy structure,** which I recommended using on p. 131 as a way of pleasing teachers. There's a lifeless, risk-free structure that just gets by. If you're asked to take a position on an issue, it would be to

State a thesis.
Explain, support, and illustrate.
Restate and draw conclusions.

If you're asked to compare and discuss two quotations on a single topic, it would be to

Restate the two quotations in your own words.
State your agreement or disagreement with the first.
State your agreement or disagreement with the second.
State your personal position on the topic.
Summarize.

Find a structure that's livelier. The difference is obvious from the first sentence. Here's a formulaic opener, from a test essay on individualism: "*Smith and Thompson both raise important issues about individualism." Here's the eye-opener: "The boys of Delta Sigma had a party last night (and the night before, and the night before)."

**Push your essay into personal narrative form.** Everyone tells stories better and faster than they write reasoning processes. Almost any abstract topic can be turned into personal narrative. If the topic is individualism and loneliness, write about a time when you were alone, or a time when you couldn't get any privacy. If the topic is guilt, write about a time you dealt with guilt or saw someone deal with it.

**Concretize and particularize.** Literacy tests must give a prompt that *anyone* can respond to, so there's a good chance that it will be a huge abstraction like friendship or education. Use the skills of Chapters 11 (p. 171) and 14 (p. 221) to concretize and particularize the abstraction.

Begin concretizing and particularizing with the first sentence: If the topic is loneliness, begin with a place where you like to go when you're alone or a person you know who thrives on solitude or craves a crowd. If the topic is friendship, begin with a particular friend, a particular act of friendship.

**Avoid the clichéd response.** On any topic there is a thesis of least imagination, the one that will be used by all the writers who can't find anything better to say:

> *On individualism:* It's important to have some private time and space, but it's important to be able to function as a social being too.
>
> *On guilt:* Guilt is a good thing because it keeps people on the straight and narrow, but it can get out of hand and become self-destructive.
>
> *On friendship:* Everybody needs a friend, and a friend is someone you can depend on in the clutch.

The clichéd response dooms you to mediocrity—figure out what it is and resolve to avoid it. Do something else, or use the anti-cliché exercise (p. 283) to argue against it:

> Individualism is an American curse and an illusion, responsible for most of our culture's ills.
>
> Guilt is the voice of the Establishment telling you that you acted like a person instead of a clone.
>
> The only thing of real value a friend can give is permission to be yourself.

**Go beyond agreeing or disagreeing.** If you're asked to respond to a provocative statement, the natural reaction is to agree or disagree. That's a dead end because after you vote yea or nay, the essay's over. Instead of voting, ask yourself, "What experience have I had with this issue?" and "What do I want to say about it?" Review the Stew Theory (p. 269) to move yourself beyond voting.

**Have a thesis.** Even if it's a cliché, a central idea will save you from just saying a bunch of things about the topic, which never makes a good essay.

# Chapter 22

# COLLABORATIVE WRITING

The first time an instructor asks you to write an essay as a member of a group, you'll probably say, "Oh dear god, no, please!" My students dread it and often try to drop the course the instant they hear they'll have to do it. That's natural. But once you get used to it, writing alone can seem empty and lonely.

## How to Make the Collaborative Experience Work for You

**Understand why your teacher is having you do it.** When I announce that assignments in my classes will be collaborative, students line up to tell me why it's a bad idea. It takes more time than solo writing. Some people do all the work, and the loafers coast. Your grade is dependent on strangers. All of which is perfectly true. So why do it?

Teachers assign collaborative writing for two reasons. First, almost all of the writing done in the business world is collaborative, the product of teams. Bosses make corporate writers do it because *collaborative writing produces better results than solo writing does.* Groups do more creative work and find better solutions to problems than individuals do. Of course, each writer wishes she were off doing it by herself, but that isn't the point.

Second, collaboration is a wonderful learning device. If you get together with three classmates and discuss the assignment, agree on strategies for fulfilling it, argue with each other about ways to go, come to consensus, write a draft, then revise and peer edit as a group, you'll learn more than you possibly can by writing alone in your room.

**Subjugate the ego.** Schoolwork can be very egocentric; collaboration isn't. The question now is no longer "What's *your* answer," but rather "What's *the best* answer?" Yes, collaboration involves you in a lot of arguing and compromising, and you end up with an essay that doesn't feel much like you. Good. When students complain that their partners forced them to say something other than what they wanted to say, I think to myself, "If your personal vision couldn't sell itself to two *friends,* how much use can it be to a bunch of *strangers*?"

**Give up your sense of fairness.** You can't guarantee that every member of the team will pull his own weight or get a grade proportional to his contribution. Good. School cares hugely about fairness, but the world of work only cares about getting the job done. Let collaboration be your introduction to two of the world's most honored principles: Life isn't fair, and you're not in control.

**Pick your collaborators carefully.** If you're assigned partners, make do, but if you can choose, the most important step in the collaborative process is picking the best people as partners. Don't work with the student nearest you, the least intimidating, or the cutest. Everybody knows which three people in the class are really on top of things—grab them.

**Schedule carefully.** Collaboration takes a lot of time—at least twice as long as writing alone. And you can't work whenever you want to, because much of the work can only be done when everyone can get together. So commit the group to a rigid working schedule up front, and stick to it.

**Be responsible.** People's grades are riding on your doing what you say you'll do. I've had students cry in my office as they realized that their self-destructive behavior just earned their classmates F's.

**Write everything down.** Everyone wants to talk and no one wants to record. Make a record of all group conversations—appoint a secretary, use a tape recorder, or take turns keeping notes.

The trickiest part of collaboration is working together so that everyone's contribution is valued, no one gets bullied, and so on. The next few principles address that.

**Be flexible but assertive.** Flexibility is what my students say they like best in a partner. It means an ability to listen to others, to accommodate, to compromise. It means you don't come to the first group session with your mind made up and a determination to make the project go your way.

But it's easy to be too nice. The value of collaboration lies in the diversity, and if you strive above all things to avoid conflict, you'll become passive and the bully will dominate. Creativity needs a little friction. State your views vigorously; then listen to others and let the group come to a decision.

**Pick a leader.** Democracy is a nice idea, but it doesn't work. Since someone is really the leader anyway, make it official.

Don't pick the person who thinks she knows the answer or who is the smartest; pick the best *manager,* the one most skillful at organizing, listening, and helping people get along.

**Don't seek consensus too early.** Forcing early decisions just slams the door on exploration and growth. So have a long, formless brainstorming period before asking for answers or votes.

I learned about the error of seeking early consensus the first time I was on a jury. When we retired to deliberate on our verdict, I suggested that we begin the discussion by voting, guilty or innocent. Wiser people said, "Don't—let's just kick stuff around for a while first." And it was only later that I realized that if we had voted first, two terrible things would have happened: All the diverse views in the room would have been reduced to a sterile two, guilty or innocent, and people would have gotten committed to their vote and become antagonistic.

**Avoid the tyranny of the mediocre.** The worst thing a collaborative team can do is decide to avoid bad feeling by adopting only the decisions that everyone feels completely comfortable with. That way produces white bread. My dad used to say, "A fair business deal leaves all parties feeling a little cheated." The bold, striking, innovative solution should leave a lot of people feeling a little uneasy, a little at risk.

**Alternate between group sessions and solo work.** If you spend all your working time in a group, people will turn into bullies, sycophants, or outcasts. To avoid that, work together for an hour; then have each member go off and write up thoughts and reactions to the conversation; then come together and share what members have generated on their own.

There are three moments in the process when team members should definitely work solo:

*No one comes to the first meeting empty-handed.* Require that all members bring thoughts on paper. If a member comes empty-handed, he'll become an echo and you'll lose the benefits of his perspective.

*Don't draft by committee.* Let one or two team members draft; then critique what they've written.

*Everyone peer edits the first draft alone.* Hand out copies of the first draft and have every member come to the next meeting with revision suggestions written on the draft. Otherwise, members will become rubber-stampers.

**Divide the labor.** Some students think it's cheating to do this, but it isn't. Some people are good drafters, some good brainstormers, some good line-editors, some good proofreaders, some good devil's advocates. Some write good dialogue, some write good thesis statements, some are good at abstracting, some at research, some at number-crunching. Let each team member do what she does well.

**Explore alternatives to conventional essay form.** Multivoice projects lend themselves to nontraditional modes of presentation. Maybe a dialogue or debate would work. Consider interviews, screenplays, fairy tales, musicals.

## Typical Collaborative Work Schedule

Here's a hypothetical by-the-numbers collaborative experience. Unless your assignment is a big deal and you have a lot of time, you probably won't need such an elaborate structure, but it's nice to know it's there if you need the discipline.

1. Long before the assignment is made, you cruise the class for partners, getting the best students to commit to working with you on the next project.
2. Immediately after the assignment is made, you gather with your collaborators to compare schedules and schedule all meeting times. You schedule at least three: one for brainstorming, one for planning the first draft, and one for peer editing and revising the first draft. The first meeting is in two days. Everyone swears to jot down first thoughts between now and then—nobody comes to the meeting empty-handed.
3. In the next two days, you kick things around in your brain and write them down as they come to you, without getting committed to anything.
4. At the first meeting, you brainstorm. All the rules of brainstorming in Chapter 3 are in force: No one is wrong, and so on. All members share the notes they brought; no one is free to listen passively. Someone takes notes or tapes the session for transcribing later. The group picks a leader, or one emerges. The group delegates tasks if the project permits. You decide if another brainstorming session is needed. If not, you agree that each member will bring his version of the first draft to the next meeting. You arrange to photocopy the meeting notes and get copies to all members to aid them in their drafting.

5. At the next meeting, everyone reads everyone else's draft silently, making comments in the margins and noting good things worth keeping. Discussion follows. Someone takes notes. A sense of the collaborative draft emerges. Someone is appointed the task of drafting it and is given all the drafts and the meeting notes to guide him.
6. The third meeting is held wherever the draft writer's word processor is. Each member silently reads a cleanly typed, double-spaced copy of the new draft. A peer-editing session follows. The author of the draft revises on the word processor while others coach. Time is set aside for mechanical line editing and checking against the course format, and changes are done on the word processor. Everyone proofreads a copy of the manuscript, and corrections are typed in. Some thoughtful person produces a fresh cartridge for the printer, and a final handsome copy is run. Someone spots a typo everyone missed, so you reprint that page.

It's time to go home, and the assignment isn't even due until the day after tomorrow!

# Chapter 23

## RESEARCH

A large part of academic writing is gathering and synthesizing data, so you need research skills. Data may be found in the field (interviews and questionnaires) or in the lab (experiments), but the two most common places to find it are in the library (books and articles), and on your computer screen (databases and Web sites). We're going to talk about how to use these last two.

Before we jump into the exotic world of research guides, abstracts, and keyword searches, let's get one thing straight: You don't have to reinvent the wheel. Thousands have gone down this road ahead of you, and many of them have left detailed instructions for you. Research assistance comes in at least five forms:

**Your instructor.** She works with the research materials in your field every day and can probably recite them off the top of her head for you.

**Librarians.** These wonderful people go to school for eight to twelve years just to learn how to help you find what you're looking for. Don't be reluctant to ask for help—they *love* this stuff.

**Your library's support system.** Any academic library should have student tours, free research guides in various disciplines (often called something like "How to Find Information on a Poem"), live seminars on topics like using the electronic databases, and online tutorials in research methods.

**Web sites and "help" programs.** More and more these days, research is done online, and the virtual world is working hard to help you use itself. Scholarly databases are incorporating self-help tutorials, organizations representing academic fields are creating Web sites in how to do research in the discipline, and libraries are creating Web sites to guide you in using their collections.

**Your classmates.** When you think about it, it's nuts to have twenty-five students over at the library, each struggling to master the same body of research skills on her own. Divide the labor; share the results.

## Using the Library

Think of the library as being made up of two parts: 1) the texts, those books, articles, and encyclopedia entries that contain the actual stuff you're looking for, and 2) search tools, instruments like catalogs, indexes, and bibliographies that help you scan the texts and find which ones have your stuff.

### The Texts

Libraries traditionally divide their holdings into five sections: books, references, newspapers, government publications, and periodicals. You find your way around each by means of its own search tools.

**Books** are the part of the library we think of first. They reside in the *stacks,* and you find your way around them by means of the *main catalog,* which is probably electronic and accessed through a keyboard in the library's reference area or through your computer at home if you have a modem hookup to the University Web site. You can look in the main catalog under the author's name, the book's title, or the subject. Unless you seek a specific title or author, you'll be most interested in the *subject catalog.* You type in keywords, just as you do surfing the Web. You might consult the nearby *Library of Congress Subject Headings,* a big book that helps you use keywords the catalog recognizes. For instance, if you look under "Home Heating," it may tell you to type in "Heating—Home."

Books are the easiest part of the library to find your way around in, but they're a poor source of information, for two reasons. First, since it takes years to write, publish, and catalog a book, any information in the book stacks is at least several years old, so the information can easily be out of date. Never use a book as a research source without checking the publication date and deciding if it's too old to be relevant. Second, books are aimed at wide audiences, so they're usually broader in scope than a journal article, and you have to wade through lots of pages before you know if a book is going to have the information you seek. Use books when you want a broad introduction to a subject, like the history of England, but in more detail than an encyclopedia would give you.

One good thing about books is they're physically present on the shelves and grouped by topic. So when you find one book that's helpful, the books on either side might be helpful as well. Always examine the books to either side of any book you take from the stacks. You can't do that in a database.

The **reference section** of the library houses all the encyclopedias, dictionaries, almanacs, and other volumes devoted to basic information. There you can look up the mailing address of your favorite author, find out how to say hello in Swahili, get a list of all the works Beethoven composed, get a quick plot summary of *Moby Dick*, or find out the side effects of the drugs the doctor prescribed for you. Use it to locate almanac-type facts, to get a brief introduction to a topic—for example, What is socialism?—or to find book-form bibliographies and research guides. Everything in the reference section should be listed in the main catalog, but don't rely on it: Ask a reference librarian to point you to the section housing books in your field. Then browse.

**Newspapers** usually have their own section in the library. The virtues of newspapers are obvious: They're up to date, the articles are about very specific topics, and they're written in plain English. But they have two major drawbacks. First, they're very hard to find your way around in, because they're almost impossible to index. Second, they're undocumented—you rarely can tell who wrote something or where the data came from. I suggest you use newspapers only if you're looking for something you know is there—if you know that the *Los Angeles Times* had a big article on your topic on page 1 on April 12 of this year—or if the newspaper has a good index. The move to electronic databases has helped here. It used to be that only newspapers like the *New York Times* and the *Christian Science Monitor* were indexed, but now even my local small-town weekly is.

Governments produce a constant stream of publications on everything under the sun. These **government documents** are usually a world unto themselves in the library, a maze of pamphlets, fliers, commission reports, and the like, often without authors, dates, or real titles, often identified only by serial number, usually listed only in their own catalog and not in the main catalog. This section of the library, like the others, is converting rapidly to a Web-based format. In the year 2000, roughly one-third of U.S. government publications were paper, one-third Web-based, and one-third microform (like camera film). With each passing year, the percentage of paper publications shrinks and the percentage of virtual publications grows.

Using the government publications is an art. Often one reference librarian specializes in them; start with her help.

The **periodicals**—the magazines and journals—are by far the most useful section of the library for most researchers. The information is up to date, specific, and usually well documented and well indexed. If the library has a print subscription to a periodical, the very recent issues are usually out on racks where people can browse in them, but the older ones are collected—usually all the issues from a single year or two together—bound as books, and shelved in their own section of the stacks. More likely, you'll access the articles through an online database the library pays to get into. My library has 2,000 print journals and 11,000 electronic journals, and soon will have next to no print journals.

## Library Search Tools

The best article or book in the world is useless to you if you don't know of its existence. The academic world knows this, so it has developed an industry that does nothing but produce tools to help you find what you're looking for. All these search tools come in print form (books) and electronic form (Web sites and databases). There are four basic sorts: bibliographies, indexes, abstracts, and research guides.

A **bibliography** is a list of titles of works on a subject and publication details that tell you how to find them. Often indexes are called bibliographies, which may be confusing.

An **index** is like a bibliography except it's usually a multivolume, ongoing project, with a new volume every year or so. The 2004 volume lists publications in the field for 2003, which means that if you want to see what's been published over the last ten years, you may have to look in ten different volumes.

Bibliographies and indexes just list titles and information on where to find them, but an **abstract** will give you a one-paragraph summary of the work, which can save you from frequent wild goose chases.

The best of all is a gift of the computer age, the **full-text database**. This is a bibliography that contains the complete text of the articles it lists. When you find an entry that looks promising, you click on it and it appears on your screen. If it's useful, you can print it out right there—glorious! So you want to use full-text search tools when you can, abstracts as a next best, and bibliographies and indexes as a last resort. Any electronic database your library owns will tell you if it's full-text always, sometimes, or never. Some databases are "full page," which means you're looking at a photocopy of the original printed page, and some are "full text," which means they merely scan and reproduce the written words, so you may not get graphics.

Search tools, like encyclopedias, have subjects, and they range from very broad to very specific. The broadest are bibliographies of all topics, like *The Reader's Guide to Periodical Literature*. It will tell you what has been published on your topic in any given year in any of several hundred popular magazines and journals. Use it if you want to know what *Redbook* or *Esquire* published on your topic.

Some search tools are devoted to broad academic areas:

*The Humanities Index*
*The Social Sciences Index*
*Business Periodicals Index*

Others are devoted to specific disciplines:

*Music Index*
*Index Medicus*
*Biological and Agricultural Index*
*Child Development Abstract and Bibliography*
*Psychological Abstracts*
*Abstracts of English Studies*

There are search tools in sub-disciplines, like Victorian poetry, movie reviewing, and neuroenzyme chemistry. Often the leading journal in a discipline publishes a yearly index of work in the field.

A **research guide** does more than list entries; it's a real instruction manual on doing research in the field. It may summarize or critique the sources it lists, review the bibliographical materials available, give an overview of what's being done in the field, and even suggest fruitful new lines of inquiry. Research guides are sometimes devoted to very specialized topics: There's one on the minor nineteenth-century novelist Elizabeth Gaskell, for instance. If you can find a reference guide to your subject, and it isn't out of date, begin your research there.

The most underutilized research tool in the library is the special kind of index called a **citation index**. It lists every time one author or work has been referred to by another. That's all it does, but that's much more than it appears. When you find a work that is useful in your research, look it up in a citation index, and the index will in effect hand you a list of all other researchers who found that work useful too—in other words, a bibliography of everyone working on your research question.

## Researching from a Terminal

With each passing year, the search tools we've been talking about and the sources they help you find are less likely to be print and more likely to be electronic and accessed through a terminal. A good electronic search tool, or "search engine," can search the majority of the entire World Wide Web—over 550 billion documents—in about ten seconds and give you a list of what it found in order of usefulness. It lets you call up the full text of the sources in seconds, tells you what the call number of the journal is if your library has it, arranges for a fax of the article to be sent to you immediately if your library doesn't have it, and prints out anything it can access or saves it to your computer or diskette. Most libraries will let you do all this from home via modem. Electronic search engines are often updated *daily*. They can reduce research time for a typical term paper from weeks to hours, and you will learn to love them.

Their only drawback is that they're electronic, so they're as alien and intimidating at first as any other computer program. Take steps to deal with your cyberphobia:

**Ask for help.** Reference librarians now spend most of their time leading novices step by step through their first experience with electronic searches.

**Find and use the manual.** Since libraries are flooded with panicking novices, they usually work hard to put plain-English user's guides right next to the terminals. More and more, electronic search tools have a link to online tutorials—look for a "Help" icon.

**Take a class.** Most libraries run live seminars for beginning researchers.

**Don't wait until the term paper is due.** Software is fun to noodle around on, but it's loathsome if you need to master it in the next thirty minutes. So go to the library when time isn't pressing and toy with the search tools: Look up articles about your favorite actor; find the three best databases on your latest hobby.

**Find a tutorial Web site.** More and more, academic libraries are putting tutorials on how to use electronic research materials on the Web. UC Berkeley's is at www.lib.berkeley.edu/TeachingLib/Guides/Internet/FindInfo.html.

The terminology for electronic research is in flux and very confusing, a world of URLs, metasearch engines, Boolean logic, vendors, servers, domains, and so on. Let's talk about what you really need to know.

## Databases

There are two kinds of places your keyboard will take you: databases and Web sites. Databases are more useful to you in school, because that's where most of the serious research is published. A database is essentially the old periodicals section of the library in digital form. It's typically available only by subscription, so your library will buy rights to use it and you will access it through your library's Web site, often using a password. The database may be an index—a list of entry titles—or it may be an abstract, in which case you get paragraph summaries of entries. But more and more databases are *full-text,* meaning you can call up the complete text of an entry at a mouse click.

Your library may offer you a choice among fifty databases. Which ones should you use?

**Ask the librarian.** Tell her what you're working on and ask her to recommend a database. She'll steer you to the most user-friendly, comprehensive one available at the moment.

**Start with full-text databases only.** They'll cut your work time by about 90 percent. If and only if what you need isn't there, use the abstract indexes next and the plain indexes as a last resort.

**Choose a degree of breadth.** Each database covers a certain territory. Some, like Academic Search, survey all academic fields. Some, like Wiley Interscience, are devoted to broad areas like science or the humanities. Some are devoted to single disciplines or issues like literature or feminism. Some are indexes to individual journals or newspapers. The more you know what you're looking for, the more focused a database you want.

**Look at the time frame.** What years does the database cover? In the old days, the problem with bibliographical tools was they were often months or years out of date. Now we have the opposite problem: Since the data is so vast and is coming in constantly, databases often chuck older information before it's really old. Many databases only contain entries from the last few years. And some databases, believe it or not, contain no entries from the most recent few years (usually two). Depending on your project, such databases may be useless to you.

**Use more than one database.** No database searches all available documents on a topic, so if you want to be thorough you'll use several of them.

**Choose a level of sophistication.** Some databases cover only cutting-edge academic and professional articles. Some cover popular magazines. Some cover newspapers. Pick one that talks on your level. If you're writing on the politics of radical mastectomy, there's no point in trying to decipher the *Index Medicus* when *Newsweek* or *Redbook* will speak your language.

Once you're inside, you order a database to search in one of two ways. You can do keyword searches, the way you do in an Internet search, where you pick a word or two central to your project and ask the search to retrieve every entry that uses those words. Just as often, you'll want to work from the topic *index* at the beginning of the database, select a topic ("English literature" or "sports"), which will lead you to a list of journals in the field, and then search individual journals by the keyword method.

### Web Sites

Web sites are different from the articles in databases. They're on the World Wide Web; they have URLs (Internet addresses, like "amazon .com"); they're usually free to anyone with an Internet connection. There is no editorial control, so they range in credibility from serious academic publication to Debbie-cam trash. Databases are little more than the old academic world of journal articles made digital, but Web sites are the new frontier, with an MTV sensibility.

By far the most important thing to remember about using the Web is that no one screens what you're receiving in any way, so you'll have to judge the worth of a site. Any psychopath can create a Web site and distribute his ravings, so never assume that the content of a site has any inherent credibility whatever. Virtual guides to the Net often include guides for evaluating Web sites: UC Berkeley's guide is at www.lib.berkeley.edu/TeachingLib/Guides/Internet/Evaluate.html.

You search the Web in four ways: via subject directories, search engines, subject gateways, and Web site links. **Subject directories** are like indexes: They begin by presenting you with a list of topics or subject categories: sports, current events, health. You choose a topic and follow the directions. Yahoo! is the most famous subject directory. Even though everyone calls it a search engine, it isn't. Subject directories are usually run by editors, so the quality is usually higher but the coverage smaller, since editorial judgment takes time.

**Search engines** (Google, AltaVista, Excite) are what everyone thinks of when they think of electronic searches. When you log onto the Internet you probably get a string of them across your screen, and you need only click on one and ask for a keyword search. If they're not there, type in the URL: www.google.com, for example. No search engine searches all of the Web, each engine stresses different subject areas, and each engine uses a different search logic. Therefore, it's worth your time to duplicate your search in a few of them. Because search engines are run by computer programs, not people, they can't think and will give you tons of dross along with the gold. Some search engines are better than others. Google seems to be the best right now, but ask your librarian for a recommendation. UC Berkeley's Web site lists the different Web search engines' different characteristics, at www.lib.berkeley.edu/TeachingLib/Guides/Internet/SearchEngines.html.

**Subject gateways** are little known and harder to find, but they're the most academically minded search tools. They're directories devoted to narrow fields, typically run by editors who are specialists—thus the quality is very high. If you can find one, start your research here. Find them by looking at your library's list of research tools under a topic like "Anatomy" or by asking someone in the field, like your instructor.

Once you've found a search tool and gotten to the keyword stage, you're ready for the moment of artfulness: designing the search parameters. When people first use search tools, they're excited by the fact that a ten-second search can turn up 10,000 "pages" (as sites are called on the Web). Soon they realize that this fecundity is a curse. You don't want 10,000 pages; you want the five useful ones. The trick is to design a search that calls up as few pages as possible without missing any important ones.

Here's how novices do it wrong: You're writing a paper on Tiger Woods, the golf pro, so you type into the search engine *Tiger Woods golf pro.* You get back a list of every page with any one of those words used prominently, all fifty million of them, including all references to tigers, wood, golf, or professions. Here's how you do it right: You learn the database's search language, a short series of instructions about how to conduct searches, instructions communicated by words and symbols: most commonly *+, –, "", and, or, not,* *, and capitalization. With many search engines, typing in *+ "Tiger Woods" + "golf pro"* will bring up only those pages with *both* the complete phrases "Tiger Woods" and "golf pro." Commonly, five minutes spent learning two or three rules in the search language can reduce a hit list from 100,000 to 4. Languages differ from one search tool to another, and each tool should have a help page with the necessary tutorial. If you can't find one or get help from a librarian, consult www.lib.berkeley.edu/TeachingLib/Guides/Internet/Strategies.html.

The most powerful search tool on the Web, and the easiest to use, turns out to be none of the three we've seen so far; it's the **links** contained within Web sites. Almost every site on the Web has several links to related sites—the virtual equivalent of a recommended reading list. If you can find one useful Web site, its links will probably give you several more, and each of those will give you several more. Sometimes the links are *hyperlinks,* highlighted keywords throughout the Web site text that automatically take you to other sites; sometimes they're listed in a "Related Web Sites of Interest" list at the end of the site or in the main menu.

# Chapter 24

# USING SOURCES

Since in academic writing you're constantly using other people's texts to support your case, a large part of the art consists of smoothly weaving other people's words and thoughts into your own paragraphs. There are three ways to do that: summary, paraphrase, and quotation. I list them in order of difficulty, hardest first, and in order of desirability—summarize most, paraphrase next most, and quote least.

## Summary and Paraphrase

Summarizing is another word for abstracting (Chapter 7). Professionals summarize a lot, often reducing a large article or report to a single sentence. You read Patrick Hartwell's twenty-two-page essay called "Grammar, Grammars, and the Teaching of Grammar" (*College English,* February 1985) and you sum it up in the term paper this way: "Formal grammar instruction has no positive effect on language performance (Hartwell)." That style will allow you to bring in several sources in a single paragraph.

Paraphrasing is saying someone else's content in about the same number of your own words. It's what you do when you tell a friend what another friend told you. Patrick Hartwell writes, "In 1893, the Committee of Ten put grammar at the center of the English curriculum, and its report established the rigidly sequential mode of instruction common for the last century." I might paraphrase: "American schools have assumed that education should center around grammar instruction ever since 1893, when an influential report by a U.S. government committee decreed that they should."

Why paraphrase when it's easier to quote? For two reasons. First, Hartwell's purposes and audience aren't exactly mine, so his words shouldn't exactly suit me. If you consistently find that others say what you want to say better than you can, worry that you've lost sight of your work's own purposes. Second, I'm not sure I understand the quote until I can say it in my own words.

# Quotation

## Why and When to Quote

Quoting is good because it constantly reminds you that you need to back up your claims. But it's easy to quote too much. Instead of thinking and writing, you are simply transcribing the thinking and writing of others. So limit your use of quotations. A paper should never be more than one-fifth quotation by volume. Never quote a passage just to reproduce what it *says*. Rather, quote only when the *words themselves* are important. Quote only the few words you absolutely need: As a rule of thumb, *be reluctant to quote an entire sentence.* See pp. 298–299 for practice.

## How to Quote

Students like quoting entire sentences and passages because they're easy to punctuate:

> Hoffmeister captured the essence of Lang: "When the dust has settled and we can see him standing clearly before us, we see that the real Lang is not really comic, but tragic."

If you must do this, *don't connect the quote to your previous text with a period or a comma:*

> Wrong: *Everybody knows that drinking and driving don't mix. "Alcohol confuses the mind and slows down the reflexes."

> Wrong: *My opinion is that they think in another frame of mind, "I've got mine, to heck with you, Jack."

Instead, add a conjunction:

> Everybody knows that drinking and driving don't mix, *since* "alcohol confuses the mind and slows down the reflexes" (Willard, 1980; p. 34).

Or use a colon:

> My opinion is that they think in another frame of mind: "I've got mine, to heck with you, Jack."

Or interpolate a phrase like "He says" or "Hernandez put it like this":

> My opinion is that they think in another frame of mind. They say, "I've got mine, to heck with you, Jack."

If the quotation takes up more than three lines of text, indent the entire quotation and leave space above and below it.

Quoting whole sentences is wasteful, however, so we aren't going to do it, in which case you must learn to punctuate a quoted phrase within your own sentence. The trick is *to make the quotation match the grammar of its surroundings.* In other words, the passage must make logical and grammatical sense with or without the quotation marks. So make sure the quotation has the same number, tense, and person as the text around it. If the sentence is in past tense, the quotation will probably have to be in past tense. If the sentence begins by calling Hamlet "he," the quote will have to call him "he" too, even if the quote is spoken by Hamlet. This rule is just a version of our general rule about parallelism on p. 185. Here's a quotation that goes awry:

> Wrong: *When George sees his mother, he doesn't know "how I can tell her of my pain."

To check yourself, read the sentence without the quotation marks and see if it makes sense:

> Wrong: *When George sees his mother, he doesn't know how I can tell her of my pain.

You can solve the problem in two ways:

1. *Use less of the quote (pp. 298–299):*

   > When George sees his mother, he just isn't able to tell her about his "pain."

2. *Rewrite the quotation slightly to make it fit.* Surround the changes with square brackets (not parentheses):

   > When George sees his mother, he doesn't know "how [he] can tell her of [his] pain."

## Documentation

### Why and When to Document

Scholars care greatly about the sources of your insights and your information. The daily paper or *People* magazine almost never tells you where its facts come from, because no one seems to care very much, but to a researcher reading your academic writing, your facts are only as good as the place where you got them and your conclusions only as good as the facts they're based on. Scholars call telling the reader where you found the information *documentation, citation, referencing,* or, loosely, *footnoting*.

What needs to be documented? There are things that come out of your own head—personal feelings, opinions, memories. Those things don't need documentation. Everything else you write or say needs documentation, since you owe it to some outside source. You heard it somewhere or read it somewhere or saw it somewhere. Those things aren't yours; they belong to the people who told them to you. You must give the owner credit in a citation.

There is one exception to all this: You don't need to document data that's common knowledge or easily verifiable. If you claim that Tierra del Fuego is at the southern tip of South America, you needn't document it because your reader can verify the fact in any atlas. But if you assert that Tierra del Fuego has tactical nuclear weapons, you'd better tell the reader where you found out. Thus all quotations must have citations, since it's never obvious where a person's words came from.

Document for two reasons. First, to have accountability. If your reader doesn't know where the information came from, he can't evaluate your sources or see if you're using them well, and thus he can't trust you. Second, to avoid plagiarism, the number one pitfall of the research paper (p. 292).

Students are often shocked by how rabid researchers are about documentation; they say, "But if you do that you'll be documenting every other sentence!" That's right. Lit reviews (p. 302) often have six citations a paragraph.

## How to Document

Let's assume you've just quoted from one of your readings and you want to tell the reader where the quotation came from. We used to cite via *footnotes* at the bottom of each page. That format is extinct, killed by its own incredible inefficiency. Taking its place are several citation systems specific to individual disciplines (the UC Berkeley style guide covers six!). We'll practice the two most common formats: MLA citations, which are used by most of the Humanities, and APA citations, used by most of the sciences. Afterwards, we'll talk about CGOS, the latest citation format for online publication.

Both of our citation formats use brief information in parentheses in the text as a kind of shorthand cue to bibliography entries at the end of the paper. You write, "In fact, Earth has been invaded three times by aliens ( )," and between those parentheses you put just enough information to let the reader find the fuller information in the bibliography. The two systems give different cues, and consequently they format the bibliography differently as well.

**MLA citations.** The Modern Language Association has established a citation system used by scholars in literature and allied fields. It puts in its parentheses the author's last name and the page number. That's all—no punctuation, no "p.," no nothing:

```
In fact, Earth has been invaded three times by aliens
(Smith 12).
```

This tells the reader to look through the bibliography until she gets to a work by Smith; there she'll find out the author's full name, the work's title, the publisher, date of publication, and anything else she needs in order to find a copy of the source herself.

In any of these citation systems, the basic rule is to put in parentheses the minimal information the reader needs to find the bibliography entry. So if your text tells the reader the author's name, the parentheses don't have to:

```
Smith showed that Earth has been invaded three times
by aliens (12).
```

But if there is more than one Smith in the bibliography, you'll have to tell the reader which one you mean:

```
In fact, Earth has been invaded three times by aliens
(J. Smith 12).
```

And if Smith has more than one title in the bibliography, you'll have to tell the reader which one you mean by including an abbreviated version of the title:

```
In fact, Earth has been invaded three times by aliens
(Smith, Aliens 12).
```

It's often easier to include that sort of information in the text itself:

```
Jolene Smith, in Aliens Among Us, argues that Earth
has been invaded three times by aliens (12).
```

If you're working with plays, poems, long works divided into books, or any text where the page number isn't the most useful way of directing the reader to the spot, give her whatever is. For a play, give act, scene, and line numbers; for a poem, give line numbers; for a long poem divided into books, give book and line numbers:

```
Hamlet blames himself for his "dull revenge" (4.4.33).

The people on Keats's urn are "overwrought" (42) in
more than one way.

We're reminded by Milton that Adam and Eve don't cry
for very long when they leave the Garden of Eden
(12.645).
```

Hamlet's line occurs in Act 4, scene 4, line 33, Keats's comment in line 42 of "Ode on a Grecian Urn," and Adam and Eve's tears in line 645 in Book 12 of *Paradise Lost.*

When you find yourself in a situation not quite covered by the rules, just use common sense and remember what citations are for: to get the reader to the bibliography entry. If the work has no author, you'll have to use the title as a cue:

```
In fact, Earth has been invaded three times by aliens
(Aliens Among Us 12).
```

If the title gets bulky, it's cleaner to put it in the text:

```
"Studies of UFO Sightings in North America, 1960-1980"
offers strong evidence that Earth has been invaded
three times by aliens (12).
```

Or use a short form of the title, if it's unambiguous:

```
In fact, Earth has been invaded three times by aliens
("Studies" 12).
```

In the MLA system, at the end of the paper you make a list of all the sources you've cited and title it "Works Cited." Each source is listed once, and the sources are in alphabetical order by authors' last names. The sources are unnumbered. The first line of each entry is unindented, but all other lines are indented five spaces. In the entry, you include all information the reader might need to locate the source itself (*not* a particular page or passage in the source). Here's a typical entry for a book:

```
Smith, Jolene. Aliens Among Us. New York: Vanity
     Press, 1991.
```

Here's a typical entry for a magazine article:

```
Smith, Jolene. "Aliens Among Us." UFO Today 14 Jan.
     1991: 10-19.
```

The title of the article is in quotation marks; the title of the whole volume is underlined (or in italics). All information about volume numbers, issue numbers, seasons (for example, the Fall issue), days, months, and years is included. The page numbers are the pages the article covers, not the pages you used or referred to in the citations.

**APA citations.** The American Psychological Association has a citation system that is used by many of the social sciences. Sometimes called the name/date or the author/year system, it gives the author *and the year of publication* in parentheses, and usually omits the page number:

```
In fact, Earth has been invaded three times by aliens
(Smith, 1991).
```

APA encourages you to put the author's name into the text, put the year in parentheses immediately following the name, and put the page number (with the "p.") at the end of the sentence if you choose to include it:

```
According to Smith (1991), Earth has been invaded
three times by aliens (p. 12).
```

Because the APA scheme asks the reader to find sources by author and year, you must structure the entries in the bibliography (which the APA calls References instead of Works Cited) so the year of publication immediately follows the author:

*For a book:*

```
    Smith, J. (1991). Aliens among us. New York: Van-
ity Press.
```

*For an article:*

```
    Smith, J. (1991, January 14). Aliens among us.
UFO Today, pp. 10-19.
```

There are lots of little ways in which this format differs from MLA's, beyond the location of the year. For instance:

1. Only the author's first initials are used, not the whole first name.
2. Only the first letters of titles and subtitles and proper nouns are capitalized, but, just to make things hard, names of periodicals (like *Science Weekly*) are capitalized conventionally.
3. Titles of articles or chapters, which have quotation marks around them in MLA style, have none here.
4. APA uses "pp." before the page numbers for magazine articles, but not for articles in professional journals (no joke!); MLA never uses it.
5. APA indentation is the opposite of MLA's: indent the first line of the entry only.
6. MLA uses punctuation differently, in several little ways.

In an author/year scheme, if you have several works by the same author, list them in chronological order, the earliest first. Distinguish between items in the same year by assigning letters: 1990a, 1990b, and so on. If the source has no author, begin the entry with the title and alphabetize it as if it were an author.

As soon as you start making citations, you realize you have a thousand unanswered questions about format. Do you write the date of a magazine "December 2," "Dec. 2," "2 December," or "12/2"? Do you underline record album titles or put them in quotation marks? If you have four authors, do you list them all or just list the first and write "et al."? Don't try to memorize answers to all such questions; instead, remember five principles:

1. *Use common sense and blunt honesty.* If you're entering something weird and you're not sure how to handle it, just tell the reader what it is. If it's a cartoon, write "Trudeau, Gary.

'Doonesbury.' Cartoon," then the usual newspaper information. If it's an interview, use "Interview" as your title. If it's a private conversation or a letter, write "Private conversation with author" or "Personal letter to author."

2. *Err on the side of helpfulness.* When in doubt about whether to include information—a government pamphlet's serial number or a TV show's network—put it in.
3. *Be consistent.* Once you do it one way, keep doing it that way.
4. *Get a style manual or research guide.* Citation format is pure convention, so you can't deduce it, and it's complex, so it takes the better part of a book to cover it. Some manuals are published by the organizations that set the rules. For literary writing, the MLA publishes *The MLA Handbook for Writers of Research Papers.* For psychology and other soft sciences, the APA publishes the *APA Publication Manual.* Biology uses *The CBE Style Manual* from the Council of Biology Editors. Social historians use Kate Turabian's *Manual for Writers.* Columbia University publishes *The Columbia Guide to Online Citation.* Other manuals, like Karen Pavlicin and Christy Lyon's *Online Style Guide: Terms, Usage, and Tips,* are not associated with any single format.
5. *Find a Web site.* Web sites are numerous, up to date, and free. Professional organizations always have them. MLA's Web site is at www.mla.org/www_mla_org/style. APA's is at www.apastyle.org/elecref.html. Columbia University's is at www.columbia.edu/cu/cup/cgos/basic.html.

   Sometimes these organizations want you to buy the book, so are chary with their information. Often you get more help from more disinterested sources, like libraries—(UC Berkeley's citation guide is at www.lib.berkeley.edu/TeachingLib/Guides/Internet/Style.html) and helpful individuals. For help with APA style, check a Web site like www.psywww.com/resource/apacrib.htm and see what I mean. A Google search using your citation style as a keyword will get you started.

## Citing Online Sources

Electronic research has created a monstrous headache for all writers using citations. Consider for a moment the key elements of a traditional citation: author, title, publishing date, place of publication (city and publisher), and page number(s). A Web source may well have none of these. Whichever of them the source does have can change overnight, since most electronic texts can be updated and altered to any degree at any time. Citing such ephemera can feel like writing on the surface of a rushing river. To keep your head above water, obey the following general rules:

1. See if the source itself gives you citation instructions. More and more, encyclopedias and other sources online include a header that begins with something like "Cite this article as . . ." You can just copy it down.
2. Unless otherwise instructed, use the traditional citation format as a template and make the electronic citation conform to it as closely as possible. For instance, if there is no title for the piece, ask yourself, "What is the nearest thing to a title here?" and put it in the title's place. Personal email isn't titled, but it usually has a subject line (a.k.a. the "re" line) when it appears in your mail cue, and that will serve.
3. The less bibliographical information you have on a source, the less you should use it at all. Even online, a work of integrity tends to have an author with a real name, some sort of page numbering system, a publication date, and a permanent existence in some stable archive. If your source has none of these, maybe you shouldn't be taking it seriously.
4. Print at least the first page of any electronic source you use—it will preserve the reference data across the bottom or top.
5. If you use an electronic version of a print source (like a newspaper article from a database), do not cite the print version—acknowledge in your citation that you used the electronic form (since the page numbers are different, for one reason).

When making parenthetical references to Internet sources where key elements of author, date, or page number are unavailable, make the following substitutions:

*For the author:* Use the file name (for instance, cgos.html).
*For the date of publication:* Use the date of last revision or the date of access.
*For the page number:* Typically use nothing.

And when building bibliographies, obey the following guidelines specific to each of our two citation formats:

**MLA citations.** An entry for an electronic source contains the following information, in this order, when available:

1. Author's name
2. Title of work—using the subject line for emails
3. Print publishing information, if the work originally appeared in print
4. Title of Web site, database, periodical, and so forth
5. Name of editor, compiler, or maintainer of site
6. Version number or volume and issue numbers
7. Date of publication or latest update

8. Name of subscription service or name of library used to access file
9. Name of list or forum
10. Page or section number
11. Name of site sponsor
12. Date of access
13. URL

See model entries on p. 338 and following.

**APA citations.** List the following elements in this order, when available:

1. Author
2. Date of work or date last modified
3. Title
4. Information on print publication
5. Type of source, in brackets: for instance, [Online], [Online database], [CD-ROM]
6. Name of vendor and document number, or "Retrieved (date) from the World Wide Web:" and the URL

See model entries on p. 338 and following.

## Model Citations

Here are templates for common bibliography entries, in MLA and APA format.

*A book with an edition number and multiple authors:*

MLA: `Tremaine, Helen, and John Blank. Over the Hill. 10th ed. New York: Houghton, 1946.`

APA: `Tremaine, H., & Blank, J. (1946). Over the hill. (10th ed.). New York: Houghton Mifflin.`

*A book with an editor:*

MLA: `Blank, John, ed. Over the Hill. New York: Houghton, 1946.`

APA: `Blank, J. (Ed.). (1946). Over the hill. New York: Houghton Mifflin.`

*A book with an author and an editor or a translator:*

MLA: `Blank, John. Over the Hill. Ed. Helen Tremaine. New York: Houghton, 1946.`

APA: Blank, J. (1946). Over the hill. (H. Tremaine, Ed.) New York: Houghton Mifflin.

MLA: Blank, John. Over the Hill. Trans. Helen Tremaine. New York: Houghton, 1946.

APA: Blank, J. (1946). Over the hill. (H. Tremaine, Trans.) New York: Houghton Mifflin. (Original work published 1910).

*A government pamphlet:*

MLA: United States. Dept. of Commerce. Highway Construction Costs Per Mile, 1980-1990. #32768. Washington: GPO, 1991.

APA: U.S. Department of Commerce. (1991). Highway construction costs per mile, 1980-1990. (DOC Publication No. 32768). Washington, DC: U.S. Government Printing Office.

*Anonymous article in a well-known reference work:*

MLA: "Alphabet." Collier's Encyclopedia. 1994 ed.

APA: Alphabet. (1994). Collier's Encyclopedia.

*Anonymous newspaper article:*

MLA: "Man Bites Dog." New York Times 25 Dec. 1999: D3.

APA: Man bites dog. (1999, December 25). New York Times, p. D3.

*Television show:*

MLA: Company's Coming. ABC. KZAP, San Francisco. 13 Oct. 1998.

APA: Company's coming. (1998, October 13). San Francisco: KZAP.

*Computer software:*

MLA: The Last Word. Computer Software. Silicon Valley, CA: DataBase, 2002.

APA: The Last Word [Computer software]. (2002). Silicon Valley, CA: DataBase.

*Lyrics from a record album or compact disc:*

MLA: The Ruttles. "Company's Coming." Live Ruttles. CD. RCA, 1964.

APA: The Ruttles. (1964). Company's coming. On Live Ruttles. [CD] New York: RCA.

*World Wide Web journal article:* (These model citations have been taken verbatim from Nick Carbone's *Writing Online,* 3rd Edition, Houghton Mifflin Company, Boston and New York, 2000):

MLA: Lewis, Theodore. "Research in Technology Education: Some Areas of Need." Journal of Technology Education, 10:2. Spring 1999. 2 Aug. 1999 <http://scholar.lib.vt.edu/ejournals/JTE/v10n2/lewis.html>.

APA: Lewis, T. (Spring 1999). Research in technology education: Some areas of need. Journal of Technology Education, 10:2. Online journal. Retrieved August 2, 1999, from the World Wide Web: http://scholar.lib.vt.edu/ejournals/JTE/v10n2/lewis.html

*Personal email:*

MLA: Russell, Sue. "E180 Fall 1999." Email Interview with Author. 10 June 1999.

APA: The APA discourages listing in the reference list any source that can't be accessed by the reader. Cite personal emails in the body of the text.

*Database:*

MLA: U.S. Census Bureau. "Quick Table P-1A: Age and Sex of Total Population: 1990, Hartford-Middletown, CT." 1990. Lkd. Home page at "Population and Housing Facts"/"Quick Tables." U.S. Census Bureau, American FactFinder. 10 June 1999 <http://factfinder.census.gov>.

APA: U.S. Census Bureau. (1990). Quick Table P-1A: Age and Sex of Total Population: 1990, Hartford-Middletown, CT. [Online, follow links Population and Housing Facts, then Quick Tables]. U.S. Census Bureau, American FactFinder. Retrieved on June 10, 1999, from the World Wide Web: http://factfinder.census.gov

**The Columbia Guide to Online Style.** The CGOS represents a recent attempt to establish a simple, universal approach to online citations. It's of primary interest to writers publishing online. Your instructor may want you to use it exclusively, use it just for your online sources, or not use it at all. Its details are set forth on the CGOS Web site and in the *Guide* itself (p. 334). It comes in a form for the humanities—an adaptation of MLA style, and a form for the sciences—an adaptation of APA. Its main differences from those two formats are three:

1. The text of the citation is aligned at the left ("left-justified"), with no indentations, since indenting translates badly in online publishing.
2. The URL is set up as a hyperlink, so the reader can simply click on it and access the source. To make that possible, the date of access is moved to the end and the URL is printed without angle brackets (<>).
3. There's no indicator that the source is virtual—that is, no "retrieved from the World Wide Web" or "Online"—since the Internet is assumed to provide the source.

Here's the online journal example from p. 338 done in the two CGOS styles:

CGOS for the humanities:

Lewis, Theodore. "Research in Technology Education: Some Areas of Need." Journal of Technology Education, 10:2. Spring 1999. http://scholar.lib.vt.edu/ejournals/JTE/v10n2/ (2 Aug. 1999).

CGOS for the sciences:

Lewis, T. (Spring 1999). Research in technology education: Some areas of need. Journal of Technology Education, 10:2. http://scholar.lib.vt.edu/ejournals/JTE/v10n2/ (2 Aug. 1999).

## EXERCISES

1. You've written a term paper citing the following sources. Make two end-of-paper bibliographies, one in the MLA citation system and one in the APA.

a. A book called *Down the Spout,* by Ellen Strand, published by Windward Press of Cleveland, Ohio, in 1983.
b. A book called *Studies in the Grotesque,* by Thomas Nixon and Andrew Gore, published by Androgyne Press of Boothbay, Minnesota, in 1971.
c. A book called *Literacy Revisited,* edited by Margaret Dumont, published by Rearguard Press of New York City, New York, in 1986.
d. An article called "Are We Helping the Russians Without Knowing It?," written by Ellen Strand, in *The Voice of the Nation* magazine, Volume #3, Issue #12, dated December 1982. The article begins on page 75 and ends on page 86.
e. An article called "Negative Camber: Three Approaches," by Morris Wills, in a book called *Suspensions and Their Maintenance,* edited by Stirling Ross and published by Graves and Digger Publishing Company of Houston, Texas, in 1964. The article begins on page 12 and ends on page 212.
f. A pamphlet from the federal government, with no identified author and no date, called "Wind Shear and Its Effect on House Trailers," printed by the Government Printing Office in Washington, D.C. It bears the number 3769 and "Department of Transportation" on the title page.
g. An anonymous article called "Byte Dogs Man," in the *Chicago Tribune* newspaper on November 12, 1975, on page 4 of Section C.
h. A personal email message sent to you by Phil Anthropy with the subject line "Developments on the Enrollment Front," sent on December 3, 1997, and received by you the same day. Phil's email address is Shellshock@Macgate.csuchico.edu.
i. An entry on "Greenland" in the *Britannica Online* version of the *Encyclopedia Britannica,* which has a publication date of 1994–1997 and which you accessed on January 12, 1998. The encyclopedia's Internet address is http://www.eb.com. The "Greenland" article's address is http://www.eb.com:180/cgi-bin/g?keywords=greenland&clrBtn=Clear.
j. An article called "Boredom in School: a Myth?", published in *College Today,* a journal, in the October 1999, issue, vol. #35. It covers pages 12–18. You found it in a database called Academic Issues, which your university library accesses via a vendor called SKOOL. You accessed it on November 7, 2001. The vendor's URL is <www.SKOOL.com>.

k. An article called "Sex Is Out," which you found in a Web site called *Today's Trends*. The article was published on January 3, 2002 and written by Brittany Shalala. You accessed it on January 27, 2003. The Web site URL is <www.trendy.com>. The article URL is <www.trendy.com/sex/07/html>.

2. Imagine that the following sentences each cite one of the sources in exercise 1, sentence *a* citing source *a*, sentence *b* citing source *b*, and so on. Add parenthetical citations to each sentence in each of our two citation formats. For example, the first sentence with a citation in MLA format might look like this: "Strand showed that American plumbing has a working life of only five years (12)." Invent page numbers as you need them.

a. Strand showed that American plumbing has a working life of only five years.
b. Gore and Nixon argued in 1971 that "the grotesque is merely the realistic turned on its head."
c. "Literacy is a fiction."
d. Since 1945, our foreign policy has unwittingly played directly into the hands of the Soviets.
e. In 1962, the average negative camber of a Formula One race car was 7 percent.
f. The federal government has concluded that no commercial trailer can be expected to withstand winds above 60 mph.
g. Actually, a man once was pursued by a computer—on November 11, 1975, in Flint, Michigan.
h. A colleague assures me that judging by her experience, college students are more familiar with recent American history than they were ten years ago.
i. Contrary to popular belief, Greenland isn't very green.
j. Only 3 percent of college students report they are "extremely bored" by their classes.
k. Celibacy is cooler than NHL jerseys right now.

3. Make a bibliography in CGOS format, using items a–k of Item 1 above.

# Chapter 25

# THE RESEARCH PAPER

A research paper is a large—ten to thirty pages—project that gathers information primarily from written materials. It's often called a term paper if it's due at the end of the term, as the culmination of the semester's work.

## Setting Yourself a Good Task

Since a term paper takes ten times as long to write as an essay, you must work ten times as hard to make sure you're not wasting your time.

When I was in the seventh grade, I wrote my first term paper, on Russia. I slaved over it. I paraphrased lengthy passages from articles on Russia in several different encyclopedias and collated them. I cut out dozens of pictures of Russians farming from back issues of *National Geographic.* I traced maps with little hay ricks indicating grain-producing areas. In the report I always referred to Russia as "the Union of Soviet Socialist Republics," because it filled more space. I got an A. And at no time did it bother me or the teacher that I didn't know what Russia was. A few years later I was mildly surprised to discover it was a country, like the United States.

For many students, that's what writing a term paper is: a pointless exercise in page filling. Resolve at the outset to prevent it from being that for you. You do this by designing a real, worthy, doable research project. Such a project has seven features:

**Like all good seeds, a term paper is a task to be performed.** It is a question to be answered, or a thesis to be defended, but never a topic, because a topic is a noun and nouns are useless.

**Your paper has an audience,** a potential reader whom you can describe in detail.

**Your paper is useful to the reader.** He's going to go out and do something with it: choose a heating source for his new house, set up a compost pile, select a treatment for his disease. The audience whose needs you care about the most is you, so try to ask a question whose answer *you* can use.

You'll know the moment the project has ceased to be useful to someone: when you find yourself copying down information from a source just because it's "on your topic," with no sense of how you're going to use it or why it matters. When that happens, stop and ask yourself again who's going to use your work and how they're going to use it.

**The task is achieved primarily through information gathering,** not by expressing your opinion. We said this about academic writing in general (pp. 291–292).

**The subject is something you know enough about to ask intelligent questions.** If you write about something you're totally ignorant of, you'll be almost forced into hiding your ignorance, writing on topic instead of task, pointless information-gathering, and plagiarism. The good project is one you know enough about to know what still needs knowing. I've sailed for a few years, bought a couple of sailboats, and dreamed of buying others, so I know that recently a number of new alternatives to outright buying are being made available to the family sailor: chartering, joining a sailing club, and buying, then leasing back to the seller. What are the advantages and disadvantages of each of the three? I don't know the answer, but I know the question needs asking.

**Your project does something no other source has quite done for you.** If you find a book or article that simply does your task, beautifully and finally, you're out of business. You must find a new task, or you'll have nothing to do but plagiarize the source.

Approach the problem in two ways. First, write about what's new. Study the latest advances in a field, before other writers have worked them over. Don't write about how to buy a mountain bike; write about the advantages and disadvantages of the new generation of mountain-bike air-suspension forks. Second, narrow the audience. If you write on alternatives to fossil fuels, a host of writers will have been there before you. If you're writing on the comparative virtues of different kinds of home heating for someone who's building a small cabin in Trinity County, California, considering the area's peculiar wood fuel supply, power company rates, and local building codes, and your reader's floor plan and budget, it's unlikely that it's been done. If you write on anorexia, everything seems to have been said already; but if you write to freshmen anorexics attending college away from home and talk about the special pressures of that environment on that particular personality type, you're more likely to find new ground to break. And narrowing the audience will make it easier to remember that this work is something someone will *use*.

**The task is neither too big nor too small.** "The term paper must be twenty-five to thirty pages," the instructor says, and you just know what's going to happen. Either you'll pick a topic that runs dry after eight pages and you end up padding and stretching, or to prevent that you'll pick a gargantuan topic like U.S. foreign policy and never finish the background reading. How can you find the task that is the right size?

First, any *topic* is too large, because the amount of information on any topic is endless, however narrowly the topic is defined: There's an endless stream of information on Russia, but the stream on Moscow is equally endless, and so is the stream on the Kremlin. Second, any almanac-type question is too small: "How many people in this country actually escape prison via the insanity plea?" Interesting question, but after you write down "On the average, thirty-five a year," the report is over.

Beyond that, any task that fits our other criteria will prove to be the right size, once you master the skills of Chapter 9 for making a prompt expand or shrink as the need arises. You don't define a thirty-page task at the outset. Rather, you pick a task and begin; as you read and write and think you say, "This is getting to be too much—I have to cut back," or "I'm getting to answers too quickly—I've got to enlarge my scope." And you shrink or expand to suit. If my sailboat chartering versus leasing versus club joining paper proves too much, I can write about the pros and cons of chartering only; if it proves too little, I can write about all possible ways to get into sailing, including crewing for other boat owners, or discuss the cost of sailing, including insurance, maintenance, and hardware options. If I'm writing on how effectively the Food and Drug Administration monitors drug testing and marketing and that proves too large, I can write on whether the FDA dropped the ball on NutraSweet; if it proves too small, I can write about whether federal regulatory agencies generally do their jobs and whether they do more harm than good.

## Getting Things Organized

Term papers are largely exercises in handling data avalanches. You need a system for handling bits. Bits are pieces of information: facts, figures, quotes, thoughts from you, titles of works to be read. You need to be able to find a bit in your notes, cluster and recluster bits quickly, tell whether or not a bit has been used in the report yet, and cite the bit in the final draft. Here's how.

**Up front, decide whether to gather data via computer or by hand.** There are advantages either way. The computer's advantages are that it encourages you to think in terms of *filing* from the outset, and it makes reshuffling bits easy, via copying and pasting. Its drawbacks are that you can only see one screen's worth of data at a time, so you lack an overview, and it can be hard to find individual items. Also, much of your note-taking will be done while you're in the library, so you'd need a laptop computer. The advantages outweigh the drawbacks, and you'll find yourself working with a computer more and more and a paper notepad less and less.

**Record all bibliographical data as soon as you begin to take notes.** If it's a book, write down the authors' full names, the complete title of the work, the publisher, and place and year of publication. If it's a periodical, record the volume number, issue number, and date. Record the page number(s) where the things you're taking notes on appear, and absolutely everything else you might need to find it again later, including the library call number or URL. It's tedious, but five minutes now will save you an hour when you need the information a month from now.

**Invent a system for marking bits you've used in the report and bits you haven't.** You must be able to look at a dozen bits and say, "Those seven I've used; those five I haven't." But don't check off the used bits by deleting them or throwing them away—keep your data intact so you can rethink it, use it elsewhere, and proofread it later. Use highlighting pens or boldface the used bits.

**Invent a cueing/categorizing system for your notes.** You need a way of labeling your notes so you can tell what they're about without rereading them. Some people use keywords: When they've taken notes on an article, they head the notes with a few keywords (or phrases) identifying the article's main issues. If you're writing on alternative heating sources, you might read an article hostile to wood-burning stoves and end up with a list of keywords like "wood-burning stoves," "air pollution," "shrinking resources," and "health hazards." If three weeks later you want to deal with the health hazards of indoor open fires, you simply make a stack of all note cards bearing the "health hazards" keyword and your data is ready to go. Word processors help by making it easy to copy and paste a fact or quotation in ten or twenty different categories.

**Build cubbyholes**—physical or electronic sites to house notes according to topic or keyword. If you're not using a computer, get a lot of manila folders or shoeboxes.

**Put each bit on a separate piece of paper if you're not working on a computer.** That way you can literally shuffle and reshuffle your data. You can take notes on slips, like 3×5 cards, or you can use full-size pages and then attack them with scissors.

**Never let the bit and its bibliographical data get separated.** As you move a quote or a stat from cubbyhole to cubbyhole, keep all info on where it came from attached to it.

**Don't forget to brainstorm.** As you strive to control the data avalanche, don't get so organized that you forget the lessons of the earlier chapters: Writing and thinking are messy, recursive businesses, and you need a lot of loose time to wander and discover. Don't take too much control. Especially don't try to do one task at a time. Writing is multitasking, and you do a creative task best when you're busy doing others. For instance, don't resolve to do the background reading, then draft, because both reading and writing are ways of thinking, and each will propagate the other—read and write simultaneously and continuously throughout the term paper process.

## Format

Since a term paper is bigger than an essay, the format may be more elaborate, with several elements that shorter papers usually don't have:

*A title page,* on which you give title, your name, the date, and usually the course name and number and instructor's name
*A table of contents*
*Appendices,* where you put the raw data the average reader won't want to read
*Graphics*—pictures, tables, graphs—either in appendices or throughout the paper
*A list of illustrations* following the table of contents, if you have graphics throughout the work
*A letter of transmittal* on the front, addressed to the receiver of the report, saying in essence, "Here's the report"
*An abstract* before page 1, summarizing the paper for the reader who only has a minute
*A bibliography* or Works Cited list at the end
*Section headings:* "Introduction," "Conclusion," "Discussion," "History of the Problem," "Three Possible Solutions," "Recent Advances"

There are models of most of these features in the sample term paper following. Use those models as templates unless your instructor has her own format.

Don't fall in love with format for format's sake. Many beginning researchers see format apparatus as an easy way to make a term paper look like a big deal. Don't do that—keep apparatus to a minimum.

## Graphics

If your research involves numbers, you'll probably find yourself using graphics: charts, tables, graphs. There are lots of regulations about how to handle graphics, but they're all variations on one rule: Remember your reader, and make things easy on her. In other words, always present data so it's easy to read, understand, and put to use. News magazines like *Time* and *Newsweek* are masters of that art, so study their graphics for lessons in effective presentation. Here are four principles to follow.

**Graphics are not self-explanatory.** Be sure to tell the reader exactly what he's looking at and what it means. Title the graphic informatively, label its parts clearly, and explain whatever needs explaining, in footnotes below the graphic or in the report's text right above or below the graphic.

**Avoid overload.** A graphic's power is in its ability to dramatize and clarify a point or show the relationships between a few bits of data. If you try to make a graphic do too much, its power is lost. Better three graphics making three points clearly and forcefully than one spectacularly ornate graphic making three points at once and obscuring all of them.

**Number all graphics,** unless you have only one. That way you can readily refer to the graphic by saying, "as shown in Figure 1."

**Express ideas as drawings.** We understand pictures better than numbers, so whenever possible express your data as a drawing, not as columns of numbers—use figures instead of tables, technical writers would say.

Let's pretend we're reproducing the results of an agricultural experiment on the relationship between fertilizer application rates and plant growth. The experiment took five groups of identical plants and gave each a different amount of fertilizer, then measured the growth after a month to see what dosage produced the most. Here we have the data expressed in a table:

| **Group #** | **1** | **2** | **3** | **4** | **5** |
|---|---|---|---|---|---|
| (mg/gal): | (10) | (20) | (30) | (40) | (50) |
| Growth (in inches) | 1.2 | 3.1 | 5.0 | −1.1 | −3.7 |

Here we have the data expressed in a figure:

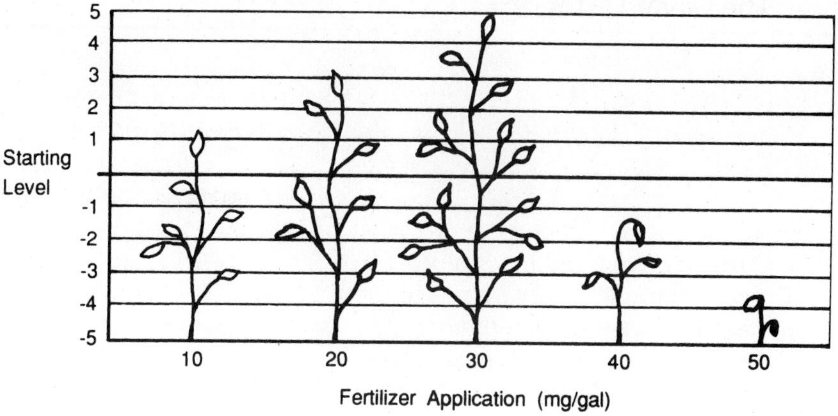


Isn't it easier to see the point in figure form?

# A Model Research Paper

## The Cover Letter

1010 Arbor Drive
Chico, CA 95926

December 9, 2000

Jack P. Rawlins
Professor
California State University, Chico
Department of English
Chico, CA 95929

Dear Dr. Rawlins:

Please accept the attached term paper, "Don't Let Your Computer Make You Sick," as my final writing project for the class English 175-3.

Thank you for your consideration.

Sincerely yours,

*Nancy C. Praizler*
Nancy C. Praizler
Astudent@aol.com
(530) 555-8922

## The Title Page

Don't Let Your Computer Make You Sick

by

Nancy C. Praizler

for Jack Rawlins

English 175-3

December 9, 2000

## The Abstract

Extended computer use can cause serious and debilitating health problems, but these problems can be prevented. Health problems are both physical and psychological. Psychological problems fall into two categories: stress-induced problems and addictions. The most common physical problems are eye strain, cumulative trauma disorder (especially carpal tunnel syndrome), "sick building syndrome," back problems, and neck problems. In each case there are measures you can take to prevent the problem from occurring and remedies to use once the problem occurs. Since computers are here to stay, we must learn to treat them like any other tool and protect ourselves from their hazards.

## Contents

Contents

Praizler 1

Paying for Computer Usage

While work has required us to perform like machines--digging ditches, assembling cars, or typing manuscripts--we tend not to think of ourselves as machines when we do work at a computer. Yet many of us sit in front of a computer monitor--a video display terminal, or VDT--for eight or more hours a day and expect our bodies not to be affected. In fact, computers have been in our workplaces long enough for us to know that they can lead to serious and debilitating health problems. Fortunately, research has been done on the causes of the problems and remedies to them.

Health problems associated with computer use come in two forms: physical problems and psychological problems.

The most common physical health problems associated with use of computers are eye strain, cumulative trauma disorder (CTD), "sick building syndrome," back and neck strain, all of which can lead to headaches (Scheuermann 94), tiredness, short-term memory loss, depression (Murray), and irritability (Free 7).

Praizler 2

Psychological Health Problems

Psychological problems generally fall into two categories: stress-induced problems and addictions. Stress, caused by information overload, long hours in front of a VDT, and decreased face-to-face contact, has been called the "new industrial epidemic" by Britain's Trade Union Congress. It can lead to insomnia, irritability, anxiety, and fatigue (Kleeman), as well as more serious health problems like heart disease, cancer, and strokes (Stress). As we increasingly use computer services like e-commerce on the Internet, we have less of the "authentic psychological encounter" (Lauer 1) we need, and feel lonely and disconnected from people. E-commerce "dehumanizes America" (Mitchell 2A), and threatens to spoil the "homeyness of the hometown stores" (Mitchell 2A), which refreshes us.

Addictive problems have emerged with the use of the Internet in particular. In August 1999, the London Sunday Times reported that people who surf the Internet for more than four hours per day are likely to be "clinically ill and need medical treatment" (Harlow). Great Britain has funded treatment of this illness, just as it funds treatment for alcoholism and gambling addictions.

Praizler 3

Physical Health Problems

Extended computer use exposes us to a very long list of potential physical attributes. Fortunately, there are precautions we can take and products we can buy that help prevent injury and illness, and give relief when damage is done.

Eye Strain

Eye strain affects 10 million people each year (Scheuermann). Its symptoms are "eye fatigue, dry itchy eyes, blurred vision, and/or headaches" (State of California 6). The problem is caused by glare from overhead lights or bright windows, a monitor screen that is too close or too far from your eyes, poor brightness and contrast on your VDT screen, and focusing on your VDT screen for long periods without a break (State of California 6).

You can prevent eye strain by making workstation adjustments, changing your behavior, and exercising and massaging your eyes and temples. First, prevent the glare. Use antiglare computer filter on your VDT, then place your monitor at a right angle to the window producing glare (State of California 5). Second, set the brightness and contrast on your VDT for the sharpest clarity and keep the screen

Praizler 4

clean. Third, exercise your eye muscles by looking away from the monitor every ten minutes and focusing on an object at least twenty feet in the distance. Blink often and "gently massage the bony area around each eye using short circular motions" (State of California 6). Next, gently massage your temples.

There are also products available to ease the strain on your eyes. Full-spectrum bulbs, treated with a special coating to make the light resemble sunlight, ease eye strain and reduce fatigue according to studies (Harmony 24). These bulbs come in globe and fluorescent types, so you can replace both your desk lamp bulb and the fluorescent bulbs overhead.

Another type of lamp to prevent eye strain is called the Eclipse Computer Light. It sits on your VDT and has a special fluorescent bulb which points upward into a reflector panel. You adjust the panel until the light is on your screen and keyboard. People who have used it report that it is very pleasant to work around and doesn't produce any glare (Warner 02G).

Cumulative Trauma Disorder

Cumulative trauma disorder (CTD), also known as repetitive-stress injury, increased 467 percent between 1991 and 1995 (Greim 8B). The disorder usually affects hands and arms, and is caused by repeating a motion such as typing on a computer keyboard. CTD is a group of disorders which include carpal tunnel syndrome, tendonitis, tenosynovitis, thoracic outlet syndrome, and ulnar neuritis (State of California 11).

Carpal Tunnel Syndrome

Carpal tunnel syndrome, the most common CTD problem, is a disorder of the median nerve. As the nerve passes through the carpal tunnel in the wrist into the hand, the sheaths that surround the tendons in the narrow tunnel swell and press against the nerve, causing pain (State of California 11). If your first three fingers are painful, numb, and tingle, especially at night, your arm muscle strength is diminishing, or you have a burning sensation in your hand, you may have the disorder.

Prevention of carpal tunnel syndrome is much easier than correction of the disorder, which often involves surgery. To prevent the problem, set up your workstation so that your wrists are straight when you sit upright in your chair with your arms on your keyboard. Keep your wrists straight when you type but move them freely, don't pound, and rest your hands for a brief period every fifteen minutes while typing or writing (State of California 13). Use a wrist rest--a padded bar--to support your

Praizler 6

wrists when you lower them, which should be infrequently, and place your computer mouse at elbow height so you can keep your wrist straight when you reach for it. (State of California 2). Also, alternate among different tasks so that you avoid long periods of repeating the same movement.

Treatment of carpal tunnel syndrome comes in many forms. Steroids may be injected into the wrists, or anti-inflammatory drugs taken. Holistic practitioners recommend ingesting Vitamin B-6, which reduces the fluid in the carpal tunnel so there is more space between the tendons and nerves. Also, arnica gel, ginger, and cold packs can help, as can acupuncture (Greim 8B).

"Sick Building Syndrome"

Electronic devices like computer monitors emit low-level electromagnetic waves. We encounter these emissions daily. They are in visible light, radio waves, microwaves, infrared radiation, ultraviolet rays, X-rays, and gamma rays (Air Force 58). Derek Clement-Croome and John Jukes claim that low-level electromagnetic radiation from computer monitors causes "sick building syndrome" which is characterized by itchy eyes, tiredness, headaches, backaches and irritability and depression (Free 7). In addition, the makers of a device designed to counteract the emissions declare that "prolonged daily exposure to the electromagnetic fields generated by the TV and computers results in a variety of physiological and neuropsychological disorders" ("Feedback" 100).

Various products to block electromagnetic radiation are appearing on the market. There is the alpha oscillator, which Clement-Croome and Jukes claim can reduce the symptoms of sick building syndrome by between 27% and 44% if it is attached to one's computer monitor (Free 7). Another product is the magnetic oscillator, whose product name is the Tecno AO antenna. It emits a "corrective compensating signal that neutralizes the polluting effects of screen magnetic stress and provides electromagnetic biocompatibility between screen radiation and the user" ("Feedback" 100).

A third product is the solid-state diode. This device maintains the natural electrical current of your body when you are bombarded with "foreign" electromagnetic waves from your computer monitor (Cook). The diodes come in different forms. Some can be affixed to your VDT, others are carried on you. Some are designed as jewelry and are worn as pins or pendants. Prices for the diodes range from $15 to $25.00.

The fourth product takes a different

Praizler 8

approach. The Asahi Chemical Industry Company has created a fabric made from silver-coated nylon filament and polyester fibers which promises to block "97-99% of high-frequency electric fields of up to 1,000 megahertz," which includes those emitted by personal computers (Asahi 11). The fabric is used in garments and can be washed or dry-cleaned without losing its effectiveness (Asahi 11) and costs about $20 to $25 per meter. Two other companies are producing fabric that shields its wearer from electro-magnet radiation: Teijin Ltd. and Kanebo Gohsen Ltd. (Asahi 11). While it is too early to know if these devices are truly effective, they may be worth trying if you are feeling sick when you are using your computer but you don't know why.

Back Problems

Our bodies are not designed for sitting for long periods without moving, which is what we often do when we sit for hours at our computers. Studies show that, since the 1970's, we are doubling every decade the amount of sick time we are taking off for back pain (Hutchison 6). In addition, "the largest single recorded cause of long-term sick leave" (Hutchison 6) is back injury. "Fifteen million working days a year are lost . . . due to . . . back problems" (Hutchison 6). It is estimated that a quarter

Praizler 9

of a million back problems were the result of conditions in the workplace, such as chairs with inadequate back support and long periods in fixed positions--"usually in front of a computer" (Hutchison 6).

If you are one of many who sits at work all day, you can protect your back by adjusting your monitor so that it is at eye level, sitting in a chair with an adjustable back rest, using a document holder so you don't have to move your neck as you look from your document to the monitor screen, and sitting with good body posture (Hutchison 6). Your head should be balanced over your shoulders and hips, your spine supported with a slight arch by the back of the chair. Knees should be at the same level or slightly lower than your hips, and your feet should be supported comfortably on the floor or on a foot rest in front of your knees (State of California 3). When you're waiting for your printer to print, relax the upper part of your body, or get up and walk around. Take a break from your computer before you become fatigued, and change tasks as often as possible.

Neck Problems

Neck pain, while less debilitating long-term than back pain, can lead to injuries like pinched nerves if ignored. Unfortunately, we

Praizler 10

often accept neck pain as an inevitable part of work, but we shouldn't.

To prevent or alleviate neck pain, adjust your workstation set-up. First, your computer monitor should be raised so that your eyes are level with or slightly below the top of the screen (State of California 13). If you wear bifocals, position the screen a little lower so you can read it with the reading part of your glasses. Second, move the monitor so that it is a comfortable reading distance from your eyes, about 12-18″. Third, sit up straight and don't bend your neck forward when you're working. Fourth, do some neck-stretching exercises. For example, while sitting at your desk, place your right hand on the top of your head. Gently pull your head toward your right shoulder. Breathe and relax while you're doing this. Hold the stretch for about twenty seconds. Repeat this stretch three times, then change hands and gently pull your head toward your left shoulder (State of California 23).

The Bottom Line

Computers are here to stay. We can't or won't live without them. Unfortunately, using them can be harmful to us. That harm is often hard

Praizler 11

to see, the product of slow, insidious damage over weeks, months, or years, but the accumulated consequences can be dire. Since computers contribute to a sedentary lifestyle, pinning us in our chairs in front of monitors for hours, we must work harder to make time to exercise. Since they are addictive, we must discipline ourselves to limit our time using them and make time to interact with other people. Since invisible emissions from our monitors may be making us sick, we must install protective devices to counteract the harmful emissions. Since the companies we work for are uninformed about workstation ergonomics, we must educate ourselves and them so we can adjust workstations that support our bodies. Above all, we must remember that a computer is a tool, and, as with a drill press or table saw, we must learn to use it properly and safely, so that we may enjoy its benefits without paying a great price in pain and injury.

Praizler 12

Works Cited

"Asahi Chemical Creates Fabric to Block Electromagnetic Waves." The Nikkei Weekly, 10 Nov. 1997: Section: New Products, Science & Technology, 11. Academic Universe. Lexis-Nexis. Meriam Library, California State University, Chico. 1 Dec. 2000 <http://web.lexis-nexis.com/universe>.

Cook, Wayne, and Cook, Wanda. "Diodes." (Product Brochure). 24 July 1987.

"Feedback." New Scientist, 6 Feb. 1999: 100. Academic Universe. Lexis-Nexis. Meriam Library, California State University, Chico. 1 Dec. 2000 <http://web.lexis-nexis.com/universe>.

Free, Rosemary. "Hi-Tech Cause of Office Illness." The Herald (Glasgow), 14 July 1999: 7. Academic Universe. Lexis-Nexis. Meriam Library, California State University, Chico. 2 Dec. 2000 <http://web.lexis-nexis.com/universe>.

Greim, Lisa. "User-Unfriendly: Computer Operators Should Take Precautions Against Injuries Incurred at Work." The Denver Rocky Mountain News (Denver, CO.), 8 June 1998: Section: Business; Ed. F: 8B. Academic Universe. Lexis-Nexis. Meriam

Library, California State University, Chico. 1 Dec. 2000 <http://web.lexis-nexis.com/universe>.

Harlow, John. "Health Experts Say Net Nerds Are Sick People." Sunday Times (London), 22 Aug. 1999: Section: Home News. Academic Universe. Lexis-Nexis. Meriam Library, California State University, Chico. 1 Dec. 2000 <http://web.lexis-nexis.com/universe>.

Harmony. (Product Catalog.) Gaiam, Inc. Colorado. 1999.

Hutchison, Anne. "Watch Your Back or Pay the Price." The Scotsman, 26 Feb. 1999: 6. Academic Universe. Lexis-Nexis. Meriam Library, California State University, Chico. 1 Dec. 2000 <http://web.lexis-nexis.com/universe>.

Kleeman, Walter B. "The Politics of Office Design." Environment & Behavior, Sept. 1998: Vol. 20(5): 537-549. PsycINFO. INFOTRAC. Meriam Library, California State University, Chico. 2 Dec. 2000 <http://infotrac.galegroup.com>.

Lauer, Charles S. Publisher's Letter. Modern Healthcare, 19 July 1999: 0. Academic Universe. Lexis-Nexis. Meriam Library, California State University, Chico. 1 Dec.

2000 <http://web.lexis-nexis.com/ universe>.

Mitchell, Larry. "Candidate's Forum Hears Chico's Hopes and Fears About E-commerce." Enterprise-Record (Chico), 13 Nov. 1999: 2A.

Murray, Ian. "VDU Radiation Making Office Workers Sick." The Times (London), 14 July 1999: Section: Home News. Academic Universe. Lexis-Nexis. Meriam Library, California State University, Chico. 2 Dec. 2000 <http://web.lexis-nexis.com/ universe>.

Scheuermann, Larry, Scheuermann, Sandra B., and Zhu, Zhiwei. "Open Your Eyes to Healthy Computer Use." Business and Management Practices; Safety + Health: 158, 6 (Dec. 1998): 94-96, ISSN: 0891-1797. Academic Universe. Lexis-Nexis. Meriam Library, California State University, Chico. 1 Dec. 2000 <http://web.lexis-nexis.com/ universe>.

State of California. Department of Personnel Administration. Computer User's Handbook. March 1997.

"Stress, the Health Hazard of Modern Life." Medical Industry Today, 25 Oct. 1996: Section: Trends to Watch. Academic

Praizler 15

Universe. Lexis-Nexis. Meriam Library, California State University, Chico. 2 Dec. 2000 <http://web.lexis-nexis.com/universe>.

"The Spectrum, in Brief." Air Force Magazine, Oct. 1999: 58. Academic Universe. Lexis-Nexis. Meriam Library, California State University, Chico. 2 Dec. 2000 <http://web.lexis-nexis.com/universe>.

Warner, Jack. "Tech Tools; Monitor Attachment Sheds Light on Eyestrain." The Atlanta Journal and Constitution, 24 Jan. 1999: Section: Personal Technology, 02G. Academic Universe. Lexis-Nexis. Meriam Library, California State University, Chico. 1 Dec. 2000 <http://web.lexis-nexis.com/universe>.

# Part Six

## A TREASURY OF ESSAYS

Here is a collection of my favorite student essays. They're divided into five groups: personal essays, informative essays, argumentative essays, academic essays, and four essays on dieting. They're for your pleasure and inspiration. Read them to get the hang of essay writing; enjoy them; get turned on to write by them. Imitate them and steal from them. After each essay I'll say a word about why I like it so much.

## Personal Essays

### TOP CHICKEN

KATIE JAQUES

The recess bell shrills and we are outside like so many pistol shots heading for the monkey bars. Out of the shuffling and shouting two distinct lines emerge, one at each end of the metal battleground which looms several feet above our collective heads. I glance cockily at the other team and begin counting. My match is the fourth girl down, Julie Grovner. She is a chubby brunette cry-baby who, for show and tell one Friday, brought in miniature bottles of eau de toilette for each of us girls. A complacent smile spreads across my face. Too easy, I decide.

We have won the first two matches and lost the third, and now it's my turn. I climb up the side ladder and take hold of the overhead bars, slippery as iron snakes, hanging like suspended railroad tracks against the cloudless ten o'clock sky. I methodically swing first to the right, then the left, wiping each opposing hand dry of accumulated sweat as I do so. The yellowed oval calluses gracing each palm attest to my huge success as a chicken fighter, and I note them with a quick sense of pride.

At an observer's terse shriek, *"Go!"*, I lurch forward, anxious for battle. Julie sways toward me more slowly, her stubby legs flailing wildly. I can practically smell her fear and see, from the corner of my eye, her black patent leather shoes as they arc widely in a feeble attempt to encircle my waist. Swinging broadly to the right, I escape her grasp and can hear the shouts from the other kids getting louder, fueling my desire to win even more. To be pulled down to the black playground surface at this point is to lose my reputation. I set my teeth and curl my toes up tightly inside my brown stained oxfords in anticipation.

Julie can feel the pressure too, and releases, for one second, her left hand in order to wipe it dry, grimacing with strain as she does so. Quickly, hand over hand, I close the gap between us and tighten my long legs about her thick waist, squeezing my victim like a merciless boa constrictor.

The shouts are deafening now. Julie's brown eyes widen in surprise as she attempts to return her free hand to the bar. Noting this, I instinctively lock my ankles together behind her arched back and begin to pull her downward, watching her one remaining hand slowly relinquish its grip, knowing all too well the Indian burn sensation the metal generously imparts to the loser's palm.

Emitting a loud squeal, Julie drops to the charcoal turf ashamed and slowly hobbles over to her own side unacknowledged. Amidst the hoopla, I quickly monkey-walk back to my own team, unable to repress a victory grin that stretches from ear to ear. Climbing down and taking my place at the back of the line, I casually pick at an old callus with a shaking hand, barely noticing my aching thighs, counting out my next opponent.

*I love how Katie captures the enormous importance of childhood experience. The battle on the bars takes on the weight of D-Day. Words count here: "Julie drops to the charcoal turf ashamed and slowly hobbles over to her side unacknowledged" is rich with resonant verbs, adjectives, and adverbs, and the last word is worth more than most entire paragraphs. "Too easy, I decide" is a wonderful example of the power of the unexpected staccato sentence.*

## BIGGER IS BETTER

MORGAN F. HEUSCHKEL

Like many people in this country, I drive my own car. Well, perhaps "car" is a misnomer. I actually drive a boat. A land yacht. It's a 1984 Mercury Grand Marquis—four-door, beige, and big enough to require its own zip code. Ten years ago, I would have laughed at the mere thought of driving such an oversized behemoth. But things have changed. I have changed. I'm almost embarrassed to say it, but I actually like my car. I really like my great big American car.

I certainly didn't start out that way. I had spent most of my youth being driven around in small imports, like the Nissan and Mazda owned by my parents. Both were most sensible and economical cars. Then, at age 23, I inherited my grandmother's Grand Marquis (I guess when you're a grandparent you can drive what you want). I balked, even in the face of this unconditional generosity. "Drive this . . . this tank?" thought I, while my friends zipped around town in their Volkswagens and Toyotas. Never! But drive it I did.

It took some getting used to. At first I got agoraphobia sitting in the front seat, and it took half an hour to scrape off the bumper sticker that read "Retired and Loving It!" I had one or two minor "incidents" before I fully learned the Mercury's perimeters. But, please, don't tell my mother—I blamed any and all body damage on irresponsible, anonymous drivers backing into the car in the parking lot at Penney's while I was shopping for blouses. However, I can now parallel park in places like San Francisco with such grace and acumen that bystanders often burst into spontaneous applause. No, really. And soon I found myself warming to the Creature.

For one thing, the Merc had some undeniable practical virtues. It could seat six without even blinking, and was obscenely comfortable. It had a stereo like a concert hall and automatic everything—windows, seats, mirrors, brakes, steering, you name it. The suspension practically levitated over speed bumps and potholes and did ninety miles per hour like a walk in the park, albeit a very fast one. And I'm safe. Thirteen years ago safety features like anti-lock brakes and air bags weren't the relatively standard additions they've become today, so the Mercury went without them, but it more than made up for them by surrounding me with two tons of solid beige steel and at least twelve feet of breathing space between me and either the nose or the tail of the car. Garbage trucks bounce off me.

But the matter went beyond pragmatics. I began to relish the unapologetically un-P.C. nature of the car. In this age, when smoking has the same social cachet as baby seal slaughtering, the Mercury has three (yes, three) sets of lighters and ashtrays. My mother's '92 Mazda didn't even come with a lighter. And mileage? While I never did any formal number crunching on the subject, a rough estimate places the car's mileage at around eleven miles to the gallon, under the most optimal of conditions (say, the hand of God pushing you down the freeway). If you're used to driving and being driven around in smaller cars, it can take a while to get used to being behind the wheel of a car with such . . . presence. There is much to be said for what a big car can do for your self-image. It is not coincidence that many larger American cars are reminiscent of armored personnel carriers. While tooling down the road, imagine that you are A Most Powerful Person. What would you do to solve the budget crisis? How about that nasty little mess in the Middle East? Go on, give those kids at the bus stop a presidential wave and a flash of your famous smile. Chomp on a big see-gar. There, feels good, doesn't it? Try getting that sense of empowerment from a Hyundai.

I began to notice that smaller, more economical cars were no longer attractive to me. While eyeing the ads in magazines and newspapers, I would pass over the colorful spreads on Sentras, Accords, and Tercels, and home in on the layout for the new Oldsmobile Cutlass Sierra. On the street, El Dorados and Impalas would sing to me. And when I got to borrow a friend's 1982 Cadillac Brougham de Ville for a week while he was on vacation, I thought I'd died and gone to heaven. Azure blue, with wondrous lines and a body in pristine condition, this monster and I spent a glorious week touring the countryside. Replete with leather interior, four built-in lighters, and every button, knob, and gadget known to man, the Cadillac showed me that there were even bigger, more luxurious fish to fry than my little Grand Marquis.

Sure, people can call cars like mine "gas guzzlers," "space hogs," and "boats," but are theirs the voices of economic and ecological practicality, or the green-tinged song of jealousy? Tired and grumpy from years of bumping knees, noses, and elbows in the cramped interiors of their "practical" cars, these people turn their ire on us, the drivers of luxury liners, in an attempt to salve their pride. Might I suggest, good people, that you put aside your indignation and mistrust and consider taking a drive on the wide side? Borrow your Aunt Ethel's yellow Cadillac for a week and discover the joys of driving big. Sit behind the wheel of that cavernous expanse of leather and steel and knobs and dials, of foot wells roomy enough to make a basketball player giggle and a trunk so big you need a miner's helmet to see it all. See if your heart doesn't melt just a little.

*This is a masterpiece of the "This is me" essay style. Morgan has no bigger agenda than to share a part of her heart with us. The result is pure joy. Behind the words about cars and grandmothers lie several large messages: Aren't people wonderful? Isn't life grand? Isn't writing fun? Aren't I glad to be me? Now admit it—wouldn't you love to go to lunch with Morgan and chat about just* anything?

## HAMMERHEAD AT THE TRAIL'S END

RAEN WILLIS

Gold can be found in unlikely places. Lovers of live music know this. They prowl the clubs, and even the streets, waiting for lightning to strike. It's blind luck, really. But you have to put yourself out there.

Wednesday night at the Trail's End, a small working-class tavern in a small town, Oregon City, just outside of Portland. There are dozens of such neighborhood taverns in the Portland area, corner pubs, where absolutely nothing has been spent on the ambience and it's all about the music. The place feels convivial even when there are only four or five people in the house and one of them's the bartender and one's the waitress.

Wednesday night is blues jam night—a very mixed bag. Anyone who wants to play gets to, either sitting in with the house band, or with other musicians who drop in, or a combination of both. Like Forrest Gump's chocolate box, you never know what you're going to get. We head over, expecting nothing. It's a cold midweek night in early March and the rain is coming down, so it's no surprise that the crowd is small—there are as many musicians milling around on the stage as there are patrons in the audience, but these working-class jazz buffs are loyal and enthusiastic.

We're surprised to find that the entire second set has been given over to some guy none of us has ever heard of, named, of all things, "Hammerhead." No last name. We joke about the name. It doesn't look promising. We get into the house band, just four guys unknown outside of a twenty-mile radius who light it up nightly at the Trail's End—Ray Davis's smooth, inventive lead guitar, Scott White's hard-kicking bass work, Jeff Alviani's inspired, mobile keyboard, all resting on Tom Drew's solid percussion. You never heard of any of them. Mark Knophler's Sultans of Swing in the flesh.

Hammerhead arrives, his overcoat flapping around his gaunt six-foot-five frame, long grayish-black hair hanging around a sculptured and eloquent face. He strides to a table and folds himself down. His body language speaks of a long and intimate association with alcohol or something worse, and the fight to put it behind him. He orders what looks like a club soda.

He unfolds from the chair and steps up on the stage with his band. He starts with the downbeat, and right away his harmonica playing is molten yet controlled. He has our attention and our respect.

But what gets me is his vocals. When he starts singing, I know immediately it's the real deal. There are plenty of competent blues singers, but this is something else—like Paul Butterfield, with that slurred-to-dead-center in his phrasing, the rich, shadowy voice that honors the sadness and the struggle to endure that is the blues. You can't learn to do what Hammerhead is doing. You can practice and hone it and be mad to have it, but somehow you have to live it or you don't ever get it this deep. It isn't decorative or pretty—it's got more important things to do. On the up-tempo songs it's a dancy slide of pocketed sensuality, and on the slow ones it's a cinder-cone rising from seething hurt.

When the set is over, Hammerhead gives the stage over to the jammers who have been filtering in over the last hour. They start to play—some good vocals, guitar, and alto sax work. The guys are working hard and having fun, but it's just pretty good, and I need the magic right now. I get up to leave and approach Hammerhead on my way out. He's facing the wall next to the stage, attending to his harp. I walk up behind him and touch his elbow to get his attention, tell him how much I loved what I'd heard. His guardedness instantly softens, and he thanks me kindly. Then I walk out into the rainy dark. I've never heard of Hammerhead since.

*This essay reminds me of two important lessons about personal writing. First, even though the essay is about Topic X (in this case, Hammerhead's music), it's really about Me, the writer. We're learning as much about Raen as we are about Hammerhead. Second, the best personal writing is quietly argumentative. There's a case being made here: that musicians work hard and make great art and are largely ignored in American culture, and that it's a tragedy.*

## GRADUATION THEATER

MARIE ROW

I'm forty-one years old. I've had a long time to envision this scene. I've imagined it with several different scripts. The most common image that surfaces, though, is where I give a little rendition of Bette Davis's "I did it myself" speech.

She said that, once, on a talk show. She shared an imaginary Academy Award speech with the audience, one where she stood in front of the podium, held up the award, and said, "I did this myself." Instead of rattling off a long list of thank you's to who was there, who had helped, who had supported et cetera, et cetera, she departed from tradition by simply and clearly claiming the trophy as her own. She was quite brazen and bold about the whole thing, in her Bette Davis daring and defiant way.

That's usually how I imagine myself on my graduation day, following in the footsteps of this actress renowned for her vivid portrayals of diabolical schemers and eccentric heroines. I am reminded that I do not want to meekly walk up shrouded in my black gown, smiling, and shake an administrator's hand, only to grasp my diploma, pose for the camera, and then retreat to my section to search for my folding chair. I want to take that diploma and declare to the world that it is mine because I earned it. I want to use that spotlight to thank the person really responsible for my success. I'm dedicating my diploma to me. I did this myself.

I did it when my grandmother voiced, "I never thought I'd see the day" when I pressed on beyond high school, to my stepmother's secret delight. I did it when my step-cousin stated, mildly surprised, that I didn't seem at all mentally handicapped as I had been described. I did it after it was helpfully suggested by my relatives that trade school was the height of challenge that I could handle. And I did it after Dad declared as fact that no one my age makes it through college.

I did it after my husband announced that it would be best for all concerned if I'd stay home and tend to him and our soon-to-arrive son. I did it after my divorce, when my boyfriend felt it would be good for the relationship if I continued working a slightly lower-paying, lower-status job than his, one that would guarantee that I never threatened the unchanging and comfortable status quo. I did it when I completed my Associate of Arts degree, and my cousin relented and agreed that we had better have a celebration, seeing as how, for me, it was probably the end of the line.

I did it attending three different colleges as my family moved seven times. I did it while mothering three children and holding seven jobs to support them. I did it pregnant. I did it at night after work when the kids were asleep. I did it by attending a new University while one son started high school and another started pre-school. I did it when I was unemployed. I did it the November the refrigerator broke down, and when the car finally gave out along the side of the road during finals. I did it after the Lancaster earthquake left me host to the spore *Coccidiodes immitis*, also known as Valley Fever. I kept doing it after I lost my home. I kept doing it after I had survived the modern cures for breast cancer, and after my daughter died and was placed in a small desert grave.

I did it when I was exhausted, scared, and lonely.

After ten scholarships, transcripts patched together over

twenty-one years, and a 3.85 grade point average, I have finally done it. I am going to receive that elusive Bachelor of Arts diploma. And when it comes to the thank you's, well, Bette, move over. I am prepared to take my place.

*This is an anti-cliché essay (p. 283), and it draws its power from its willingness to defy convention: "I will not say what I am expected to say." Any time you do that you run the risk of being disliked, and Marie risks coming off egotistical or hostile. I think she triumphs over those risks, proving in the meantime that in any situation there's always something new, personal, and powerful to say—even in a valedictory address, the world's most tired set piece.*

## HOW TO TALK TO YOUR KIDS ABOUT DRUGS

ROSA LEVY

If you get to that day when you have kids and they grow up a little and they want to know about drugs, do you tell them? Do you tell them all of the things you did, starting at age sixteen, when you met Suzie and Jenn and started drinking and smoking cigarettes and driving around in your car all night or sitting down by the river talking about boys and sex (which you had never had then, but it wouldn't take long—your friends were always bragging that they had slept with so many and teasing you that you hadn't, and you felt small and silly even when you drank beer and drove your car fast and stopped going to school for a while)? Will you tell them how drinking made you sleep with boys who were mean to you, how you would go to anyone then, how your mother (good, smart, bewildered mother, who always taught you to make your own way, never thought you would be mean and dumb and waste your life and mind and body as if they were a worthless burden to you) waited up for you at night afraid that you had died and then screamed "I don't know what you are turning into" and you screamed back that you hated her because the last thing you would ever be able to do was admit that who you were turning into was somebody you hated too? And maybe if you told your kids this story when they were young enough that they still had that kind of perfect adoring love for their parents then later when they got mad and mean they would remember that story and not want to lose themselves or you, even if it is only for a little while.

There are other stories too, increasing in depravity (or at least intensity)—do you tell those? How at the first college you went to you met Megan and Mark and started to smoke pot and then drop acid and eat those bitter little mushrooms but it was an intellectual, spiritual experience then or so you all liked to say and so you would take acid and look at trees and talk about books and ideas and lie in the park twirling perfect flowers over your head and go to concerts in dark halls with day-glow amoebas crawling the walls and the music exploding through you and it always seemed like everyone should be hallucinating, like you had discovered the true Tao of life, but that there is a lesson here too because it ended with flunking out of college, with a dull head and sad-achy, realizing that another year or so had passed and you still didn't know how to make yourself happy by working and making stuff that lasts and that every time you fail even a little bit you remember it, so that the next time you try to do something your past reminds you how easily you gave up before? So maybe your kids will look at you and see all that wasted time, and how the drugs never did open you up so much as divide you into pieces of people and that sometime you still have to collect the pieces off the floor and stuff them into clothes and try to walk around like you are whole, hoping nobody can see the places where you are coming apart.

Do you tell the last tale, the one that hurts the most, which you probably shouldn't tell them because most days you can barely tell it to yourself, because there are some things that can be forgiven and some that can't, some that hang around and hover at the edges of sleep, smack you awake and gasping knowing that whatever you do, you were once this person capable of these things and that knowledge never goes away? So do you tell them how you were married and somehow you didn't want to be married any more so you started to sleep with Eddie, and Eddie sold but mostly used cocaine, and somehow you started doing it with him in his bedroom in his mother's house while she slept and how for ten minutes at a time you got to be this superstar in your own life, and how the two of you moved on to amphetamines and would get high and walk all over the city, laughing and talking about life as if it were this curious, trifling thing and ordering food in restaurants and walking out without eating it and figuring you must be the smartest people in the world to have discovered something so easy and fun that hurts no one and they say isn't addictive? Or about the inevitable divorce and how you began begging money from all your friends until they ran from you and all you cared about was getting high, until finally you went to Europe to escape everything, especially yourself, who you hated for ever thinking there was a way out of living besides getting up and facing yourself every day unblinking, and drugs, which you hated for taking sweet people and smart people and good people and destroying them by telling them that horrible lie that living a life that is sometimes quiet and disappointing and ordinary isn't good enough, that you need a life where you get to be a superstar? Maybe that is the thing to tell them, the one thing, and maybe you don't even have to sacrifice yourself, maybe you can just tell them that there are ways to escape your life for a minute or two and that these ways can feel incredible for a minute or two but the loss is that you trick yourself into believing that there is a way out of the work and drudgery that sometimes is life, and that if you trick yourself too many times you may not remember how to look at life on a spring day and see the sun shining and feel all the wonder of that growing and not need anything to make you feel how beautiful and perfect that moment is.

*I'm always encouraging you to ask of your work, "Did it take any risks?" If you aren't sure what that means, take this essay as a model. It's constantly breaking rules and defying boundaries. It's a personal essay and an argument at the same time. It seems to be rambling talk, but it's a very hard kind of thing to write. Our reaction to Rosa keeps getting more and more complex, because her view of herself is so multifaceted. She describes her weaknesses with so much skill that we both accept her self-loathing and admire her for her courage. And what courage this essay has! Not only the courage to discuss the author's sins in the raw without sentiment, but also the courage to take the reader on an exhausting roller coaster. And notice that while it's utterly fresh and original, it's a redressing of two of the oldest clichés in essay writing: "Just say no to drugs" and "Don't make the mistakes I made as a youth."*

## SALAD WARS

LEO WHITE

Elizabeth takes a bite of her sandwich and looks at me. I am grimacing. "You should try it," she says.

I look at this sandwich. It has what look like blades of grass sticking out of the side. Some sort of by-product of oats and soy is oozing juices onto the flowered plate.

"No, thanks," I reply.

"You're just afraid of food that's good for you," she says. "This is really tasty, I swear."

Elizabeth is my roommate. We share a refrigerator together. My side is full of butter, eggs, cheeses, an occasional meat patty, whole milk, and sour cream. I notice that most of her food is much more brown than mine. She says that's because it's full of nutrition and protein. I tell her it's because she doesn't cover anything up. She just smiles and eats a spoonful of tofutti.

Before we were roommates we used to go out and really dine: rich Alfredo sauces, fruity cabernets, tiramisu and ice cream, cappuccino. Now she says she needs to cleanse her temple.

Cleansing her temple means hummus. It means millet and barley and rice milk. Elizabeth eats like Gandhi now, and, though I love her, joining her is a sacrifice I can't force on myself.

Elizabeth has now made Udon noodles with tofu pesto sauce. She has sprinkled wheat germ on her spinach salad and is sipping ginseng tea by candlelight. "Come on, Leo, try some," she urges me, smiling and looking at me over a fork full of . . . something. I am grimacing again. "No, thanks," I say again.

The next morning she is up early. From my bed I can hear her humming something. The juicer squeaks, the blender whirs, the oats roll. I turn toward the wall and go back to sleep.

When I finally wake up, there's a note for me: "Meet me at the cafe for lunch, love, Elizabeth." I grind the French roast into a gritty pulp and strain myself a thick mug of coffee. Then I pour a bowl of Cocoa Puffs into a mixing bowl and reach for the milk. It's sour and lumpy, so I mix a little half and half with water and eat my breakfast.

In my first class, I am a jittery wreck, at the same time exhausted and wired. My hands sweat and my eyes are heavy. In my next class I fall asleep.

When I see Elizabeth at the cafe she is smiling again. Her eyes are bright and she is sipping coffee. "Decaf," she explains to me before I can ask.

"So what's up?" I ask through a yawn.

"Well, this morning I finished that art project I've been working on, and then I did some research for a paper that's due next week, and after lunch I'm off to work."

"Sheesh," I mumble.

"How about you?" she asks.

"Oh, uh, I just woke up."

"Didn't you go to class?"

"I *was* in class."

She grins at me again. The waiter comes for our order. I've been eyeing that flap-jack special, or maybe the four-cheese omelette. "I'll have the spirulina whip with a side of echinacea and a mung bean salad, please," Elizabeth says to the waiter.

I grimace, fold the menu, lean back in my chair, look around, tap my finger on the table, and smile back at her. "Me, too," I tell the waiter.

I feel better already.

*I like a lot of things about this essay. Leo has a sweet light sense of humor about himself. The essay goes beyond the obvious "my roommate is a health nut" thesis—it has more to do—and it resists "telling" at every turn. The language is rich without flourishes: "Cleansing the temple means hummus" is a sentence I wish I had written, and the phrase "the oats roll" is worth savoring.*

## Informative Essays

### AVOIDING THERAPY

BARBARA OTT

When my daughter tried to get married two years ago, I ended up in therapy twice a week. I failed miserably as mother of the bride. I was hell on wheels.

Luckily the wedding fell through, and I'm getting a second chance. Once again I am mother of the bride, but this time I'm weathering it well and there is no therapist in sight (I do have his business card nearby, however). I have discovered the three rules that will help any distraught mother survive her daughter's wedding preparations. Not only will the three make the wedding go smoothly; they will actually strengthen the bond between you and your daughter and lay the groundwork for your future career as a mother-in-law. In fact, you will find them useful in all your interactions with your adult children.

Rule #1: Settle on a fixed sum of money for the wedding—no more, no less—and give it to your daughter up front with no strings attached. This is not easy. It's your money, you want the control, you know what's best, etc., etc. Visions of large sums of money squandered on live doves and ice sculptures dance in your head. But if you don't do this, the alternative is worse. My daughter and I argued about the cost of every single decision: How much should the reception room cost, was this band worth the money, how many people simply had to be invited, how cheap could the buffet be without humiliation? There were no answers, so each decision was arrived at by war. I had the A-bomb: the checkbook. She had the weapons of screaming, tantrums, and hatred. We glared at each other across the DMZ, both miserable. We both ended up in therapy to save the relationship.

In therapy I learned two things. One, it's okay to trust your daughter. Two, what she decides is not a judgment on you—she is responsible for her choices. The second time around, armed with these lessons, I handed her the check and said, "It's yours, have at it!" Now we talk, we laugh, we're still friends.

Rule #2: Let go of every fantasy you have about your daughter's wedding—let her decide everything. You might think that once you've given up control of the money this would follow naturally, but silly you! All your unfulfilled dreams will emerge from the place where you stuck them out of sight long ago and told yourself you were done with them; suddenly you will have hundreds of "good ideas" about how this affair should be conducted. Be vigilant; watch out for any idea that begins, "But I always thought . . ." "I always thought you'd wear my wedding dress." BEWARE! "I just assumed that you'd be inviting all the cousins." DANGER! "Certainly the bride and groom will wear clothing." QUICKSAND! In my first wedding, I became dehydrated from crying over the loss of all those little dreams I had been nursing about how my daughter's nuptials would go, dreams my daughter didn't share. This time around, letting them go and letting her make all the decisions has been blissful. So what if she doesn't use Grandma's hanky for something old? So what if all the groomsmen have Mohawks? It's your daughter's show—enjoy it from the sidelines, as a member of the audience.

Rule #3 follows naturally: Accept your role as "gofer." A gofer offers no advice—a gofer does what she's asked to do, as efficiently as possible, without adding extras, however swell those little touches may seem to you. When your daughter needs someone to call the dressmaker for an alteration appointment, you do NOT suggest that maybe the hem should be whip-stitched—no, no! You simply call, make the appointment, and tell your daughter the information—that is all. You fetch netting for favors, you pick up thank-you notes, you cheerfully stand in line at the post office to get two hundred stamps. And then you say sweetly, "What else can I do?"

You may feel like this isn't doing your job as a mother; you're avoiding your adult responsibilities: You're depriving your daughter of your valuable wisdom. Nonsense—all you're doing is giving up power over another adult. And that's good for her, because it will ensure that your daughter assumes the responsibilities you lay down. And it's good for you, because being responsible for others isn't fun, however much you are used to it. Best of all, it will mean that, on the day of the wedding, you and your daughter can look at each other with love and pride instead of resentment and frustration. And, last but not least, you can put some of the money you've saved on therapy sessions toward the wedding present.

*What a classic model for how to start an informative essay this is! Barbara lays down three important principles: 1) you'll suffer big-time if you don't know this stuff; 2) I did it all wrong my first try, so I know whereof I speak (and I deserve your empathy); and 3) our self-important follies are really pretty funny (so it's okay to relax a little). It gets everything off on just the right foot.*

## SCRATCH THAT ITCH

BENNETT LINDSEY

You feel that burning, untamable desire again. You know you shouldn't do it. It will only make it worse. You try to think about something else. You rock back and forth in your chair. Finally you give in and scratch that mosquito bite. For a brief moment, you experience pleasure akin to orgasm—then you realize you've only made the problem worse. Now the bite hurts twice as much and in a few minutes it will be swollen and infected. Luckily, there is no need to ever go through this misery again. There are several simple preventatives that will encourage those vile bloodsuckers to keep their distance or minimize the damage if the preventatives fail.

Everyone's favorite bug repellent is a spray can of chemicals, like Off! Unfortunately, these products are sticky and gooey and stink and are generally carcinogenic. The better they work, the worse they are for you. The most effective, and therefore the most lethal, is DEET (diethyl toluamide). You can buy bug repellent that is 100% DEET, or any smaller percentage—just read the ingredients label. It's wise to carry DEET on trips into serious mosquito country, just for those emergencies when nothing else works and your back is to the wall.

But there are less toxic, less repulsive products. Any bug spray that is citronella-based is safe to use, feels OK on the skin, and is effective enough to keep off all but the most voracious bugs. There are two schools of thought on the smell. Some consider it aromatic; others hate it. Wear it to an outdoor concert and you'll find out which group your neighbors are in. Citronella in any form works, so you can use citronella candles on your picnic table. Other plant products that produce smells that mosquitoes don't like are tea tree oil, eucalyptus oil, and any citrus juice.

You can protect yourself over the long term by altering your diet. Mosquitoes bite you because they like the way your sweat smells, and that is largely a product of what you eat. To take yourself off the mosquito menu, avoid refined sugar and alcohol and consume foods rich in thiamin (vitamin B1): brewer's yeast, molasses, and wheat germ, all of which are good for you in other ways. Or simply take a vitamin B pill. The old wives' tale that garlic keeps vampires away turns out to have a grain of truth in it—ingesting garlic or rubbing it on your skin turns mosquitoes off. You can add it to almost anything you eat, and it will only cost you your social life. Mexicans, who have learned to cope with mosquito swarms of Biblical proportions, swear by the tequila diet—after a couple of Tequila Sunrises your problems will be gone, or at least you won't be conscious of them anymore. Anything that smells good—perfume, hair spray—is to be avoided.

You can bathe in chlorine—mosquitoes don't like the smell any more than people do. A dip in a heavily chlorinated pool should do the trick. Or you can smoke. It's horrible for you, so if you don't want the cancer you might consider hiking with a friend who has the habit and just standing downwind. A campfire will have the same effect at night without the health hazards.

If none of this seems appetizing, wear clothing. Modern outdoor clothing is so light and breathable that you can wear it on even hot summer days. You can even buy mosquito-net hats from outdoor catalog companies, if you don't mind the fashion statement. But determined mosquitoes will bite right through thin cloth, so you may end up bug-spraying your shirts and pants. Or you can hang your clothes in that evening campfire. And choose dull-colored clothing—mosquitoes like bright colors.

If the barricades fall and you do get bitten, there are several things you can do to minimize the damage. As with all bites, begin by washing the area. Then apply one or more of the following lotions or poultices: baking soda, goldenseal, tea tree oil, walnut oil, Vitamin E oil, charcoal, a slice of onion, or good old calamine lotion. Take lots of Vitamin C. And don't scratch! Your mother told you the truth: if you pick at it, it will never get well.

*This is a straightforward informative piece of writing. Its usefulness is obvious and low-key. Bennett wisely doesn't try to make more of it than it is; he just organizes the information well and adds a lightly amusing, pleasant tone. And he's framed the essay core with a funny opener and a good punch line.*

## THE SPROUT ROUTE

WINSTON BELL

You take nutritional supplements. You exercise and eat well-balanced meals. You've even started doing more of your grocery shopping at the health food store. What's missing from your program? Home-grown sprouts. Sprouts are the richest source of whole-food nutrition on the planet, and by far the easiest to grow on your own.

Sprouts are nutritious because they're alive when you eat them. Living foods supply something you can't get anywhere else: enzymes, living organisms that break down food so the nutrients can be absorbed. When you eat living foods, the enzymes needed for digestion are included in the food, but with cooked, aged, or processed foods, your body has to add enzymes from its own limited supply. As enzymes are depleted, your body loses vitality and numerous health problems arise. Living foods are also a rich source of essential nutrients—proteins, vitamins, minerals, sugars, and oils.

The easiest and most practical way to get living foods onto your plate is by growing your own sprouts. You don't need to be a scientist or even a gardener. Sprouts demand very little care, so they're perfect for the person with limited time or space—in other words, all of us. It's simple: soak the seeds, rinse them, and watch them sprout. It takes a few minutes a day, and you don't have to wait long to enjoy the fruits of your labor—a seed will germinate into a mature sprout in one to seven days. And sprouts reduce your time in the kitchen, because you don't cook them.

Sprouts are cheap. You can buy seeds for a couple of dollars per pound. That pound will grow into many, many pounds of wonderfully healthy food. And the materials for your sprout farm are cheap and never have to be replaced.

Cooking with sprouts is easy. Just throw them into almost anything you're making, as little or as much as you like. You can start in the traditional way, by adding them to sandwiches and salads, but soon you'll want to think outside the box. Sprouts can be used in juices, yogurts, cheeses, dressings, breads, and desserts. Eventually you can base your entire diet on sprouts, since living foods can provide your body with everything it needs.

Sprouts have many advantages over those other healthy staples, raw fruits and vegetables. If you buy your fruits and veggies at the store, they are already days old and most of their enzymes and nutrients are gone, since foods retain their life force for only three days after harvest. And if you try to grow them yourself, the commitment of time, money, energy, and space is enormous—vegetable gardening isn't a sidelight, it's a career.

Sprouting takes almost no space, and since it takes place indoors, you have no problems with weather, irrigation, pest management, soil conditioning, or disease control.

You can buy sprouts in the store, but you want to grow your own, for lots of reasons. First, the sprouts you buy in the grocery store are old, so a lot of their enzymes and nutrients are history. Second, growing your own means you can experiment with different varieties and combinations, which will give your body a wider range of nutrients—your local store probably only stocks one or two kinds of sprouts. Third, seeds are much cheaper than sprouts. And fourth, sprouting is fun.

So what do you need? First, seeds. Buy organic seeds in bulk at the health food store. For a well-balanced diet, grow more than one kind of sprout. You can sprout almost any kind of seed, but start with the seven traditionals: almond, mung bean, sesame, sunflower, alfalfa, and wheat. Next, buy some wide-mouth canning jars and non-toxic screening material at the homeware store. Cut the material into circles, put water and seeds into the jars, put the rings from the lids over the jar mouths (throw away the flat part), and screw the rings down tight over the mesh. Now all you need to do is rinse the seeds two to four times a day and harvest your sprouts when they are a few inches long. You'll probably want to buy Ann Wigmore's *The Sprouting Book*, which will give you more detailed instructions, lots of nutritional information, and delicious recipes.

*This essay is half argument, half informative. Winston has found a great voice—he's passionate about his subject, he's aware of us readers and our wants, and he wants to make things perfectly clear. He's thoroughly likable, so he's easy to agree with. He also has the courage to have no conclusion. I told you it works (p. 128). By the way, you have to pronounce "route" as "rowt" to make the title work.*

## EUROPE AND THE STARVING STUDENT

ANDREW ROE

If you think the prospect of traveling to Europe is out of the question because you're only a "starving student," then you've never been more wrong in your life. I went for five months and took only $2050.00, but still managed to see and experience the many wonders it has to offer. There was a lot of Europe that I didn't get to see, but still I can say, "I've been there!" Follow me closely, and I will show you just how easy it is.

The first thing you need is motivation. If you lack the desire, you'll never get there. If you really believe that on such and such a date, you'll be flying at thirty-five thousand feet above the Atlantic Ocean, destination London, you're halfway there.

Next, it's important to start saving money early. Don't keep going out every weekend; consider every single dime you spend here will be one less that you can spend there. Friends may try to persuade you to go out with them: "Hey, don't grow roots on that couch, Man, let's drink some brewskis!" Let your "cultural alarm" take over and think about being in Europe. Tell yourself and tell your friends that you have other goals than just living for the moment. Smile, relax, and pop in a video. May I suggest "American Werewolf In London"?

There's a basic formula to figure out how much money you should take with you. If you plan on staying for six months, then save every penny you make for six months. This money is your "spending money." This will pay for your food (which you can purchase and cook in the youth hostel kitchens, as I'll explain), local transportation (which could be free if you use your thumb), and entertainment.

Now that you mentally know you're going, it's time to set up a plan for getting there. Airlines are obviously the most efficient in terms of time and money, but you must be careful to not get duped by purchasing the first ticket a travel agent offers you. Newspaper advertisements will quote airline fares running from $699.00 and up. Travel agents will sometimes quote fares as high as $2000.00! The key to finding a ticket for the starving student is to be persistent. You need to search in the classified ad sections of major newspapers in the large international American cities like Los Angeles, New York, or Chicago. Under the "for sale" column there is a section specializing on air tickets. Don't be surprised if you see sporting events and concerts for sale in this section too. People sell either actual discounted airline tickets or travel discount coupons for up to 70% off. This is how I purchased a ticket on Pan Am and ended up paying only $400 round trip. You can also save money by traveling in the off-season—usually winter—when demand is low and the ticket prices drop. The places you want to visit will be less crowded then too. Remember, always buy a round trip ticket—it's cheaper, and some countries may not let you in if they think you're not planning on leaving.

Now your tickets are taken care of; where are you going to stay? This is the easy part. Pick up your telephone and ask directory assistance for the local branch of the International Youth

Hostel Foundation. Call them! The IYHF was created in the early part of the century for people just like you, young people who want to travel but can't afford the ritzy hotels such as the Grosvenor in London. The cost for a night in a hostel ranges from about $5–$11. You sleep in dorms with anywhere from four to twenty people. Most dorms aren't co-ed, but some have "couple quarters"—if you're traveling with your significant other you'll have to reserve them far in advance. Hostels have lockers for stowing your gear, rentable for mere pocket change. Bring your own padlock—they don't provide them.

Hostels are an experience. You may not be like all of the people you're sleeping with, but you all have a few things in common: You're young and you're a traveler in a foreign land. Trust me, this will create some of the best and most interesting friendships you could ever hope for. IYHF requires a membership fee—somewhere between $20 to $30 for a one-year membership. Buy the membership, or you may find yourself arriving at a hostel and hearing what Jesus heard: "Sorry, there's no room at the inn."

Where do you want to go? If you want to specialize in just one country you should get a train pass for that country only. For example, I purchased a Britrail Pass good for thirty days' travel throughout England, Scotland, and Wales. For only $200, this gave me unlimited train travel, anywhere, any time in Britain. If you want to travel all over Europe, the Eurail Pass is the one for you. Usually, the cost for Eurail is based on how long a term you want. Passes come in either fourteen-day, twenty-one-day, one-month, two-month, or three-month terms. A sixteen-day pass will cost you about $280, a three-month pass about $700. I know it sounds expensive, considering you can probably get your airline ticket cheaper, but remember: you want to "see" Europe. Trains offer you a relaxing windowseat on the countryside, where you can sit back and soak it in.

From my own experience, I think it's best to decide exactly where you want to go. Instead of buying a Eurail Pass, if there is one particular country you'd like to emphasize, get a pass only for that country and allocate some extra funds for buying train tickets to the other major European cities you wish to visit. The advantage of not buying a Eurail pass is that you don't have to be on any "schedule" when traveling. I bought my Britrail Pass for $200 and then spent only $300 on regular train tickets. After going through eighteen different cities and towns in Britain, I traveled direct to France (stopping in Paris and Reims), Germany (stopping in Cologne, Essen, and Berlin), Holland (stopping in Arnem and Amsterdam), and Belgium (stopping in Brussels and Ostend), and finally returned to England. This took five months. I was on my own schedule and didn't need to purchase the Eurail for $700. If you want to make a "whistle-stop tour," get the Eurail Pass, but remember: If you fall in love with the place you're in and decide to stay, your pass will expire and you will have wasted a lot of money. Don't forget to purchase the Eurail Pass here in the U.S.—you can't buy one in Europe.

Eurail is a standard price, so it's OK to go to a travel agent for this. For a national pass such as Britrail, contact the Embassy for the country of your choice. They will provide you with the information you need. Once again, you must purchase the pass in advance.

Let's review: motivation, travel fund, airline tickets, youth hostel membership, and train passes. You, the starving student, are almost in Europe. It wasn't that difficult, was it? When you're about to leave, make sure to get your money in the form of traveler's checks so if your money is lost or stolen, you can get it back. Another helpful hint is to change your currency here before you leave. Get some traveler's checks in British pounds, German deutschmarks, French francs, etc. You'll get a better foreign exchange rate.

I have left one item to the end so you won't forget: Get your passport! Without it you don't go anywhere. You can apply for one at your local post office, or passport office if you live in a big city—call U.S. Customs if you're not sure where to go. It can take up to three months to process the papers, so start early.

These tips are for the starving student, the young traveler who wants to see the world as it really is. If you want to see Europe from the window of the London Marriott, then disregard this traveler's advice. If you are that open-eyed young one, then I say, "Happy traveling and bon voyage!" When you get back you too can say, "I've been there!"

*Andrew demonstrates the power of the narrowly defined audience and purpose. European vacation travel is a gigantic topic, so Andrew chops it down to easy-to-handle size by writing only about travel preparations, and only for the young traveler going to Europe for the first time on a shoestring.*

## THE LAST STOP FOR AMERICA'S BUSSES

JOHN MERCER

After waving off my friends, I just stood there, dwarfed by the enormous message towering over me: "International Border, Welcome to Mexico." Taking a deep breath, I tossed my duffel bag over my shoulder and headed for the bus station. It was here that I was forced to make my first decision. A large blackboard displayed the names of various cities in alphabetical order. To the right of each name were times and prices. "Primero and Segundo," I read, thinking to myself, "First and second class . . . I wonder what's the difference?"

Mexico, like all countries, has its own system of bus transportation. To help you get started, I've summarized the functions of the four bus classes below. With a little time and a lot of patience, you'll soon be bussing your way across Mexico like a local.

The woman at the counter was helpful and fortunately spoke a little English. First-class busses have toilets, air conditioning, and fewer stops; second-class busses don't. Naturally, considering a thirty-six-hour bus ride, these items are no longer luxuries; they're necessities. Within fifteen minutes I had bought my ticket and boarded the bus for Guadalajara, first class . . . or so I thought. An hour later, I was fidgeting in my seat after four unsuccessful attempts at the restroom door. I remember thinking, "The poor bastard must really be constipated"; then I remembered I was in Mexico and knew that wasn't possible. Someone finally stopped me and explained the facts: the restrooms don't work; they never have worked; they never will work.

The same can be said for the air conditioning. In all fairness, the first-class bus does have fewer scheduled stops; however, due to the lack of facilities, it's always making those necessary unscheduled stops. Realistically, there's only one reason to travel first class: You won't normally find the crowds that plague the cheaper second class.

I probably wouldn't have ever tried a second-class bus if it hadn't been for the first-class bus strike which left me stranded in Puerto Escondido. Preparing myself for the worst, I was pleasantly surprised. Although the busses are uglier and lack the maintenance of the first, passengers have the comfort of knowing the drivers are first-rate mechanics. Second class has more scheduled stops, but they have little effect on arrival times. Like the tortoise racing the hare, the bus sputters along at a consistent pace, seldom far behind in the end. The atmosphere is pleasant, probably due to the open windows and fresh air.

It was this favorable impression of second class that led me to try third class, and for this I'll always be grateful. The third-class bus stations are separate from the previous two, and are normally found in the sections of towns best avoided by people with white faces. However, for those of you who have the time and aren't easily discouraged, you may find the heart of Mexico lies along the paths they forge. They're almost free, because they're government-subsidized. If you're in a hurry or trying to get someplace, forget it. But if you like the thought of listening to Bob Marley tapes through distorted speakers while traveling in a modified school bus so old it may have taken your grandparents to school, stay seated—you're in for a ride. The routes are treacherous, sending the bus bouncing and rattling up and down roads without signs to places without names. Along these roads, most of which are dirt, you will come face to face with people who have spent their entire lives camping out. I remember their stares, looking at me like someone might look at moldy food discovered in the back of the refrigerator. I suppose the story of the man with the white face who was seen on the bus that day may still be told at night by the fire or among the women doing wash at the banks of the river. I will always remember the people and places I found while riding the third-class bus.

The fourth and last class of busses are the city busses. They're the cheapest way to tour a city without getting lost. Like all city busses, they spend the day doing laps. So don't hesitate; jump on, toss the driver a C-Note (about five cents U.S.), and relax.

> *Here's a nice example of basic information enriched by a lively and complex personality. To John's simple informative message he adds the dramatic* in medias res *introduction, the narrative structure, and rich physical details ("listening to Bob Marley tapes through distorted speakers"; "I suppose the story of the man with the white face may still be told at night by the fire . . ."). He portrays himself as a slightly inept gringo falling into this wisdom against his will. That helps with a problem all informative writers face: the reader's fear of the unknown. John is saying, "I blundered my way through, so you can do it."*

## WHY FALLING IN LOVE FEELS SO GOOD

JUDY KRAUSE

After a few years of marriage, I realized I had married the wrong person. We had nothing in common. All the magic was gone. So I got divorced, and have deeply regretted the time I wasted in the marriage and the pain the divorce caused my kids and family.

Why did I make the mistake in the first place? How could I have been so blind? I was a typical young American adult when I married. My parents had been married thirty years to each other. I wanted to be married. And I was in love. Surely that was the sign. If I was in love, that must mean he was the man for me.

I was making the same mistake that thousands of Americans

make every year. Perhaps if I'd known just a little more about the physiology of love, I'd have done a better job picking a partner, and my children wouldn't have had to live in two homes. If we teach our children more about love, perhaps the astronomical divorce rate in this country will come down a little.

The simple truth is, Nature programs us chemically to select the wrong partner, or at least the first partner. I discovered this while reading a wonderful book about women's physiology and psychology, *A Woman's Book of Life*, by Joan Borysenko, Ph.D., where I learned about the relationship between the infatuation stage and one's ability to pick a mate. Here's what happens. When a human meets a member of the opposite sex, her old reptilian brain makes a few quick checks to see if he would be a suitable mate: Is he strong, is he healthy, does he smell right? If the old brain is satisfied, it orders her limbic system to kick in, where a neurotransmitter called phenylethylamine, or PEA, is released. She doesn't realize what is going on, but she's in mating mode, and with one look of interest from the lucky guy, her infatuation mechanism takes over.

PEA gives you those wonderful "in love" feelings—the wild euphoria, the skyrocketing libido, and the self-esteem you've always craved. Suddenly the world is wonderful, you're wonderful, the other person is wonderful. Suddenly you can stay up making love until the wee hours with your boyfriend and go to work the next day looking fresh. Suddenly you are understanding, generous, tolerant, and loving toward everyone. PEA makes you unable to reason, you know it, and you like it—what did reason ever do for you? And then PEA gives you the big lie: It says to you, All these wonderful feelings are proof that your new partner is the one. You feel this good because he is so right for you. And you'll always feel this way.

It's all a lie, because PEA remains in your system for about six months after meeting Mr. or Ms. Momentarily Right—then it leaves, and you return to earth, and you see your partner for the first time without the benefit of chemicals. Who is that person? And did you really promise to spend the only lifetime you have with . . . that?

This system worked well when we lived in caves, people needed to mate constantly to provide fresh population reserves, humans lived until they were thirty, couples stayed together long enough to raise the children, and smell was a fairly good indicator of partner potential. But times have changed, and Mother Nature hasn't caught on. With divorce rates at about 50% in this country, wouldn't it be great if we told each other, and especially our kids, what's really going on? If we published the knowledge that it's a chemical we're in love with, not a person, that the chemical's sole purpose is to mislead us into a committed relationship we'll regret, and that it doesn't last, we could be on our guard.

How do we spread this information? The perfect vehicle already exists—sex education classes in high school. Let teens know about the infatuation stage and PEA. Tell them their feelings are marvelous and to be celebrated and enjoyed, but they are unique to a 3–6 month period and are in no way something to base life-long decisions on. They will learn that choosing a life partner should be done after the infatuation stage has passed, or at least calmed down. If young people hear this, maybe the next generation of children won't consider living between two homes a normal lifestyle.

*This essay has a great sense of what Chapter 15 calls the "argumentative edge"—it's saying loudly, "I think you need this information—it will save your life." It reminds us that informing is not a boring recitation of facts; it's tossing the reader a life preserver. Its sense of "should" is so strong that a case could be made for putting it in the argumentative essay group.*

## Argumentative Essays

### WHY I NEVER CARED FOR THE CIVIL WAR

SHAWNI ALLRED

I got mostly A's and a few B's all through high school and have managed, for the most part, to do the same in college. I'm sure that most people, when they hear that, are thinking, "That means she's really smart." Well, I'm not stupid, but I don't know near as much as people think I know. I just learned how to pass tests. I got an A in history, but I couldn't tell you where the first battle of the Civil War was fought. I got an A in geometry, but I couldn't in a million years tell you the area of a circle. There are many things I "learned" that have vanished from my memory, thanks to some flaws in the teaching system.

The set-up is always the same. The teacher lectures, and the students take notes. I'm thinking of one class in particular, a history class. We went from the Pilgrims to Harry S. Truman in twelve weeks. I was bored out of my mind. I tried so hard to care about the soldiers in the Civil War, but with the teacher outlining the lecture on the board and citing facts as though he were reading from a cookbook, my passion for them was lost. As a result, I remembered what I needed to remember to pass the test, but then it was gone.

The tests reinforce the problem. Comprehensive, timed tests encourage short-term memory. The students, knowing all along their grades will rest heavily on tests, study for the sake of passing the test, not for the sake of learning. They stay up late the night before, cramming as much information into their minds as they can. And it works. They pass the exams and get rewarded. Unfortunately, that A or B is often only a measure of the student's ability to cram.

Is this what we want education to accomplish? To teach students how to cram? Or to teach them to remember the Civil War like it was a recipe? I hope not. I hope the aim is to teach students information they will remember, that means something to them, information they can teach others and use themselves for the rest of their lives. The first step to improving the quality of education is for educators to agree that these are their primary objectives. From there, the solutions to achieving these goals are exciting and endless.

Controlled discussions could be used in place of lectures. For example, if my history class could have had us sit around in a circle and bounce ideas off one another, I might have gotten to the heart of what the Civil War was all about. We could have asked each other questions like, Why did we allow slavery? How do you think the slaves felt? What would you have done if you were one of them?

Even more creative is the idea of using experience as the basis for learning. A friend once had a class where the students acted out the Salem witch trials. Some were judges, some townspeople, some witches. He says he'll never forget that part of history. Another friend had a philosophy class where students walked into strange classrooms and stood inside the doorway until they felt the stares of the other students, in order to understand what Sartre meant by "the Look."

Finally, we could grade, not on timed tests, but on class involvement, homework, and maybe take-home exams. Students would feel they were being rewarded for getting involved in their education, not for becoming experts in test taking.

The question remains whether teachers are willing to step out of old ways of teaching. Some already have. It's because of one teacher I had in the fifth grade that I remember the names of the micro-organisms that live in a drop of pond water. We went to the far end of the playground and scooped up the muddy green water all by ourselves and took it back to the classroom to look at it under a microscope. There were paramecia, volvoxes, and amoebas. I remember.

*I love the way Shawni respects her personal experience. She says to herself, "I know that much of my schooling was a waste of time, because I was there." She trusts her ability to tell which teaching approaches work for her and which don't. And the conclusion is a work of art. "I remember." It gives me a little chill every time I read it.*

## A MORAL VICTORY?

ANGELA COOP

In 1984, a group of white male police officers brought suit against the city of San Francisco, alleging that they were the victims of reverse discrimination. They maintained that they had been passed over for promotion in favor of less qualified women and minority officers because of the city's affirmative action policy. The U.S. Supreme Court has recently refused to hear their case.

This action is seen by some as a victory for women and minorities, but, if the allegations are true, isn't it really a loss for us all? The law prohibiting discrimination is intended to ensure equal opportunity for everybody. No group is exempted. It doesn't mean equal opportunity for everybody except white males.

I'm not a white male, but I've been married to one for fifteen years, and I've seen a lot through his eyes. My husband is a mechanical engineer. He's a professor now, but he worked in industry for seven years, and he had a consulting business for six years while he taught, so he has a good understanding of his place in the professional world. Unfortunately, reverse discrimination is nothing new to him. It's a fact of life. Employers are forced by federal equal-opportunity quotas to give preference to Hispanics, blacks, and women.

My sister is also an engineering professor. Although she teaches in the same system with my husband, her experience has been vastly different. Basically, what she wants she gets. It's that simple. It has to be that way, because the quota system makes her a sought-after commodity, and her employer can't afford to lose her.

It took my sister a long time to appreciate the injustice of this. For years, she felt like she deserved everything she got, even though other professors actually quit working in her department because she was treated so favorably. Somehow she felt like she was rectifying the problem of sexism in the workplace, a goal so virtuous as to be worth any cost.

When I talked to my sister last week, she was excited because her department was interviewing the wife of one of my husband's friends. The department doesn't actually have an open position, but the University has funding for a certain number of faculty who meet "specific criteria." As luck would have it, this woman, who normally wouldn't be considered because of her lack of experience, is black. She's irresistible!

We feel an awful sense of collective guilt in this country for what we've done to women and minorities, and we should. We've behaved inexcusably. Affirmative Action policies were developed in an attempt to make up for those past injustices. But do we really think we can right past wrongs by creating new ones? It's said that those who forget history are condemned to repeat it. I would never propose that we do that. But I think it's time to forgive ourselves and move on.

*I love the way this essay moves through its material with complete sureness but no sense of thesis plop or wooden outline. It's an anti-cliché essay (p. 283), or was when it was written, and it sets the reader up for the surprise thesis nicely in paragraph one by inviting the clichéd response. The conclusion is a lovely lesson in how to end without summary restatement.*

## THE GOOD MOTHER

KAREN ARRINGTON

If you're raising a child and it's going beautifully, you can pat yourself on the back for doing a great job. But it's possible there's another explanation. And if you find yourself sitting in judgment of mothers who appear to be doing the less-than-perfect job, don't convict too quickly. You may find in a few years that you've been condemning yourself. It happened to me.

I had my first child when I was twenty-three. I sailed through my first initiation into motherhood with flying colors, approving nods from elders in grocery stores, and rave reviews at family reunions. My son was bright, sweet, mature, and well-behaved. He was creative, clean, not spoiled, and nicely dressed. He was a testament to my superior mothering skills—what else could it be?—and I was quite proud of a job well done. I was set apart from those stressed mothers in supermarkets barking short-tempered commands at their out-of-control offspring and receiving cool glances from the other moms.

I couldn't understand how mothers could be reduced to tears by small children, or how they could have trouble asserting their parental authority. Spanking, of course, was out of the question, and any civilized and competent parent would refrain from this medieval atrocity. It was obvious to any onlooker that my majoring in Child Development and working in the mental health field had paid off. I was the one other mothers asked for advice. And after twelve years of motherhood, I could walk the talk. Or so I thought.

I had my second child when I was thirty-six. The tempo of my life was very different. The nightly feedings weren't as easy to accommodate to, and I had to return to work after only six weeks. Determined to offer this child the same amenities as I had my first, I dutifully split my lunch break in half so I could tear home to nurse him. My sitter shook her head in amusement, or amazement, and said that I had brought new meaning to the term fast food.

Ryan was born May 5, and he grew curls that flipped up over his ears resembling horns. I had joked that he was my little Taurus, my bull, and indeed when pressed or angry he would drop his head and lower his eyebrows, stopping just short of pawing the ground. But he was a beautiful, happy, and very sociable baby, and I was still giving my arm a work-out patting myself on the back.

Then he turned two. At this point, his crying took on a new velocity and pitch that would after a time leave his brother and me grimacing with our hands to our heads. However cute at first, his stubbornness was relentless and began to pose major problems. When opposed, he would become inconsolable, his crying escalating.

I was, however, resolved to be the capable, intelligent mother equipped to shape this young one's psyche. When the going gets tough, the tough moms get going. I consulted psychologists and counselors. I read more books on parenting the strong-willed child. And I attended parent meetings where parents and authorities shared experience and advice.

While I was seeking out better methods to form Ryan's personality, I didn't realize how much he was reshaping mine. I found myself resorting to yelling, snapping, and even—unbelievable—spanking. I had become the recipient of the chilly and disapproving glances in the grocery store aisles.

Ryan changed every concept that I held about myself as a mother and a person. He changed my views about parenthood, children, and personality. He showed me that children are not simply empty slates awaiting impression; they are active participants in their environment, making their own imprints on the world, evoking response from their caregivers. I have had to redefine my goals as a parent, and recognize that infants are born with distinct personalities intact. My job is to guide what is there by nature, not create the perfect person with my superior nurturing skills. I have less power than I thought. And all those simple absolutes about who I am—I'm not a spanker, for instance—now seem open to debate and dependent on context.

Now that I am pursuing a teaching career, these discoveries have gained a new relevance. As a teacher, I expect to put my best foot forward and bring students along in their learning in every way available to me. But, as with Ryan, I can't determine what my students will walk away with, what mark they will leave, or who they will be. Their own personalities will make those choices. I can do a good job and the results might not show it. That is important to know, because to bank on your own image as Super Mom or Super Teacher is to set yourself up for a devastating reality check.

My enlightenment has also changed my relationship to my peers. I listen to students in my University classes loudly voicing their oh-so-sure opinions on all subjects and passing judgment on others, including parents, from their unassailable position of ignorance. At family gatherings, my outspoken in-laws and cousins do the same. I once might have joined them, but now I look and listen longer before I speak. I sit back more quietly, and, if not more wisely, then surely more humbly.

And now when I meet disheveled mothers in the supermarket vocalizing shrill, ignored refrains to their progeny, I don't automatically react with silent pity for the kids, as I once did. I'm slower to assign blame, and I ask if my condolence for those unlucky children couldn't be better replaced with compassion for mothers who may find themselves struggling to understand and cope with the complex little people who have graced their lives.

*I have great respect for essays like this one. Karen speaks to us from a deep and gutsy place. She's saying, "I had my own simplistic, idealized view of myself handed to me in pieces, and I'm going to relive the pain of that in public so you can share in the wisdom I gained." Sometimes writing is good because the writer is good—honest, daring, generous. We should appreciate the gift.*

## SOCIAL DICTATORS

SARAH INNES

I just got through reading another of those letters to the editor trashing public smokers. It reminded me of why I started smoking in the first place. Smoking, while admittedly dumb and dangerous, also serves a valuable social function: to separate the straight-laced from the self-destructive, the health nuts from the oral compulsives, and the social dictators from the marginalized outsiders. The latter in each case being, in my experience, more fun all around than the former—edgier, less emotionally stable, more sensitive to the pains of the world, less guarded. In this health-obsessed age, where the ultimate goal is preserving the perfectly toned body and wrinkle-free face well past the years when anybody wants you around anyway, smoking has become the demon of choice for the herb-chomping baby boomer storm troopers, determined to exterminate everything vaguely frivolous or politically incorrect by means of a combination of repressive laws and—considerably worse—sanctimonious throat-clearing and moralizing. I would like to say a few words in defense of the few hapless smokers left.

What I think our letter-writer needs is a little perspective. In response to business owners allowing smoking on their premises, she declares, "I don't believe we can <u>ever</u> filter out <u>all</u> the smoke that <u>might</u> get into our lungs." First, never listen seriously to anyone who underlines frequently. After all, I can decide which are the important words for myself. Second, such panic-stricken statements wildly overestimate the danger of second-hand smoke, which is a real threat only to people who live with a smoker who smokes in their living area. People who do are in fact more vulnerable to disease than people who don't, and smoking parents should take great care not to foist their cigarette smoke on their unwitting children, for instance. But the anti-smoking zealots go much farther, and would have no one smoke in public under any circumstances, on the off chance that <u>some</u> chemicals (see, now she's got me doing it) may remain in the air and later infiltrate their innocent lungs.

This is actuarial madness. All life is a risk. Everything we do endangers us to some extent. Driving a car, for instance, has a vastly greater likelihood of injuring us than catching a whiff of someone else's smoke for a half hour. As does riding a bike, eating butter, using a kitchen knife, or doing the zealot's very favorite thing, going for a hike in the hills. Most of the substances that we wallow in every day are toxic to some degree. The gasoline we enjoy pumping destroys our brain cells. The water we drink is full of deadly trace metals. The food we eat has many kinds of carcinogenics thoughtfully included in them by Mother Nature. Why do so many people focus on the unhealthy habits of a ragtag band of nicotine junkies and largely ignore the oil companies destroying ecosystems with their spills, nuclear power plants deforming the children across Europe, agriculturalists augmenting our aquifer with biocides, and factories spewing millions of gallons of toxic waste into our rivers and bays?

Perhaps because it's so much easier—and more pleasurable—to point the finger directly at the powerless schmuck sitting next to them at an outdoor café than it is to take on the big boys, who bite back. Or perhaps it's because the oil companies et al. buy them off by giving them gas at less than two dollars a gallon and lettuce for a buck a head. Or perhaps because what a lot of people really want isn't cleaner air or healthier lives, but the sweet sense of control they get from dictating another person's behavior. After all, a zealot could do this world more good by switching from his ponderous gas-guzzling SUV to a fuel-efficient gas-electric hybrid than by eliminating all the second-hand smoke in all the outdoor cafés in the world, but I haven't noticed the stampede starting yet.

Next our letter-writer argues, "Allowing public smoking sends the message to our children that it is an acceptable addiction." Well, first, smoking is acceptable, barely, by the law of the land. Second, addictions aren't necessarily actionable, as every Pepsi fiend or watcher of daytime soaps can attest. But more important, who are these children, so impressionable, so without an internal moral guide or judgment or free will, that anything they see anyone doing will automatically register as acceptable behavior? I dread to think what will happen to these pliable folk when they watch TV and see an endless stream of killings, adulterous liaisons, and car crashes. Will they conclude that crashing their car is "acceptable"? While I agree that smoking next to other people's children is tacky, why should I be responsible, in my own space, for what messages these children construct from what they observe? And where does such reasoning end? Is our letter-writer going to lean over to the well-tanned person next to her and say, "Excuse me, but could you please use sunscreen from now on? I'm worried that the message your reckless exposure to harmful UV rays is sending to my children is that it's acceptable to get skin cancer"? The world is a messy place, full of messages you probably don't want your children to hear, but you can't screen them all out. I don't think the goal of a parent should be to shelter kids from every glimpse of human error, weakness, or vice in the hopes that the kids will be fooled into some grandiose delusion of human perfectibility. Instead, teach the kids to think and make choices.

Smokers, one must concede, have given up a lot in this war. We've given up restaurants, airplanes, all public offices, and now even bars—bars, the last haven of hedonism and tolerance of bad behavior in the world! Now it is time for the other side to give a little. Our requests are few. If you drive by a sleazy bar with a name like "Last Chance" or "The Pastime" and you happen to see someone smoking, don't call the cops. You can assume that everyone in there has consented of their own free will to bathe in carcinogens, and it's really none of your business. And if you walk by a smoker in the park, don't cough and sputter as if your luncheon weenie has just lodged in your windpipe. Just exhale deeply (call it "yogic breathing" if that helps), resolve to run another lap, or take an extra shot of wheat grass juice at the spa. Your health will be fine—and what's more you'll breathe easier knowing you've taken a step toward tolerance in the world.

*This is a classic, time-honored approach to the essay, for two reasons. It's a reaction to something Sarah ran across in her daily reading, and it's an anti-cliché: It critiques a currently popular belief or behavior—it says, "We're all going around believing X, but maybe we should stop and rethink the wisdom of that." I also like it because it has the courage to be snotty.*

## AIDS HITS HOME

JEFFERSON GOOLSBY

I got the bad news about my fifteen-year-old nephew a couple of days after he was told the bad news himself. My brother—his dad—was visiting us down in the valley and told the rest of the family. It was hard to believe. My nephew seemed so young and healthy, the star of the high school basketball team in a small mountain community of two thousand people where everybody knew everybody. It couldn't happen to him. That's what we all said. Yet it had. The AIDS epidemic had reached this small, remote town in full force.

Was he HIV positive? Not at all. In fact, he was a virgin. But a group of well-intentioned educators from the big city decided to be "pro-active" and drove up to my nephew's town and planted the fear of HIV and AIDS in the hearts and minds of all the local school kids. They even brought along an HIV-positive gay male to bear witness to the looming devastation. AIDS had come to this town in all its horror. Not the disease—just the propaganda.

It reminded me of when I was twelve and had inflicted on me my first sex education course, though anti-sex education would have been a more suitable title. After we boys were mysteriously segregated from the girls, my flustered male teacher threaded up a peculiar filmstrip showing outline drawings of a flaccid penis. For no specific reason, animated arrows indicated that something called "semen" would flow from the "scrotum" and exit. After this meaningless film, unrelated to anything I called life, we were shown something with more impact. Two guys who worked in an auto garage were talking. One spoke of how it hurt when he "urinated." "You've got VD!" said his buddy in horror; "Venereal disease."

Sex and VD. Semen and disease. Hand in glove. Back to back. As inevitable as the turn of the seasons.

Thirty years later, the words are different but the pattern is the same. When an American child approaches the age of sexual activity, our schools enter a crisis management mode and quickly tell him or her, "If you have sex, disease will follow." It used to be that if you masturbated, you'd go mad. Now the stakes have been raised: if you have sex, you'll die. The educators told my nephew that a single sexual exposure could result in infection; there was no cure; death was almost inevitable; not even a condom could totally, absolutely, with complete certainty guarantee protection from the scourge. Run, run for your lives! By what unknown logic a sexually active gay male supported this argument was not entirely clear.

I wistfully recalled the sex education I had witnessed while living in Sweden. There, sex education begins at age five. Sex is viewed as a healthy, wonderful, natural human activity. When children reach a sexually active age, they are calmly and accurately informed of health risks. No horror shows. No foretellings of doom. No revolting videos of deformed genitals.

What sort of people would consider it rational to teach young people at almost zero risk that sex can kill them? What sort of person would take pleasure in turning sex into a thing of fear and dread? I think we know what sort of people do this, and their numbers seem to be growing.

Is the chance of dying of AIDS real? Yes, as is the chance of dying from flash floods, airplane crashes, stranger abduction, lightning, poisonous jellyfish, and esophageal obstruction. How great is the risk? For my nephew, the risk approaches zero—much less than the risk of death by lightning, inconceivably less than the risk of death by car collision. He is much more likely to die from heart disease caused by the margarine on his breakfast table. Certain, very limited groups of people living highly specific lifestyles and practicing highly specific behaviors are at risk. By all means, put the fear of god in them if you can. But nobody in my nephew's town has AIDS. Even here at our local campus, where 14,000 college students frolic, most of them with sexual abandon, every year, there has been exactly one single HIV diagnosis—ever.

But we don't tell young people that if they practice anal sex with multiple partners or share needles they are at risk. We don't tell them that 95% of HIV or AIDS patients are gay men. We tell them that every young person in the room is hanging by a thread—fall victim to your base appetites and have sex, and die. And we don't show them videos showing the horrid remains of people struck by lightning or detail the agonies of a person dying from the deadly sting of a poisonous jelly fish.

Why is this so? Because it isn't about disease or risk or protection; it's about keeping young people from having sex, by telling any lie we think might work. It's about brainwashing a young man so that when he looks across the room and sees that sweet, pretty girl sitting there, he sees images of sickness and wasting instead of, lord save us, pleasure and joy. And it's a lie. Why do we do it? Why do we do it?

*This is an anti-cliché essay (p. 283) that demonstrates a lot of guts. Sex is such a difficult subject to handle that few of my students ever touch it. Jeff gets it just right—no smirking, no squirming. And what a lovely trick opening—I fell for it completely, and I bet you did too.*

## Academic Essays

### "GALAXY QUEST" AND THE USES OF LITERATURE

ANTOINE LAVIN

"Galaxy Quest," the 2001 hit science fiction movie comedy, works on many different levels. It is a parody of science fiction television, a subtle commentary on our culture of celebrity, a moving tale of personal redemption, and a complex, carefully worked out exercise in plotting. But in addition, it offers an answer to questions that English majors get asked often: "What's so important about movies and TV? Isn't it all just entertainment?"

Everybody can see that "Galaxy Quest" is affectionately teasing the TV series "Star Trek" and its annual conventions and obsessive fans. These fans know the floor plan of the USS Enterprise, both Kirk's and Picard's, by heart and argue about the home life of the lava monster in Episode #42.

It's also a study of the American worship of celebrity and the horror of being "washed up." In the story, the actors in the original TV series "Galaxy Quest" were once stars, but the series was cancelled many years ago, and now they squeeze a living out of humiliating appearances at mall openings and annual "Quest-Cons." At these depressing gatherings, they are forced to face their uselessness and has-been status again and again.

It's also a retelling of the ancient myth about discovering your best self. Jason Nesmith (played by Tim Allen, doing a hilarious take-off of William Shatner), the actor who played the captain in the original "Galaxy Quest" series, is a drunk full of self-pity when the movie begins. He is approached by an alien race called the Thermians, who have been monitoring old "Galaxy Quest" reruns from space and naively think that the transmissions are "history." The Thermians ask "Commander Taggert" (Nesmith's character's name in the old series) to lead his crew on a mission to rescue their people from the evil space villain Sarris. Thinking it is some kind of public appearance, he accepts. He is terrified when he discovers what is really going on, but he finally discovers that he can be a space captain. He does have the makings of a hero inside him.

The movie is also fun to watch just because the plot is so well put together. The best example of this is the character of Brandon, the ultimate Trekkie nerd who appears again and again throughout the movie trying to engage "Taggert" in conversations about trivial technical problems from old episodes, like exactly how the dilithium crystals were wired to the thruster tubes to re-ignite the engines in Episode #12. Brandon appears to be in the movie only to represent the Trekkie mentality, but it turns out that he has a larger role to play. The Thermians give "Taggert" a communicator. Brandon, being a good Trekkie, has his own fake communicator, which looks just the same. Taggert and Brandon collide and exchange communicators by accident. When Nesmith needs key information about the layout of the space ship in order to defeat the bad guys, Nesmith uses his communicator to call Brandon. Brandon then gets his fellow nerds together and their expert knowledge of the ship's layout saves the day.

These four reasons make the movie outstanding all by themselves. However, the movie has something more to offer. It also teaches us something about being human and experiencing literature, and how the two are interrelated.

The Thermians tell us that in their past history they had constant wars and bloodshed. Then they began receiving the transmissions of the Galaxy Quest "history." The world of "Galaxy Quest" is full of fairness, equality, and peace, like the world of "Star Trek." There is no racism or war. The Thermians decide to model their society to be like the world of "Galaxy Quest," so they imitate everything they see, including all the sets, costumes, etc. The result is a world of perfect kindness, honesty, and brotherhood. They don't understand lying, for example. Cooperation is the norm. The Thermians also literally become human in form. They use image projection so they can appear as human to the human crewmembers.

We are invited to laugh at the Thermians and their naïve misinterpretation of TV images. However, beneath the joke lies an important theme. What the Thermians are doing is learning to be good, kind, and civilized by watching TV. They see an idealized, goody-goody image of human behavior, they embrace it as their ideal, and so they try to make the ideal come true in their own lives. They succeed completely. Everything they make while imitating the TV show works: the space ship, the beryllium sphere that powers the ship, the communicators, etc. There is no logical way this can happen, since there is no way to invent the technology, but if we see their success as a symbol for the way humans use literature, it makes sense. In the real world, the Thermians cannot really make a space ship that flies, but humans can read a book, see the image of a hero or saint, and choose to live their lives according to that model.

In fact, the human race has been doing exactly that since the beginning of history. Literature is a model humans use to inspire them to live the right kind of life. People read about (or watch) Gilgamesh or Perseus or James Bond and they say, So that is how I am supposed to live my life. Or, so that is how I am *not* supposed to live my life. Consequently, the character and his world become real, as the world of Galaxy Quest becomes real when the Thermians make it real. The world of James Bond becomes real when a generation of American males read the James Bond books or watch the movies and spend the rest of their lives trying to dress, walk, and talk like Bond.

Each of us is like the Thermians. We are lost, we don't know how to behave. We don't know how to get along with each other. We don't know what life is supposed to look like. The males don't know what it means to be male. The females don't know what it means to be female. Therefore we follow the Thermian plan. We experience literature. There we select models, and dedicate our lives to imitating them. We define ourselves as cowboys, swashbucklers, *femmes fatales*, war heroes, daring spies, damsels in distress, or faithful wives. By magic, it works. Whatever we choose, we become. The world of imagination becomes real because we will it to be real. Just like the Thermians, we project an artificial image of ourselves and live in the projection.

The power of this magic is amazing. The Thermians literally remake their world. Literature is always doing this. In England in the nineteenth century, Lord Byron wrote poems about a Satanic character called the Byronic hero, and the next few generations of literary people in England spent their lives acting the part and seeing the world as the Byronic hero saw it. In America in the Fifties and Sixties, two generations of young people devoted their lives to acting out the role of Holden Caulfield in *The Catcher in the Rye* or James Dean in "Rebel Without a Cause."

Now we can answer the question we started with. What is so important about movies and TV? They are the templates we use to construct the fantasy we call our lives. We can choose any fantasy we like. The consequences of our choice are enormous. Generations of American men have paid the price for choosing as their template the Gunslinger, and generations of American women have paid the price for choosing as their template Cinderella. The Thermians chose their template wisely, so they lived in peace and harmony. What choices are you making?

*I appreciate this essay for making two assumptions: 1) that popular art (movies, TV) is complex, artful, and deserving of serious examination, and 2) that literary criticism is about big, important things. Antoine goes far beyond the typical student pose of "I'm saying these things about this movie to be saying these things about this movie." He has something very important to tell us about how we live our lives. That movement from the specific subject (the movie) to large life issues is at the heart of most good academic work.*

## SOME ALTERNATIVES TO BURNING RICE STRAW

JAIME RAYNOR

In California a controversy has raged for years over whether or not to allow rice farmers to burn the straw left over after harvest. The California Air Resources Board and most California citizens don't want the farmers to burn, because burning pollutes the air and makes many residents of agricultural areas suffer from allergies. The farmers argue that they must burn because burning is cheap and gets rid of molds and diseases that wreak havoc on the rice crop.

The State Government is currently trying to find a solution to the problem. At present their only solution is to compromise and let the farmers burn a fraction of their straw but not all. This is only a temporary solution. If farmers are allowed to burn only 20% or 25% of their fields, they are still polluting the air and people are still getting sick. A satisfactory, long-term solution is still being sought. Senate Bill 318, which regulates the amount of rice straw that can be burned, mandated a committee to explore the different ways to put rice straw to use or get rid of it in ways that don't involve burning.

At first glance, burning can appear both necessary and justifiable. Rice crops are highly susceptible to diseases, and even large amounts of pesticides have been found ineffective in controlling them (Why Par. 2). And rice burning is hardly the only culprit in California's pollution problem. When interviewed, rice farmer Lyle Job argued, "I don't understand why the government wants to restrict us when all the agricultural burning—wheat, corn, oats, and others, not just rice—is only 2% of all the pollution in the air. Cars pollute the air more than agriculture does, and the government doesn't tell drivers they can only drive their car 10,000 miles a year."

Despite these arguments, there are presently several methods in place which provide workable alternatives to rice burning. Many of these methods have been used by enlightened rice farmers for years with success, while others are very new.

Lundberg Family Farms in Richvale, California, has been growing organic rice using non-polluting technology for years. Most simply, Wendell Lundberg explained in a personal interview, when a rice field gets diseased Lundberg's simply lets the field go unplanted for a year. Another alternative is to rotate crops. That way when a field becomes infected, a crop can be grown that isn't susceptible to the disease for a year.

Rice stubble can also be worked back into the soil instead of burned. The Lundbergs crush the stubble with huge rubber rollers, then work the stubble into the soil with a chisel (Straw Par. 4). All these procedures cost more than conventional burning, and many farmers are therefore resistant to them, but they work and the gains to our health and air are worth the cost.

Ecologically friendly ways of handling rice stubble have other benefits. The Lundbergs flood their fields after working the straw into the ground. This gives migrating birds such as geese, ducks, and swans a place to rest in mid-migration. It also benefits hunters in the area, because the time when the fields are flooded is around the same time when hunters are getting ready for duck and pheasant season. The flocks of birds actually help decompose the straw by trampling it (Straw Par. 4), while their excrement provides "natural fertilization" for the crops, which the Lundbergs call "vital to the soil building program" (Soil Par. 4).

Traditional farmers who embrace these new methods are going to have to adopt a larger view of the agricultural cycle. The Lundbergs explain, "Most farmers consider the soil to be merely an anchor for the plant's roots, and treat it as a sterile medium in which they attempt to control growth, weeds, insects, and diseases with chemicals and burning" (Soil Par. 1). The Lundbergs view the soil as a living organism (Soil Par. 1). For instance, they plant nitrogen-fixing legumes as a cover crop during the winter after the rice season is over (Soil Par. 2). The nitrogen from the legumes helps grow better rice without the Lundbergs having to resort to polluting chemical additives.

If farmers don't want to go to the expense of plowing rice straw into the ground or letting fields lie fallow for a year, there are other ways to avoid burning. First, straw can be bailed like hay and used as a construction material. Second-generation rice farmer Rick Green is using baled rice straw to build houses (Sirard IB3). Green explains his methods in this way:

> The straw is set upon a concrete base, placing it out of contact with the ground and moisture, its worst enemy. Once the straw is stacked two bales high, a metal plate is placed across the top to cinch down the bales. At eight feet, stucco is poured over the project, making it look like an adobe wall.

The resulting walls are fifteen inches thick and have an astounding insulation rating of R-53, according to Green: "When it's 105 degrees outside, the inside of the house is about 70 degrees," he says (all Sirard IB3).

Building houses out of rice bales is currently still more expensive than using lumber, but only because we pretty much give the lumber companies our forests for free. Since rice straw is almost limitless in supply, a waste product, and annually renewable, doesn't it make more sense to use it and save the trees we have left?

Another way to market rice stubble is to bury people in it. Hard as it may be to believe, Will Maetens has begun selling rice straw coffins (Gabrukiewicz B3). A six-foot, eight-inch coffin of compressed rice straw costs only $375, compared to conventional coffins, which run anywhere from $2,000 up. This is a great idea for those who are not so well off, who want to be buried in a more natural way, or who like the idea of becoming one with the earth.

A third way of marketing rice stubble is to turn it into fuel. The city of Gridley in Northern California recently secured a letter of intent from BC International of Boston to construct a plant in their town, at a cost of $60 million, for the conversion of rice straw to ethanol (Gonzales E1). This may prove to be the best solution to the burning problem so far. If it works, it will not only solve the problems associated with rice burning, but will also help solve our energy problem and create needed jobs in economically depressed rural areas.

With all these alternatives to burning, and more on the way, it seems that burning is unnecessary. The alternatives may cost a little more now, but as industries like rice home building and ethanol become established, that should change. And even if it doesn't, the benefits of these alternatives are so many and so great, for the farmers and the community, that I feel the time has come for rice farmers to give up their old ways and turn away from burning.

**Works Cited**

Gabrukiewicz, Thom. "Businessman's Rice Straw Coffins Designed for Ecologically Correct." *Sacramento Bee* 8 Dec. 1997: B3.

Gonzales, Anne. "Pesky Rice Straw Could Fuel New Business for Gridley." *Sacramento Bee* 28 Sept. 1997: E1.

Job, Lyle. Personal interview. 1 Nov. 1998.

Lundberg, Wendell. Personal interview. 31 Oct. 1998.

Sirard, Jack. "Rice Farmer Constructs Walls of Waste." *Sacramento Bee* 22 June 1998: IB3.

"Soul Enrichment." *Lundberg Family Partnership with Nature.* 1 Dec. 1998 <http://www.lundberg.com/partnership/soil.html>.

"Straw Incorporation." *Lundberg Family Partnership with Nature.* 19 Oct. 1998 <http://www.lundberg.com/partnership/straw.html>.

"Why Burn Rice Straw?" *Rice Disease: How an Old Flame Burns Them Out and Protects Our Crop.* 17 Oct. 1998 <http://riceproducers.com/whyburn.html>.

*This essay has a fine sense of its own importance. Jaime is saying, "I'm not writing this just to fulfill an assignment. Hey, people are choking to death out there on that smoke, and there are lots of things we can do about it!" It's also about an issue close to home—Jaime and his readers are actually breathing that stuff.*

## WHY PEOPLE KILL

DAVID SMITHERS

Taking the life of another human being is a simple thing to do, and if we believe TV, rap music, and the movies it's also pretty natural. But it isn't, at least not for most people. Two books, *On Killing* by David Grossman and *Why They Kill* by Richard Rhodes, illustrate this idea. Both authors are in agreement that it is an innate quality of mankind to resist killing another human being. Yet ours is a history of nearly constant warfare and violence. The authors explore this paradox as they attempt to explain how people overcome their inherent unwillingness to take another's life.

*On Killing* explores killing that is sanctioned by authority, as in the military, and *Why They Kill* investigates nonsanctioned killing such as criminal murder. In examining these two books, we see that military killing is very different from criminal acts. Killing in the military is mainly done in groups, and the killer is ordered to kill by his superiors. Yet despite these powerful sanctions, soldiers are still highly reluctant to kill. Major General S. L. A. Marshall studied this issue throughout World War II and concluded, "The average, healthy individual has such an inner and usually unrealized resistance towards killing a fellow man that he will not of his own volition take life if it is possible to turn away from that responsibility" (Marshall 23). The same was found to be true of World War II pilots. The Army Air Corps found that 30 to 40 percent of all enemy planes destroyed in combat were shot down by less than 1 percent of American fighter pilots.

Grossman's research shows that this resistance to killing holds true not only for World War II but for all the wars that he studied. These studies have led him to conclude that the average man will not kill even at the risk of his own life or in defense of what he holds dear. Grossman flatly states, "Looking another human being in the eye, making an independent decision to kill him, and watching as he dies due to your action, combine to form the single, most basic, important, primal, and potentially traumatic occurrence of war" (12). On its face this conclusion seems counter-intuitive, since plenty of people are killed in wars, but Grossman explains that until Marshall started interviewing combatants immediately after battles no one really understood what actually happened on the battlefield. As with sex, there were lots of myths but no scientific data. Grossman is convinced that the data supports his contention that the aversion to killing is so strong that men will go to almost any lengths to avoid it.

Grossman also believes that it is the act of killing, not the threat of being killed, that is the cause of psychological damage seen in veterans of war. For example, in World War II more than 800,000 men were classified as 4-F due to psychiatric reasons. Over 500,000 soldiers suffered psychiatric collapse. During the Arab-Israeli War, almost a third of casualties on both sides were due to psychiatric problems. In a World War II study by Swank and Marchand, it was determined that after sixty days of continuous combat 98 percent of surviving soldiers became psychiatric casualties of some kind. These figures, according to Grossman, are not explained by lack of sleep or food, exposure to the elements, or fear, but by the burden imposed on men by having to kill fellow soldiers. Grossman cites several examples of enemy soldiers who come upon each other unexpectedly and instead of attempting to kill each other go their separate ways.

How does the military overcome this powerful resistance to killing? A number of methods are utilized. Grossman shows there are four factors in getting soldiers to kill on command: the proximity of the authority figure, the killer's respect for the authority figure, the intensity of the authority figure's commands, and the perceived legitimacy of the authority figure's authority.

According to Grossman, military leaders demand obedience. Soldiers kill not as individuals but as a group. Thus the individual soldier has a sense of anonymity. Furthermore, crowds have the effect of intensifying behavior. Actions one would not take alone become possible in a crowd. A combat unit disintegrates as a fighting unit when it suffers 50 percent casualties; at this point the individual soldiers no longer feel a part of a larger whole and their will to kill evaporates.

Grossman argues that modern soldiers are psychologically conditioned to overcome the resistance to killing in three ways: desensitization, conditioning, and denial defense mechanisms. Desensitization involves teaching soldiers to view the enemy as inhuman and thus worthy of killing. Conditioning is the application of Pavlovian and Skinnerian programming techniques. Instead of shooting at targets on target ranges, soldiers are run through training exercises where they wear full battle gear and shoot at lifelike targets of enemy soldiers that fall convincingly after being shot. Afterwards the successful shooters are praised and rewarded. Denial mechanisms are rehearsed fictions that help numb the pain of killing. Veterans of the Falklands War said they thought of the enemy as simply more man-shaped targets from the training exercises, for instance.

Most frightening is Grossman's observation that all three of these conditioning techniques are presently being employed by our civilian population of young men on themselves, in the form of violent video games and action movies. This, Grossman argues, explains the startling statistics on aggravated assault by young people in America. Murder by youths age fifteen to nineteen increased by 154% between 1985 and 1991.

Richard Rhodes has a different approach to the subject of killing. As a criminologist, he studies civilian killings, and his view is based on the work of criminologist Lonnie Athens, who studied this topic for years.

Rhodes begins by rejecting all traditional explanations for violent crime—poverty, race, mental illness, child abuse, and gender. He specifically rejects the idea that violent behavior springs from low self-esteem, arguing that in fact violent members of society have an exaggeratedly high sense of self-esteem. He also rejects Grossman, and argues that video games and violent movies do not make people violent. According to Rhodes, people become killers because they are socialized to be killers from the time they are very young children. Athens refers to this process of education as "violentization," or violent socialization. Without undergoing this process, people simply do not become killers.

Athens breaks down the process of violentization into four steps: brutalization, belligerency, violent performances, and virulency. He further breaks brutalization down into three steps: violent subjugation, personal horrification, and violent coaching. Violent subjugation occurs when an authority figure—parent, spouse, or gang leader—uses violence to compel the subject to submit to his authority. Personal horrification occurs when the subject witnesses someone highly valued—a friend, a sibling, a parent—undergoing violent subjugation. Violent coaching occurs when the subject is assigned the role of novice by a trusted authority figure who takes on the role of instructor in violence.

The second stage, belligerency, occurs when the subject decides that violence is necessary or resolves to use it by attacking people who provoke him. In the third stage, violent performance, the subject crosses the point of no return and uses violence against someone. After his violent performance, the subject is changed in his own eyes and the eyes of those around him—he is seen as a different person. He becomes overly impressed with his own performance. He resolves not to tolerate provocation from anyone, and moves from using violence as a defense to being the aggressor.

He now moves to the final stage, virulency. He is now a ticking time bomb, just waiting for an opportunity to demonstrate his violence. He is willing to attack anyone, with minimal provocation and with intent to commit great harm.

Rhodes uses his theory to account for the statistics of violence in a number of different contexts. He examines the personal histories of several famous violent Americans—Mike Tyson, Lee Harvey Oswald—and finds the theory holds true for all of them. He relates the extremely high rate of violence in the Middle Ages to violent medieval child-raising methods. Louis IV, for instance, was subjected to beatings virtually every day for simple infractions such as not removing his hat in the king's presence. Rhodes examines violent primitive cultures like the Gebusi of New Guinea, and points out that their homicide rates are often incredibly high compared even to those of American cities. And finally Rhodes considers Viet Nam, where the level of atrocities committed by American troops reached unprecedented levels, as a result of new military training methods, Rhodes argues.

Rhodes concludes that the best place to prevent the creation of new criminals is in the schools. He states, "A good school can go a long way in making up for a bad family" (124). He condemns writers like James Dobson who advocate using corporal punishment on children, and finds conservative Christianity guilty of perpetuating violence against children because it is based on the Bible, which was written in a barbaric era when physical violence was the primary means of settling disputes and thus endorses violent subjugation. He also argues that the penal system needs to make changes in how it handles criminals. A distinction should be made between violent criminals, whose programming is complete and who are beyond redemption, and non-violent criminals, who pose no physical threat to society.

Grossman and Rhodes are in basic agreement about their central thesis, that getting humans to kill other humans is extraordinarily difficult and requires a methodical, sophisticated training program. But the political cultures of the military killer and the criminal killer are far different from each other. The military killer is recognized as good and necessary in all cultures; the criminal killer has no place in any social system, from anarchist to fascist. Thus Grossman and Rhodes have nearly opposite reactions to their thesis. The whole thrust of Grossman's book is about getting a man in his role as soldier to perform the act of killing well. The military looks for ways to remove the obstacles in the way of killing, and thus seeks to establish authority figures and pecking orders that will distribute the guilt of killing and allow the killer to bear it, for instance. Grossman's view is basically that the modern military isn't doing this job well enough, and that as a consequence our young soldiers refuse to kill or suffer excessively afterwards. Rhodes sees the opposite problem: our society is teaching the wrong people to kill—civilians—and teaching it with great success. If both men are right, then ironically our society is failing by teaching killing both too well and not well enough.

Yet there is comfort in the message of both men. Violence is learned. People are not born violent, and in fact resist violence intensely. Thus society is in control of its own violent behavior. If we want to reduce violence, we need only change the programming we give our young people. But do we want to?

**Works Cited**

Athens, Lonnie H. *The Creation of Dangerous Violent Criminals*. Urbana: University of Illinois Press, 1992.

Grossman, David. *On Killing*. New York: Little, Brown, 1997.

Marshall, S. L. A. *Men Against Fire: The Problem of Battle Command in Future War*. Gloucester, MA: Peter Smith, 1978.
Rhodes, Richard. *Why They Kill: The Discoveries of a Maverick Criminologist*. New York: Knopf, 1999.

*This is a classic compare-and-contrast essay, and it's a good example of academic tone. The voice is impersonal, reserved, scholarly—yet the sense of personal purpose is still strong. This isn't just an exercise in data synthesis—we need to know this stuff, David is saying, if we want to stop the bloodshed. David has wisely kept the canvas to be covered small—instead of trying to survey the entire literature on the subject, he's just comparing the approaches of two interestingly different men. That's smart, because it keeps the project doable.*

## Four Essays on Dieting

*Chapter 17's Stew Theory (p. 269) says that everybody has something of her own to contribute to any topic. Here is living proof: four essays about dieting, each finding its own thing to say in its own voice. Dieting is one of the most tired topics in composition classes, yet each of these four writers finds something lively and fresh to say about it. By the way, the first essay was inspired by Dave Barry's newspaper columns.*

### BERUMEN ON DIETING

ANDRA BERUMEN-GOODWIN

Many of you women out there are seriously thinking about going on a diet. OK, all of you are. The long winter months of being wrapped safely in multiple heavy layers are dwindling, and the thought of being seen in a swimming suit is enough to strike you dead where you stand. Before you begin, there are many things you should know.

Dieting is hard. That's why it's called "dieting" and not "being happy" or "having a nice time."

Dieting makes no sense. I mean, really, America is the land of plenty, so what kind of sick, twisted person would want to deny herself those Ding Dongs many people worked so hard to manufacture, package, and market? As you begin your diet, say, "I am nuts" three times out loud.

A diet usually finds its source in one of three Incidents:

1. The Fluorescent Incident. This involves undressing in a bathroom with an unforgiving fluorescent light, one that could reveal new pits and craters on the moon if it were ever sent into space. You try to throw a heavy object through the glass, but you're too out of shape to lift it.

2. The Scale Incident. This involves tiptoeing around the bathroom carefully avoiding the scale, losing your balance, and falling helplessly onto the dreaded truth-teller, where the numbers burn the hateful information into your retinas.

3. The Guess Incident: This involves trying to squeeze into last year's favorite pair of jeans, which fit perfectly back then, while lying face up on your bed, knees bent, inhaling more deeply than you ever did at those college reggae concerts, while feeling the last button slip from your plump sweaty fingers.

Diet Fact: what you buy you will eat. It's easy to tell yourself when you're shopping that you'll save the chocolate morsels for when you make those tollhouse cookies next year, but the fact is they'll be gone tonight. It's easy to tell yourself you're buying the butter and full-fat sour cream for *him*, the lazy boob who can't control his appetite and doesn't care what he looks like at the beach since no one is looking anyway, but the fact is they'll end up on your toast and your enchilada.

Diet Fact: it doesn't matter how low your weight gets, but how low it stays. There is an inverse law working here: the faster a diet takes off pounds, the more likely the pounds will return. The fast diets all work through pills and deprivation. No wonder no one can stay on them! These diets breed yo-yo weight swings and, worse, eating disorders. Instead of taking a pill or eating nothing but plain spaghetti for two weeks, think in terms of substituting healthy alternatives for your fat-producing menu items. Eat whole-grain bread instead of processed white, for instance, and fat-free milk for regular milk. And make the change permanent. Don't grit your teeth and eat whole-grain bread for a month, or until the ten pounds come off; eat it for life.

To diet is to haunt the diet section of your local bookstore. There are very few Americans who have not published a diet book. Any diet book is guaranteed to make you lose about twenty-five dollars, and not much else. Since the number of diet books is infinite, you can work backwards: decide what you like to eat, and go look for a diet book that swears that eating exactly *that* will melt off the pounds. If you believe that book sales equal merit, three diets are so popular that you'll want to give them a look: the Zone Diet, the Cabbage Soup Diet, and the Atkins Diet. Here's what you're in for in each case:

1. The Zone Diet. This diet requires great will power and free time—just to read the gargantuan book. The diet is relatively

sane. You eat fruits and nonstarchy vegetables and avoid grains and starchy vegetables. You can eat anything in moderation, and you are allowed three meals and two snacks a day. Nothing too terrible there. You have to like number crunching and obsessive counting—compulsive personality types will thrive. If you love your pasta, look elsewhere.

2. The Cabbage Soup Diet. This diet has the virtue of simplicity. You eat a special soup that is very low in calories. The more you eat, the more weight you lose. This is a good diet for people who get confused easily, or who really like the idea of being able to eat as much of *something* as they want, and don't care what the something is. The problem is, the soup isn't very tasty. It consists of scallions, bell peppers, tomatoes, celery, cabbage, Lipton soup mix, bouillon, and V8 juice (see, I just saved you the $25 for the book). Doesn't sound too bad, right? Until about the fourth week of the diet. See the second Diet Fact above. Also, cabbage smells, and endless amounts of it seem to produce an adverse reaction in the human bowel. All in all, if you have no taste buds, live alone, have no pets to offend, and like being in the bathroom, the cabbage soup diet is for you.

3. The Atkins Diet. This is the one that has lit up the phone lines at the radio talk shows. Want to lose weight while eating butter, spareribs, and rack of lamb? Sounds impossible, but it's not, according to Dr. Robert Atkins, who made millions from the Atkins Diet. This diet is founded on the principle that "fat does not make you fat"—carbohydrates do. The diet simply says, avoid all carbohydrates and consume all the protein (meat, cheese, eggs) you want. The dieter's dream come true.

So does it work? In a word . . . yes. You will lose weight, especially during the first two weeks. Is it good for you? Probably not. While you're losing weight, you are also jacking up your cholesterol level, stuffing your arteries, and inviting the mother of all heart attacks. But, hey, you'll look good on the operating table!

Most diets fail. Most dieters end up weighing what they did when they started. Do not despair. Diets are like boyfriends—if they didn't let us down, what would we have to talk about among ourselves?

## THE PRICE OF SHRIMP

RHONDA VANDIVER

A recent article in *People* magazine observed that over 45% of Americans are overweight. The magazine laid the blame for this tragedy at the foot of the American consumer. We don't exercise enough, we don't eat healthily, we don't do this or that. True enough. But to lay the blame for America's obesity problem entirely on us couch potatoes is a dangerous oversimplification. Part of the problem is on display down at your local grocery store.

Pick up a box of Top Ramen noodles at Safeway and check the price. On sale, you can score them for about ten for a dollar. Fantastic! What a great buy, you mutter to yourself as you cruise past the canned foods and head into the produce section. You reach for the asparagus. Holy Mother of God! Three dollars a pound! A war wages in your psyche. Top Ramen is cheap and terrible for you, full of the trans-fats all dieticians have at the top of their To Be Avoided list. Asparagus is very healthy. Ramen prepares in a couple of minutes. Asparagus takes time. Your daughter hates anything green. Hmmmm. The average American probably won't debate that very long. Top Ramen wins out over the shrubbery any day.

Americans eat junk because it's faster and cheaper, not because they crave obesity. Most of us would rather be eating those leafy green salads and grilled prawns the diets preach, but lettuce is two dollars a head and takes time, and prawns are twenty dollars a pound. Burger King will feed you and your family dinner for around eight bucks, if you go with the 99-cent specials. The fiber in the lettuce will reduce your risk of colon cancer and the omega-three fatty acids in the prawns will lower your risk of heart attack, while the Burger King meal will shoot up to 250 grams of artery-clogging fat into your family's collective arteries, but who has the time to care? And there's no clean-up.

Quick food is cheaper than healthy food, always. The American Medical Association in conjunction with Discovery Health has done several studies of food prices in American supermarkets. They conclude that healthy food is generally three times as expensive as the less healthy alternative. For instance, a hamburger at McDonald's, made with meat and sauces high in fat, costs 49 cents on burger day. Lean ground beef in the grocery store is $2.50 a pound. Veggie burger patties are twice that.

Why is this pricing system allowed to exist, in a culture where everyone is on a diet and hundreds of thousands of people are swallowing any dangerous pill that promises to make pounds vanish? Some of it is the result of the nature of food production. Organic food, which is better for you than nonorganic, is more expensive to grow and harvest. Organic agriculture produces smaller yields per acre, so an organic farmer must charge more for a pound of her produce. Most of the higher cost, however, can be attributed to pure greed. It's all about the Benjamins at supermarket chains. Safeway considers tofu a specialty item, which means they know that customers who want it really want it, and will pay a lot for it. Healthy food is also more expensive for supermarkets to handle. To Safeway, the perfect item is Twinkies, sealed and loaded with preservatives and happy to sit on the shelf for decades waiting for a customer. Most important, low volume makes products expensive. McDonald's can sell hamburgers for 49 cents because they sell a billion a day. If Americans bought a billion slabs of tofu a day, it would be cheap too.

There are solutions to this problem. Most supermarkets are corporations, and corporations are very sensitive to public opinion and negative publicity. Furthermore, most supermarkets work together, negotiating prices with other supermarkets to prevent competition and keep demand high. This means we can effect change if we work together, and if we can change one store we'll change all of them. And, since prices come down as volume sales go up, we can help by encouraging everyone to buy more and more healthy food. After all, once computers cost hundreds of thousands of dollars, and now they're in three-dollar wrist watches.

The Movement is just getting started. A women's health group has lobbied for investigation into food pricing, but their campaign has stagnated due to general lack of interest. We have to change that. Web sites like Discovery Health and the Food and Drug Administration site have links that contain information about the problem and possible solutions, along with addresses of major grocery retailers you can use to express your displeasure.

As long as the problem exists, we will continue to face an ugly choice: eat well, and pay through the nose, or eat junk and save. It isn't easy watching the wallet empty, but think of it this way: you aren't just spending three dollars for asparagus; you're saving $50 a month on diet pills, $28 on the latest fad diet book, $55 a month for your exercise club membership, $350 for the treadmill . . .

## A GOOD ITALIAN GIRL

REBECCA TUMLINSON

"Tell me what you eat, and I'll tell you what you are," Brillat-Savarin once said. In that case, I was a good Italian girl. I was pasta, lasagna, and tiramisu. And, like any other good Italian girl, I was what my grandmother called "pleasingly plump." Little did I know that my plumpness, which everyone thought was so adorable when I was eight, would become the bane of my existence. The over-eating that won me smiles and praise among my family didn't play so well in the outside world.

I grew faster than other girls. When my best friends were graduating from pink chemises, I was picking out underwire bras. The extra weight, the too-noticeable bust combined with a natural awkwardness to produce a shy kid who hid from the stares and criticisms of high school by seeking comfort where my family taught me to find it—in food. That, of course, made the problem worse, which made my desire for food worse, and so on. I was in the fat person's death spiral.

Desperate to shed the bulk, I tried diets. But I always ended up defeating myself. I would cheat, sneaking food from the fridge when I was home alone. The food often tasted as dry as sawdust to me, but I couldn't stop. All it really brought me was a sense of guilt and failure that made my problems worse.

After high school I attended a junior college where I learned a way out. My acting teacher, who had once been obese himself, recognized my syndrome and offered me some advice: "Start writing about it," he said. "Only then are you going to know what is causing you to overeat. You can't change a behavior until you know *why* you do it."

Like most wise counsel, this sounded dumb to me, but I gave it a try. I began to scribble every time I felt hungry or found myself wanting food. What I found after a month of note taking surprised me. I ate in moments of boredom. When I was done with homework or chores, when I was staring at unfilled time on my hands, I headed for the fridge. I ate when I felt down, or lonely, or unappreciated. I felt like I had just found the lost city of Atlantis. *It wasn't about food. It wasn't about hunger.* I was using food as a substitute for what I really craved—physical stimulation, emotional comfort, companionship. If I could just find a way to give myself what I really wanted, I could skip the snacks.

Now I knew what to do. When I felt the urge to hit the fridge, I got busy. I went outside and swam or played with my pets. I called up friends and asked them to go for a hike in the hills. The more I did these things, the more I wanted to do them. I bought a treadmill and used it. I bought a set of freeweights and began lifting at home. I got interested in cycling and began riding regularly with other riders. The snowball was really rolling now. I have recently taken up yoga and meditation.

It hasn't been an easy few months, and I'm not nearly finished with my journey to a healthy weight, but I have lost twenty-five pounds and have never felt so confident or so happy. I don't have to count calories, avoid anything fried, or live on fat-free cottage cheese either. I am still the same enthusiastic eater I've always been. Food is one of life's pleasures, and for me no diet would ever work if it turned eating into a grim, negative denial experience. But now I eat to refuel my body, not to drive away the demons.

You may not eat for the same reasons I ate. Whatever your reasons, if you overeat, you can't control it until you know why. So when you feel the urge to eat, grab that pencil and notepad and start writing. Ask yourself, "What am I feeling? How is my life right now? What do I really want right now? What do I really hope to gain by eating?" Only when you know how you've learned to think about food can you critically review that thinking pattern and choose to replace it with a healthier one.

## THE LAST WORD ON DIETS

ZEKE TOBIAS

Obesity seems to be one of those things like politics that everybody wants to talk about but nobody wants to fix. The bookstores are groaning with the weight of diet books. Women's magazines have a monthly weight-loss section. People are having themselves mutilated with painful and expensive surgery to lose weight. We're spending billions of dollars on low-fat pizzas and diet sodas. We're bingeing and purging and bingeing and purging. Eating disorders have become the hottest cash cow in American medicine, after liposuction. Every food item in the grocery store has had a diet built around it. The Grapefruit Diet! The Kale Diet! The Pennzoil Diet! And we keep getting fatter and fatter.

Enough already. Thirty years of research into weight loss can be summarized in one sentence: eat fewer calories and fat than you burn, and you lose weight; eat more calories and fat than you burn, and you gain weight. So eat less and exercise more. End of story. Don't like it? Too bad. If you still don't get it, reread these two paragraphs until you do.

# Author/Title Index

The following index lists all the student and professional writings that appear in *The Writer's Way*. The first index lists works by author's name in alphabetical order. The second index is organized by mode and lists each work by title.

## Essays by Author

## Essays by Mode and Title

### Personal Essays

## Informative Essays



## Argumentative Essays

## Academic Essays



## Term Paper

# Subject Index

# Understanding Plagiarism

## A STUDENT GUIDE TO WRITING YOUR OWN WORK

# CONTENTS

## CHAPTER 1


## CHAPTER 2


## CHAPTER 3


## CHAPTER 4

# CHAPTER 1

## Introduction

### What is in this guide?

This booklet is designed to help students avoid the pitfalls of plagiarism. Chapters cover the correct way to credit sources, quote, cite, paraphrase, summarize, create a list of references, and more. Knowledge checks are provided at the end of each section for review.

### Why is this guide important to you as a student?

What do you want from college? You probably want to succeed in your classes. The last thing you want is to fail a class for cheating or plagiarizing by mistake. If you are unfamiliar with the practices and rules of incorporating work from other sources, then you will find this guide a useful resource.

You can use the knowledge checks in each chapter or the quiz at the end of the booklet to practice all the skills necessary to use resources correctly. We've tried to make it as clear and simple as possible. Citing correctly can be confusing. Most colleges have very specific requirements about giving references, depending on the subject or instructor. Citing correctly is more involved than inserting footnotes or listing references at the end of a paper. This guide provides information and samples of the kinds of citations that are necessary to correctly reference different types of academic work.

### What is plagiarism?

**Plagiarism** is using someone else's work and passing it off as one's own. The term comes from the Latin word *plagiarius*, which means *kidnapper*.

This means that if a student uses another writer's work without giving credit, it may be considered deceptive even if it is an honest mistake. Knowing the definition of plagiarism and when to cite sources is the best way to avoid problems.

### When should you credit another author's work?

Because many things such as information, pictures, and music are now so easy to copy from the Internet, it's more tempting than ever to find and use those materials for free. How can you tell when it is appropriate to use something without a citation and when it isn't?

Generally any time you use someone else's work as a source of ideas or inspiration, credit is required. There are a few exceptions, such as when the information is common knowledge. An example of common knowledge is the fact that Christopher Columbus crossed the Atlantic Ocean in 1492. To be safe, if you consult a source and that source's ideas become part of your work, then you need to cite that source. If you use a direct quotation, then you need to reproduce it accurately and to cite it correctly. These practices will prevent inadvertent plagiarizing, and this guide will provide the basics to get you started.

> ***Tip***
> **When you consult a source, cite it correctly!**

There are also limitations to how much of someone else's work can be used as part of an assignment. Exclusively, excessively, or inappropriately using another author's work by copying paraphrasing, summarizing, or directly quoting is plagiarizing. It is important to use your own words and ideas in a paper. One suggested rule of thumb for acceptable use of content in a submitted assignment is up to 10 percent, provided it is properly cited (Zaharoff). Make sure to check your instructor's preferences.

Many students worry that their own words do not sound as professional as those used by the original author. But that fear ignores the point of using a source in the first place. Instructors do not give assignments so students can give them back another author's work. Instructors do not expect the same quality of work from a novice as from an expert. College is a place of learning. If instructors wanted to read only the professional author's words and ideas, they could go directly to the original source and skip the student's work.

The whole point of having you use sources is to enable you to learn from those sources and to develop your own writing and analytical skills. It's important for you to work with ideas and to express them in writing so you can develop your own writing style, perspective, and voice. This is a big investment of time and effort. Often when students risk plagiarizing, they haven't allowed themselves sufficient time to complete an assignment. These types of miscalculations can lead to trouble.

## Know the rules.

Because academic honesty and the validity of a college degree are vitally important to institutions of higher learning, schools create codes or policies governing instances of

> ***Tip***
> **Know the rules about plagiarism; ignorance is no excuse.**

dishonesty. Many of these policies are listed as Academic Integrity, Academic Honesty, Honor Code, Cheating, Student Conduct Code, or Plagiarism. The codes may consist of a list of rules definitions, specific behaviors, procedures, and consequences of academic dishonesty. It is your responsibility to know the rules of your institution and to follow them. Rules are usually published in school catalogs and considered a part of the enrollment agreement for the college. If you have any questions about academic policies, then check with your instructor or the dean's office to get the facts.

When instructors suspect plagiarism, they will follow steps prescribed by the institution to address the problem. These steps include contacting the student and forwarding a report to the dean or a disciplinary committee, which will probably conduct a hearing.

Consequences to the student can include failing the assignment or the course, as well as being given community service or some other restitution to the campus community. Some students have been unhappily surprised to learn that the consequences for a first-time offense of plagiarism can be as severe as expulsion from the institution. Being caught as a plagiarizer is humiliating, can directly affect a student's progress toward a degree, is costly, and is entirely avoidable.

## Knowledge Check: True or False?

1. Most students who plagiarize do so inadvertently.
2. Students cannot be accused of plagiarizing if they don't know the citation style expected by the instructor.
3. Using sources for educational purposes means that those sources are exempt from citation rules.

## Answers

1. (True) Don't be one of them. This can be a costly mistake!
2. (False) It is your job to find out.
3. (False) All sources should be cited.

# CHAPTER 2

# How to Avoid Plagiarism

***12 Tips to Avoid Plagiarizing***

1. Do your own work, and use your own words.
2. Allow yourself enough time to research the assignment.
3. Keep careful track of your sources.
4. Take careful notes.
5. Assemble your thoughts, and make clear who is speaking.
6. If you use an idea, a quotation, paraphrase, or summary, then credit the source.
7. Learn how to cite sources correctly both in the body of your paper and in your List of Works Cited.
8. Quote accurately and sparingly.
9. Paraphrase carefully.
10. Do not patchwrite.
11. Summarize, don't auto-summarize.
12. Do not rework another student's paper or buy paper-mill papers.

## Do your own work, and use your own words.

College gives you the opportunity to be exposed to new ideas, to formulate ideas of your own, and to develop skills to communicate your ideas. Strengthening your writing skills requires hard work and practice, but you will learn thinking and communicating skills that will benefit both your studies in college and your career.

Expressing a thought in your own words may seem overwhelming. The difficulty may stem from not understanding the language, not understanding the research material, or a lack of confidence in expressing ideas and concepts. Don't be discouraged that your paper may not sound as professional as you would like. By creating and practicing your own personal style, you will improve your ability to state ideas clearly and support arguments, and your vocabulary will increase.

These skills are not built by using another researcher's or student's words or by paying a service to write a paper for your class. Attempting to cheat on your paper cheats you the most because you are depriving yourself of the thinking, learning, and writing practice that would have benefited all of your classwork and beyond. But cheating also creates the risk of humiliation and punishment. Most professors are so familiar with the work in their field that they can spot a fake quickly. New plagiarism detection methods are also making it easier for professors to catch cheaters electronically. And as discussed in Chapter 1, all institutions will punish students who plagiarize. Doing honest work is the way to avoid the humiliation of being accused of cheating.

## Allow yourself enough time to research the assignment.

Often students who are caught plagiarizing claim that they didn't have time to do the work. This excuse rarely works. Allow sufficient time to do all the steps necessary in an assignment. The best way is to plan for each part: selecting the topic, doing the research, then writing and refining your ideas. Minimizing the time it will take to do the work, or procrastinating because you feel that you do better work when you are anxious, will easily create trouble.

The most productive strategy is to begin the assignment as soon as it is given and try to complete it early. This allows you to adjust the schedule if you encounter any research difficulties, provides time for questions or clarification, and offsets other events that can interfere or cut into study time. If you are unsure about how to plot out your time for each step, then ask your instructor to help you plan your schedule.

## Keep careful track of your sources.

As you look through books, articles, and electronic materials, you will be able to identify which content is relevant to your paper. The sources that you decide to take notes from are the ones you will need to keep careful records of.

Create a master list of all your sources that contains detailed bibliographic information for each item. (You will need to record the author; title of article or book; publisher, periodical title, electronic medium, or URL; date, and page number. See Chapter 6 for a detailed list of the information you will need and the format you will need to provide it in.) As you conduct your research, you will likely add or delete sources from this list, but keeping it current and complete will make your work much easier when it comes time to format the list into your formal List of Works Cited (for MLA papers) or Reference List (for APA papers). This list of references will enable the readers of your paper to locate the exact content you discuss in your paper-as well as to assist you to find it again, should you need to.

## Take careful notes.

Some students find they take more complete notes (and can easily refer back to their sources) if they make photocopies of the relevant pages from their sources. If you decide to use this method, for print sources, such as articles and books, copy the copyright page and relevant content pages of each source. Make sure the page numbers or other identifiers are visible on each page. For electronic sources, such as the websites, databases, CDs, or even web logs, print out both the home or copyright page and the relevant content pages, making sure that identifiers such as the URL and the date, or page numbers, are visible.

If you take notes on note cards or in computer files, then make sure to keep a detailed record of where each note came from and take down the information carefully and accurately.

Next scrutinize your resources, thinking about the ideas expressed, noting and recording the relevant points, and adding to the notes your reactions, questions, and thoughts. If you find a particular phrasing that you want to quote, then highlight it to separate it from the regular notes.

## Assemble your thoughts, and make clear who is speaking.

As you write the first draft of your paper, make sure you are expressing your thoughts and ideas in your own voice. Use the thoughts or words of others only to support your own thoughts, *not to make your point for you*. Your writing should make clear at all times who is speaking.

Decide from your notes whether you need to quote, summarize, or paraphrase the source. (See Chapters 3, 4, and 5 for a discussion of each method.) Then make sure to introduce the guest voice (the source) and explain why the source's information is relevant to your topic.

## If you use an idea, a quotation, paraphrase, or summary, then credit the source.

When you draft your paper, if you are stating another person's thought, then make clear where that thought came from. Identify the source of all borrowed content in your paper, even if it's from a blog on the Internet. Your readers need to know where to find the original source if they want to explore the idea further.

Identify your source by inserting a brief parenthetical citation in the paper where the source's content appears, and then list the complete source information at the end of the paper. Follow the documentation style directed by your instructor (usually MLA or APA; see Chapter 6 for examples.)

## Cite sources correctly, both in the body of your paper and in your list of Works Cited.

A **citation**-that is, stating the source of an idea, a conclusion, or a specific collection of information—of another person's work is the highest form of respect that a serious writer can make. It is also the single best way to avoid accusations of plagiarism and cheating. Properly citing sources involves acknowledging them both in the body of your work (when and where your writing borrows from a given source) and in a list of all the sources at the end of your paper.

Citation styles differ by subject or discipline. There are styles for English, the Social Sciences, the Humanities, and the Sciences. Check with your instructor or writing center for the proper format style of your writing project.

See Chapter 3, Quotations; Chapter 4, Paraphrases; Chapter 5, Summaries; and Chapter 6, Citations, for basic models of citations. Guidebooks such as MLA, APA, and Chicago, which are available in most bookstores, provide models for all common types of sources. Online citation generators (see Chapter 8) can also help you with listing references in the correct format.

## Quote accurately and sparingly.

Quotations should be used *only to emphasize your own point*, which you have already stated in your own words. A good quotation from an original source can underscore a theme and introduce thoughts or direction, but quotations should be relevant, necessary, accurate, and limited.

Using too many direct quotations (more than ten percent) is a sign both that you have not developed your own idea enough and that you are relying on others to make your point for you. Over-quoting is also an opportunity for plagiarism to creep in. If you are using several sources, then limit how much those sources contribute, and give correct citation and credit every time you use them.

## Paraphrase carefully.

The practice of taking another writer's sentence and then looking up words and replacing them with synonyms is a common way for students to think they are paraphrasing from a source. (See Chapter 4.) Merely changing some of another writer's words, or reversing the order of the clauses in the sentences, is still copying. This is another way students can inadvertently plagiarize. Use paraphrase to state in your own words what another writer believes or argues.

## Do not patchwrite.

**Patchwriting** consists of mixing several references together and arranging paraphrases and quotations to constitute much of a paper. In essence, the student has assembled others' works with a bit of embroidery here and there but with very little original thinking or expression. Turning in work that has been woven into a quilt with patches arranged together constitutes plagiarism. Instead, work on developing a position and bringing in sources to support the viewpoint or argument that you are presenting.

A way to avoid patchwriting is good preparation. Read the material several times to make sure you understand what the source is saying; then put it aside and think about it. Analyze the readings and what they mean, and then try to organize the main points. Create an outline of what you want to say, and then go back and pull in the supporting information from the sources. Good writers think of the reader as listening to what is being said; this process will help you create and organize your own, original work.

## Summarize, don't auto-summarize.

Most word processors have an automatic summarize function that can take fifty pages and turn them into ten. The problem with this feature is that it condenses material by selecting key sentences. Therefore a summarized version is still in the exact words of the original source, only shorter and not necessarily making the same point as the original. The auto-summary feature is intended for writers to summarize their *own* work, *not* the work of others. If a student uses any portion of the auto-summary from another writer's work, then it is plagiarism.

If you wish to summarize another writer's work, then describe briefly in your own words the writer's idea (identifying who that writer is and providing a citation to the work) and state how it relates to your own ideas. (See Chapter 5.)

## Do not rework another student's paper or buy papermill papers.

Don't cross the line from looking at someone else's paper as an example of how to do the assignment, to the action of using it as original work. Reworking someone else's paper is plagiarism. It also shows that the student is unwilling to think for him- or herself.

Similarly, buying papers from paper mills, or paying for someone else to write a paper, is obviously dishonest and is a clear example of plagiarizing and cheating. Databases of written papers are often kept by colleges and by plagiarism detection services, so instructors who have a question about the authenticity of a student's paper can easily verify its source.

## Knowledge Check: True or False?

1. One way to avoid plagiarizing is to give yourself enough time to do a good job on the assignment.
2. As long as you put everything in quotation marks, you are not plagiarizing.
3. Getting a paper from a friend or the Internet is a good way to get a head start on your assignment.

## Answers

1. (True) Most people who plagiarize use poor time management and even worse judgment.
2. (False) If you quote more than 10 percent of your paper, you may be graded down for over-quoting.
3. (False) Using a friend's paper or an Internet paper is plagiarizing and considered to be academic cheating.

# CHAPTER 3

## Using Quotations

Using quotations is an effective way to support your arguments and add credibility to your research paper. Quotations are most useful when they highlight or help to refine a point you are making. Inserting too many quotations in your paper distracts your readers from the argument you are trying to construct, and makes your paper sound as if you are letting others speak for you, so use quotations selectively and sparingly.

You can use a **direct quotation** (a word-for-word repetition from another source) or an **indirect quotation** (a recasting in your own words of the ideas of another person-see Chapters 4 and 5). Each time you insert a direct or indirect quotation into your paper, you must add a citation to the source at the quotation. This in-text citation follows an abbreviated, parenthetical format that points your reader to the full citation in a Works Cited or References list at the end of your paper (see Chapter 6).

Quotations can be used in various ways within a research paper. This chapter will cover some of those uses and the proper citation styles needed for each.

Follow these basic rules for using quotations:

- Use quotations sparingly.
- Make sure the quotation exactly fits the idea of your paragraph.
- Make sure direct quotations stay identical to the original passage. Do not change the wording, the spelling, or the punctuation of the original passage.
- Cite the source! Include a parenthetical citation for all quotations.
- If a direct quotation is longer than four lines, use a block quotation.

### Using direct quotations

A direct quotation is an exact copy of the original author's work. Make your point first, and then enclose the quote in quotation marks (or if it is long set it apart as a block quotation) and provide a parenthetical citation directly after.

**Example: parenthetical citation, MLA**

The MLA style of citing a quotation includes the author's last name followed by the page number directly after the quotation. Note that no comma separates the name from the page number.

> Personal growth is a painful process, and part of that process is taking personal responsibility for your actions. This includes remembering that "you can't talk your way out of problems you behaved yourself into" (Covey 186).

**Example: parenthetical citation, APA**

The APA style of citing the same quotation includes the publication year as well as the author's last name and page number. Note that no comma separates the name from the date, but that a comma does follow the date and that the abbreviation *p.* precedes the page number.

> Personal growth is a painful process, and part of that process is taking personal responsibility for your actions. This includes remembering that "you can't talk your way out of problems you behaved yourself into" (Covey 1989, p. 186).

Notice that in both cases the citation is included in the sentence, with the period after the citation.

**Example: author's name in text, MLA**

You can introduce the name of the author in the text and then cite the page number for reference.

> Noted author Stephen Covey suggests that to be effective, one must "begin with the end in mind" (97).

**Example: author's name in text, APA**

Note that the APA style includes the year of publication directly after the author's name and the page number at the end for easy reference.

> Weeks (1994) believes that "we need to celebrate diversity, not fear it or perceive it as a threat" (33).

## Quoting a secondary source

When using research sources it is common to find that the original author has quoted a **secondary source**, another author, in his or her work. The following example shows such a quotation and the proper citation for it.

**Example: secondary source, MLA**

The addition of *qtd. in* (for "quoted in") shows that this quote by Jung was found in a secondary resource, written by Byrne.

> Psychology has had its masters of theory and quite a bit of humor as well. C. G. Jung, a noted psychologist, once claimed, "Show me a sane man and I will cure him for you" (qtd. in Byrne 453).

## Using ellipses to show omissions and brackets to show insertions

An **ellipsis** (shown by three evenly spaced periods: ...) is a break or omission of words within a direct quote. Using only part of a quotation is common practice, especially if the entire quotation is too long or cumbersome. But make sure to use ellipses cautiously so you don't present the author's words out of intended context.

**Example: ellipses to show omitted words from the middle of a quote**

> We can now plainly and painfully see that "components of human interaction ... often lead to conflict" (Weeks 33).

**Example: bracketed insertion to make a sentence correct**

Sometimes a quote will be worded in a way that could read awkwardly or make an incomplete sentence when inserted in a paper. If you need to add a word or phrase within a quotation to make your sentence grammatically correct or clearer, then put brackets around your insertion.

> There are many examples of how "components of human interaction... [can] often lead to conflict" (Weeks 33).

In this instance the word *can* was added to clarify the thought for the reader.

## Block quotations

A quotation from poetry, plays, or any text longer than four lines should be set apart in a block quotation format. A block quotation is indented about one inch (ten spaces) from the left margin and double-spaced. A block quotation needs no quotation marks and is introduced by a complete sentence. Often a colon, rather than a period, follows the introductory words.

***Tip***
**Block quotations do not require quotation marks.**

**Example: block quotation, MLA**

The block quotation is introduced by a sentence that contains the author's name, ends with a colon, and uses ellipsis to show that it is not complete. Note that the page number is in parentheses after the period.

> As Jess Tavares explains, older students face different challenges when returning to school:
>
> As an older student, returning to the academic world was quite a shock. I hadn't seen a classroom in twenty-five years. But with a new backpack, pens, and a bill from the bookstore that equaled my rent, I sat in my very first college class, ... scared to death I could not pass the tests I had just set for myself. (2)

## Knowledge Check: True or False?

1. Quotations must be used in original form.
2. Quotation marks are required for all direct quotations.
3. Brackets indicate that a word has been added that is not in the original text.

## Answers

1. (True) Quotations should be identical to the original passage.
2. (False) Block quotations do not require quotation marks.
3. (True) Brackets show that text was added to the original passage.

# CHAPTER 4

# Paraphrasing

## What is a paraphrase?

A **paraphrase** is a restatement of an author's writing by using your own words and accurately conveying the original information. You would paraphrase an author when you want to explain the content of his or her passage while maintaining your own voice and rhythm. You might also paraphrase after you have introduced a source earlier in your paper and wish to continue to discuss that source's ideas without needing to quote the source verbatim.

The length of a paraphrase should be about equal to the length of the original work. (By contrast, a summary - as explained in Chapter 5 - describes in just a few words the ideas or points made in another author's long passage or large work.)

It is vital that the paraphrase not alter the original meaning of the source. Adding words that distort the intention of the author or leaving out significant parts of what the author was intending misstates that author.

A paraphrase, because it's an indirect quotation, always requires a parenthetical citation. See the MLA and APA examples below.

To restate an author's ideas accurately but in your own words and writing style can be difficult. You might be tempted to shift some words around from the original, but doing so would be plagiarizing because those words and the idea still belong to the author. Remember that improving your writing skills is part of the goal of using others' works. Instructors want you to learn to write and think, not just to hand back what someone else has created.

***Tips***

**DO**

1. Use your own words.
2. Present the author's ideas without changing, adding to, or deleting from the original meaning.
3. Make the paraphrase about equal in length to the original.
4. Give credit to the source.

**DON'T**

1. Keep the author's sentences and just replace the words with synonyms.
2. Flip-flop clause and leave the words the same.
3. Lose track of original sources.

## Accuracy is vital.

One way to develop paraphrasing skills is to read the material several times to make sure that you understand completely what the writer is saying. Next, put aside the author's work and try to explain the passage in your own words. This will help you to develop a personal voice and style. Compare the explanation with the original and decide whether it is accurate and conveys the original ideas. Consider whether something is missing that a person who didn't read the first passage would need to know in order to understand it. Make sure to explain for your reader how the paraphrased content relates to your idea. Once you have worked the paraphrase into your draft, be sure to cite the original.

## Always give credit to the source of an idea.

It may be confusing when and how to add a citation to the original source. A good practice to follow is if a sentence or idea came from an outside source, then it should be acknowledged with a parenthetical citation.

# Sample paraphrases

**Example 1: paraphrase with citation, MLA**

**Original work**

> Poll after poll indicates that one of the primary concerns of contemporary U.S. citizens is violence. Terrorism is obviously one part of this concern, but there is also considerable concern about nonterrorist forms of violence. Violence among the nation's youth is especially troubling and difficult to explain. This difficulty is frequently the reason that social psychologists are often asked to make sense of seemingly senseless acts of violence. Why are there so many shootings in the U.S. high schools? Why are there so many gangs, and why are they growing at such alarming rates? (Potter 1999)

**Incorrect paraphrase**

> Survey **after** survey show **that one of the** big things that people in the **U.S.** worry about today is **violence. Terrorism is** clearly a reason **but there is also** a lot of worry **about** other **forms of violence. Violence** from the young people in this country **is** very confusing **and** hard **to** understand. **This** problem **is** often **the** issue **that researchers** are frequently required to explain incomprehensibl violent crimes. What is the reason for the number of gun related crimes in schools in America? Is it because the number of **gangs** are going up?

In the above example the writing style of the original piece was copied. It was plagiarized, not paraphrased. Sentence by sentence, the information is exactly restated using different words. The substituted words in exact sequence are underlined. The sequence of each idea and structure of each sentence is the same, and words have been replaced with synonyms. In some cases original phrases have been kept in order (shown in **bold**). This patchwork paraphrasing merely uses a thesaurus to find synonyms for words in the original text, but everything is essentially identical. Finally, there was no indication of the source of this paraphrase.

**Correct paraphrase**

> Many recent **polls** have suggested that people in the United States are very concerned about **terrorism** and other acts of **violence**. Increasing violence, including **shootings**, among **high-school**-aged children is one of these concerns. People in the community want to understand why this is happening. **Social psychologists** have been asked to explain this troubling trend. It is difficult to understand why young people may be joining **gangs** and committing acts of violence in greater numbers. (Potte 306)

This example maintains the ideas of the original piece, but the style of writing is different. Instead of following an identical sequence to the original work, the correctly paraphrased paragraph conveys the information but does not pull out words and substitute them with synonyms. It uses some of the words from the original to accurately present the author's ideas and is complete in presenting the original author's ideas, but it uses the student's own original sentences. It also cites the author of the original work.

**Example 2: paraphrase with citation, MLA**

**Original work**

> At first glance, there appears to be little justification for telling the story of California's early Indian wars. Aside from the brief Modoc conflict of 1873, and possibly the Mariposa war of 1851, few people are aware that California had any Indian troubles during the Gold Rush days of the 1850's. Certainly the Far West never had a Custer's Last Stand or a grand retreat such as that made by Chief Joseph of the Nez Perce. Here were no Sitting Bull or Geronimo, no spectacular uprisings, like Adobe Walls or Beecher's Islands. On the contrary, many California tribes were generally peaceful by nature, few having even a war club or a tomahawk as part of their culture. Yet in California, the bloodiest drama in the settlement of the West took place, a brutal disruption and destruction so devastating that by the 1870's many native groups were extinct. (Secrest xi)

**Incorrect paraphrase**

> <u>Unless you know about the events, you would think there isn't much reason to write about what happened</u> in the **Indian wars** in **early California**. There were two conflicts, one in **1873** with the **Modoc** and another in **Mariposa in 1851**. <u>But most people don't know anything about California having trouble with Indians during the</u> **1850's Gold Rush**. The **Far West** <u>didn't have any famous Indian conflicts like</u> **Custer's Last Stand** or any other Indians that were well known like **Chief Joseph of the Nez Perce, Sitting Bull, or Geronimo**. <u>It didn't have Indian revolts like</u> **Adobe Walls or Beecher's Islands**. <u>In California the Indians were peaceful and didn't carry weapons</u>. <u>But California had the</u> **bloodiest** <u>wars in the</u> **West**. <u>It was harsh and destructive and annihilated the Indians to the point where by the 1870's many of the groups were dead and gone</u>.

This paragraph is plagiarized. Notice that the writing style of the original piece was copied. Sentence by sentence the information is restated using different words, and the sequence of each idea and sentence is the same. In most cases, words have been substituted for synonyms (see <u>underlined</u>). In some cases words have been kept (see **bold**). This is another example of patchwork paraphrasing. In addition, no indication of the source of this paraphrase is provided in the text.

**Correct paraphrase**

> If history books are to be believed, there is little to say about the California Indian conflicts. Indeed it would seem that all of the great battles such as Custer's Last Stand and the great chiefs took place far away. While history shows us the Gold Rush and its effect on California, it also leaves us with the false impression that California Indians were peaceful, with no weapons or conflicts with the intruding whites. This type of historical omission negates the devastation and annihilation that the California Indians suffered; annihilation so complete "that by the 1870's many native groups were extinct". (Secrest, xi)

In this example the ideas of the original piece are maintained, but the style of writing is different and belongs to the writer of the paper. Instead of following an identical sequence to the original work, the correctly paraphrased paragraph conveys the information but does not pull out words and substitute them with synonyms. It still uses some of the phrasing from the original, but this instance is identified by quotation marks and is used to accurately convey and emphasize the ideas of the original author. It also cites the author of the original work.

To avoid the errors of adding information that wasn't in the original work or omitting something important to the original meaning, carefully track your sources and acknowledge them in your writing. You need to correctly present the meaning, and you need to cite the source accurately. Sometimes it is difficult to try to work with many different ideas, but remember that your professor is very familiar with many of the ideas and sources you'll use and can help you work out how best to present them.

## Style of citation for paraphrases

Like direct quotations, the only difference between APA and MLA styles is the citation at the end.

**Example: parenthetical citation, MLA**

MLA style includes the name of the author and the page number. This example shows a block quotation.

> ...Yet in California, the bloodiest drama in the settlement of the West took place, a brutal disruption and destruction so devastating that by the 1870's many native groups were extinct. (Secrest xi)

**Example: parenthetical citation, APA**

APA style includes the name of the author and the date of publication. This example shows a block quotation.

> ...Yet in California, the bloodiest drama in the settlement of the West took place, a brutal disruption and destruction so devastating that by the 1870's many native groups were extinct. (Secrest, 2003)

Provide the complete information in your Works Cited or References list at the conclusion of your paper.

## Knowledge Check: True or False?

1. Keeping the writing style of the original passage when you paraphrase is appropriate as long as you change most of the words.
2. Correct paraphrasing includes a citation for the original source after the paraphrased passage.
3. A paraphrase should be roughly the same length as the original.

## Answers

1. (False) This is a common mistake students make because they don't know the rules and they lack confidence in their own writing ability. You should restate the writer's idea in your own words.
2. (True) Always acknowledge when you've used ideas from someone else, no matter whether it's a clause, sentence, or paragraph.
3. (True) The paraphrase restates another person's idea in your own words.

# CHAPTER 5

## Summarizing

### What is a summary?

A **summary** condenses the idea of the original author while retaining the message of the original passage. A summary enables you to comment briefly on another writer's ideas and to express how they relate to your own ideas. Summarizing shortens the length of the original passage, whereas paraphrasing nearly matches the original in length.

***Tips***

DO

1. Be accurate to the original meaning.
2. Cite the original source.
3. Make your summary significantly shorter than the original.
4. Use your own words and explain how the writer's ideas relates to yours.

DON'T

1. Copy the original writing style; use your own.
2. Replace the original words with synonyms.
3. Change the meaning of a passage.

To summarize another writer's passage, read it several times-taking notes if necessary-to make sure you understand what the writer is saying. It might help to read the passage aloud so you can hear the words. Then say to yourself, "In other words, ..." and complete the thought. If you find that you are using almost as many words to explain or express the thought, then you need to revise it and make it simpler and briefer. Reduce the original passage to its basic idea. And make sure to explain for your reader how the writer's idea relates to the point you are making in your paper.

# Sample summary

**Original work**

> Polls show that large majorities of Americans believe that anyone who works hard can succeed, and even higher percentages of Americans say they admire people who get rich by their own efforts. Those who fall behind, meanwhile, are often blamed for their misery. In a typical recent survey finding, three quarters of Americans agreed with the statement that if a person is poor, their own "lack of effort" is to blame. In other words, Americans tend to make moral judgments about people based upon their level of economic success. Everybody loves a winner, the saying goes, and nowhere is that more true than in America. Winners are seen as virtuous, as people to admire and emulate. Losers get the opposite treatment for their own good, mind you. As Marvin Olasky, ... has said: "An emphasis on freedom should also include a willingness to step away for a time and let those who have dug their own hole 'suffer the consequences of their misconduct.'" The prevalence of a sink-or-swim mentality in the United States is unique among Western democracies, as is the belief that individuals have so much control over their destiny. Elsewhere people are more apt to believe that success or failure is determined by circumstances beyond individual control. Scholars attribute the difference in outlook to the "exceptionalism" of American and, especially to the American Dream ethos that dominates U.S. culture - an ethos at once intensely optimistic and brutally unforgiving. (Callahan 124-25)

**Incorrect Summary**

> Polls show that large majorities of Americans believe that anyone who works hard can succeed, and even higher percentages of Americans say they admire people who get rich by their own efforts. Winners are seen as virtuous, as people to admire and emulate. Elsewhere people are more apt to believe that success or failure is determined by circumstances beyond individual control.

The above summary was created using the autosummarize feature of Word set for 25 percent. It selects key sentences from the original document and puts those sentences together to form an abbreviated copy. (Note that the auto-summarize feature is intended for writers to provide summaries of their *own* work, not the work of others.) This is *not* an acceptable summary because it is entirely copied, word for word. It is plagiarism. It does not change the writing style of the original author, nor does it give credit with a correct citation to indicate the source. Additional problems with this method of summary may be the altering of the original meaning of the piece. Note that the original piece was about the difference between how Americans view winners and losers, but the summary does not mention how losers are viewed. That thesis has not been mentioned in the summary. It is important to connect a summary to the point you fire making in your paper and the reason why you referred to the source you are summarizing.

**Correct summary**

> According to Callahan, American culture, unlike other Western democracies, takes the moral perspective that success is the result of individual effort. According to polls, a person's success is considered to be a product of his or her labor and thus deserved. Conversely, a person's poverty or failure is viewed as the outcome of his or her lack of sufficient effort and therefore also deserved. (124-25)

In the correct summary, the ideas of the original passage are maintained, but the style of writing is different from the original passage. The summary is shorter than the original. The summary conveys the main points of the original, but it does not copy full sentences or pull out words and substitute them with synonyms. It still uses some of the words from the original to accurately present the author's ideas. When you use a summary is a paper, make sure it clearly addresses your thesis or argument and that you cite it correctly.

## Knowledge Check: True or False?

1. You can keep the writing style of the original passage when you summarize as long as you significantly shorten the length and leave out some of the original.
2. Correct summarizing includes a citation for the original source next to the summarized passage.
3. A summary should convey the same meaning as the original.

## Answers

1. (False) A summary should be in your own words and writing style but convey the message of the original. Do not use auto-summarize for someone else's work because it is just an abridged copy.
2. (True) Always acknowledge when you've used ideas from someone else, no matter whether it's a clause, sentence or paragraph, paraphrase or summary.
3. (True) Do not alter the meaning, just express it concisely and in your own words.

# CHAPTER 6

# Listing the Works Cited

As you draft your paper and decide how to use your final sources, you will assemble a complete list of the references that you use in your paper (as discussed in Chapters 3-5), and you will need to format that list of Works Cited and present that list at the end of your paper. This chapter presents the basics of how to format your reference list items in the MLA and APA styles, which your general coursework will likely require. You can find more detailed examples in your textbook, from your school's library or writing center, and from electronic resources such as those listed in Chapter 8.

***Tip***
**Always check with your instructor for the documentation style that he or she requires.**

## Content of citations

While the information presented in all styles is the same, the order of the information and how it is shown can be quite different. The basic information contained by all citation styles includes the following:

- Author name
- Title of article, essay, book, or Web site
- Publisher information
- Year of publication
- Place or form of publication

## Basic format of citations

All documentation styles place the list of references at the end of the paper. Follow these basic formatting rules for all citation styles:

- Arrange all citations in alphabetical order by the author's last name.
- Arrange authors' names in a multiple-author work exactly as they appear in the source.
- Reverse the first author's name so that the last name appears first.
- Double-space your list of references, the way you double-space your paper.
- Indent the second and subsequent lines of a citation by 1/2 inch or 5 spaces, so the author's name always appears by itself at the left margin.
- Include in your list of references only the works that your paper refers to.

Always check with your course instructor for the preferred citation style. (See Chapter 8 f sources of citation styles for specific subject areas such as mathematics, biology, physics, and s on.) This guide does not discuss footnotes, as parenthetical citations are emphasized.

## MLA citations: Books

The basic MLA style of citation for a book is as follows:

- Author last name first, first name followed by a period.
- Book Title underlined, followed by a period.
- City of publication followed by a colon.
- Publisher's name followed by a comma. Use only the first name of the publisher, and abbreviate University Press to UP.
- Year of publication followed by a period.

**Example: single-author book**

Maguire, Gregory. Wicked: The Life and Times of the Wicked Witch of the West. New York: Harper, 19

**Examples: multiple authors of a book**

When you are citing a book that has two or three authors, list them in the order that they appear on the title page. Invert the first author's name but not the names of the second or third author. Separate all the authors by commas.

For a book by four or more authors, MLA allows the listing to include all authors listed in order *or* just the first author followed by the Latin words **et al.** (which is short for *et alii*, meaning "and others"). Check with your instructor about the form that he or she prefers.

**A book by two authors**

Norman, Michael, and Beth Scott. Historic Haunted America. New York: Tor, 1995.

**A book by four or more authors**

Kauffman, James, Mark Mostert, Stanley Trent, and Daniel Hallahan. Managing Classroom Behavior. Boston: Allyn, 2002.

*or*

Kauffman, James, et al. Managing Classroom Behavior. Boston: Allyn, 2002.

## MLA citations: Articles or essays

You might use an article from a periodical or an essay from an anthology. While the basic stru ture of citations for articles is the same as for books, there are some significant differences. Yo need to list both the title of the article or essay and the journal or book that it was published

**Example: essay in an anthology**

The information in a citation of a source from an anthology follows this order:

- Author of the article or essay (last name first) followed by a period.
- "Title of the article or essay" in quotation marks, followed by a period.
- Title of the Book underlined, followed by a period.
- Comp. (for Compiled by) or Ed. (for Edited by).
- Author of the book (first name first), followed by a period.
- City followed by a colon.
- Publisher followed by a comma.
- Year followed by a period.
- Page range (hyphenated) followed by a period.

Anson, Chris. "Taking Off." Finding Our Way: A Writing Teacher's Sourcebook. Ed. Wendy Bishop and Deborah Coxwell Teague. Boston: Houghton, 2005. 44-51.

For citations from an anthology or magazine, always include the page numbers.

**Example: article from a magazine**

Magazine or journal articles include the month of publication in the citation. Note the abbreviated month and the colon following the year.

Myers, Michaela. "Pole Results." Horse Illustrated Feb. 2005: 68-74.

**Example: article from a journal**

Note the volume number following the journal title, the year in parentheses, the colon following the year, and the inclusive page numbers.

Paulos, Lyn. "Sexuality in Women: Feminism in Conflict." Women's Studies Weekly 1 (2000): 15-20.

## APA citations: Books

The APA style contains the same information as MLA, but it formats the content differently, putting more emphasis on the date of publication. The basic APA style of citation for a book is as follows:

- Author, last name first, then first initial, followed by a period. For a work by more than one author, invert all names, use initials instead of first names, and insert an ampersand (&) before the last author.
- Year of publication in parentheses, followed by a period.
- Book title *italicized* (capitalize the first word of the title, the first word of the subtitle, and any proper nouns), followed by a period.
- City and full publisher's name, separated by a colon and followed by a period.

**Example: book**

Maguire, G. (1995). *Wicked: The life and times of the Wicked Witch of the West.* New York: HarperCollins.

## APA citations: Articles

The basic APA style of citation for a journal article by a single author is as follows:

- Author last name, and first initial followed by a period. For a work by more than one author, invert all names, use initials instead of first names, and insert an ampersand (&) before the last author.
- Year (in parentheses) with a period.
- Title of article (capitalize only first word and first word after a colon, no quotation marks), followed by a period.
- *Title of journal in italics* followed by a comma.
- *Volume number in italics* followed by a comma.
- Full page range of article, followed by a period.

**Example: journal article by a single author**

Paulos, L. (2000). Sexuality in women: Feminism in conflict. *Women's Studies Weekly, 1,*15-20.

**Example: journal article by two to five authors**

Paulos, L., & Walker. K. (2005). Understanding twin rivalry: A case study. *Sibling Circular, 10,* 70-72.

Menager, R., Herch, S., Lewis, G., & Walker, K. (2005). Friends and family. *Relations, 5,* 21-24.

## MLA and APA citations: Online sources

Provide the following information for online sources:

- Author (if available).
- Title of Web page.
- Title of full work (if available).
- Date of work (if available).
- File number (if available).
- Date that you accessed it.
- URL or Web address.

**Example: MLA online citation**

The MLA citation shows the author's full name and the date after the title. Note that the year of publication is followed by a period, that the date of access is inverted and abbreviated and that no punctuation follows it, that the URL is put in angle brackets, that the line break of the URL falls after a slash, and that a period follows the URL.

Warlick, David."Landmarks Citation Machine: The Landmark Project. 2000.19 Mar. 2005
<http:// www.landmarkproject.com/citationmachinelindex.php>.

**Example: APA online citation, no print source**

APA electronic citations likewise follow the rules of normal APA style of formatting such as capitalization, first initial, year placement, and italics. Note that the retrieval date is spelled out, that a comma follows it, and that no punctuation follows the URL. If the URL extends to more than one line, then break it only after a slash or a period.

Lee. I. (1998). *A research guide for students: Research, writing, and style guides.* Retrieved
March 19,2005, from http://www.aresearchguide.com/styleguides.html

**Example: APA online citation, print source**

McCabe, D. L., Trevino, L. K., & Butterfield, K. D. (1999). Academic integrity in honor code and non-honor code environments: A qualitative investigation. *Journal of Higher Education,* 70, 211-234. Retrieved May 19, 2003, from http://www.questia.com/SM.qst

***Tip***
**Always include the date of access, because Web sites often change.**

**Example: online citation, no author, MLA style**

If the Web site does not have an author or organization listed, then list the title of the Web site. Include the date of publication if available and the date of access.

Some Web sites are sponsored or maintained by universities or companies and do not list authors for their Web materials. If that is the case, list the university or company name in the author space of the citation.

DSPS Policies and Procedures. 2003. Santa Barbara City College. 3 Jan. 2004 <http://www.sbcc.edu/dsps/>.

**Example: online citation, no author, APA style**

*DSPS policies and procedures.* (2003). Santa Barbara City College. Retrieved January 3, 2004, from http://www.sbcc.edu/dsps/

## List of cited works

At the end of your paper, make sure to provide the complete list of works that you have cited in the body of the paper.

**Example: MLA Works Cited**

Works Cited

Anson, Chris. "Taking Off." Finding Our Way: A Writing Teacher's Sourcebook. Ed. Wendy Bishop and Deborah Coxwell Teague. Boston: Houghton, 2005. 44-51.

DSPS Policies and Procedures. 2003. Santa Barbara City College. 3 Jan. 2004 <http://www.sbcc.edu/dspsl>.

Kauffman, James, Mark Mostert, Stanley Trent, and Daniel Hallahan. Managing Classroom Behavior. Boston: Allyn, 2002.

Maguire, Gregory. Wicked: The Life and Times of the Wicked Witch of the West. New York: Harper, 1995.

Myers, Michaela. "Pole Results." Horse Illustrated Feb. 2005: 68-74.

Norman, Michael, and Beth Scott. Historic Haunted America. New York: Tor, 1995.

Paulos, Lyn. "Sexuality in Women: Feminism in Conflict." Women's Studies Weekly 1 (2000): 15-20.

Warlick, David. "Landmarks Citation Machine." The Landmark Project. 2000. 19 Mar. 2005 <http:" www.landmarkproject.comlcitationmachine/index.php> .

**Example: APA References**

References

*DSPS policies and procedures.* (2003). Santa Barbara City College. Retrieved January 3, 2004, from http://www.sbcc.edu/dsps/

Lee, I. (1998). *A research guide for students: Research, writing, and style guides.* Retrieved March 19, 2005, from http://www.aresearchguide.comlstyleguides.html

Maguire, G. (1995). *Wicked: The life and times of the Wicked Witch of the West.* New York: HarperCollins.

McCabe, D. L., Trevino, L. K., & Butterfield, K. D. (1999). Academic integrity in honor code and non-honor code environments: A qualitative investigation. *Journal of Higher Education,* 70, 211-234. Retrieved May 19, 2003,from http://www.questia.comlSM.qst

Menager, R., Herch, S., Lewis, G., & Walker, K. (2005). Friends and family. *Relations, 5,* 21-24.

Paulos, L. (2000). Sexuality in women: Feminism in conflict. *Women's Studies Weekly, 1,* 15-20.

Paulos, L., & Walker. K. (2005). Understanding twin rivalry: A case study. *Sibling Circular, 10,* 70-72.

## Knowledge Check: True or False?

1. Works Cited or References should be single-spaced.
2. Only works actually cited in the body of the paper should be listed in the Works Cited or Reference pages.
3. References or Works Cited should be listed in alphabetical order by author's last name.
4. Each reference item can be provided in any style (MLA, APA, etc.) as long as it's complete.

## Answers

1. (False) All references should be double-spaced.
2. (True)
3. (True)
4. (False) All of the references should follow the style used in the body of the paper. The choice of style is determined by the academic subject (unless instructed otherwise by your professor).

# CHAPTER 7

## Practice Quiz

**1. Cheating may include**
a. plagiarizing or copying without attribution.
b. using an essay or paper from someone who has previously taken the course.
c. using answers to an exam from someone who has previously taken the course.
d. all of the above.

**2. Plagiarism is**
a. quoting someone else's work and giving credit to them.
b. using someone else's ideas, work, sentences, research, or information and presenting it as your own.
c. using original ideas in your written work.
d. using Web sources.

**3. Citation of sources is required**
a. whenever paraphrasing or summarizing another author's idea.
b. only in the works cited section of your paper.
c. when using your own ideas in an original paragraph.
d. a and b.

**4. The word *paraphrase* means**
a. to replace original words with synonyms.
b. to maintain the writing style of the original author.
c. to give an exact idea of the original author's meaning in your own writing style.
d. to give a general, but not exact, idea of the original author's meaning.

**5. A paragraph is not properly paraphrased when**
a. only a few words are different.
b. you express in your own words the general idea of what the author is saying.
c. the sentences have been rearranged but not changed much.
d. a and b.
e. a and c.

**6. Correct summarizing includes**
a. a copy of the original writing style.
b. replacing the original work with synonyms.
c. the accurate meaning of the original work but significantly shorter than the original.
d. using the autosummarize feature of your word processing program.

**7. Citation of sources is required**
a. when quoting a source in your paper that you use word for word.
b. when browsing the internet.
c. when describing another writer's idea in your paper.
d. a and c.

**8. Over-quoting in your work**
a. shows you have not synthesized or analyzed the material from your resources.
b. is acceptable because it shows the amount of work and research you have done.
c. means using too many direct quotes from your sources.
d. a and c.
e. a and b.

**9. John's paper is based on several different sources,**
including a research paper from a friend who took the same class last summer. Seeing that his friend's research closely matches his own, does John need to cite his friend in his final draft?
a. No, he just needs to cite the other sources.
b. Yes, anything John consults and incorporates needs to be cited.

**10. Look at the original and choose which paraphrase is correct.**

**Original**

> Because there are many ways to cheat, and there is temptation to do so, students may assume that this is something that everyone is doing. Surveys of college students show that cheating is a common occurrence, and some students consider it an accomplishment to get away with this type of behavior. These kinds of attitudes and behaviors are unethical and have consequences. (Menager-Beeley 2003)

a. Students can be tempted to cheat by the many resources available to them that make it easy. They may believe that a majority of students cheat in some form or another. Surveys done in colleges suggest that cheating is more rampant than once thought and that students see it as a triumph to cheat and not get caught. This shows a serious lack of ethics in behavior and can lead to repercussions from the academic institution. (Menager-Beeley, 2003)

b. Because there are so many different ways to cheat, and temptations for students are great, a lot of students think everyone is doing it. Students surveyed say that cheating is a common occurrence and it is an accomplishment to get away with it. This kind of attitude is unethical and can have some consequences.

## Answers:

1. d 2. b 3. a 4. c 5. e 6. c 7. d 8. d 9. b 10. a

# CHAPTER 8

# Additional Sources of Information

The following links are subject to change. They were accessed March 25-26, 2005.

## Web site with information on documentation styles, general

**University of California, Berkeley**
<http://www.lib.berkeley.edu/TeachingLib/Guides/Internet/Style.html>

## Web sites with information on documentation styles, by discipline

**Anthropology**
<http://www.aaanet.org/pubs/style_guide.htm>

**Biology**
<http://www.wisc.edu/writing/Handbook/DocCBE.html>

**Chemistry**
<http://pubs.acs.org/books/references.shtml>

**Legal**
<http://www.law.cornell.edu/citation/>

**Math**
<http://www.longwood.edu/mathematics/stylesheet.html>

**Physics**
<http://www.aip.org/pubservs/style.html>

**Sociology**
<http://www.calstatela.edu/library/bi/rsalina/asa.styleguide.html>

## Free Citation Generators

**Landmark's Citation Machine**
<http://www.citationmachine.net/>

**Style Wizard**
<http://www.stylewizard.com/>

## Reference Tracking, Subscriptions, and Free Trials

**Easy Bib**
<http://easybib.com/>

**RefWorks**
<http://www.refworks.com>

## Links for Articles on Plagiarism

**Center for Academic Integrity**
<http://www.academicintegrity.org/links.asp>

**Plagiarism.org**
<http://www.plagiarism.org/articles.html>

**Samford University Library**
<http://library.samford.edu/topics/plagiarism.html>

**University of Indiana**
<http://www.indiana.edu/~istd/definition.html>

## Print Resources, Style Guides

American Psychological Association. *Concise Rules of APA Style*. Washington: APA, 2005. <http://www.apa.org/books/>.

Gibaldi, Joseph. *The MLA Style Guide for Writers of Research Papers*. 6th ed. New York: MLA, 2003. <http://www.mla.org/store/>.

Huth, Edward J. *Scientific Style and Format: The CBE Manual for Authors, Editors and Publishers*. 6th ed. New York: Cambridge UP, 1994. http://www.councilscienceeditors.org/publications/style.cfm>.

University of Chicago Press Staff. *The Chicago Manual of Style*. 15th ed. Chicago: U of Chicago P, 2003. <http://www.chicagomanualofstyle.org/about.html>.

# CHAPTER 9

## Works Cited

Byrne, Robert. *The 2,548 Best Things Anybody Ever Said.* New York: Galahad, 1996. Sec. 453.

Covey, Stephen. *The Seven Habits of Highly Effective People.* New York: Simon, 1989. 97, 186.

Melville, Herman. Quotation 4797 in *Cole's Quotables.* 30 Mar. 2005 <http://www.quotationspage.com/ quotes/Herman _Melville/>.

Potter, W. James. "Is Media Violence Harmful to Children?" *Taking Sides: Clashing on Controversial Psychological Issue.* 13th ed. Ed. Brent Slife. New York: McGraw, 2004. 306.

Secrest, William B. *When the Great Spirit Died: Destruction of the California Indians, 1850-1860.* Sanger: Word Dancer, 2003.

Tavares, Jess. "Returning Students." Scholarship essay. May 2002.

Weeks, Dudley. *The Eight Essential Steps to Conflict Resolution.* 2002. New York: Tarcher-Penguin, 1994.33.

Zaharoff, Howard. "A Writer's Guide to Fair Use in Copyright Law." *Writers Digest* Jan. 2001. 3 Mar. 2005 <http://www.writersdigest.com/articles/zaharoff_fair_copyright_law .asp>.